Cleavages, Institutions and Competition

ECPR Press

The ECPR Press is published by the European Consortium for Political Research in partnership with Rowman & Littlefield International. It publishes original research from leading political scientists and the best among early career researchers in the discipline. Its scope extends to all fields of political science, international relations and political thought, without restriction in either approach or regional focus. It is also open to interdisciplinary work with a predominant political dimension.

Cleavages, Institutions and Competition

Understanding Vote Nationalisation in Western Europe (1965–2015)

Vincenzo Emanuele

ROWMAN &
LITTLEFIELD
INTERNATIONAL
London • New York

Published by Rowman & Littlefield International, Ltd.
6 Tinworth Street, London SE11 5AL, United Kingdom
www.rowmaninternational.com

In partnership with the European Consortium for Political Research, Harbour House, 6–8 Hythe Quay, Colchester, CO2 8JF, United Kingdom

Rowman & Littlefield International Ltd. is an affiliate of Rowman & Littlefield
4501 Forbes Boulevard, Suite 200, Lanham, Maryland 20706, USA
With additional offices in Boulder, New York, Toronto (Canada), and Plymouth (UK)
www.rowman.com

British Library Cataloguing in Publication Data
A catalogue record for this book is available from the British Library

ISBN: HB 978-1-78660-673-0
PB 978-1-78661-308-0

Library of Congress Cataloging-in-Publication Data
Names: Emanuele, Vincenzo, 1986– author.
Title: Cleavages, institutions and competition : understanding vote nationalisation in Western Europe, 1965–2015 / Vincenzo Emanuele.
Description: New York : Rowman & Littlefield International Ltd, [2018] | Includes bibliographical references and index.
Identifiers: LCCN 2017048488 (print) | LCCN 2017060082 (ebook) | ISBN 9781786606747 (electronic) | ISBN 9781786606730 (cloth : alk. paper) | ISBN 9781786613080 (paper : alk. paper)
Subjects: LCSH: Voting research—Europe, Western—Cross-cultural studies. | Political parties—Europe, Western—Cross-cultural studies.
Classification: LCC JF1005 (ebook) | LCC JF1005 .E53 2018 (print) | DDC 324.94/055—dc23
LC record available at https://lccn.loc.gov/2017048488

∞™ The paper used in this publication meets the minimum requirements of American National Standard for Information Sciences—Permanence of Paper for Printed Library Materials, ANSI/NISO Z39.48–1992.

Printed in the United States of America

A mia madre che mi ha trasmesso l'amore per la storia
e a mio padre che per primo mi ha spiegato la politica

Contents

Figures and Tables

FIGURES

TABLES

The methodologically aware comparative social scientist is always subject to fears and doubts and is frequently not self-assured and sometimes even unhappy scholar. . . . Constantly worrying about the combination of an esprit de finesse with an esprit de géométrie, the comparativist must balance both in the full knowledge of the risk of falling under Pascal's dictum: '. . . les esprits faux ne sont jamais ni fins, ni géomètres'. Comparativists, in short, must always justify their research choices.

Stefano Bartolini, *The Political Mobilization of the European Left*, 2000

Abbreviations

ADM	Average district magnitude
AR1	First-order autoregressive parameter
CRII	Cumulative regional inequality index
CV	Coefficient of variation
E	Local entrant measure
EEA	European Economic Area
EFTA	European Free Trade Area
EMS	European Monetary System
ENEP	Effective number of electoral parties
EU	European Union
EURII	Index of European institutional integration
FGLS	Feasible generalised least squares
GEE	Generalised estimating equations
GLS	Generalised least squares
IPR	Index adjusted for party size and number of regions
IVreg	Instrumental variable regression
LPD	Left partisan density
MAD	Mean absolute deviation
MSD	Mean squared deviation
OLS	Ordinary least squares
PCSE	Panel-corrected standard errors
PNS	Party nationalisation score
PR	Proportional representation
PSNS	Party system nationalisation score
RAI	Regional Authority Index
SCVw	Standardised and weighted variability coefficient
SMD	Single-member district

sPNS	standardised party nationalisation score
sPSNS	standardised party system nationalisation score
TSCS	Time-series-cross-section
TUD	Trade union density
TV	Total volatility
VIF	Variance inflation factor

In some figures, countries have been abbreviated following the ISO Alpha-2 Country Code: Austria (AT), Belgium (BE), Denmark (DK), Finland (FI), France (FR), Germany (DE), Greece (GR), Ireland (IE), Italy (IT), the Netherlands (NL), Norway (NO), Portugal (PT), Spain (ES), Sweden (SE), Switzerland (CH), the United Kingdom (UK).

Preface

This book has the purpose to analyse the evolution of vote nationalisation in Western European party systems over the past fifty years and to look for an explanation, by providing a far-reaching assessment of the macro-constellation of factors involved in this process.

Vote nationalisation is conceived as the level of territorial homogeneity of the electoral support for a given party or, at the aggregate level, in a given party system. The more the support for a party (or for a group of parties) is homogeneous among the territorial units of the country, the more that party (or that party system) is nationalised, and vice versa. From this conceptualisation, it derives that vote nationalisation is a matter of degree and concerns the within-country territorial variations of party support. Therefore, it is not something that can be achieved once and for all. Even if the most important steps towards the formation of nationalised electorates and party systems were reached during a specific period of time – between the end of the nineteenth century and the end of World War I – the extent to which a given party system is more or less nationalised varies through time, and this variation depends on many different factors.

What has been the evolution in the levels of vote nationalisation during the past fifty years in Western Europe? Have Western European party systems been characterised by a continuing homogenising process of electoral behaviour, consistent with the evidence detected in previous studies (Rose and Urwin 1975; Caramani 2004)? Or, on the contrary, have there been a reverse of this trend and a resurgence of some territorial distinctiveness leading to the opening of a denationalisation process? Moreover, which are the factors that can account for vote nationalisation's variance across Western European polities? Is it conceivable that the structure of the competition – albeit hitherto neglected – plays a major role in the explanation of vote nationalisation, to the detriment of the much more emphasised social and institutional factors?

The following chapters, after having outlined the theoretical and methodological framework from which this work moves, aim at answering these questions. By adopting a macro-comparative perspective, I develop a systematic study of the territorial configurations of party support and their determinants by focusing on the 230 parliamentary elections occurred in sixteen Western European party systems from 1965 to 2015.

The goal is that of combining the fascinating comparative and macro-historical perspective (Lipset and Rokkan 1967; Rokkan and Urwin 1982; Caramani 2004) with an original empirical research, in order to put forward a comprehensive understanding of the territorial structuring of Western European party systems, their cross-country differences, their changes through time and the determinants of these variations. Since this book deals with social cleavages, institutional arrangements and party competition, it lies at the core of comparative politics, and, more specifically, at the intersection between the subfields of party system studies and electoral studies.

Notwithstanding the increasing attention paid by scholars to vote nationalisation, most studies have, in turn, focused on different regions of the world, or on purely methodological aspects of this process (i.e., the development of new measures of vote nationalisation), or they have provided purely descriptive accounts without building an empirical model of explanation, or they have simply disentangled the effect of specific predictors without providing a broad overview of the phenomenon. This book is, to the extent of my knowledge, the first attempt to deal with the evolution of the territorial variation of party support in the specific context of Western Europe, by using a recently developed index of vote nationalisation (Bochsler 2010) that corrects most of the biases of the previous measures and by building a rigorous quantitative analysis.

Given that, as Bartolini (2000: 2) puts it, the comparativists 'must always justify their research choices', it is necessary to state why it is important to study vote nationalisation, its changes through time and the factors affecting it. As emphasised by Rose and Urwin (1975: 46), the territory of the state is one of the 'fundamentals' of the political system, and the degree to which the territory is homogeneously represented is not only a more or less fascinating descriptive information but also a crucial research question for political scientists – a research question whose answer is fraught with consequences for the political system. Indeed, the level of vote nationalisation in a given country may have implications that go far beyond the mere electoral viewpoint, affecting the democratic process at large, as witnessed by the growing number of scholars focusing on its consequences for the political system. The concept of vote nationalisation is closely linked with historical macro-processes such as democratisation and nation building, and, as underlined by Rokkan (1970: 227), it is a central element of the formation of a political and democratic citizenship. Whether or not political parties are able to represent nationwide interests and voters' preferences is an essential question for the proper functioning of the representative process, affecting the legislative careers and the executive-legislative relations (Jones and Mainwaring 2003: 144). Moreover, it also has important consequences for the policy outcomes, in terms of scope and direction of the expenditures and the services provided by the central government (Castañeda-Angarita 2013; Crisp, Olivella and Potter 2013; Hicken, Kollman and Simmons 2016), and for the ability of the government to attract foreign investments (Simmons et al. 2016).

Above all, the level of vote nationalisation in a country may affect, in the long run, the preservation of democracy (Diamond 1988; Stepan 2001) and the maintenance of the nation-state (Rose and Urwin 1975: 46). Indeed, the prolonged existence of a denationalised pattern of electoral competition, with territorially concentrated parties that are unable to represent voters' preferences on a national scale, puts the national unity at serious risk. Even the Western European context, where nation building and democratisation are apparently taken-for-granted processes, provides examples of such risks: most of all, the Belgian system, divided along the linguistic line between the Dutch-speaking community of Flanders and the French-speaking community of Wallonia, still seems 'on the eve of disintegration' (de Winter and Dumont 1999), and the new record-breaking 541 days occurred to form a new government after the 2010 election witnesses the growing problems of coexistence among the different parts of Belgian politics. To a lesser extent, the claims of secession carried out by Scotland and Catalonia have old roots but, given the increasing support gained by the nationalist parties in the two regions, they have recently acquired a renewed strength, and the independence of these regions is actually a concrete issue at stake.

The book is divided into three main parts and eight chapters.

Part I deals with the theoretical and methodological framework and consists of two chapters. chapter 1 reviews the theory of nationalisation, provides a necessary conceptual clarification and reconstructs the historical process of formation of national electorates and party systems occurred in Western Europe during the early phases of electoral competition. chapter 2 outlines the research design of the book, introduces the main research questions, operationalises the dependent variable and clarifies the spatial and time scope the data and the method employed in the empirical analysis.

Part II is devoted to the analysis of vote nationalisation trends in Western Europe in the past fifty years. In particular, chapter 3 analyses the levels of vote nationalisation in Western Europe and their variations, both cross-country and over time. Moreover, a specific focus on national variations – through the analysis of the different patterns of vote nationalisation for each of the sixteen Western European countries under study, as well as for the most important parties of each country – can be found in the appendix at the end of the book.

Part III – composed of five chapters – aims at detecting the macro-constellation of explanatory factors of vote nationalisation. Each of the first three chapters of this part introduces a different set of potential predictors and tests its impact on vote nationalisation. Specifically, chapter 4 introduces the macro-sociological determinants, chapter 5 presents the institutional constraints and chapter 6 deals with the factors linked to the structure of the competition. Finally, the hypotheses raised in the previous chapters and the related preliminary evidence find a far-reaching assessment in chapter 7 that builds an overall explanatory model of vote nationalisation, also looking for temporal and national variations in the explanatory capacity of the predictors. The concluding chapter, chapter 8, summarises the main findings of the book and the related implications.

Acknowledgements

This book comes out as a transformation of my PhD thesis. It has been a long, fruitful and sometimes even troublesome path, started about six years ago. Since the first draft, this book has been rewritten more than once, not only, as one can easily imagine, for the integration and the update of the empirical data but also because I felt the necessity to reshape and enrich the book consistent with the evolution of my academic path. Being at the conclusion of this journey, I have only to thank all the people who have helped me to devise this research.

To begin with, I thank Giliberto Capano, who has been the coordinator of my PhD, and all the other scholars who, especially when I was at the early stages of development, provided me with precious pieces of advice to put the research in the right direction: in particular, I wish to warmly thank Claudius Wagemann, Stefano Bartolini, Piergiorgio Corbetta, José Ramón Montero and Cees van der Eijk.

Throughout all these years, my research activity has primarily taken place within the CISE (Italian Centre for Electoral Studies), a scientific research team directed by Roberto D'Alimonte and coordinated by Lorenzo De Sio, which I am honoured to be part of. Roberto D'Alimonte has forged a competent group of colleagues and friends, thus making the CISE a pleasant environment and also a place for continuous discussions and improvements. The opportunity to take part in the CISE meetings provided me with hints and guidelines that have been fundamental in developing this book. Therefore, I am grateful to Roberto D'Alimonte, who has been a mentor and a source of inspiration over all these years; to Lorenzo De Sio, for his invaluable and constant scientific support; and to the other members of the CISE, Matteo Cataldi, Nicola Maggini and Aldo Paparo.

Furthermore, I thank Nicola Martocchia Diodati for his precious methodological pieces of advice. I also thank the anonymous reviewers of ECPR Press.

Above all, warm thanks shall go to two people without whom this book would have hardly been born.

Bruno Marino deserves a special mention for his accurate reading of the entire manuscript and for providing me with constant opportunities for fruitful scientific discussions.

Last but not least, I want to thank my former PhD supervisor and today co-author of many pieces of research, Alessandro Chiaramonte. Across all these years, he has been more than a mentor to me. A noticeable part of my knowledge regarding the topics I deal with in this book is a consequence of his day-by-day teaching. From the very beginning, he has shown constant support towards my research. I have shared with him both the enthusiasm and the difficulties related to my research path. He has carefully revised the whole manuscript, and his suggestions have been decisive. Apparently, I bear full responsibility for the errors and the shortcomings of this work.

Part I

THEORETICAL AND METHODOLOGICAL FRAMEWORK

Chapter 1

Theoretical background

The task of this chapter is to outline the theoretical framework of this work. It constitutes the indispensable starting point for the empirical analysis to be carried out in the second and in the third part of the book. In the following pages, I review the basic elements of the theory concerning the nationalisation of politics as it has been studied and problematised over the past fifty years.

What is vote nationalisation? How have scholars studied it? Is it just a conceptual definition or is it also a historical process? And, if it is also a historical process, when did it happen? Which were the factors that generated it?

These questions are only some of the issues that are addressed in this chapter. Moreover, this chapter does not exclusively deal with the theoretical aspects of the current research, since it is also devoted to underline the main limits of previous studies on the topic that this book tries to overcome and solve.

The structure of the chapter is as follows: the first section, 'A multidimensional concept', briefly presents the different conceptualisations used in the literature to define this phenomenon and gives account of the main debated points among scholars; finally, it provides a theoretical clarification of what vote nationalisation means. The second section, 'The historical process of nationalisation in Western Europe', analyses, by adopting a macro-sociological approach, the historical process of nationalisation in the specific context of Western Europe, which is the spatial context covered by the research. The third section, 'Historical sources of deviations: Parties for religious, territorial and agrarian defence', explores the most relevant deviations, which have differentiated the territorial configuration of national party systems, thus determining a partial or total failure of the nationalisation process. Finally, the fourth section, 'Limits of previous studies', lists and briefly reviews the previous empirical research on the topic.

A MULTIDIMENSIONAL CONCEPT

Generally defined as 'the uniformity or universality of attitudes and political behaviour within nations' (Caramani 1996: 206), and strictly related to the process of homogenisation of political characters, the term 'nationalisation' assumes a polyhedral physiognomy, characterised by numerous viewpoints and perspectives, and it has been conceptualised in different ways by the scholars who have dealt with the topic. As Morgenstern and Pothoff emphasise, the concept of nationalisation has 'suffered from a conflation of terms and imprecise, if not ambiguous, definitions' (2005: 18).

The theory of the nationalisation of politics first developed in the American setting and originated from Schattschneider's (1960) analysis on the genesis of the US party system, where the term 'nationalization of politics' can be originally found.

Analysing the US party system, where, for more than thirty years (from 1896 to 1932), national political life was dominated by the Republican Party, Schattschneider notes that the electoral support for the two major parties was characterised by strong territoriality, with the Democratic Party dominating the southern states but not able to compete with the Republican Party in the rest of country, so much that in 1896, there was a real competition between the two parties in only six states, thus creating uncertainty about the final result, while in all the other states the apparent supremacy of either the Democratic or the Republican Party did not allow for competitive spaces. This situation radically changed in 1932, when the high degree of territoriality of American politics dissipated because, since that moment, it has been dominated by national rather than local questions: the Depression and the New Deal first, and later World War II and the Cold War, shifted the attention of voters towards national issues. Therefore, according to Schattschneider, nationalisation of politics consists of the turn from local ('sectional' in the author's words) to national politics, and it is meant as an increased competitiveness[1] of elections, with the main national parties contesting elections in each state.

As underlined by Caramani (1996: 207–8), from Schattschneider's reflections it derives that nationalisation is composed of three different elements: a *dynamic* element (nationalisation as an historical-temporal process), a *social* element (nationalisation as a structural and cultural change) and a *spatial*[2] element (nationalisation as an increasing similarity between geographical areas and territorial-administrative units within nations).

Later on, other authors deal with the theme of nationalisation of politics. Stokes (1965; 1967), like Schattschneider, regards the phenomenon as the progressive increase in the importance of national issues and empirically tests his hypotheses by analysing turnout rates and party votes in the United States and Great Britain. Moreover, he introduces a further dimension to operationalise the concept of nationalisation, that is, the correspondence of the change (in turnout levels and votes for a given party) from one election to the next one between the national level and a given number of constituencies. Thus, the higher the number of territorial units that show a change against the national trend (i.e., a party loses votes at national level but grows in many local constituencies), the lower the level of nationalisation.

An instrumental study on this topic is the systematic clarification provided by Claggett, Flanigan and Zingale (1984). Moving from the discussion of Schattschneider's and Stokes's contributions, the authors distinguish three different and coexisting aspects of the concept of nationalisation. First, it is a process of convergence in the levels of partisan support, namely of progressive homogenisation of turnout and support for political parties. Second, the concept of nationalisation expresses the propensity of the electorate to refer to political forces, issues and leaders located at the national level, rather than at the local one: it concerns the tendency of voters to be influenced by national political stimuli as, for example, national political leaders rather than local candidates. Third, nationalisation means a uniform response of voters to these stimuli coming from the national level: the response (operationalised as the swing between two subsequent elections) could be uniform or nonuniform. In the case of perfect nationalisation, a party that, for example, increases three points at national level compared to the previous election has a similar increase also in all the territorial units of that country.

As far as the first aspect is concerned, nationalisation has to be considered a macro-phenomenon, namely a process affecting the macro-level, thus implying increasing similarity among territorial units and not among individuals. Many authors emphasise this aspect in their definition of the concept. In his study on the nationalisation of the American politics,[3] Sundquist (1973: 332–37) states that it means 'the convergence of party strength' characterised by a reduced variance around the average of the two largest parties' votes across states. Agnew (1987; 1988) links the first and the second dimensions of Claggett, Flanigan and Zingale's definition, identifying nationalisation as the process through which 'allegiances are transferred from the local to the national community and the major political parties receive support that is equally distributed across the national territory and fluctuates in equal proportion across all voting units' (Agnew 1988: 307).

The third dimension (the type of response) is the most problematic and has been used by Stokes and later by Katz (1973) as an indicator of the second dimension (the source of influence). Katz criticises Stokes's model, according to which uniform swings indicate responses to national forces, arguing that, through Stokes's model, national effects are underestimated, since nationalisation can also be extended to cover 'the degree to which different areas respond to the same electoral forces, whether or not the effects of these forces are numerically identical across space' (Katz 1973: 817). In other words, according to this interpretation, even nonuniform swings could be responses to national forces.

The problem arising from this threefold definition is therefore that, while the first aspect (related to the vote) is easily measurable through various indicators[4] and does not leave room to misleading interpretations, this does not happen for the other two aspects. Claggett, Flanigan and Zingale believe that both Stokes and Katz confuse the second dimension with the third one and, by crossing the second aspect with the third one, propose a typology where four possible situations come out. Two cases are very clear: that of typical nationalisation (forces located at national level and uniform response of the voters) and that of typical localisation of politics (nonuniform responses to locally based factors). Two other cases are instead less easily interpretable: the case of 'coincidence' (local forces and uniform response), though difficult to verify, and that of 'mediated national influences', in which nationally located stimuli are followed by nonuniform responses of voters. Since there is not a way to empirically clarify the source of stimuli (if national ones or local ones), it will be impossible to interpret the case of nonuniform swing between the territorial units of a given country (it cannot be indeed established if the causal political factors come from the national or the local level). Regarding the second and the third aspects of the definition by Claggett, Flanigan and Zingale (1984), measuring the level of nationalisation is therefore problematic. For this reason, according to Caramani (2004: 42), the homogeneity of electoral behaviour (the first aspect) is a parsimonious indicator of the nationalisation of broader political aspects.

Morgenstern, Swindle and Castagnola (2009: 1322) effectively epitomise this lengthy discussion by distinguishing between a *dynamic* dimension of nationalisation, that is, 'the degree to which a party's vote in the various districts changes uniformly across time' (the third aspect in Claggett, Flanigan and Zingale's definition as well as Stokes's definition), and a *static* or *distributional* dimension of nationalisation, namely, 'the degree to which a party has broad appeal across the nation' (the first aspect in Claggett, Flanigan and Zingale's definition as well as Schattschneider's viewpoint). The dynamic dimension focuses on the comparison of parties' votes between two subsequent elections, while the static or distributional dimension compares parties' votes across districts in a given election.

Recently, Lago and Montero (2014: 193) summarise another controversial issue related to the concept of nationalisation, by stating that 'the nationalization of party systems can be both understood as a process or as an outcome'. Contributions about nationalisation conceived as a process are provided by Caramani (2004), whose deep analysis about the historical process of nationalisation in Western Europe will be reviewed in the next section; by Cox (1997), who calls it 'party linkage', namely, the process by which politicians contesting elections in different districts get to run under a common party label; and, similarly, by Chhibber and Kollman (1998: 330), according to whom 'party aggregation' is defined as the process by which politicians coordinate candidates and/or voters in order to aggregate votes across districts and to create national parties.[5] Nonetheless, Lago and Montero prefer to consider nationalisation as an outcome that 'involves the replacement of local parties with national parties' (2014: 194), or, according to Kasuya and Moenius (2008: 126), nationalisation 'refers to the extent to which parties compete with equal strength across various geographic units within a nation. Strongly nationalised party systems are systems where the vote share of each party is similar across geographic units (e.g., districts, provinces, and regions), while weakly nationalised party systems exhibit large variation in the vote shares of parties across sub-national units'.

In this study, I adopt a 'distributional' definition of vote nationalisation, meant as *the level of territorial homogeneity of party support*. Moreover, throughout this study, nationalisation will be mainly considered as an outcome based on election results (the level of vote nationalisation in a given country at a given election). It concerns within-country territorial variations of party support, and it can be measured at party level or country level, by aggregating the scores of the parties that contest the election in a given system. The more the support for a party (or a group of parties) is homogeneous among the territorial units of the country, the more that party (or that party system) is nationalised, and vice versa. From this conceptualisation it derives that vote nationalisation is a matter of degree (a party can have a high or a low level of vote nationalisation and so does a country). However, the 'process' perspective will not be discarded. The historical process of nationalisation of politics in Western Europe is a crucial starting point of this study, as I show in the next section. Moreover, the 'process' perspective will be adopted whenever there will be a comparison of trends of nationalisation or denationalisation over time, related to individual countries or the overall sample.

As regards the scope of nationalisation, I agree with Caramani (1996: 208), according to whom the two concepts of nationalisation of politics and nationalisation of the vote are in a relationship of genus and species, and, therefore, we can infer the first from the second, the vote being an important catalyst of other political behaviours. Furthermore, I prefer to use the term 'vote nationalisation' instead of the conventional 'party system nationalisation' so as to emphasise that this book studies the levels of nationalisation resulting from election results and not simply from party's territorial coverage: according to this latter, a party system is nationalised if parties present lists or candidates in each district, while vote nationalisation implies that parties receive similar share of votes in each district.

THE HISTORICAL PROCESS OF NATIONALISATION IN WESTERN EUROPE

In the specific European context, the most systematic contribution about the vote nationalisation process, from both a theoretical and an empirical point of view, is provided by Caramani (1996; 2004). His conceptualisation of vote nationalisation is primarily influenced by Rokkan's definition of 'politicization'. Rokkan does not directly address the issue of nationalisation in his works, but, analysing the move towards the national integration of Norwegian politics, he identifies four steps of change, the last one being that of 'politicization', namely, 'the breakdown of the traditional system of local rule through the entry of nationally organised parties into municipal elections' (Rokkan 1970: 227).

According to Caramani, the nationalisation of politics is a major long-term political phenomenon which deals with the historical evolution from highly localised and territorialised politics – that characterised the early phases of electoral competition – towards the formation of national electorates and party systems and carried out through the progressive reduction of the territoriality of political cleavages. Quoting a meaningful extract at the beginning of his work (2004: 1):

> Through nationalization processes, the highly localised and territorialised politics that characterised the early phases of electoral competition in the nineteenth century is replaced by national electoral alignments and oppositions. Peripheral and regional specificities disappear and sectional cleavages progressively transform into nationwide functional alignments. Through the development of central party organisations, local candidates are absorbed into nationwide structures and ideologies. Programs and policies become national in scope and cancel out – or at least reduce – the scope of local problems, with the most relevant issues being transferred from the local to the national level. These processes of political integration translate in the territorial homogenization of electoral behaviour, both electoral participation and the support for the main party families. Nationalization processes therefore represent a crucial step in the structuring of party politics.

The starting point of Caramani's analysis is represented by Rokkan's (1970) macro-sociological study on the territorial structuring of the European party systems as well as by previous empirical analyses about regional differentiation in Western nations (Rose and Urwin 1975; Ersson, Janda and Lane 1985) and the substantial set of studies on the nation-building process and the consequent centre-periphery conflict in Europe (Daalder 1966a; Tilly 1975; Torvsik 1981; Rokkan and Urwin 1982; 1983; Flora 1999).

As far as the timing of the process is taken into account, the formation of national electorates and party systems and the progressive homogenisation of party support in Europe took place in the early phases of development of electoral competition, between the end of the nineteenth century and World War I. By the 1920s, the electoral competition was already fully nationalised, and the period after World War II brought about a long pattern of fundamental stability of territorial configuration with only a slight tendency towards further nationalisation (Caramani 2004: 73–81). Caramani brings much empirical evidence to support this finding, concluding that the timing of the process is directly related to the famous 'freezing hypothesis' formulated by Lipset and Rokkan (1967: 50), according to whom, around the 1920s cleavage structures and the related partisan alignments crystallised and remained stable in the following decades. This finding proves consistent with the research by Rose and Urwin (1975: 45) who emphasise that 'nationalization of party competition had already occurred by the start of the postwar era'.

The timing of the process is crucial to understand its causal factors and their role in shaping the process. As far as these causal factors are concerned, Caramani's theoretical scheme is based on the three fundamental dimensions concerning the structuring of the political space: state formation, democratisation and nation building (2004: 195).

To begin with, the process of state formation has historically concerned the definition and the closing of external state boundaries and the related definition of the citizenship. There are two different types of boundaries: geographical and sociocultural ones. The geographical boundary building regards the definition of the territorial space on which the state is sovereign, while the sociocultural boundary building entails the delimitation of the membership in the state community and the development of a national identity. In the nation-state, these two dimensions are merged in the concept of citizenship. Using Hirschman's terminology (1970), this strengthening of external boundaries resulted in a reduction of the *exit* options.[6]

Second, the process of democratisation concerns the development of mass politics and party competition through the diffusion of the institutional channels of representation[7] and the progressive extension and equalisation of voting rights to previously excluded citizens. Quoting Hirschman again, democratisation favoured the development of territorial *voice* channels.

Finally, the nation-building process refers to the centralising effort, led by the nation-building elites, to penetrate the country's peripheries and achieve their political mobilisation, economic integration and cultural standardisation. Through the nation-building process, therefore, the different geographical areas of a given country become more homogeneous[8] and 'issues, organisations, allegiances, and competences' are progressively dislocated from the local to the national level (Caramani 2004: 32). By doing so, political cleavages, which shape the expression of *voice* in the political system and structure the constellations of party alliances and oppositions, lost part of their former territoriality.[9] As the nation-building process is successfully carried out, the old territorial lines of conflict (originated by ethnic, linguistic or religious divisions), characterising the early phases of electoral competition, are replaced by functional cleavages[10] that cut across territorial units, thus opposing segments of population into the same territory according to interest and ideologies instead of set against different territories of a given country. Nationalisation of politics therefore consists of the weakening of internal territorial boundaries (cleavages) or, using Hirschman's terminology again, in the reduction in the territoriality of *voice* options.

These three macro-processes (state formation, democratisation and nation-building) and their political consequences (reduction of exit options, development of internal voice channels and progressive reduction of their territoriality) structured the European political space and fostered the evolution of European countries towards the emergence of a nationalised pattern of electoral competition.

Nonetheless, these processes have not always been entirely successful: in some polities, the nationalisation process has not been fully achieved, while in some others, it has completely failed, thus leading to the exit option[11] or to the territorial expression of voice, as the next section shows.

As mentioned before, the expression of voice in a political system is shaped by the structure of constellations of party alliances and oppositions arisen from social cleavages. The genesis and evolution of party systems in Europe during the nineteenth century and the beginning of the twentieth century can be explained by the interaction between two processes of revolutionary change: the National Revolution and the Industrial Revolution (Lipset and Rokkan 1967).

The National Revolution is the precondition for the deepest and bitterest cleavages since such cleavages are based on values and cultural identities: the centre-periphery cleavage and the state-church one. These two cleavages triggered the rise, first in Britain and then in other European countries, of Liberal and Conservative parties which contributed – in a more relevant way than all other parties – to nationalise the electoral competition, as well as of ethnoregionalist and religious parties which were responsible for the major deviations from the pattern of homogenisation.[12]

The Liberal parties were the main actors in the historical evolution towards the centralisation of the state, the integration and cultural standardisation of the peripheries, the democratisation of political institutions and the secularisation and separation of government from religious influences (Caramani 2004: 199). The Liberals, therefore, embodied the 'centre'[13] and the 'state' sides in the two cleavages emerged from the National Revolution.

On the other side, the Conservative parties represented the reaction of the aristocratic elites, which aimed at restoring the royal authority weakened by constitutionalism and parliamentarianism and at preserving the old order threatened by liberal reforms. Moreover, the Conservatives strived against the secularisation carried out by the Liberals and supported the religious moral order and church's privileges. By emerging within the political space well before other party families, the Liberals and the Conservatives took part in the early phases of electoral competition, attempting to mobilise that small portion of citizens who had the right of vote, thus being the first parties to spread throughout the European countries their (still embryonic) forms of party organisations and thereby playing a central role in the nationalisation of the electoral competition. This point can be easily understood by considering that the opposition between Liberals and Conservatives was of a nonterritorial but of a functional nature, namely based on specific interests (liberal and secular reforms versus the defence of aristocratic and ecclesiastic privileges).

Therefore, before the inclusion of mass working electorates and the spread of Social Democratic parties, towards the end of the nineteenth century, many Western European countries had already experienced the development of a nationwide party competition, based on the functional opposition between Liberals and Conservatives.

Although less decisive than the National Revolution, even the Industrial Revolution, with its related cleavages (rural-urban and class ones), has been an important determinant of the nationalisation process. The industrialisation has produced a massive demographic migration from the peripheries towards the urban and industrial centres, bringing into contact masses of individuals coming from different regions in the same new industrial environment. Furthermore, the parallel development of new forms of mass communications has had a substantial impact on the transformation of cleavages from territorial into functional ones. Social divisions have persisted, but they have been much more cross-cutting and did not project themselves on the territory.

In the wake of this historical transformation, a strong factor of vote homogenisation was the rise of Socialist and Social Democratic parties which stemmed from the class-cleavage and developed between the last thirty years of the nineteenth century and the first fifteen years of the twentieth century. After the enlargement of voting rights to previously excluded citizens, these parties mobilised large masses of newly enfranchised workers, and in a few years they reached a stable level of support, around 30 per cent (Caramani 2004: 212), thus becoming crucial actors of Western European politics. Like their electoral growth, their territorial spread and the homogenising effect on the overall level of vote nationalisation were rapid. After the entering of Social Democratic parties, which were an expression of the class cleavage, 'a homogenizing cleavage' (Caramani 2004: 196), the European political space definitely structured in functional terms,[14] leading to the predominance of a left-right pattern of competition between these parties and the Conservatives and 'bourgeois' coalitions which contested the extension of voting rights to the working classes and the growth of the welfare state.

It follows that Western European electorates and party systems became increasingly homogeneous under the pressure of two main factors, one related to macro-sociological factors and the other related to parties' competitive strategies. On the one hand, there was the supremacy of the functional left-right conflict and the consequent reduction of the territoriality of political cleavages (Caramani 2004: 247), determined by the process of cultural integration and then reinforced by that of social mobilisation. On the other hand, there was the spread of electoral competition carried out by the two historical families of Liberals and Conservatives that started to contest each district and challenge each other in the respective strongholds, thus drastically reducing the territoriality of the vote.[15] On this latter point, Caramani (2004: 231) argues that the process of nationalisation is also 'the result of political parties themselves and of their strategic-competitive action aiming at winning the highest number of seats'.

Moreover, other intervening institutional factors, such as the extension of suffrage and the incorporation of the masses into political life (enfranchisement), as well as the introduction of proportional electoral formulas in Europe, only took place after the achievement of a nationalised competition. The enfranchisement extended the process of nationalisation to the masses, but it was the result of the supremacy of earlier processes triggered by the National and, to a lesser extent, by the Industrial Revolution rather than of mass politics through the extension of suffrage. At the same time, PR systems were introduced after World War I, when nationalisation processes were already attained. 'Rather than having been a factor of homogenization of party support, therefore, PR appears to have been a factor of *stabilization*[16] of territorial configuration in Europe' (Caramani 2004: 246).

HISTORICAL SOURCES OF DEVIATIONS: PARTIES FOR RELIGIOUS, TERRITORIAL AND AGRARIAN DEFENCE

After having analysed the historical process of formation of national electorates and party systems in Europe and having detected the main determinants of this process, by following Rokkan and Caramani's macro-sociological framework, this section focuses on the deviations from the main pattern of nationalisation, namely, the long-lasting variations in the within-country territorial configurations of party support. The following pages aim at identifying the most important sources of diversity in the territorial structures of Western European party systems and at looking for the existence of some common patterns and regularities that have concurred to determine the total, or partial, failure of the nationalisation process in these contexts.

In the European landscape, three major sources of deviations from the main pattern towards territorial homogeneity have emerged: parties for religious, territorial and agrarian defence.

Parties for religious defence

Parties emerged to defend the church's interests were the result of the National Revolution (and especially of the state-church cleavage). The diffusion and the electoral fortunes of these parties greatly vary across Europe. The critical juncture for the subsequent differentiated development of these parties was the Reformation (Rokkan 1970: 116). In homogeneously Protestant countries (like Britain and Scandinavia), the state-church conflict was resolved long before the advent of mass democracy and democratisation: the Reformation led to the development of national churches in opposition to the Roman Catholic one. Temporal and spiritual institutions were therefore allied 'in the defence of the central nation-building culture' (Rokkan 1970: 112). This historical development has facilitated the diffusion and the penetration throughout the country of the national culture and language (also thanks to the translation of the Bible in national languages) and prevented the rise, in Britain as well as in the Scandinavian countries, of large Protestant parties for the defence of the national church. In these contexts, the alliance between the nation builders and the church has been challenged by the rise of peripheral nonconformist movements of religious dissidents with orthodox Protestant beliefs, emerged as a reaction against the secularised tendencies of the ruling elites. These movements, although in many cases have only been peripheral minorities, have been the only source of 'religious' deviation in homogeneously Protestant countries.

Conversely, in the Counter-Reformed countries, the protection of Catholic Church's interests has led to the formation of parties for religious defence (as the large Christian Democratic parties of Austria, Belgium and Italy) or to the inclusion of religious issues into the political manifestos of broad conservative fronts (like in France or Spain). In all these homogeneously Catholic countries,[17] parties for religious defence have represented the 'right' side of the functional Liberal-Conservative opposition,[18] and, as a result, just like the Conservative parties, have shown high levels of vote nationalisation.

The most important source of territorial deviation among the parties emerged for religious defence can be found in the religiously mixed countries (Germany, the Netherlands and Switzerland). Here both Catholic and Protestant parties have emerged, and the religious affiliation has acquired strong territorial connotations, with the Catholic minority being rooted in some areas (Bavaria in Germany, the southern provinces of Limburg and North Brabant in the Netherlands, the southern cantons of Switzerland) and the Protestant majority in the rest of these countries. As a consequence, these kinds of confessional parties have exhibited heterogeneous territorial configurations of support. On the contrary, the interconfessional parties of these religiously mixed countries (as the Christian Democratic Appeal in the Netherlands) have been very homogeneous from the territorial viewpoint, since their appeal to religious values has cut across the cleavage between Catholics and Protestants.

Parties for territorial defence

The second major source of territorial deviation in Europe, and undoubtedly the one accounting for the largest within-country territorial differences, has been represented by the ethnoregionalist party family,[19] stemming from the centre-periphery cleavage, which in turn resulted from the National Revolution.

The process of nation building generated territorial and cultural conflicts that sometimes have been solved through secessions and boundary changes (e.g., the dismemberment of the Hapsburg Empire, the Irish secession from England in 1922, the secession of the Catholic Belgian provinces from the Low Countries in 1830) and in some other countries have led to the formation of territorial parties that have survived the nationalisation process. According to Caramani (2004: 185), parties for territorial defence include parties originating from the centre-periphery cleavage that have emerged in the process of state formation and nation building (e.g., the Basque Nationalist Party); parties born from ethnolinguistic cleavages (e.g., the Flemish People's Union); parties claiming stronger administrative autonomy but not centred on cultural identity (e.g., the Italian Northern League); parties created as local branches of larger national parties or allied with them (e.g., the Bavarian

Christian-Social Union). Although the supremacy of the left-right dimension has favoured the nationalisation of party systems all over Europe, cultural cleavages have survived the advent of class politics and have hindered the process of national integration. Parties that stemmed from ethnic and linguistic cleavages – the main survivors of preindustrial cleavages (together with the aforementioned religious cleavage) – have become the main sources of territorial diversity in Europe.

Many factors and conditions have been emphasised by the literature to account for the emergence and the survival of territorial parties in Europe (see in particular Rokkan 1970; Torvsik 1981; Rokkan and Urwin 1982). Among all these explanations, a set of common factors must be considered for the birth and consolidation of territorial oppositions: (a) the cultural fragmentation of the country (religious and/or ethnolinguistic fragmentation); (b) a strong concentration of the counter-culture within a distinct and clear-cut territory; (c) the presence of few and tenuous ties of communication and alliance towards the national centre and of more and stronger ties towards external centres of cultural and/or economic influence; (d) a low degree of economic dependence from the political centre/metropolis; and (e) a polarising cleavage structure (in particular, urban-rural and religious cleavages reinforcing the centre-periphery one). An accumulation of such conditions makes the emergence and survival of federalist, autonomist, separatist movements and parties more likely to occur.

All countries where parties for territorial defence have emerged are characterised by cultural heterogeneity. Most of them are heterogeneous from an ethnolinguistic standpoint: Belgium (with the linguistic split between the Dutch-speaking Flanders and the French-speaking Wallonia), Spain (with the Castilian challenged by many peripheral dialects and languages, above all Catalan and Basque), Finland (with the sizeable Swedish-speaking minority), and, to a lesser extent, Great Britain (with the ethnic claims of peripheral nationalisms in Scotland, Wales and Northern Ireland) and Italy (with the German and French-speaking minorities, respectively, concentrated in the two border regions of Trentino-Alto Adige and Valle d'Aosta). Moreover, Switzerland is a heterogeneous country both in religious and in ethnolinguistic terms (although only the religious dimension has been translated into the party system). In all these countries, the ethnolinguistic groups are concentrated in clear-cut territories. In many of them, the peripheries have been tied to external centres of cultural and/or economic influence (Germany and France for Switzerland, the Netherlands and France for Belgium, Sweden for Finland, Austria and France for two Italian regions, Ireland for Northern Ireland). In many cases, the peripheries are economically prosperous and industrialised while the political centre is backwards (it is the case of the northern regions in Italy, the Catalan and Basque regions in Spain, the Flanders region in Belgium). Finally, the polarising cleavage structure reinforces the territorial cleavages in some countries (as in Belgium), whereas in other cases the criss-crossing of cleavage lines dampens the territorial oppositions (as in Switzerland).

Parties for agrarian defence

The last major source of deviation from the main pattern towards the formation of nationalised party systems in Europe was represented by the rise of agrarian parties which have stemmed from the urban-rural cleavage.

The critical juncture for the beginning of this process was the Industrial Revolution: it produced a spectacular growth of world trade, the spread of new technologies and the widening of the markets through the opening of the old protectionist barriers, and, as a consequence, it triggered increasing mass migrations towards the industrial cities. As stated by Rokkan (1970: 107), this process 'generated increasing strains between the primary producers in the countryside and the merchants and the entrepreneurs in the towns and the cities'. This cleavage was characterised by a hard core of economic conflict (disputes over the commodity market, the tariff barriers and the prices of agricultural products), but it also reflected 'an opposition between two value orientations: the recognition of status through *ascriptions and kin connections* versus the claims for status through *achievement and enterprise*' (Lipset and Rokkan 1967: 19).

Parties for agrarian defence[20] did not emerge everywhere in Europe but only in some countries where certain conditions occur. The first two conditions were the structure of alliance formed by the central core of nation builders and the organisation of the rural society at the time of the extension of suffrage. These two conditions were closely related. Agrarian parties were movements for the defence of small and medium-sized units of production against the predominance of the cities into the national political life. Therefore, 'agrarian interests were most likely to find direct political expression in systems of close alliance between nation-builders and the urban economic leadership' (Rokkan 1970: 126) and in systems where land tenure was not dominated by large estates. These two fundamental requirements rule out many countries from the possibility of emergence of agrarian parties: in Britain, Germany, Spain and Austria, land ownership was organised in large estates and 'the concentration of power and the social role of great landowners put the landed economy in a much stronger position' (Caramani 2004: 219) and increased the centre-builder's payoffs of alliances with landowners.[21]

In addition, there were cultural and religious conditions to be respected: parties for agrarian defence developed 'where there were important cultural barriers between the countryside and the cities and much resistance to the incorporation of farm production in the capitalist economy of the cities' and also 'where the Catholic Church was without significant influence' (Rokkan 1970: 128). These cultural and religious factors were absent in some other countries, such as Belgium and the Netherlands, which instead fitted the first two aforementioned conditions, since the centre-builders were allied with urban interests and family-size farming predominated.[22] Nevertheless, in both countries, small farming was closely tied to urban economy (Lipset and Rokkan 1967: 45). Moreover, the religious condition leaves out France[23] and Italy,[24] where the Catholic Church acted as an agency of rural mobilisation in the countryside, including the defence of rural interests into large Catholic-Conservative fronts which rarely found direct political expression through the emergence of peasant parties.[25]

The third and last important condition for the emergence of agrarian parties in Europe was the weakness of the cities at the time of the decisive extension of the suffrage. Only a few countries comply with all these circumstances: the Scandinavian ones[26] and the Protestant cantons of Switzerland. While in some other countries small farmers' and peasants' parties emerged during the interwar period but rapidly disappeared after World War II, or were absorbed by broader Catholic-Conservative fronts (Caramani 2004: 220),[27] it is only in Scandinavia and Protestant Switzerland that large and time-resistant agrarian parties have developed.

The largest European agrarian party has been the Finnish Agrarian League, and, even today, its successor (the Centre Party) is usually the first- or the second-largest party in the country. In the other three Scandinavian countries, there have been strong traditions of independent peasant representation and widespread rejection of the cultural influence of the encroaching cities. In Denmark, Norway and Sweden, the agrarian movements have initially been included into broad 'Left' fronts including nonconformist religious dissidents and radicals against the urban and conservative centre-builders.[28] More specifically, in Denmark a genuine agrarian party has never emerged since the urban radicals have left the original opposition front and the Liberal Left (*Venstre*) has remained an agrarian-based party; on the contrary, in Sweden a distinct party for the defence of the agrarian class emerged, but its interests were threatened by the uniquely rapid transition of the country from agrarian to modern industrial society and by the consequent internal migration of the population from the rural to the urban areas (Hancock 1980: 186–87; Christensen 1997: 395); finally, in Norway the agrarian party had their strongholds in the western and southern peripheral regions, where the agrarian claims welded themselves with the three historical 'counter-cultures'[29] (Rokkan 1967; Rokkan and Valen 1970; Aarebrot 1982).

Out of the Scandinavian context, a large rural party has only developed in Switzerland, where the need for protecting the farmers' interests against the urban predominance has led to the formation of the Farmers, Artisans and Citizens' Party (later Swiss People's Party), deeply rooted in rural Protestant areas around Zurich and Berne.

Once they have emerged and consolidated into the national party system, these large agrarian parties have substantially contributed to reduce the within-country territorial homogeneity and to deviate from the vote nationalisation pattern. Yet, the overall territorial impact of this cleavage has massively reduced through time: in the wake of the urbanisation process and the continuous decline of the rural population, the Nordic agrarian parties have transformed since the 1950s into 'centre' parties with a broader interclass appeal, emphasising new issues such as environmentalism and power decentralisation to regional authorities (Knutsen 2004: 155); in Switzerland the agrarian party transformed itself into a right-wing populist and Conservative Party in 1971. Accordingly, both in the Scandinavian and in the Swiss cases, the territorial support for these parties has become far less heterogeneous and no longer able to develop a substantial failure of the nationalisation process.

LIMITS OF PREVIOUS STUDIES

Although the issue of vote nationalisation has long and deep roots in both the American and the European scholarly traditions (*see* the above sections), Jones and Mainwaring (2003: 139) stated the necessity to address 'an under-analysed issue in the comparative study of parties and party systems: their degree of nationalization'. It seems that their appeal has been successful: during the past years, scholars have paid increasing attention to vote nationalisation, with the publication of several articles on the topic. Yet, many of these articles have a predominant methodological purpose since their main goal is to propose new measures of vote nationalisation. Amongst such articles, we can remember the ones by Cox (1999), Moenius and Kasuya (2004), Kasuya and Moenius (2008), Bochsler (2010), Golosov (2014), Lago and Montero (2014) and Morgenstern, Polga-Hecimovich and Siavelis (2014).

Regarding the articles that bring about some empirical findings, some of them treat vote nationalisation not as an outcome but as a predictor, exploring its ability to affect the scope of public policies (Crisp, Olivella and Potter 2013), the composition of central government expenditures (Castañeda-Angarita 2013), the provisions of the public healthcare service (Hicken,

Kollman and Simmons 2016), or the consequences for foreign direct investment (Simmons et al. 2016), or deal with vote nationalisation as a contextual feature affecting individual voting behaviour (Maggini and Emanuele 2015; Morgenstern, Smith and Trelles 2017).

Moreover, many of the empirical works devoted to study vote nationalisation and its determinants do not specifically focus on Western Europe but on Latin America (Jones and Mainwaring 2003; Harbers 2010; Alemán and Kellam 2016; Su 2017), Africa (Golosov 2016a), Eastern Europe (Nikoleny 2008; Sikk and Bochsler 2008), federal systems of government (Chhibber and Kollman 1998; 2004; Roberts and Wibbels 2011) or cross-regional studies mixing together democratic and authoritarian regimes (De Miguel 2016; Lago and Lago 2016; Golosov 2016b).

The articles related to Western Europe generally aim at disentangling some specific elements associated to vote nationalisation, such as the link between decentralisation and vote nationalisation (Lago and Lago 2010; Lago 2011; Schakel 2012; Simón 2013) or the relation between institutional arrangement (in terms of executive system and electoral system) and vote nationalisation (Morgenstern, Swindle and Castagnola 2009; Golosov 2016c). All these contributions rely on Western Europe and reach some important achievements but do not provide a comprehensive explanation concerning the empirical determinants of vote nationalisation.

The only published work that tries to achieve such a result is *The Nationalization of Politics* by Caramani (2004). His comparative analysis relies on Western Europe and studies the processes of formation of national electorates and party systems since the early phases of electoral competition. Nevertheless, Caramani's work has some serious flaws that this book tries to overcome and solve, as shown in the next chapter, which is devoted to outlining the research design of this book.

First of all, Caramani's analysis – as well as most of the ones cited earlier – is based on indicators of vote nationalisation that are biased for a number of reasons, thus undermining the reliability of his empirical results. On the contrary, this book relies on the sPSNS, recently developed by Bochsler (2010) and generally considered the most reliable measure of vote nationalisation. Second, Caramani's data do not go beyond the mid-1990s, while this book covers all general elections held in Western Europe until 2015. Therefore, Caramani's work is not able to take into account many relevant social, institutional and political changes that have occurred in Western Europe during the past two decades. Third, and foremost, Caramani's work remains on a purely descriptive level, and it does not provide an empirically based explanation about the determinants of vote nationalisation – a gap that is eventually filled by part III of this book.

Chapter 2

Research design

This chapter presents the research design of the book. In the following sections, I discuss the methodological framework: from the operationalisation of the dependent variable to the spatial and temporal scope of the book, up to the type of data and method employed in the empirical analysis. Moreover, I raise some important questions that find a proper response in the second and the third parts of this work, that is, respectively, in chapter 3, dedicated to showing the vote nationalisation patterns in Western Europe and in the chapters devoted to the search for an explanation of those patterns (from chapters 4 to 7).

More specifically, this chapter is organised as follows: the first section, 'Research questions: Assessing and explaining vote nationalisation', introduces the two research questions which are the starting point of the analysis; the second section, 'The dependent variable: How to measure vote nationalisation?', presents – after a critical review of the previous measures employed by the literature on the topic – the dependent variable and its operationalisation; the third section, 'Space and time', specifies the spatial and the temporal horizon of the research, while the fourth section, 'Data collection', discusses the data employed and their underlying criteria; the fifth section, 'Method', examines the method used for the test of the hypotheses; finally, the last section, 'The independent variables: The macro-constellation of factors', briefly introduces the macro-constellation of the independent variables.

RESEARCH QUESTIONS: ASSESSING AND EXPLAINING VOTE NATIONALISATION

As emphasised in the previous chapter, according to Rose and Urwin (1975) and Caramani (2004), the fundamental steps towards the formation of national electorates and party systems took place before World War I, thanks to the impact of macro-processes like cultural integration and social mobilisation. Then, since the 1920s, there has been a long pattern of stability, with only a slight tendency towards further territorial homogeneity.

However, nowadays these findings should be put into question, for two main reasons. First, most of the previous studies on territorial variations in Western Europe have been carried out by operationalising the outcome (the level of vote nationalisation in a country) through the use of some biased measures, as shown in the next section. Thus, the possibility that these studies have achieved some misleading results is anything but a discarded perspective.

Second, as mentioned in chapter 1, Caramani's research – the most important analysis of vote nationalisation in Western Europe so far – uses data that do not go beyond the mid-1990s. Therefore, his analysis is not able to take into account properly many relevant social, political and institutional changes occurred in Western Europe during the past years: let us just think about the demise of the class cleavage, the changes in party competition patterns, the increase in power decentralisation and the European integration.

To begin with, the acceleration of the decline of the class cleavage (Franklin, Mackie and Valen 1992; Knutsen 2004), which is the most 'homogenising cleavage' according to Caramani (2004: 196), is likely to have brought about consequences on the territorial structuring of the Socialist and Social Democratic parties' support. This development is obviously related to the overall 'de-freezing' of partisan alignments that consolidated during the 1920s, according to Lipset and Rokkan's (1967) theory. This process is fraught with consequences for party competition as revealed by the increase in party system fragmentation and electoral volatility (Drummond 2006; Chiaramonte and Emanuele 2015; Dassonneville and Hooghe 2015), and it has been made possible by the simultaneous presence of two interrelated phenomena: on the one hand, the electoral decline of traditional mainstream parties, which had mainly contributed to the increase in competitiveness and vote nationalisation; on the other hand, the rise of genuinely new parties (Sikk 2005) or the revival and transformation of old ones, like new ethnoregionalist parties which have been able to achieve increasing electoral success in their strongholds, thus increasing the within-country territorial variation in Western Europe.

Furthermore, the process of power decentralisation, that is, the progressive devolution of formerly state functions and power to peripheral authorities, which has been ongoing for a number of years in most Western European countries, may have affected the level of vote nationalisation, like the process of Europeanisation, namely, the adaptation of actors, organisations and institutions to the process of European integration (Hanley 2002). Both decentralisation and European integration have caused the emergence of the so-called multilevel governance (Hooghe and Marks 2001), which in turn represents a challenge to the traditional nation-state and its ability to produce autonomous laws and provide identity resources.

These are only some of the macro-processes – extensively analysed in the third part of the book – that may have affected the level of vote nationalisation in Western European countries during the past years. Indeed, vote nationalisation is not something that can be taken for granted or an outcome that is reached once for all. Conversely, being a political phenomenon, it is continuously influenced and determined by a complex macro-constellation of factors that, in turn, change through time.

My investigation moves from two main research questions. The first aims at assessing the evolution of the vote nationalisation process during the past fifty years. Have Western European party systems been characterised by a continuing homogenising process of electoral behaviour, as Caramani (2004) suggests? Or, on the contrary, can we notice a reverse of this trend and a resurgence of some territorial distinctiveness that lead to the opening of a denationalisation process?

The idea of a trend reversal in the process of vote nationalisation has been recently underlined by several authors[1] (Broughton and Donovan 1999; Hopkin 2003; Szöcsik and Zuber 2012), and such an eventuality has been already prefigured more than twenty years ago by Caramani himself, when he stated that 'a process of denationalization and of regionalisation cannot now be excluded' (1996: 220). To address this question, my first task is that of mapping the level of vote nationalisation in Western Europe, showing its cross-national variation as well as its trend towards change or stability through time.

The second research question is related to the explanation of the outcome. Which are the best predictors of vote nationalisation, their changes through time and their national variations? Is it conceivable that political factors, linked to the structure of the competition – albeit hitherto neglected – play a major role in the explanation of vote nationalisation, to the detriment of the much more emphasised social and institutional factors?

I will look for an overall explanation, thus detecting some decisive factors regardless of time and space. Nevertheless, I will also try to identify which factors are not important in the overall explanation but are temporally or country specific, thus providing some additional explanation of the variance.

The starting point to address this second research question is represented by the growing literature on the topic. On one side, Caramani (2004) emphasises the impact of macro-sociological factors on nationalisation, although he does not empirically test his working hypotheses. In a similar vein, Ersson, Janda and Lane (1985) and Knutsen (2010) stress the valuable impact of variables related to the social structure on the explanation of within-country territorial variations. On the other side, in recent studies many other scholars suggest the importance of institutional factors, such as the level of decentralisation (Chhibber and Kollman 1998; 2004; Brancati 2006; Harbers 2010; Lago 2011; Lago and Montero 2014) and the type of electoral system (Cox 1997; Cox and Knoll 2003; Morgenstern, Swindle and Castagnola 2009; Golosov 2016c). Yet, there may be some other factors with a significant impact on vote nationalisation. I am referring to the features of the political context, namely, to the dynamics of the party system and the structure of the competition, which have undergone significant changes in the past decades.

THE DEPENDENT VARIABLE: HOW TO MEASURE VOTE NATIONALISATION?

As shown in chapter 1, during the past fifty years, a large amount of literature has addressed the issue of nationalisation and has proposed different ways to measure it.

The first scholar who provides an operational definition of nationalisation is Schattschneider (1960). As discussed in chapter 1, his definition is closely related to that of competitiveness: the higher the number of states in which the two parties compete, the more nationalised is the party system. From this first conceptualisation, it derives the use of some basic indicators of competitiveness:[2] Rose and Urwin (1975: 19) and Urwin (1982a: 41) operationalise this concept through the *number of uncontested seats*, that is, the proportion of constituencies in which only one candidate contests the seat to be returned. Similarly, Cornford (1970) focuses on the proportion of *safe seats* for each political party. A different way related to the same approach is that of measuring the *territorial coverage* of the parties (Caramani 2004: 61): the percentage of territorial units of a country where a party contests seats. Moving from the concept of nationalisation as homogeneity of the parties' supply between the areas of the country, Lago and Montero (2014) develop a slightly more complex index, the *local entrant measure* (*E*).[3] It ranges from 0 (every party contests seats in only one district) to 1 (every party contests seats in every district). The index weights for party size at the district level as a proportion of the nationwide total and for the size of territorial units (in terms of allocated seats) as a proportion of the nationwide total.

Neither the number of uncontested seats nor the degree of territorial coverage nor the local entrant measure has much to do with vote nationalisation as it has been defined in the previous chapter (the level of territorial homogeneity of the party support). Indeed, each seat could be contested at least by two parties, and each party could have a territorial coverage of 100 per cent in a given country without having vote nationalisation as conceived in this book. A perfect territorial coverage of a party is a necessary but insufficient condition of vote nationalisation. Furthermore, in electoral systems with a single national constituency for the allocation of seats (as in the Netherlands), these indices would by default show perfect nationalisation. Rather, by reasoning in economic terms, they can be defined as measures of homogeneity on the supply side, while here I am interested in looking for the level of homogeneity of the electoral outcome, namely, the vote.

Among the measures that specifically focus on the nationalisation of the vote, two different groups can be distinguished: the measures that study nationalisation at a given election (the so-called static or distributional nationalisation) and those based on the comparison between two following elections (the so-called dynamic nationalisation). Among the latter, Stokes (1965; 1967) uses the swing between subsequent elections. Another way is to correlate the parties' vote share across the territorial units of a country at time t and $t+1$ (Pavsic 1985). Even in this case, however, the nationalisation of the vote – conceived as uniformity or unidirectional change between the elections – is entirely independent of the levels of support received by a party across the territorial units of a country.

The former group of measures that study nationalisation at a given election is in turn divided into three subsets: the 'inflation' measures, the indices of variance and the distribution coefficients.

The so-called inflation measures (Cox 1999; Moenius and Kasuya 2004; Kasuya and Moenius 2008) compare the number of parties both at the national and at the local level. Chhibber and Kollman (1998; 2004) measure the level of party system nationalisation by calculating the difference between the effective number of electoral parties (ENEP)[4] at the national level and the average of the ENEP in the different local units. This measure is called *Deviation*,[5] and, the higher it is, the less the system is nationalised, because it means that the national party system is nothing but the aggregation of local party systems which are very different from each other. The basic idea is that a party system can be said to be 'nationalised' if 'the same parties compete at different levels of vote aggregation' (Chhibber and Kollman 2004: 4): the higher the difference between the ENEP at the national level and the mean of the effective number of parties among the different regions of the country, the lower the level of nationalisation of the party system (and the higher the 'inflation'). However, 'whereas the indicator might be useful for single-seat district systems, it has its limits for PR systems, when in each district many parties compete' (Bochsler 2010: 159). Starting from Chhibber and Kollman's measure, Cox (1999: 155–56) develops the *Inflation score* which normalises the *Deviation* for the effective number of parties at the national level. Allik (2006) creates the *index of party aggregation*, which is the complement of Cox's measure, since it varies between 0 (minimum party aggregation) and 1 (maximum party aggregation). Moenius and Kasuya (2004) build a slightly more complex index, called *Inflation*.[6] As for the other 'inflation' measures, if the average number of parties at the local level is lower than that at the national level, there will be inflation. In the opposite circumstance, there will be deflation. The authors themselves (Kasuya and Moenius 2008) then propose a weighted version of the same index which now takes into account the different size of territorial units (in terms of votes cast). All in all, despite taking into account, to some extent, the electoral outcome, the measures of inflation are not able to give account properly of the homogeneity of electoral behaviour among the territorial units, but only of the difference in the number of parties between national and local level.

The indices of variance, instead, are based on the dispersion of the party values at the regional level around the national mean. Amongst the many, we mention the *mean absolute deviation* (MAD) or *index of variation* by Rose and Urwin (1975: 24), the Lee index (Lee 1988), the *mean squared deviation* (MSD), the *variance* (S^2) and the *standard deviation* (S). The literature has often emphasised the limits and failings of some of these measures (*see* table 2.1 for a synthetic overview):[7] some of them do not take party size into account, and most of them do not consider the number and the size of the territorial units; furthermore, many of them are not standardised and lack an upper limit. Therefore, other measures have sometimes been preferred, such as the *coefficient of variation* (CV) that normalises the standard deviation by the mean, thus taking the relative size of parties into account. However, it retains other shortcomings, such as the lack of an upper limit and the sensitivity to the number of territorial units (the values of the CV diminish when the number of units increases). Aiming at improving its reliability, Ersson, Janda and Lane (1985: 176) propose the *standardised and weighted coefficient of variation* (SCV_w) which takes the size of the units (in terms of voters) into account, but it is biased with respect to the number of units and lacks an upper limit. This last shortcoming is not present in the IPR (*index adjusted for party size and number of regions*) by Caramani (2004: 62), as well as in the CRII (*Cumulative Regional Inequality Index*) by Rose and Urwin (1975: 30). However, even these measures are not immune from failings:[8] the IPR does not take into account the size of territorial units (Bochsler 2010: 159), while the CRII overestimates the differences in the size of regions (Caramani 2004: 63).

The distribution coefficients are by far the most reliable indices of static or distributional vote nationalisation. They conceive the nationalisation of the vote as the level of homogeneity of party support across the territorial units of a country. Jones and Mainwaring (2003) created the Party Nationalisation Score (PNS)[9] which is nothing but the inverted Gini coefficient, a widely

Table 2.1 Indicators of party system nationalisation and their shortcomings

	Reported problems (1–7)						
Index	*1. No consideration of party support level*	*2. Lacking upper limit*	*3. Does not take different sizes of territorial units into account*	*4. Lacking scale invariance ('party size problem')*	*5. Insensitivity to transfers*	*6. Insensitivity to the number of territorial units*	*7. Large local party-system bias*
a) Competition indices							
Number of uncontested seats	X		X		x	x	
Safe seats	X		X		x	x	
Territorial coverage index	X				x	x	
b) Inflation measures							
Deviation		X	X			x	x
Inflation index		X				x	x
Weighted inflation index		X				x	
c) Indices of variance							
Index of variation		x	x	x	x	x	
Mean absolute deviation/ Lee index		x	x	x	x	x	
Standard deviation		x	X	x		x	
SCV_w			X			x	
IPR			X		x	x	
CRII					x	x	
d) Distribution coefficients							
PNS			X			x	

Source: Adaptation from Bochsler (2010: 157).

used index of inequality across units. The PNS varies from 0 (the party receives 100 per cent of its votes in 1 subnational unit and 0 per cent in all the rest) to 1 (the party receives the same share of votes in each subnational unit). In order to take into account the systemic level of nationalisation, they developed the party system nationalisation score (PSNS) that consists of the sum of the PNS of each party weighted for its national share of votes. The contribution of every party to the PSNS is thus proportionate to its electoral strength.

Although it is surely superior to its existing alternatives and allows for both cross-country and cross-time comparability, PNS still retains two main shortcomings, as underlined by Bochsler (2010: 157): First, it takes into account neither the size of territorial units (measured in terms of voters) nor the different number of units (all else equal, if the number of units increases, the score of the PNS decreases). As far as the first shortcoming is concerned, it might be questionable whether the small Finnish island of Åland (26,000 inhabitants) should weight similarly to the vast southwestern province of Uusimaa (which counts seventy times more inhabitants).

The second shortcoming depends upon the availability of electoral data at the same level of aggregation. Generally speaking, 'statisticians expect that the lower the number of territorial units the less variation across them because of the larger size of units and the elimination – through aggregation – of extreme and outlying values' (Caramani 2004: 64). For instance, let us imagine that only regional-level data are available and the support for a party seems to be very homogeneous throughout the country. Yet, if lower-level data had been available, it might have been clear that this seeming homogeneity was nothing but the result of a larger within-region heterogeneity of party support, with some provinces where the party had its own strongholds and others where it was very weak. Therefore, according to the level of aggregation considered, the coefficient will assume different values.

In order to correct these two failings, Bochsler (2010: 164) developed the standardised Party nationalisation score (sPNS). Its complex formula[10] is exponentiated to 1/log (*E*) where log stands for the logarithmic function and *E* represents the effective number of territorial units (analogous to the effective number of parties by Laakso and Taagepera (1979)) and allows to take the size and the number of territorial units into account, thus solving both the failings of the simple PNS. The empirical tests made by Bochsler (2010: 164–65) on Central and Eastern European countries and by Andreadis (2011) on the 1958 Greek election show that the sPNS (and the systemic measure, the sPSNS) is by far the index with the lesser variance on scores calculated at different levels of data aggregation.[11]

Performing as the most reliable measure of vote nationalisation developed so far, the sPNS has been chosen to operationalise the dependent variable (vote nationalisation) of the current analysis.

SPACE AND TIME

This book covers sixteen national cases, namely, all Western European countries over one million inhabitants. The number of national cases is consistent with all the previous studies on the topic in this region: in particular, Ersson, Janda and Lane (1985) deal with the same sixteen countries, while Caramani's (2004) study is carried out on seventeen, as he includes Iceland also; seventeen is also the number of countries selected by Lago and Lago (2010), who leave out the Netherlands but add Iceland and Luxembourg in their analysis; finally, Lago and Montero (2014) work with eighteen countries, adding Iceland and Luxembourg to the larger sixteen countries.

As Bartolini (2000: 35) suggests, the choice of cases is a critical task and it is interlocked with the problem we want to investigate and explain: 'the choice of cases influences what we can study, and what we want to study influences what cases we should consider'. I am interested in studying the evolution of the level of vote nationalisation in the specific context of Western Europe, a geopolitical area characterised by the presence of countries with a long-term consolidated democratic rule (with the significant exceptions of Spain, Portugal and Greece where democracy has come back during the 1970s) and a certain degree of similarity concerning the historical roots of political development. Hence, I have decided to limit the spatial horizon of the current research to the Western European landscape by taking into consideration virtually all its relevant national cases. By doing this, the sample matches the population and the problem of achieving valid generalisations to a larger number of cases disappears. The purpose is, therefore, that of conducting a study of area assessing and explaining the variance of vote nationalisation in the specific historical, cultural, social and political context of Western Europe.

Given this book deals with the presence of a process of change, that is, with the evolution towards a more pronounced path of vote nationalisation or, conversely, with the beginning of a trend reversal towards the reterritorialisation of party support, it is clear that the choice of the temporal span of the analysis becomes crucial.

As shown in table 2.2, this study covers half a century of Western European electoral politics. The period under study goes from 1965 to 2015.[12] This time frame is long enough to generate temporal variations and to allow for detecting some change in the vote nationalisation patterns. Moreover, the choice to make the analysis start in the mid-1960s is not a random one. I have attempted to identify the turning point between the end of a long phase of nationalisation and the beginning of a possible trend reversal. According to the aforementioned theoretical contributions, this turning point cannot have taken place before the mid-1960s. Indeed, in 1967 Lipset and Rokkan outlined the well-known *freezing hypothesis*, that is, the theory

Table 2.2 Countries, level of data aggregation, period covered, number of elections and parties

Country	*Territorial unit*	*Number of territorial units*	*Period covered*	*N elections*	*N party cases*
Austria	*Länder*	9	1966–2013	15	67
Belgium	*Provinces*	11	1965–2014	16	157
Denmark	*Amter/Storkredse*	17/10 since 2007	1966–2015	19	152
Finland	*Vaalipiirit*	15/13 in 2015	1966–2015	14	108
France	*Régions*	22	1967–2012	12	107
Germany	*Länder*	10/16 since 1990	1965–2013	14	80
Greece	*Peripheries*	13	1974–2015	17	91
Ireland	*Regions*	8	1965–2011	14	67
Italy	*Regioni*	20	1968–2013	13	146
Netherlands	*Provinces*	11–13	1967–2012	15	109
Norway	*Fylker*	20/19 since 1973	1965–2013	13	97
Portugal	*Distritos administrativos*	20	1975–2015	15	67
Spain	*Comunidad autónomas*	19	1977–2015	12	151
Sweden	*Län*	21	1968–2014	15	97
Switzerland	*Cantons*	25–26	1967–2015	13	164
UK	*Regions*	12	1966–2015	13	129
Total			**1965–2015**	**230**	**1789**

concerning the freezing of the political cleavages and of the following partisan alignments, which consolidated around the 1920s and was still taking place in the mid-1960s.

This freezing of cleavages and partisan alignments took place in the same years in which the vote nationalisation process made its fundamental steps, before following a pattern of stability in the subsequent decades. Therefore, a clear parallelism exists between the Rokkanian theory about cleavages and the freezing of party alternatives and Caramani's theory on vote nationalisation.

Hence the decision to start the data analysis from 1965, being convinced that the beginning of the defreezing of the party system is a necessary prerequisite to detecting some kind of territorial defreezing of party support. The occurrence of the former can, in turn, lead to either a re-acceleration of the nationalisation process, with an increase of territorial similarity of party support across districts, or to exactly the opposite process, that is, the beginning of a general trend towards a pattern of increasing territorial heterogeneity of party support.

At this point, it is worth wondering since when the party system defreezing has taken place. The literature is not unanimous about the timing of this process. In particular, there are two opposite viewpoints on the topic, given by two of the most fundamental contributions on electoral politics of the past decades: the study of Bartolini and Mair (1990) and that of Franklin, Mackie and Valen (1992). According to the former ones, the freezing proposition is still valid, and their data reveal that the levels of volatility reflect '*a fundamental bias towards stability*' (Bartolini and Mair 1990: 68). An opposite viewpoint is provided by Franklin, Mackie, Valen and their contributors. They deal with sixteen Western democracies through a longitudinal data analysis aiming at testing the tightness of the links between social divisions and voting choice. The authors claim that, since the 1970s, there has been a remarkable decline of the ties between social divisions and individual voting choice, with the former that are no longer able to structure the vote choice as in the past. This evidence is the consequence of a universal process of cleavage decline (Franklin, Mackie and Valen 1992: 386). It follows that Western voters show a growing and unexpected unpredictability of their voting choices that now often tend to support newcomer parties.

As it can be easily noted, these two classics of European comparative politics could not lead to more different conclusions, pushing me even more on the chosen path, that is, that of studying the evolution of vote nationalisation process since the time of Lipset and Rokkan's work in order to test the two competitive hypotheses of further nationalisation or of reversal towards denationalisation.

This work, therefore, shows the typical features of a longitudinal long-term comparative study, in which the temporal factor plays a fundamental role. On the importance of time in comparative research, Bartolini's (1993; 2000) reflections prove enlightening. The author starts from the consideration that most of the contemporary political scientists use time not as a developmental dimension but as a strategy aimed at increasing the number of cases without increasing the number of additional control variables, thus getting several observations through time of the same case. By doing this, time becomes a simple unit-defining parameter and disappears through the aggregation of all cases (temporally or spatially defined) into a single sample. Nevertheless, this is only an 'asynchronic comparison' (Bartolini 1993: 146) which does not properly take into account the temporal variance that, like the spatial one, shows some problems to be solved. While 'cross-unit variance is normally expressed in terms of presence or absence of given properties', cross-time variance (made by observations at different time-points separated by intervals which may be more or less regular, just like the 230 elections of this study) 'is identified in terms of deviation from an estimated temporal trend' (Bartolini 1993: 153).

There are several strategies of periodisation in order to identify a given temporal trend (as, for instance, the trend towards vote nationalisation in Europe): amongst many, the identification of *developmental dichotomies* (i.e., traditional vs. modern), *transitional models* (i.e., stability-transitional disequilibrium-new stability), *sequential generalisations* (Dahl 1971; Sartori 1984) or *thresholds* (Rokkan 1970). Scholars must be careful to avoid problems of historical multicollinearity among variables: 'Multi-collinearity in temporal series of information indicates the possibility that all series will tend to be strongly associated with one another'[13] (Bartolini 1993: 157). To avoid the risks of historical multicollinearity, Bartolini suggests resorting to '*slides of synchronic comparisons through time*' (159). This method consists of the split of the chosen temporal span in some slides of synchronic comparisons in order to explain not the developmental trend as such, but rather the deviations from it, that is, the cross-unit synchronic variance in terms of relative earliness, lateness, presence, absence or intensity of a given property.

Throughout the empirical analysis, this strategy is followed by resorting to temporal splits of the sample into decades or two longer 'slices' or periods (1965–1990, 1991–2015). Far from being a mere temporal division, this periodisation has not only the merit of splitting the sample into two homogeneous temporal subsets of about twenty-five years each and to group a similar number of elections (121 and 109, respectively) but also a specific underlying meaning. The cut-off point of 1990 is indeed a crucial juncture of European history, given that it roughly corresponds to the fall of the Berlin Wall, the reunification of Germany and the start of the negotiations that would have led to the creation of the European Union through the signature of the Maastricht Treaty. This strategy allows us to explore the cross-unit synchronic variance (across parties and countries) of vote nationalisation in terms of deviations from a given developmental trend – homogenisation, stability or reterritorialisation over time – as well as to investigate the cross-time relationships between vote nationalisation and its predictors.

DATA COLLECTION

The second and the third columns of table 2.2 show, respectively, the name and the number of the territorial units in which electoral data[14] have been disaggregated for each country. The availability of territorially disaggregated data in a certain number of units is necessary to measure the level of vote nationalisation which is based on the variation of party support between the different areas of a given country, regardless of the measure used.

The criteria used for selecting the number and the type of territorial units have been that of homogeneity and, secondarily, that of data availability.[15]

As regards the homogeneity in the number of territorial units, the basic idea has been that of limiting the variation in the number of units as regards both the various countries and the different elections of each country, so as to minimise the risk of getting biased scores and to make comparisons more reliable.[16]

The number of territorial units for each national case ranges from eight (Ireland) to twenty-six (Switzerland), with an average of sixteen territorial units per country. Sometimes data were not available at the chosen level but only at a lower one, so that a regrouping of the original data has been required, in order to preserve the original purpose of homogeneity in the number of units. This has occurred in France, from *département* (88/96 units) to regions (22); in Greece, from electoral districts (56) to regions (13); in Ireland and the United Kingdom, from constituencies (respectively, 41/43 and 630–59) to regions (8[17] and 12, respectively); in Italy from *circoscrizioni* (32 during the 1968–1992 period and 27 afterwards) to regions (20); in the Netherlands, from 18 districts (*Kieskringen*) to 11/13[18] provinces; in Spain from provinces (52) to *Comunidad autónomas* (19); and finally in Sweden from electoral districts (28/29) to the 21 counties (*Län*).

The second criterion has been that of the availability of electoral data at the chosen level of territorial aggregation. In Denmark, the number of units significantly changes during the electoral period under study:[19] here data were available at the provincial level (17 units) until the 2005 election. Afterwards, a reform of the local government abolished the provinces (*Amter*) and made data at that level of aggregation no longer available, being replaced by ten larger districts since the 2007 election.

Overall, the territorial level selected for the disaggregation of the data always corresponds to a certain administrative subdivision of the country:[20] in half of the countries, data are collected at the provincial level, often with different denominations, from county to canton (as in the cases of Belgium, Denmark until 2005, Finland, the Netherlands, Norway, Portugal, Sweden and Switzerland), while in the other half they are collected at the regional level (as in the cases of Austria, France, Germany, Greece, Ireland, Italy, Spain and the United Kingdom).

The last column of table 2.2 reports the number of individual parties selected in the data set. A total of 1,789 party cases (the party at a given election) has been included in the analysis, with a mean of about 112 party cases per country (ranging from the 67 cases of Austria, Ireland and Portugal to the 164 of Switzerland). Political parties have been selected when they obtain at least 3 per cent of the votes nationwide or 4 per cent in at least one territorial unit. These two alternative criteria allow for the inclusion of both parties that are relevant at the national level and parties that are relevant at the local level. Parties fulfilling neither of these criteria have been excluded from the analysis.

METHOD

Providing an unbiased selection of the party cases is a fundamental precondition for achieving unbiased results of vote nationalisation at the country level. The index of vote nationalisation is firstly calculated at the party level and then aggregated at the systemic level. This step is crucial for the overall understanding of the general purpose of the analysis: even if nationalisation scores at the party level are important (such scores are reported and analysed in the appendix), the main goal of the research is to assess and explain the evolution of vote nationalisation at the systemic level over the past fifty years in Western European countries.

This study, therefore, adopts a 'macro' perspective, by carrying out a comparative study between political systems and their macro-structural features.

As explained earlier, this analysis combines the synchronic, cross-country variance with the diachronic, cross-time variance. Each country does not represent a 'case', but it will be considered as many times as the number of elections of the lower chamber[21] in the chosen time span of the research. The unit of analysis of the current work, which in turn represents the individual rows of the data matrix, is, therefore, the election in a given country in a given year. In other words, we are in front of a time-series-cross-section (TSCS) data set (Beck and Katz 1995; Beck 2001; 2008). TSCS data consist of comparable time series data observed on a variety of units. 'TSCS data are characterised by repeated observations (often annual) on the same fixed (non-sampled) political units (usually states or countries)' (Beck 2001: 271). Commonly applied to the study of comparative political economy (e.g., Garrett 1998), TSCS methods typically deal with a relatively small number of units observed for some reasonable length of time. Even if there are no fixed rules for the employment of a TSCS method, observations over time must be 'large enough that averages over the T time periods for each unit make sense . . . One ought to be suspicious of TSCS methods used for, say, $T < 10$. On the other hand, TSCS methods do not require a large N, although a large N is typically not harmful' (Beck 2001: 274).

Dealing with a TSCS data set, with repeated observations over time (elections) on the same fixed units (countries), problems of heteroscedasticity and autocorrelation may arise (Stimson 1985). In particular, unlike in classical ordinary least squares (OLS) regression, errors may not be independent and identically distributed, given that each panel (i.e., each country) has its own variance; moreover, errors are serially correlated, that is, the errors for a given country are correlated with previous errors for that country. In the field of TSCS techniques, Parks (1967) pioneered a feasible generalised least squares (FGLS) method, which is 'feasible' because it uses an estimate of the error process, avoiding the generalised least squares (GLS) assumption that the error process is known. Notwithstanding this correction, a path-breaking article by Beck and Katz (1995) has shown that FGLS method produces standard errors that lead to extreme overconfidence, often underestimating variability by 50 per cent or more. Moreover, FGLS requires that $T > N$ (Beck and Katz 1995: 637). In other words, the number of observations over time (in our data set, elections) for each group (i.e., country) should be higher than the number of groups. Indeed, as reported in table 2.2, the research covers 230 national elections, with a mean of 14.4 elections for each country (ranging from the 12 elections of France and Spain to the 19 that occurred in Denmark). This means that the data set has a so-called cross-sectional dominant pool (Stimson 1985), where cross section units are more numerous than temporal units ($N > T$). For this reason, FGLS is inappropriate. In these cases, Beck and Katz developed an alternative method that uses OLS parameter estimates and replaces the OLS standard errors with 'panel-corrected standard errors' (PCSE; Beck and Katz 1995: 638).

In order to tackle these issues and to deal with the presence of panel-heteroskedasticity and autocorrelation,[22] the explanatory part of the book tests the hypotheses by using the PCSE method with a first-order autoregressive (AR1) parameter, namely, the so-called Prais-Winsten regression.[23] The PCSE method has already been used by other scholars dealing with the issue of vote nationalisation and faced with a similar data matrix (Harbers 2010; Lago and Lago 2010; Schakel 2012; Su 2017).

Concluding, this work follows the comparative method for the control of the hypotheses, assisted and reinforced by the use of statistical analyses to strengthen the overall explanation. The comparative method is carried out in the next chapters through three different perspectives. The first one is the study of the overall pattern of vote nationalisation in Western Europe, by putting together all the 230 elections of the data set into the same theoretical and interpretative framework. The second perspective is the study of temporal variations which consists of the assessment of the existence of such a specific temporal trend in the evolution of vote nationalisation in Western Europe and the possible deviations from it. Finally, the third perspective is the cross-country comparison of the level of vote nationalisation among the Western European nation-states, namely, a synchronic comparison between countries and the specific evolution of vote nationalisation in each of the sixteen party systems included in the research.

THE INDEPENDENT VARIABLES: THE MACRO-CONSTELLATION OF FACTORS

After outlining the main features of the research design, there is a last, crucial point to be clarified. It regards the identification of the independent variables, namely, the potential determinants of vote nationalisation in Western Europe.

This task is extensively carried out in the third part of this work, devoted to detecting the most important predictors of vote nationalisation, thus providing a comprehensive explanation of the object under study.

This section therefore merely introduces some topics that are widely discussed later in this work. In order to explain the temporal trend of the vote nationalisation process and give account of its national variations, while keeping an interpretative framework as much parsimonious as possible, the potential explanatory factors have been grouped into three categories: the macro-sociological determinants, the institutional constraints and those related to the structure of the competition (i.e., the 'political' factors).

Figure 2.1 summarises the macro-constellation of the main potential determinants of vote nationalisation. The so-called macro-sociological determinants refer to the impact of cleavages on the vote nationalisation process. As shown in chapter 1, the theory of nationalisation emphasises the impact of the class cleavage in the structuring of functional left-right alignments of competition and the progressive development of nationalised territorial configurations in Western Europe. The class cleavage, therefore, has been a

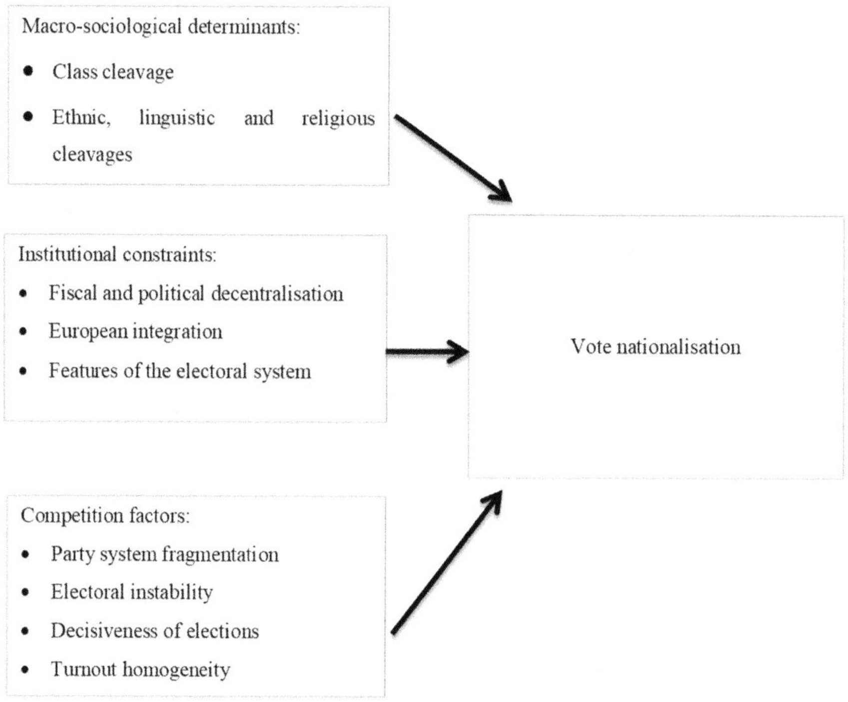

Figure 2.1 Map of the main potential determinants of vote nationalisation in Western Europe

homogenising cleavage. Conversely, among the most important causes of territorial deviations, Rokkan (1970) and Caramani (2004) underline the impact of parties for territorial defence, fostered by the presence of strong ethnic, linguistic or religious minorities in the country. Chapter 4 is devoted to detecting if these factors (class, ethnicity, language and religion) are associated with vote nationalisation and how much of its variance they take into account.

As far as the institutional constraints are concerned, many recent scholars have recently underlined the impact of political and fiscal decentralisation on the rise of ethnoregionalist parties and, as a consequence, on the denationalisation of the vote (Chhibber and Kollman 1998; 2004; Brancati 2006). Aside from decentralisation, another major change that has affected the institutional framework in the past decades has been the process of European integration. According to some scholars (Keating 1998; Bartolini 2005), the process of European integration has challenged the old nation-states, by weakening the formerly consolidated structuration of the national political space and helping to build a new European political space. This process, in turn, has fostered the resurgence of territorial politics. However, the literature on both decentralisation and European integration is not consistent, and some other authors have proposed different explanations (see, respectively, Hopkin 2003; Caramani 2004; 2015). Finally, among the institutional factors, the features of the electoral system deserve attention, even if the direction of the relationship with vote nationalisation is not entirely clear since different aspects of the electoral system provide different incentives to parties in favour or against nationalisation. Chapter 5 explores the correlations between decentralisation, European integration and electoral rules on one side and vote nationalisation on the other.

Finally, a third category, the 'political factors' may affect vote nationalisation. These factors are linked to the structure of the competition or related to the features of the party system: party system fragmentation, electoral instability, turnout homogeneity and the 'decisiveness' of elections. These potential determinants have been widely neglected by the existing literature on vote nationalisation, even if they have proved to be important factors of change of the European party systems in the past decades. Chapter 6 looks at the impact of these factors.

These three sets of explanatory factors are therefore introduced, operationalised and separately tested in chapters 4, 5 and 6, respectively. Then, chapter 7 eventually disentangles, through a multivariate regression analysis, the relative weight of the different predictors, thus showing which factors have a significant impact on vote nationalisation and instead which others are not related to it.

Part II

ASSESSING VOTE NATIONALISATION

Chapter 3

Vote nationalisation trends (1965–2015)

This chapter is dedicated to the analysis of vote nationalisation data. It assesses the results of the standardised party system nationalisation score (sPSNS) in the Western European elections during the past fifty years (1965–2015). First, more specifically, this chapter focuses on the overall pattern of vote nationalisation by putting together all the 230 elections in a general analytical model. Second, it introduces the temporal dimension in the framework to take into account the impact of the time variance and to assess the existence of a distinct temporal trend in the evolution of vote nationalisation in Western Europe. Therefore, this chapter addresses the first research question formulated in chapter 2: has there been, during the past fifty years, as Caramani (2004) suggests, a homogenising process of electoral behaviour, which started in the early phases of electoral mobilisation and democratisation, between the end of the nineteenth century and the beginning of the twentieth century, and that is still going on? Or, on the contrary, can we notice a reverse of this trend and a resurgence of some territorial distinctiveness that have led to the opening of a denationalisation process? Furthermore, this chapter deeply explores vote nationalisation data, and, through different indicators and tools of analysis, it looks like countries deviating from the overall Western European pattern.

The chapter is organised as follows: the first section, 'Empirical evidence', presents preliminary descriptive statistics of the dependent variable in terms of overall frequency distribution, country means and standard deviations; then, the following three sections are dedicated to address the core question of the chapter, namely, the relation between time and vote nationalisation. The main pattern is presented in the second section, 'Time and nationalisation: The overall pattern', while the cross-country variations from this pattern are analysed in the third and in the fourth sections, 'Time and nationalisation:

Cross-country variations' and 'Time and nationalisation: Two snapshots fifty years apart', respectively; finally the last section, 'A classification of European elections', develops a classification of European elections according to their levels of vote nationalisation.

EMPIRICAL EVIDENCE

A first sight to the nationalisation scores provided by the overall set of elections reveals some interesting evidence. Figure 3.1 plots the frequency distribution of the sPSNS for the 230 elections of the data set. As reported in the descriptive statistics in the histogram, the median value (0.858) is higher than the mean (0.816): in statistical terms it means that there is a negatively skewed curve of frequency (certified by the negative value of skewness, −1.96), with few and very low values (with the biggest negative deviations from the mean) on the left tail of the curve and a lot of values with small and positive deviations placed on the right side of the curve.

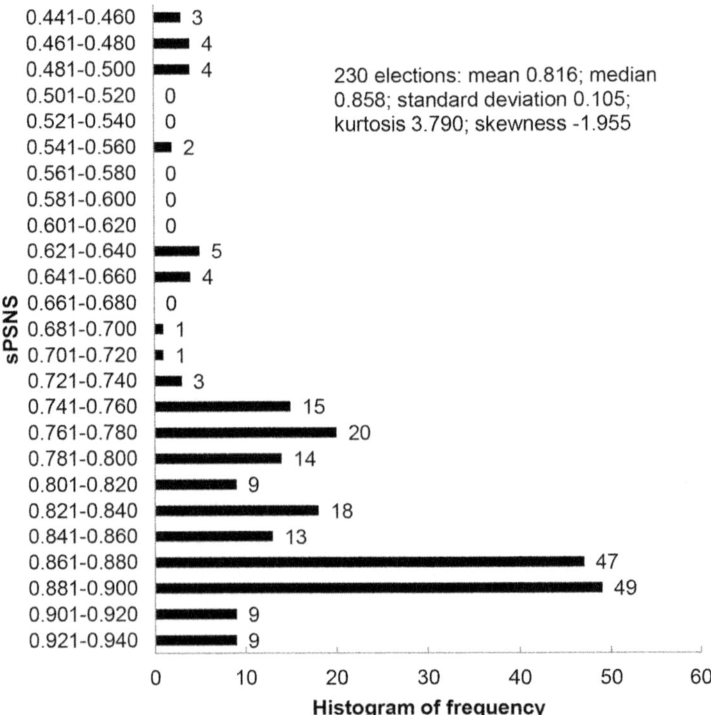

Figure 3.1 Vote nationalisation in Western Europe, 1965–2015: Frequency distribution

This evidence has an important implication: with the exception of few extreme elections – scoring a Bochsler's index lower than 0.700 (a total of twenty-three cases, all belonging to the very regionalised and territorially segmented Belgian and Swiss cases) – the vast bulk of elections has a rather high level of vote nationalisation, meaning that most of the Western European countries have strongly nationalised polities. More than 40 per cent of the observations (96 out of 230) fall between the scores of 0.861 and 0.900, showing quite homogeneous territorial distributions of the votes for the political parties competing in those elections. At the same time, figure 3.1 shows that more than a quarter of the entire sample (62 cases) falls between 0.701 and 0.820, outlining the presence of some regionalised party systems.

Starting from these first pieces of evidence (to be analysed in depth in the following pages, with the addition of many other useful tools for a less crude and more far-reaching interpretation), it is possible to detect the presence of at least two different patterns of territorial distribution of the vote in the data set, the regionalised territorial configurations (those elections with a sPSNS ranging from 0.701 to 0.800) and the nationalised ones (between 0.861 and 0.900).[1]

However, as a general premise, it must be underlined that when I talk about 'regionalised' or 'territorially inhomogeneous' countries, I refer to them only in relative terms, comparing cases that belong to Western Europe. Such countries are characterised by the presence of a long-term democratic rule (with the significant exceptions of Spain, Portugal and Greece, where democracy came back only during the 1970s) and that experienced the historical processes of mass democratisation and electoral mobilisation about one century ago. In these countries, as already stated in chapter 1, the party systems became nationalised at the beginning of the twentieth century, with the structuring of the political space around national alignments of partisan alternatives, according to the specific system of cleavages arisen in each country. During the 1920s, these party systems, by that time almost nationalised, became 'frozen' and kept intact their stable alignments at least until the 1960s (Lipset and Rokkan 1967), the period from which this analysis takes off. Therefore, it is clear that the labels of 'regionalised' or 'territorially inhomogeneous' country I use here to describe the features of some Western European countries are specifically linked to this context and not easily comparable with other areas, such as Latin America (Jones and Mainwaring 2003) or even Eastern Europe (Bochsler 2010). Countries from such regions have experienced different historical processes and, as a consequence, show different (and often, lower) levels of vote nationalisation.

Moreover, despite the fact that the sPSNS has a theoretical range running from 0 (all parties of the system cast all their votes in a single constituency)[2] to 1 (all parties of the system cast the same proportion of their votes in each constituency, and the constituencies are equally sized), the actual values lie on a more limited scale, ranging from a minimum of 0.441 to a maximum of 0.935, not far from the upper limit, and with almost 90 per cent of the elections (202 out of 230) falling in the highest quartile of the theoretical range of the variable (sPSNS > 0.750). This is more evidence of the nature of Western European party systems as nationalised polities.

After this brief overview about the distribution of the sPSNS values, I now go more into detail by showing the mean values of vote nationalisation for the Western European countries during the past fifty years. As can be seen in figure 3.2, there is a moderate variability among the countries, with almost 0.400 points of the index separating the territorially fragmented Belgium from the highly nationalised configuration of Greece, which is characterised by an impressive mean level of the index (0.910). Greece is followed by other countries showing high degree of nationalisation, such as Sweden, Denmark, Austria, Ireland and, to a lesser extent, France.

On the opposite side of the histogram, there are polities with regionalised territorial configurations. After the extreme Belgian case, Switzerland, Germany, Spain and Finland have mean values of sPSNS below the overall mean of 0.816, while the other countries, Italy, Portugal, Norway and the Netherlands, are placed between the mean and the median value (0.858), displaying an intermediate level of nationalisation.

However, these are simply average levels, and they do not say anything about the relative dispersion of values around these national means and about the pattern of stability or change (towards a more pronounced nationalisation of the vote or, conversely, a more regionalised configuration) undertaken by each country during the period under study.

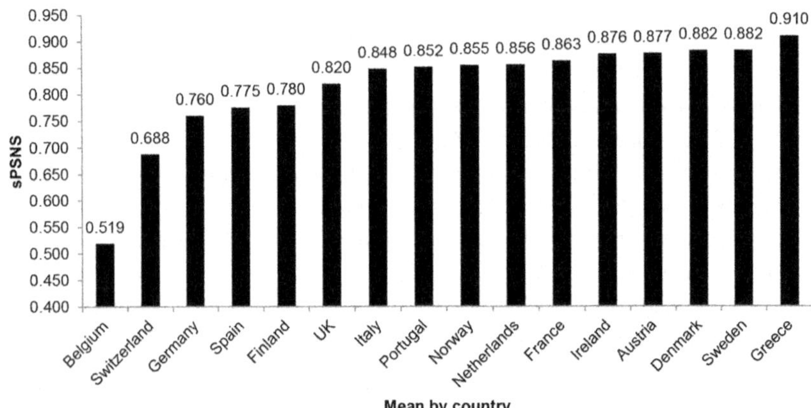

Figure 3.2 Mean sPSNS by country, 1965–2015

In order to depict a clearer picture and to compare the different national patterns of the sixteen countries, another element has to be added: the standard deviation. This latter takes into account the variance of vote nationalisation around the national mean, and it helps to detect whether the trend followed by each country during the past fifty years has been characterised by stability or change. Figure 3.3 plots the countries according to their mean level of vote nationalisation and the standard deviation of the same variable. Even if this is only an earlier stage of the analysis, some fundamental differences between the European countries can be easily identified. First, if the chart is divided into four quadrants, according to the mean value of both the sPSNS and the standard deviation of the sixteen countries (respectively, 0.816 and 0.031), a fourfold typology emerges.

According to the mean sPSNS, countries are divided among nationalised and regionalised polities, while the standard deviation provides a distinction between stable and unstable countries.

The upper-left quadrant includes countries characterised by a heterogeneous electoral geography and, at the same time, by an unstable pattern, with greater changes in the values of vote nationalisation occurred between the beginning and the end of the time span considered. Here we find the two most regionalised countries, Belgium and Switzerland. The former is a clear outlier[3] in the data set – with an extremely low mean of vote nationalisation (0.519) and with a standard deviation (0.093) that is three times larger than the mean value of the standard deviation – and it has been left out of the chart to provide a better visualisation of the other countries. Between the late 1960s and late 1970s, Belgium experienced the

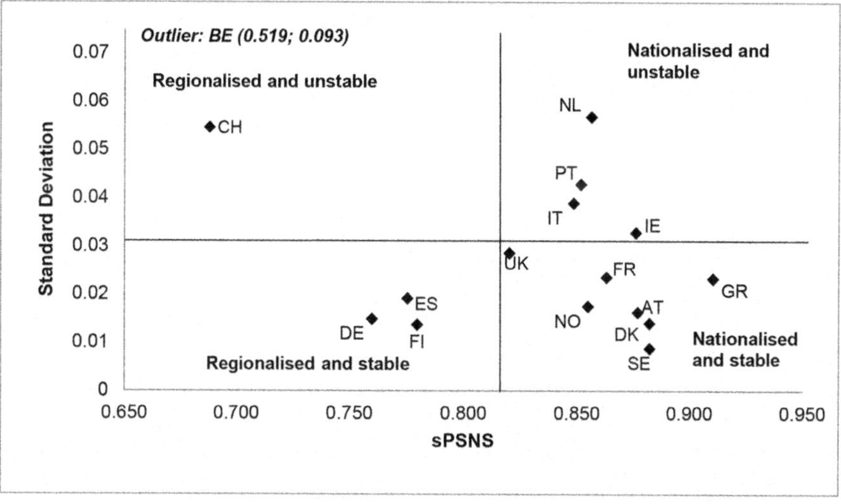

Figure 3.3 Contrasting patterns of vote nationalisation in Western Europe, 1965–2015

complete split of its previously unified party system into two systems, the Flemish one and the Walloon one, with the division of the three main parties, the Christian-Democrats, the Liberals and the Socialists, along the linguistic cleavage. On the other hand, Switzerland is a long-term culturally segmented polity, with the presence of linguistic and religious divisions: here the 'instability' is given by the increasing nationalisation of the main Swiss parties, resulting in a progressive reduction of the formerly marked territoriality.

The lower-left quadrant hosts those regionalised countries whose level of vote nationalisation has proved to be stable through time. First, we find Germany, where the presence of the biggest European regionalist party, the Bavarian CSU, strongly contributed to keeping the Bochsler's index at a relatively low level; then Finland, characterised by the prevalence of two cleavages, both of them having a high degree of territoriality: the centre-periphery one, politicised by the former agrarian party (the current Centre Party), which has been dominating the rural north of the country up to now, and the linguistic one, with the substantial minority of Swedish speakers, supporting the Swedish People's Party, concentrated in the Western, bordering Sweden, Vaasa province, in southern Finland (Helsinki and Uusimaa) and in the small island of Aland; and finally Spain, in which the national parties are still surrounded by a plethora of small regionalist parties claiming more autonomy from the central power and strongly contributing to drop the sPSNS.

The nationalised polities are located on the right side of the chart, beyond the mean sPSNS of 0.816. In the upper-right quadrant, the Netherlands, Portugal, Italy and, to a lesser extent, Ireland emerge as the most unstable polities within the most nationalised countries. The Netherlands experienced a sharp nationalisation during the 1970s, when the three main religious parties (the Catholic, the Calvinist and the Dutch reformed ones) merged into the big interconfessional Christian Democratic Appeal (CDA), thus losing the previous territorial heterogeneity retained by the three original parties; Portugal and Italy are quite nationalised polities but have experienced deviant, territorialised elections throughout their electoral history; finally, Ireland was a very nationalised country until the beginning of the 1980s, when it started a process of denationalisation of the vote due to several factors to be analysed in the next chapter.

In the lower-right quadrant, but very close to the intersection of the axes, the United Kingdom shows average values of nationalisation and dispersion. The remaining six countries, Greece, France, Austria and the three Scandinavian polities (Norway, Denmark and Sweden) are characterised – albeit with varying degrees – by an enduring stability in the territorial distribution of the votes for parties within a framework of strong homogeneity.

TIME AND NATIONALISATION: THE OVERALL PATTERN

This study has not only the purpose to discover the spatial differences, namely, the cross-country variations in vote nationalisation, but it also aims at verifying what has been, over the past decades, the trend of vote nationalisation in Europe (this last point being the first research question formulated in chapter 2).

Has there been a pattern of increasing homogeneity of electoral support as stated by Caramani (2004: 77)[4] or, on the contrary, have Western European countries faced a reversal towards a process of denationalisation of voting behaviour? To address this question, the introduction of the temporal dimension into the analysis – next to the spatial aspect that maintains its importance – is required. In order to take the cross-time variance into account, there are many strategies. As suggested by Bartolini (1993), the simplest one is to consider each unit of analysis (in our case, each election), as spatially and temporally defined in the sample (for instance, the 1968 Italian general election), and put all of them together in a model to assess the overall time path of the variable (in our case, vote nationalisation). Figure 3.4 plots the sPSNS for all the 230 elections held in sixteen Western European countries along a fifty-year timeline.

The result is straightforward: the territorial structuring of voting behaviour in Western Europe is characterised by an enduring stability through time. Interestingly, the two patterns of evolution hypothesised before have not

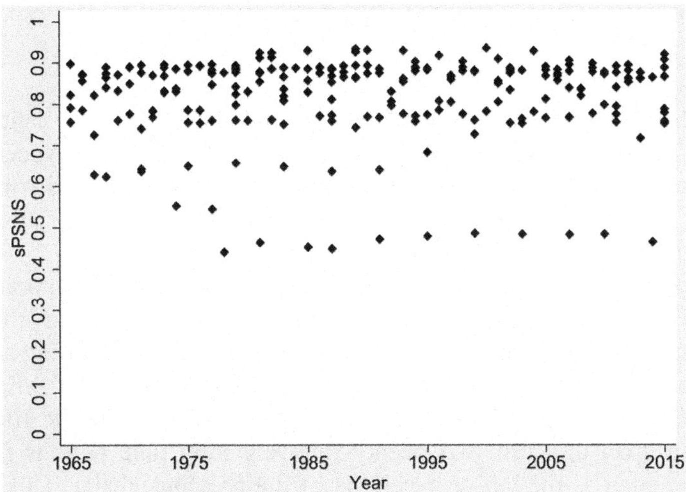

Figure 3.4 Evolution of vote nationalisation over time, 1965–2015

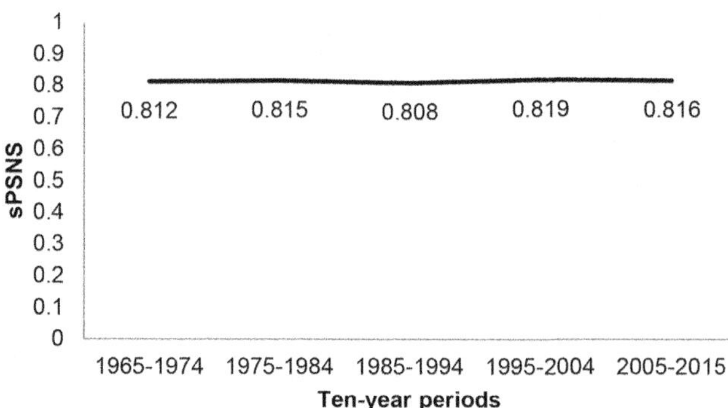

Figure 3.5 Vote nationalisation over time by ten-year periods

taken place: neither the increasing homogeneity established by Caramani in his research nor an overall trend towards a denationalisation process. There is no correlation at all between the sPSNS and time.[5] This long-lasting pattern of stability is confirmed if the fifty-year span is divided into five periods of ten years each, so as to reduce the erratic shifts of the values based on single elections. The ten-year period averages are based on the mean value for each country in each period, in order to take into account the difference in the number of elections that occur in each country during each period.[6] The results are again of impressive stability, with very limited shifts across the periods, as it can be seen in figure 3.5.

TIME AND NATIONALISATION: CROSS-COUNTRY VARIATIONS

In a nutshell, so far the analysis of the relation between time and nationalisation has shown a clear pattern of enduring stability through time. Nonetheless, in order to provide a comprehensive assessment, one needs to verify the presence of national deviations – towards nationalisation or denationalisation – from this general developmental trend.

As specified in chapter 2, in order to take into account the temporal variance in vote nationalisation and detect the deviations from a given developmental trend – which is, as seen previously, a trend of enduring stability over time – I follow Bartolini's strategy to resort to 'slides of synchronic comparisons through time' (Bartolini 1993: 159). I divide the fifty-year temporal span into just two twenty-five-year-long time periods (instead of more, such as the ten-year periods of the previous chart). This choice allows giving a substantive meaning to each period, grouping a significant number of elections for each country within each period for the sake of comparability of each country's developmental phase. The first period goes from 1965 to 1990, while the second one covers the years going from 1991 onwards.

Moreover, I also assess the overall impact of time on vote nationalisation in each country through simple bivariate correlations between time (measured in days) and sPSNS and through a more sophisticated regression technique. This latter tackles the two main problems of a pooled time-series-cross-section data structure, namely, panel-heteroskedasticity and autocorrelation. As reported in chapter 2, this is possible by estimating through the Prais-Winsten regression, namely, a regression with panel-corrected standard errors (PCSE) and a first-order autoregressive (AR1) correlation structure.

Table 3.1 reports the mean values of sPSNS and the total number of elections by country for the two periods (as well as the overall mean by country), the coefficients of correlations (Pearson's *r*) between time (measured as the number of days elapsed since the beginning of the period covered by the analysis, i.e., since 1 January 1965) and vote nationalisation and the *b* coefficients of the Prais-Winsten regression of the sPSNS on time. Moreover, figure 3.6 plots the national variations of the sPSNS over time for the sixteen countries under study.

Table 3.1 Time and vote nationalisation in Western Europe: Cross-country variations

	1965–1990		*1991–2015*		*1965–2015*			
Country	*sPSNS*	*N*	*sPSNS*	*N*	*sPSNS*	*N*	*Pearson's r*	*PCSE with AR(1)*
Austria	0.885	8	0.868	7	0.877	15	−0.667**	−0.00*
Belgium	0.550	9	0.479	7	0.519	16	−0.644**	−0.00**
Denmark	0.878	12	0.889	7	0.882	19	0.417	0.00
Finland	0.787	7	0.772	7	0.780	14	−0.328	−0.00
France	0.857	7	0.872	5	0.863	12	0.625*	0.00*
Germany	0.760	8	0.760	6	0.760	14	−0.122	0.00
Greece	0.913	7	0.909	10	0.910	17	−0.097	0.00
Ireland	0.896	9	0.840	5	0.876	14	−0.694**	−0.00*
Italy	0.875	6	0.826	7	0.848	13	−0.334	−0.00
Netherlands	0.834	8	0.882	7	0.856	15	0.674**	0.00**
Norway	0.844	7	0.868	6	0.855	13	0.930***	0.00***
Portugal	0.814	7	0.885	8	0.852	15	0.870***	0.00***
Spain	0.759	5	0.787	7	0.775	12	0.670*	0.00***
Sweden	0.888	8	0.876	7	0.882	15	−0.841***	−0.00***
Switzerland	0.643	6	0.726	7	0.688	13	0.897***	0.00***
UK	0.840	7	0.797	6	0.820	13	−0.912***	−0.00***
Mean	**0.816**	**121**	**0.817**	**109**	**0.816**	**230**	**0.037**	**0.00**

Note: * $p < 0.05$; ** $p < 0.01$; *** $p < 0.001$. In the last two columns, cells report Pearson's coefficients of correlations and *b* coefficients of the Prais-Winsten AR1 regression.

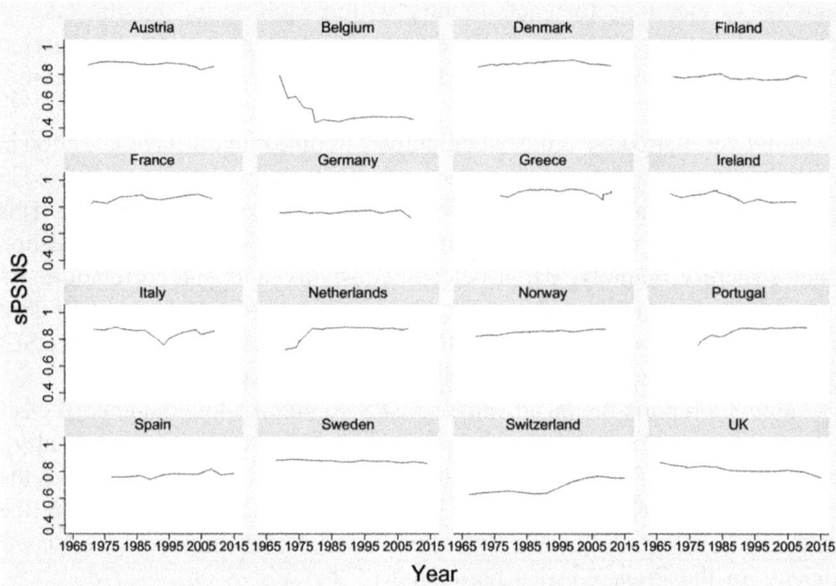

Figure 3.6 National variations of the sPSNS over time, 1965–2015

The last row of table 3.1 shows that by splitting the whole sample of elections into two subgroups, nothing changes for the average level of vote nationalisation: the sPSNS remains virtually identical to the overall mean value during the two periods (0.816 and 0.817, respectively). The overall trend through time of vote nationalisation discloses, as seen earlier, a zero correlation, and, consistently, the *b* coefficient of the regression model is not significant. However, this long-lasting stability over time hides a lot of variability showed by each country's nationalisation trends.

As regards national variations, the results should be interpreted carefully, since the number of observations is scarce (ranging from twelve to nineteen), and this negatively influences the robustness of the estimation. According to Pearson's *r* coefficients in the penultimate column of table 3.1, the sample could be split into two groups, with nine Western European nations that show a negative correlation between time and vote nationalisation, while the other seven display a positive association.[7] These correlations are not significant in some cases, but in others they are powerful. Norway, Portugal and Switzerland have experienced the greatest nationalisation processes, with a substantive decrease in the territorial heterogeneity of voting behaviour. To a lesser extent, France, the Netherlands and Spain show a similar trend. The strong negative correlation coefficients of Austria, Belgium, Ireland, Sweden and the United Kingdom reveal the occurrence of the opposite process, that is, a sharp decline of territorial homogeneity between the mid-1960s and the first fifteen years of the new century. In particular, remarkable evidence of change over time is offered by two opposite cases: in Switzerland, the average sPSNS increases by 0.083 between the first and the second period (almost three times the mean standard deviation shown in figure 3.3); in Belgium, instead, the sPSNS decreases by 0.071 between the two periods.[8] The remaining five countries do not show a significant linear trend over time, although it is possible to note a tendency towards denationalisation in Finland, Germany, Greece and Italy and an opposite, homogenising trend in Denmark.

Even if based on a few number of observations, the results of the regression model provide a solid confirmation of the findings obtained with the simple bivariate correlations. All the significant associations between time and the sPSNS are confirmed when one takes into account the potentially distorting effect created by panel-heteroskedasticity and autocorrelation of the errors.

Yet, the most attentive readers should have noted that the relative position of certain countries in the typology that emerged from figure 3.3 seems to be in contrast with their trend of vote nationalisation over time reported in table 3.1. For instance, Italy appears to have a standard deviation well over the mean and belongs to the unstable polities according to figure 3.3, but it shows no significant trend over time according to table 3.1. Conversely, Sweden, Norway, Spain and Austria show significant correlation coefficients (and regression coefficients as well) towards nationalisation or denationalisation over time, albeit falling in the 'stable' part of figure 3.3, with an overall standard deviation below the mean. This is because these two statistical tools provide different information: on the one hand, the standard deviation only gives account of the relative dispersion from the mean, without telling anything about the consistency of this change over time; on the other hand, the coefficients of correlation give us an estimate of how similarly the two variables covariate, without looking at the overall amount of change in the sPSNS occurring over time.

To improve our assessment of the cross-country variations in the relation between time and vote nationalisation, it is useful to measure the 'mean absolute interelectoral change' occurred during a period. The 'interelectoral change' refers to the variation in the sPSNS occurred in a given country between two subsequent elections. The 'mean absolute interelectoral change' is obtained by summing, for each country, the absolute values of all these variations and then dividing the result by the number of elections occurred in that country.

Even if highly associated with the correlation coefficients and especially with the standard deviation,[9] the mean absolute interelectoral change measures a different thing. Indeed, this measure takes into account all the effective variation occurred when one measures a given phenomenon (here, changes in the territorial configuration of party support). This means that if in a country the level of vote nationalisation continuously increases (or decreases) during a period but with small changes between each election and the following one (i.e., this country has a low standard deviation but a significant correlation between time and sPSNS), this will result in a comparatively low mean absolute interelectoral change. On the contrary, if the level of vote nationalisation in a given country shows high fluctuations around the mean (i.e., this country has a high standard deviation but a non-significant correlation between time and sPSNS), the mean absolute interelectoral change will be comparatively high. At the same time, as we are going to see, there could also be cases of consistency between the standard deviation and the correlation coefficients, but where the mean absolute interelectoral change tells a different story.

Figure 3.7 reports the mean absolute interelectoral change of the sPSNS in the sixteen Western European countries under study during the period 1965–2015. The results have been multiplied by 100 to facilitate the reading. For instance, the Western European average of 1.40 means that the average change occurred between two subsequent elections in the entire universe of elections is 0.014. By comparing the scores of figure 3.7 with the standard deviations in figure 3.3 and the coefficients of correlations through time of table 3.1, the above-mentioned apparently inconsistent results find clarification. Unsurprisingly, Belgium stands out again as the most territorially unstable polity, with a mean absolute interelectoral change of 2.96 (corresponding to a mean change of 0.030 in the level of sPSNS), which is more than two times above the overall mean. Italy follows as the second country with the highest mean absolute interelectoral change, not far from Belgium's level (2.65). Italy belongs to the unstable polities (high standard deviation), but vote nationalisation was not significantly correlated with time. This means that Italy shows contrasting fluctuations, alternating periods of increasing nationalisation to others of growing denationalisation: the amount of change is relevant but invisible in the correlation since it is not consistent over time.

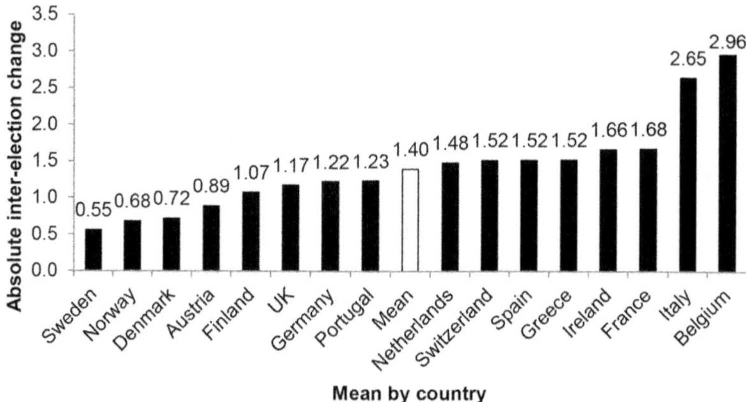

Figure 3.7 Mean absolute interelectoral change of the sPSNS by country (1965–2015)

Conversely, the opposite situation can be found in the two Scandinavian countries (Sweden and Norway) and Austria, which appear as the most territorially stable nations, albeit showing significant correlations between vote nationalisation and time. Indeed, these countries display some of the smallest levels of interelectoral change. Sweden, in particular, shows the lower mean absolute interelectoral change (0.55), almost 2.6 times under the overall mean. In these contexts, the amount of change is limited, but it has occurred consistently over time (steady vote denationalisation in Austria and Sweden, the opposite in Norway).

Nonetheless, there are also countries showing a mean absolute interelectoral change that appears in contrast with the standard deviation and, conversely, consistent with the correlation coefficient. Indeed, France and Spain belong to the group of countries with the highest interelectoral change, despite being in the subgroup of the stable polities in figure 3.3. This entails the presence of a quite relevant change, not very dispersed around the mean (low standard deviation) but substantially consistent over time (positive correlation between time and sPSNS in both countries).

Finally, Greece and Portugal are examples of countries where the standard deviation and the correlation coefficient were consistently oriented, the former towards stability and absence of relationship with time and the latter towards instability and a very strong positive correlation with time. Nonetheless, figure 3.7 surprisingly places Greece above the average interelectoral change and Portugal below it. These contrasting findings prove that a single indicator can be misleading and that the picture is often more complex and nuanced than it appears at first sight. The analysis of the mean absolute interelectoral change in the territorial configuration of party support tells us that the overall amount of change that occurred in Greece has been higher than that concerning Portugal. This change has resulted, in Greece, in fluctuations above and below the country average, without any clear direction over time; in Portugal, on the contrary, the (more limited) change has followed a clear pattern over time, with the first, very regionalised elections (with the highest negative deviations from the mean) progressively replaced by elections with very high levels of territorial homogeneity.

TIME AND NATIONALISATION: TWO SNAPSHOTS FIFTY YEARS APART

Beyond the specific trend over time and the interelectoral variation in vote nationalisation followed by each country and discussed in detail in the previous section, we need to gauge the extent of change occurred in the past fifty years of elections in Western Europe.

In order to achieve a comprehensive assessment of how the territorial configuration of each country has changed compared to the others, it is useful to take a look at figure 3.8. It compares the ranks of the sixteen countries regarding their sPSNS at the beginning of the period (i.e., in 1965 or in the year when the first election occurred) and at the end of the period (i.e., in 2015 or in the year when the last election occurred). In other words, figure 3.8 takes two snapshots of the same object (i.e., Western European countries) in a fifty-year time span. The figure is insightful since we can draw a rather clear picture of the change occurred in each country in terms of the territorialisation of party support and its relative position vis-à-vis the other countries.

To begin with, the aforementioned aggregate stability over time is confirmed by looking at these pieces of data: the average sPSNS in the first election of the period is 0.812 and it remains perfectly steady in the last election considered (0.811). Overall, half of the countries show an increase in the 2015 territorial homogeneity compared to that of 1965, while the other half displays a denationalisation. Despite this aggregate stability, the relative position of each country substantially changes and, at the end of the period, no country shows the same position in the ranking it had at the beginning.

Fifty years ago, the most nationalised country was Ireland, followed by Sweden, while the least nationalised was Switzerland, followed by the Netherlands. Today, the picture is radically different. The most nationalised country is Greece, followed by Portugal, which was the third most territorialised country at

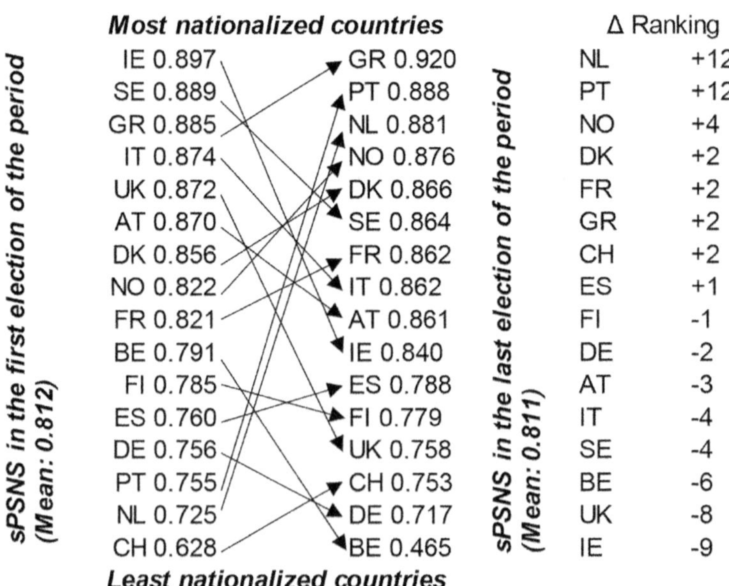

Figure 3.8 Vote nationalisation and relative rank of countries: A comparison between the beginning and the end of the 1965–2015 period

the beginning of the period. Conversely, Ireland falls in the second half of this classification, ranking only tenth in terms of sPSNS, while Sweden is only sixth, also overtaken by two other Scandinavian polities, Norway and Denmark. The bottom of the ranking is occupied – with a huge gap from the other countries – by Belgium, which in 1965 showed a level of the sPSNS somewhat close to the average. Finally, today the penultimate country in terms of vote nationalisation is Germany, while Switzerland and the Netherlands, which were at the bottom of the ranking fifty years ago, have experienced a sharp process of territorial homogenisation: for instance, today the Netherlands is the third most nationalised country in Western Europe.

The right part of figure 3.8 summarises the changes occurred within the ranking over the past fifty years. The remarkable growth in the ranking by the Netherlands and Switzerland (+12 positions for both countries) and the dramatic decline undergone by Belgium, the United Kingdom and Ireland (−6, −8 and −9 positions, respectively) create a massive overturn. Therefore, notwithstanding the presence of countries showing limited variations (e.g., Spain and Finland, going up and down by just one position, respectively), the snapshot taken today appears largely different from that of fifty years ago.

These pieces of evidence show that the territorial configuration of party support in the Western European countries has considerably changed over the past fifty years, and we need to provide an explanation for these different national trajectories – a task that is accomplished in the third part of the book.

A CLASSIFICATION OF EUROPEAN ELECTIONS

This chapter has pointed out that while there is an overall stability in the level of vote nationalisation in Europe over time, if the sixteen countries are separately taken into consideration, the general pattern of stability is replaced by a wide array of different trend lines. Western European countries, therefore, differ among each other with regard to their level of nationalisation, the extent of this variability through time and the direction of change (towards homogenisation or territorialisation). Further empirical evidence can be drawn from the quartile distribution of the 230 elections included in the sample. Table 3.2 reports for each country the number of elections that fall in the lowest quartile of the distribution (sPSNS < 0.776), the number of those falling in the two quartiles around the overall median value (0.858) and finally the number of elections included in the highest quartile (sPSNS > 0.883). It is a different way to look at the same data.

This distinction proves very useful since it provides a classification of European elections: we can consider the fifty-seven elections included in the

Table 3.2 Quartile distribution of elections according to the sPSNS, by country (1965–2015)

Country	*Lowest quartile (< 0.776)*	*Middle quartiles*	*Highest quartile (> 0.883)*	*N elections*
Austria		9	6	15
Belgium	15	1		16
Denmark		10	9	19
Finland	6	8		14
France		10	2	12
Germany	12	2		14
Greece		2	15	17
Ireland		8	6	14
Italy	1	11	1	13
Netherlands	2	8	5	15
Norway		13		13
Portugal	1	9	5	15
Spain	6	6		12
Sweden		7	8	15
Switzerland	13			13
UK	1	12		13
Total	**57**	**116**	**57**	**230**

lowest quartile as 'poorly nationalised elections' and the fifty-seven ones that fall in the highest quartile as 'highly nationalised elections'.[10] Comparing the evidence that emerges from this table with that from table 3.1 and figure 3.6, some of the results can be confirmed; nonetheless, we must notice the presence of some contrasting findings. First of all, nine countries experienced at least a poorly nationalised election and the same number had at least a highly nationalised one. Only Norwegian elections are entirely included into the two middle quartiles: this means that although Norway experienced one of the sharpest processes of nationalisation over time, their sPSNS coefficients did not change so much if considered in a broad European perspective. Switzerland is the only other country whose elections fall in just one column of table 3.2. Notwithstanding its high standard deviation and the high correlation between time and nationalisation process (highlighted previously), this country has always recorded 'poorly nationalized elections'.

Among the fourteen countries showing a certain degree of variability in the quartile distribution of elections, eleven of them have elections falling into two columns and three have elections ranging from the lowest to the highest quartile. This latter group includes Italy, the Netherlands and Portugal. These three countries experienced both poorly and highly nationalised elections but with opposite trends over time: while Italy underwent a process of denationalisation between its only highly nationalised election

(1976) and its unique poorly nationalised election (1994), both in the Netherlands and Portugal, the opposite process took place and the poorly nationalised elections are the first ones covered by the research (the Netherlands in 1967 and 1971; Portugal in 1975).

In general, five countries are overrepresented in the lowest quartile, since more than 25 per cent of their elections belong to the poorly nationalised European elections: Switzerland (100 per cent), Belgium (94 per cent), Germany (86 per cent), Spain (50 per cent) and Finland (43 per cent). Conversely, other seven countries are overrepresented among the highest quartile, which means that more than 25 per cent of their elections belong to the 'highly nationalized European elections': Greece (88 per cent), Sweden (53 per cent) and, to a lesser extent, Denmark (47 per cent), Ireland (43 per cent), Austria (40 per cent) and the Netherlands (33 per cent). These findings are consistent with the expectations: the former five countries show the lower mean of vote nationalisation, while the latter six are among the most nationalised ones.[11]

Part III

EXPLAINING VOTE NATIONALISATION

Chapter 4

The 'macro-sociological' determinants

This chapter introduces the first set of potential explanatory factors of vote nationalisation in Western Europe. This first set consists of variables related to the structure of the cleavage system in a given country. I explore the relationship between vote nationalisation and some predictors concerning the relative strength of social cleavages such as class, ethnicity, language and religion. In the analysis that follows, I briefly review the state of the art of the literature on this topic, and I present my working hypotheses that will be eventually tested in chapter 7; here, however, some preliminary findings on the relationship between the 'macro-sociological' predictors and vote nationalisation are given. Moreover, the analysis takes into account not only the overall relationship between the *explanans* and the *explanandum* but also temporal variations and national differences. Indeed, I do not want to detect exclusively whether a factor is an important determinant of vote nationalisation but also understand whether this factor maintains the same importance over time or across countries.

The structure of this chapter is as follows: the first section, 'Class cleavage as a homogenising factor', explores the relation between class cleavage and vote nationalisation and also detect its evolution over time and its national variations; the second section, 'Cultural cleavages and territoriality', is instead devoted to assessing the impact of cultural segmentation; finally, the third section, 'The macro-sociological model', puts together class and cultural cleavages to gauge the role of a comprehensive 'macro-sociological model'. Throughout the chapter, two tools of analysis are employed: regression models, to assess the relative importance of each factor in the explanation, and typologies, to explore the implications for vote nationalisation emerging from different cleavage settings.

CLASS CLEAVAGE AS A HOMOGENISING FACTOR

The macro-sociological literature (Lipset and Rokkan 1967; Rose and Urwin 1970; Bartolini 2000) has emphasised the role of social cleavages in shaping Western European party systems and, specifically, the impact of the class cleavage on the structuring of the European political space in functional terms, with opposing left-right alignments. As regards the process of nationalisation, the class cleavage, based on a functional division between the interests of the working class and those of the employers, has been a strong 'homogenising cleavage' (Caramani 2004: 196), since it has created nonterritorial nationwide alignments that have been translated in nationalised party families (the Social Democratic family and, on the opposite side, the Conservative and the Liberal families). These families have spread their support across countries, to the detriment of the territorialised party families, expression of the old ethnolinguistic and religious cleavages.

As stressed by Caramani (2004), vote nationalisation in Western Europe has been the result of a long-term process of progressive reduction of the territoriality of political cleavages. In order to assess if political cleavages still play a central role in the explanation of the vote nationalisation's variance, the temporal dimension becomes crucial. Indeed, it is possible to hypothesise that a transformation or a decline of the class cleavage might have produced important consequences in the evolution of vote nationalisation during the past fifty years. In this regard, a large amount of literature has highlighted the irreversible decline of the class cleavage[1] (Franklin, Mackie and Valen 1992; Kriesi 1998; Dalton 2002; Knutsen 2004).

In this context, it is essential to empirically assess the strength of the class cleavage and its trend through time in the sixteen countries included in this research, in order to test if the class cleavage is related to the process of nationalisation, the expectation being, following Caramani's theory, of a trend towards denationalisation as the class cleavage loses its salience.

Measuring the strength of the class cleavage in a country from a nonelectoral point of view (to avoid problems of endogeneity with the dependent variable) is quite complicated. According to Bartolini and Mair (1990: 215):

> the concept of cleavage can be seen to incorporate three levels: an empirical element, which identifies the empirical referent of the concept, . . . a normative element, that is the set of values and beliefs which provides a sense of identity and role to the empirical element, and which reflect the self-consciousness of the social group(s) involved; and an organisational/behavioural element, that is the set of individual interactions, institutions and organisations, such as political parties, which develop as part of the cleavage.

Following Bartolini and Mair (1990: 231–38) and Bartolini (2000: 262–63), the best proxy for class cleavage strength can be achieved by focusing on the level of 'organisational density'[2] – which is one of the three dimensions of a cleavage[3] – through the use of two indicators: the ratio between left parties' membership[4] and total electorate[5] (left partisan density, LPD) and trade union density (TUD), which is the ratio between union membership[6] and the total dependent labour force of a country. The source for the collection of data on left parties' membership has been the MAPP Project Data Archive (van Haute et al. 2016),[7] while TUD data have been collected from Visser (2015). Here LPD and TUD are not considered as independent determinants of vote nationalisation but as different components of a single determinant, that is, organisational density as one aspect of class cleavage strength. For this reason, following again Bartolini and Mair's strategy (1990: 237–38), I have combined the two indices into a single standardised index of class cleavage strength.[8] The new class index is nothing but the half-sum of LPD and TUD expressed in the standardised form (in other words, its observations are the half-sums of the Z-scores of LPD and TUD). In summary, the first hypothesis is as follows:

> H1: The stronger the class cleavage in society, the higher the level of vote nationalisation.

Table 4.1 shows the results of the Prais-Winsten regression – the regression with panel-corrected standard errors (PCSE) and a first-order autoregressive (AR1) parameter (*see* chapter 2) – of the sPSNS on the class index in the two time periods introduced in chapter 2 (Model 1 and 2) and in the whole period including all the 230 elections occurred since 1965 (Model 3).[9] As it can be noticed, despite the higher impact during the first period taken

Table 4.1 Regressions of vote nationalisation (sPSNS) on the class index

	Model 1	*Model 2*	*Model 3*
	1965–1990	*1991–2015*	*All elections*
Class	0.013 (0.009)	–0.000 (0.014)	0.007 (0.006)
Constant	0.810*** (0.017)	0.811*** (0.014)	0.814*** (0.014)
Wald $\chi 2$	2	0.00	1.31
N elections	121	109	230
N countries	16	16	16

Note: Prais-Winsten AR1 regression. Panel-corrected standard errors in parentheses.

† $p < 0.1$; * $p < 0.05$; ** $p < 0.01$; *** $p < 0.001$.

into consideration (1965–1990),[10] the standardised index of class cleavage strength is never significant.[11]

Therefore, from these first, preliminary, pieces of evidence, the class cleavage does not seem to be an important determinant of vote nationalisation, thus disproving Caramani's (2004) theory about the central role of the class cleavage in shaping nonterritorial nationwide alignments in the Western European countries, at least as far as the period since 1965 is concerned. Why do such unexpected results occur? The analysis of temporal and national variation can shed more light on this puzzle.

The chart in figure 4.1 plots the evolution of the class index through time. A straightforward trend towards a declining strength of the index has occurred since 1965, and the negative correlation ($r = -0.354$) is significant at the 0.001 level.[12] These results are consistent with the literature on the growing decline of party membership (Mair and Van Biezen 2001; Van Biezen, Mair and Poguntke 2012; Paulis, Sierens and Van Haute 2015) and, more generally, of the class cleavage (see in particular Franklin, Mackie and Valen 1992). Resuming Rokkan's and Bartolini and Mair's terminology, the decrease in the organisational density means that present Western European societies are by far less segmented on class basis than in the past. Conversely, as shown in chapter 3, vote nationalisation over time has followed a trend of enduring stability, and this difference may partly explain why class cleavage and nationalisation are so loosely linked.

Yet, notwithstanding this overall declining trend over time, it is possible to hypothesise that the class cleavage has not undergone an even decline as a factor of territorial homogenisation of party support across countries. Indeed,

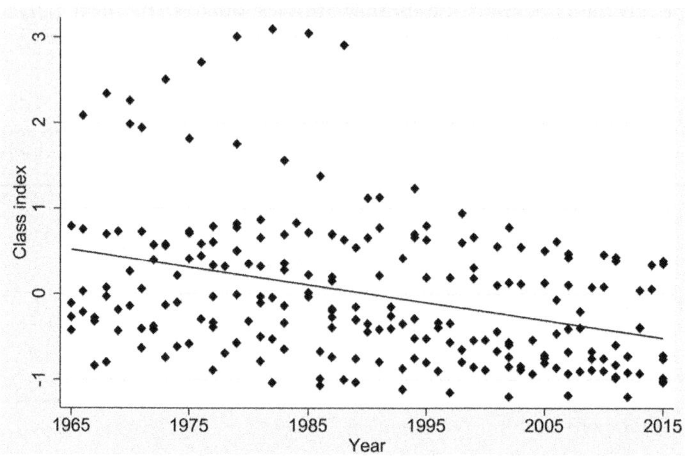

Figure 4.1 Trend of class cleavage over time, 1965–2015

an exploration of the national variations is needed to achieve a comprehensive understanding of the relation between class and vote nationalisation in Western Europe, as well as to detect whether some national contexts deviate from the main pattern.

Figure 4.2 plots the sixteen countries under study according to their mean level of vote nationalisation (the *y*-axis) and their mean level of the standardised class index (the *x*-axis). The chart has been divided into four quadrants according to the mean value of the two variables (respectively, 0.816 for the sPSNS and 0 for Class). Thus, the figure depicts a synthetic map of Western European countries as regards the relation between class and nationalisation.

The upper-right quadrant includes countries that are, at the same time, highly segmented on class basis and highly nationalised. Austria belongs to this group, thanks to its extremely high level of LPD, and so do the three Scandinavian countries, with Sweden falling close to the right edge of the figure and appearing as the country with the strongest salience of the class cleavage. Finland is located a little further down, in the lower-right quadrant, since it combines a regionalised territorial configuration with one of the highest levels of class cleavage strength. In general, the results of Austria and Scandinavia are entirely consistent with Bartolini and Mair's findings, when they argue that 'the Scandinavian countries and Austria, which may be regarded as very homogeneous in cultural terms, evidence extremely high levels of organisational encapsulation' (Bartolini and Mair 1990: 239). On the opposite side, they

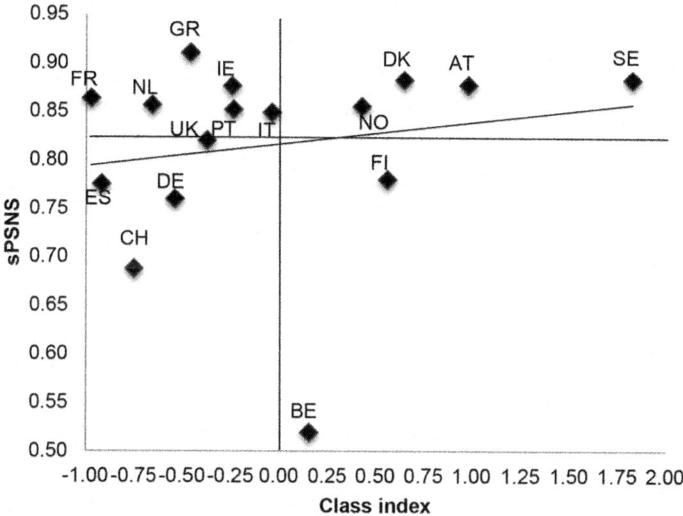

Figure 4.2 Class cleavage strength and vote nationalisation in Western Europe, mean values by country

find that France 'is characterised by the lowest level of organisational density in Western Europe' (*ibidem*). Consistently, in figure 4.2 France shows the lowest level of class cleavage strength.

The lower-left quadrant includes three countries where class plays only a minor or diminishing role and where the electoral behaviour is highly territorialised: Germany, Spain and Switzerland.

The other two quadrants are those deviating from the hypothesised positive relationship between class cleavage and nationalisation. On one side, in the upper-left quadrant, seven countries, despite a weak class cleavage, show highly nationalised territorial configurations: Greece, Ireland, the Netherlands and France and, to a lesser extent, Portugal, Italy and the United Kingdom.[13] In these contexts, the determinants of the high level of vote nationalisation must be sought elsewhere, since the class cleavage does not play a major role, contrary to what has been originally predicted.

On the other side, in the lower-right quadrant, it is possible to find – beyond the aforementioned Finland – Belgium, where a territorially divided party system goes hand in hand with a strong relevance of the class cleavage. Here, not only does Belgium appear as a dramatic case of a denationalised country but also as a case whose territorial heterogeneity has to be explained by referring to other variables (first of all, the level of cultural segmentation, as shown in the next section). What emerges, in a striking way, is the location of Belgium vis-à-vis the other countries in the chart and also with respect to the overall relationship under study (the trend line) from which Belgium impressively deviates. As stated in chapter 3 (*see* endnote 3), Belgium meets the statistical definition of 'outlier' as regards vote nationalisation.

This clarification is essential, since the presence of Belgium in the data set undermines the validity of the result concerning the overall relation between class cleavage and vote nationalisation:[14] the expected relation between the two variables is positive and the presence of Belgium – with its extremely low level of the dependent variable and, on the contrary, its relatively strong class cleavage – underestimates the effective impact of class on nationalisation. Therefore, it is useful to test again the relationship between the class cleavage and vote nationalisation after the exclusion of Belgium.[15]

The results are reported in table 4.2. The regression coefficients significantly differ from those shown in table 4.1. After the exclusion of Belgium, the overall impact the class index has on the sPSNS becomes significant at the 0.05 level.[16] Therefore, leaving Belgium aside, in the rest of Western Europe, the class cleavage has an impact on vote nationalisation, and the hypothesised homogenising effect seems confirmed.

Moreover, almost the entire increase in the strength and the statistical significance of the regression coefficient in the full model of table 4.2 compared to table 4.1 is due to the relative importance of the class cleavage

Table 4.2 Regressions of vote nationalisation on the class index (Belgium excluded)

	Model 1	*Model 2*	*Model 3*
	1965–1990	*1991–2015*	*All elections*
Class	0.022** (0.007)	0.018† (0.010)	0.012* (0.005)
Constant	0.825*** (0.010)	0.841*** (0.008)	0.832*** (0.009)
Wald $\chi 2$	10.32**	2.97†	5.68*
N elections	112	102	214
N countries	15	15	15

Note: Prais-Winsten AR1 regression. Panel-corrected standard errors in parentheses.

† $p < 0.1$; * $p < 0.05$; ** $p < 0.01$; *** $p < 0.001$.

during the first period under study. From this point of view, the results of the regressions obtained after the exclusion of Belgium are consistent with those obtained before: the class index shows a substantial and significant impact ($p < 0.01$) on the territorial structuring of party support during the first period (1965–1990), while since then its influence on vote nationalisation almost disappears.

CULTURAL CLEAVAGES AND TERRITORIALITY

While the class cleavage has historically played a fundamental role in the structuring of a nationwide electoral competition based on the functional left-right dimension, culture-related cleavages have produced the opposite result. Scholars have highlighted the role of culture-related cleavages as the primary source of 'deviation' (Rokkan 1970: 120) of the European nation-states from the path towards centralisation and homogenisation carried out by the nation-building elites. Therefore, the presence of an ethnic, linguistic or religious minority in a given country has usually led to the formation of parties for territorial defence, since this kind of conflict holds a predominant territorial nature[17] (the struggle of the culturally distinct periphery against the effort of standardisation led by the ruling elite) and translates into parties with a remarkably heterogeneous territorial configuration of support.[18]

The presence of cultural cleavages is considered an important factor of territorial differentiation of party support within countries even today. As posited by Caramani, 'The survival of territoriality in politics today can be principally explained through cultural cleavages that resisted the homogenising impact of class politics' (2005: 318). Most of the recently published contributions on vote nationalisation emphasise the role of 'pre-industrial cleavages' in shaping a territorially based electoral competition and show that the level of cultural (namely, ethnic, linguistic or religious) segmentation is positively and significantly associated with a denationalised outcome in Western Europe (Lago and Lago 2010; Lago 2011; Simón 2013) as well as in Eastern Europe (Sikk and Bochsler 2008) and Latin America (Harbers 2010).

In order to assess the relative importance of cultural cleavages within society, we need to take into account two dimensions: *cultural heterogeneity* and *territorial distinctiveness*.

Cultural heterogeneity is conceived as the degree to which individuals within society belong to different ethnic, linguistic or religious groups. The most commonly used measure of cultural heterogeneity is the *Fractionalisation index* by Alesina et al. (2003). It is defined as the probability that two randomly selected individuals in a country belong to a different group. This formula[19] is not new, since it consists of the 'one minus the Herfindahl index' formula, typically adopted by the literature on this topic before the Alesina et al. contribution, which in turn has the merit of providing a systematic measurement throughout the world of ethnic, linguistic or religious fractionalisation. The fractionalisation index ranges from 0 to 1, where 0 implies a perfectly homogeneous country and 1 indicates a country where each individual belongs to a different group. For example, a score of ethnic fractionalisation of 0.250 refers to a country where the probability of two randomly selected people to belong to two different ethnic groups is 25 per cent. The same logic applies to the linguistic and religious indices. The aggregate index of cultural heterogeneity is, therefore, nothing but the mean of the three indices.[20]

Yet, what is important to test is not only the general level of cultural heterogeneity within a nation, namely, the presence of minorities, but also the geographic concentration of such minorities, since 'geographically concentrated groups should . . . increase the distinctiveness of local electoral units' (Morgenstern, Swindle and Castagnola 2009: 1328). Conversely, if a minority is homogeneously distributed throughout the country, this is less likely to bring to the political activation of that cleavage, namely, to the formation of distinct parties for ethnic, linguistic or religious defence. The second – often neglected[21] – dimension to be taken into account is, therefore, that of territorial distinctiveness, defined as the level of territorial concentration of ethnic, linguistic and religious groups. It can be operationalised through the *Segregation index* (Alesina and Zhuravskaya 2011). It ranges from 0 to 1, where 0 means that every region has the same fraction of each group as the country as a whole and 1 means that each region is comprised of a separate group (full segregation).[22]

Figure 4.3 provides a map of the different types of cultural cleavages' structures in Western Europe.

Half of the countries are located in the lower-left quadrant, showing low cultural heterogeneity and low or absent territorial distinctiveness of the minorities. These polities can be considered culturally homogeneous

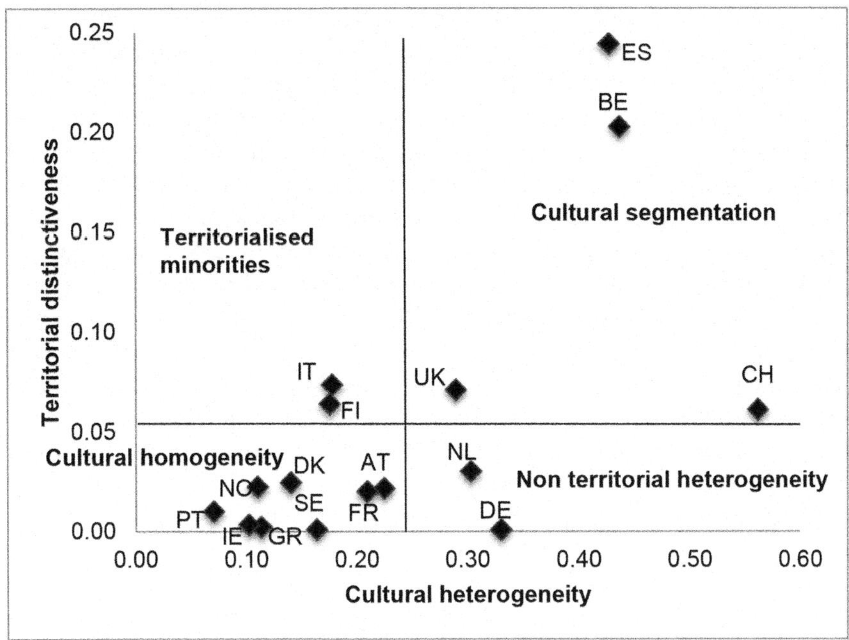

Figure 4.3 Cultural cleavages in Western Europe: A typology

societies. The lower-right quadrant hosts Germany and the Netherlands, namely, two countries where there is a high level of cultural heterogeneity, mainly due to the religious divide between Catholics and Protestants. In both countries, religious fractionalisation is around 0.7 which means that there is a probability of about 70 per cent that two randomly selected individuals belong to two different religious groups. Yet, this divide is not structured along marked territorial lines, and both religious groups (as well as non-religious people), due to long-term processes of urbanisation and secularisation, are spread across the country. Despite being the most culturally heterogeneous country in Western Europe, even Switzerland falls close to this quadrant, being barely over the average territorial distinctiveness. The opposite situation can be found in Italy and Finland, culturally homogeneous countries recording the presence of small minorities with a noticeable territorial distinctiveness: it is the case of the French- and the German-speaking minorities in Italy, concentrated in the peripheral northern regions of, respectively, Aosta Valley and Trentino-Alto Adige, or the case of the Swedish-speaking minority located in southwest Finland (*see* the appendix). Finally, the upper-right quadrant includes countries with a territorialised heterogeneity, where cultural cleavages are expected to produce major consequences on the territorial configuration of party support. Not by chance, the four countries of this quadrant are all regionalised polities. Beyond Switzerland, the United Kingdom appears culturally segmented due to the regional distinctiveness of Scotland and Wales and to the religious division between Anglicans, atheists and the two largest religious minorities of Roman Catholics and nonconformist Protestants. Belgium and Spain appear as the most culturally segmented countries and as the only ones where ethnolinguistic heterogeneity also has a substantively territorial distinctiveness. In Belgium, beyond the historical ethnic and linguistic cleavage opposing the Flemish and the Walloon regions, there has been a growing level of 'religious' conflict in the past decades between the Catholic Flanders and the secular Wallonia. In Spain, the main sources of heterogeneity come from the ethnic and linguistic diversity of the territorially peripheral regions (Catalonia, Basque Country, Galicia, etc.) opposed to the Castilian centre.

Considered together, these two dimensions of cultural heterogeneity and territorial distinctiveness shape the concept of *cultural segmentation*: the degree to which a given society is segmented across cultural divisions. Cultural segmentation is measured through a standardised index combining the two indices of fractionalisation and segregation.[23] The second hypothesis concerning the expected predictors of vote nationalisation in Western Europe is as follows:

> H2: As far as cultural segmentation increases, vote nationalisation should decrease, and vice versa.

Table 4.3 reports the results of the Prais-Winsten models where the sPSNS is regressed on cultural segmentation. The models test this relation in the overall set of elections as well as separately in the two periods, both in the full data set and in the data set excluding Belgium from the analysis. As expected, the regression coefficients show negative sign and are very strong, always reaching the highest level of confidence ($p < 0.001$).[24] Moreover, unlike the previously presented data about the class cleavage, here it seems not to be a distorting effect of Belgium. This latter is – as it will be shown in the next section – a culturally segmented country with the lowest level of vote nationalisation in Western Europe. Indeed, one might expect that the exclusion of Belgian elections would heavily reduce the strength of the association between cultural segmentation and sPSNS. Yet, notwithstanding a noticeable decrease in the *b* coefficients, the association remains powerful and all models are significant, as shown by the Wald Chi-Square statistics. Before testing this factor in a multivariate model, to control for possible spurious effects in

Table 4.3 Regressions of vote nationalisation on cultural segmentation

	Model 1	*Model 2*	*Model 3*
Full data set	*1965–1990*	*1991–2015*	*All elections*
Cultural segmentation	−0.078*** (0.022)	−0.086*** (0.014)	−0.075*** (0.015)
Constant	0.814*** (0.012)	0.816*** (0.008)	0.815*** (0.009)
Wald $\chi2$	12.76***	35.91***	24.53***
N elections	121	109	230
N countries	16	16	16
Belgium excluded	−0.061*** (0.012)	−0.050*** (0.010)	−0.052*** (0.010)
Constant	0.821*** (0.009)	0.832*** (0.007)	0.826*** (0.007)
Wald $\chi2$	26.27***	23.89***	27.82***
N elections	112	102	214
N countries	15	15	15

Note: Prais-Winsten AR1 regression. Panel-corrected standard errors in parentheses.

† $p < 0.1$; * $p < 0.05$; ** $p < 0.01$; *** $p < 0.001$.

the explanation of the vote nationalisation's variance, these first pieces of evidence suggest that *H2* might be confirmed: as far as cultural segmentation increases, vote nationalisation decreases. Consistent with previous studies, cultural segmentation remains a strong factor of territorial heterogeneity in Western Europe.

In order to account for national variations, figure 4.4 offers a synthetic map on the relationship between cultural segmentation and vote nationalisation. As in figure 4.2, regarding the relation between class and vote nationalisation, figure 4.4 has been divided into four quadrants according to the mean levels of the two variables (respectively, 0.816 for the sPSNS and 0 for the cultural segmentation index). The association between the two variables is powerful, and therefore, most countries fall into the two quadrants that respect the hypothesised negative relation, the upper-left quadrant and the lower-right one. Unlike figure 4.2, where the deviations from the main pattern were considerable, here most countries fall very close to the regression line. The only significant exceptions are represented by Spain, showing a higher level of nationalisation than that expected based on its cultural segmentation and, on the other side, by Belgium (and to a lesser extent by Finland and Germany), whose territorial heterogeneity is not entirely explained by the level of cultural segmentation. This means that in Spain and Belgium, cultural segmentation is not sufficient to account for the level of vote nationalisation since other determinants are at stake.

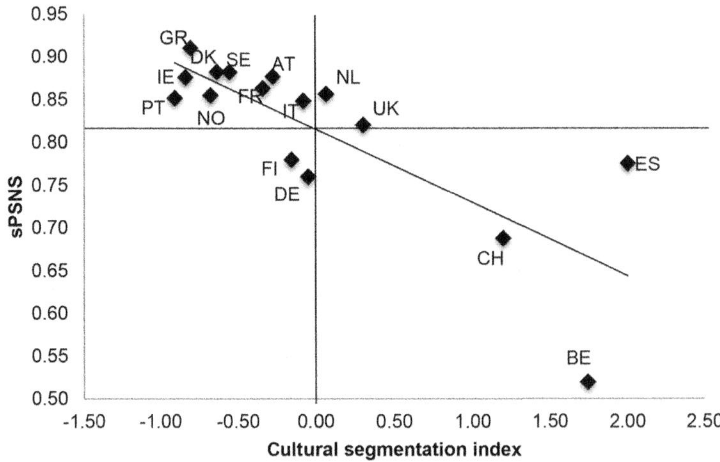

Figure 4.4 Cultural segmentation and vote nationalisation in Western Europe, mean values by country

THE MACRO-SOCIOLOGICAL MODEL

So far, the role of political cleavages in shaping the Western European territorial configuration has been analysed by separately tackling the class cleavage and the cultural ones. This final section of the chapter puts together the analyses carried out in the previous sections by presenting a 'macro-sociological model' and briefly discussing findings and implications.

The evidence discussed in the previous sections suggests that the class cleavage has not been a powerful predictor of vote nationalisation over the past fifty years. Contrary to what expected based on existing literature, emphasising its role as 'homogenising cleavage' (Caramani 2004: 196), the regression analyses have shown that, overall, the impact of class on the sPSNS is not significant. This seems due to two different factors at stake: the distorting effect exerted by Belgium on the overall set of elections and the declining salience through time of the class cleavage. By excluding Belgium from the analysis and by splitting the sample into two periods (1965–1990 and 1991–2015), the result is a positive and statistically significant impact of the class cleavage during the first period under study and a confirmation of its insignificance in the past decades. On the other side, cultural conflicts, summarised through the index of cultural segmentation, have played a major role in the explanation of vote nationalisation. Data definitely show the tight negative association between cultural segmentation and vote nationalisation: with few exceptions, as far as cultural segmentation increases, the territorial homogeneity of party support decreases. Moreover, while class, with its straightforward trend of decline over time, is able to account for the temporal variation of the relation with vote nationalisation but to some extent fails to account for differences across countries (*see* figure 4.2), cultural segmentation does the opposite. Indeed, this latter is unable to explain temporal trends (since data do not provide temporal variation) but particularly powerful in explaining cross-country differences (*see* figure 4.4).

Table 4.4 puts together the macro-sociological indices of class and cultural segmentation and regresses vote nationalisation on them. The results generally confirm the expectations, highlighting the modest role played by class and the powerful impact of cultural segmentation, whose effect is independent of Belgium's exclusion. Note that the previously observed significant effect of class in the models without Belgium now disappears once cultural segmentation is taken under control.[25]

This macro-sociological regression model has confirmed the primary role of cultural cleavages as predictors of the vote nationalisation's variance and has also shown the insignificance of the class cleavage, once being a crucial factor of territorial homogenisation and today reduced to play a marginal part in the story.

Figure 4.5 offers further evidence of these findings. The interaction between class and cultural cleavages is presented by reporting the mean levels of the sPSNS in four different cleavage settings created by cutting the chart into four quadrants according to the mean values of the class index and

Table 4.4 Regressions of vote nationalisation on the macro-sociological variables

	Model 1	*Model 2*	*Model 3*
Full data set	*1965–1990*	*1991–2015*	*All elections*
Class	−0.002 (0.009)	−0.031** (0.011)	−0.002 (0.006)
Cultural segmentation	−0.080** (0.023)	−0.091*** (0.014)	−0.076*** (0.015)
Constant	0.814*** (0.012)	0.807*** (0.009)	0.815*** (0.009)
Wald $\chi 2$	15.78***	44.13***	29.65***
N elections	121	109	230
N countries	16	16	16
Belgium excluded			
Class	0.007 (0.007)	−0.004 (0.008)	0.005 (0.005)
Cultural segmentation	−0.058*** (0.013)	−0.050*** (0.010)	−0.049*** (0.010)
Constant	0.820*** (0.010)	0.831*** (0.007)	0.827*** (0.007)
Wald $\chi 2$	26.76***	27.67***	31.15***
N elections	112	102	214
N countries	15	15	15

Note: Prais-Winsten AR1 regression. Panel-corrected standard errors in parentheses.

† $p < 0.1$; * $p < 0.05$; ** $p < 0.01$; *** $p < 0.001$.

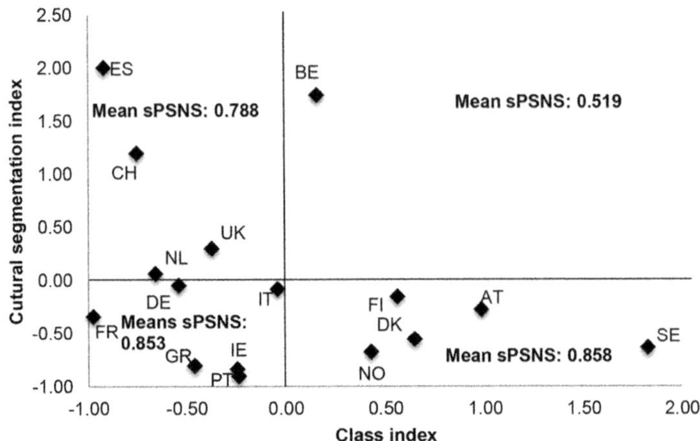

Figure 4.5 Mean vote nationalisation in four different cleavage contexts

the cultural segmentation one. Once again, the presence of cultural cleavages seems to be the only macro-sociological predictor that matters in explaining vote nationalisation's variance. Indeed, where cultural segmentation is high and class is low (upper-left quadrant), as in Spain, Switzerland, the Netherlands and the United Kingdom, the outcome is, on average, a regionalised territorial configuration of party support. The difference with the context where both cleavages are low (lower-left quadrant) is noticeable (the mean sPSNS are, respectively, 0.788 and 0.853). Conversely, a strong class cleavage setting is not able to push the party system towards a more nationalised configuration: in the Scandinavian countries and Austria, where class is comparatively strong and cultural homogeneity is high, the mean sPSNS is not significantly higher than that of the lower-left quadrant (0.858). Finally, the Western European country where cleavages play the largest role is Belgium, where the marked territorialisation of the vote is mostly due to the ethnic and linguistic divide and where class is not able to push in the opposite direction (i.e., towards increasing territorial homogeneity), since even the organisational representatives of the class cleavage (left parties, trade unions) are divided along the cultural divide.

From these considerations, one main implication can be drawn: cleavage-related factors are neither entirely able to discriminate across countries as regards their different levels of vote nationalisation nor able to give account of temporal variations. Evidence of this is not only the very low level of nationalisation in Belgium, whose mean score cannot be entirely explained by the high cultural segmentation of the country. Even the wide differences in the sPSNS detectable within the other three quadrants[26] suggest the same thing. Cleavages tell us only a part of the story, and a comprehensive explanation of vote nationalisation can be achieved only by looking elsewhere.

Chapter 5

The institutional constraints

This chapter focuses on the so-called institutional factors and their impact on vote nationalisation. By 'institutional' factors I mean all those determinants related to the institutional framework (namely, the set of rules, procedures and power structures that define the political system) within which political actors interact with one another. More specifically, I aim at assessing the impact of changes in the institutional framework on the territorial homogeneity of party support: institutional changes modify the structure of opportunities for electoral competition and, therefore, may constrain both the political supply and voting choices. As a consequence, these constraints may also affect the territorial configuration of party support in a given country.

In the following pages, I explore the effect of institutional determinants (e.g., decentralisation, the level of European integration and the features of the electoral system) on the level of vote nationalisation in Western Europe. As in the previous chapter, I do not simply test the working hypotheses concerning the overall relationship between these factors and vote nationalisation. I also assess the extent to which these determinants have a valuable impact cross-time and cross-country, also detecting the possible deviations from the hypothesised pattern.

The structure of the chapter is as follows: the first section, 'Decentralisation', introduces the first institutional determinant, that is, decentralisation, and tests its impact on vote nationalisation; the second section, 'EU integration', deals with the European integration; the third section, 'Electoral systems and vote nationalisation: An unsolved puzzle', analyses the effects of three different aspects of the electoral system on vote nationalisation; finally, the last section of the chapter, 'The institutional model', puts together all the institutional factors to gauge the role of a comprehensive 'institutional model' and its ability to predict the vote nationalisation's variance in Western Europe.

DECENTRALISATION

As stressed by Hooghe, Marks and Schakel (2010: 33), decentralisation can be conceived as 'a single, continuous dimension ranging from centralization, in which the central government monopolizes decision-making authority, to decentralisation, in which subnational governments have extensive decision-making authority that falls short of a monopoly over authority'.

During the past years, many scholars have underlined that the economic and political decentralisation negatively affects the level of nationalisation of party systems (Cox and Knoll 2003; Jones and Mainwaring 2003; Brancati 2007; Thorlakson 2007; Harbers 2010; Lago and Montero 2014; Golosov 2016b; Simón and Gunjoan 2017). Indeed, while 'voters are more likely to support national political parties, as the national government becomes more important for their lives' (Lago and Lago 2010: 5), the growth of powers held by local authorities encourages the rise of regional parties (Chhibber and Kollman 1998; 2004) and their electoral success (Brancati 2006). This is because, with fiscal and political decentralisation, local parties have fewer incentives to merge with each other to become competitive at the national level, since the 'prize' of the national government becomes less attractive. Moreover, the lower the power of the central government, the higher the incentives for voters to vote for local parties (and thus the lower the level of territorial homogeneity for the party system).[1] A similar thought is expressed by Thorlakson (2007) who argues that decentralisation gives both parties and voters incentives and opportunities to mobilise and respond to locally defined issues which may lead to the development of 'unique' party systems at the subnational level. Thus, 'centralization fosters the nationalization of party systems' (Simón 2013: 25), and vice versa.

However, some authors take on a slightly different perspective. In particular, as argued by Morgenstern, Swindle and Castagnola (2009: 1329), the effect of decentralisation on nationalisation is detectable only if the former interacts with cultural segmentation. The empirical analysis carried out by Lago reinforces Morgenstern, Swindle and Castagnola's findings: 'the reductive effect of decentralisation on nationalization increases as the size of regionally based ethnopolitically relevant groups grows' (Lago 2011: 16).

Moreover, Simón (2013: 24–25) suggests an alternative argument: 'the impact of decentralisation on the nationalization of party systems is conditional on the extent to which electoral law encourages personal voting'. This means that in a decentralised country with a very party-centred electoral law, candidates will prefer to run under a national party, 'because national labels can offer crucial added value in bringing about their electoral success'. Conversely, 'when a decentralised country has an electoral law that promotes candidate-oriented voting . . . candidates will prefer to compete without merging with a national party, and therefore, by doing this, they will erode party system nationalization' (*ibidem*). In other words, according to Simón, to gauge the role played by decentralisation, it is necessary to pay attention to the extent to which electoral rules encourage personal voting.

Finally, some authors question even the link itself between decentralisation and vote nationalisation. First of all, the so-called party-centred approach (Hopkin 2003; 2009) posits that institutional changes are mediated by parties' internal dynamics. Indeed, party organisations, with their internal history and conflicts, play a mediating role between the institutional reforms and the electoral behaviour. In this perspective, the effects of institutional changes may be limited due to the inertias of long-standing party organisation arrangements. Therefore, according to Hopkin (2009: 196), 'one should not expect a strong relationship between the degree of decentralisation and the nationalization of party systems'. Similarly, Lago and Lago (2010: 20) show 'the absence of a clear pattern connecting fiscal and political decentralisation to party system nationalization'. To add more, Deschouwer (2009: 46) concludes his analysis on Belgium and Spain by stressing that 'the results are not very encouraging for those who believe that the presence of (strong and important) regions has clear and increasing effects on national electoral politics'.

A further different viewpoint is taken by Caramani (2004): the recent decentralisation of power in Western Europe has been allegedly caused by the existence of long-standing cultural cleavages and can be conceived as a response to those territorial claims. Rather than being a factor of denationalisation, the rise of regional authority has not led to fundamental modifications of territorial electoral alignments. Moreover, 'the opening up of new channels of representation through territorial autonomy seems to have had the opposite effect of reducing the probability of regionalist voices expressed in the party system' (282–83).

Finally, Schakel (2012: 226) emphasises the 'multilevel' nature of party systems, arguing that as far as the link between decentralisation and nationalisation of party systems is concerned, one should look at the regional rather than at the national elections. His empirical analysis shows that regional authority has a robust negative effect on the level of nationalisation as far as regional elections are considered instead of the national ones, for which decentralisation shows no significant effect.

Given these contrasting theories and empirical results concerning the relationship between decentralisation and nationalisation, a first paramount step is that of finding a trustworthy way to operationalise this institutional factor.

The literature has proposed different indices in order to measure decentralisation.[2] The most rigorous and suitable one, which also allows for cross-time and cross-country comparisons, is the Regional Authority Index (RAI) by Hooghe et al. (2016). It measures the 'regional authority', namely, the formal authority, exercised in relations to explicit rules, usually, but not necessarily, written in constitutions and legislation, displayed by a regional government. The RAI consists of two macro-dimensions (*Self Rule* and *Shared Rule*) that in turn are composed of some indicators.[3] Scores are first assigned to individual regions and then, by summing the scores of each region of a country weighted by the respective population,[4] the authors build the index for each country in a given year.[5] Country scores may vary over time according to the reforms of decentralisation or centralisation carried out in each polity. The index by Hooghe et al. (2016) covers almost the whole period of this work (1950–2010) and presents 'the richest approach to political decentralisation that the literature has had to date' (Simón 2013: 31).[6]

By looking at the evolution of the RAI through time, figure 5.1 shows a tendency towards a growth of the index during the past fifty years. The correlation with time is positive and significant ($r = 0.175$; $p < 0.01$). This result is broadly consistent with the literature on this topic which underlines, with no exceptions, the presence of a massive process of regionalisation and power decentralisation which has taken place in Europe since the 1980s (Hooghe and Marks 2001: 18; Fabbrini 2008: 158). Rather, given the emphasis used by some scholars to illustrate such a process, I would have expected a stronger correlation between time and decentralisation. The weak, though significant, coefficient means that some deviations from the main pattern are likely to occur.

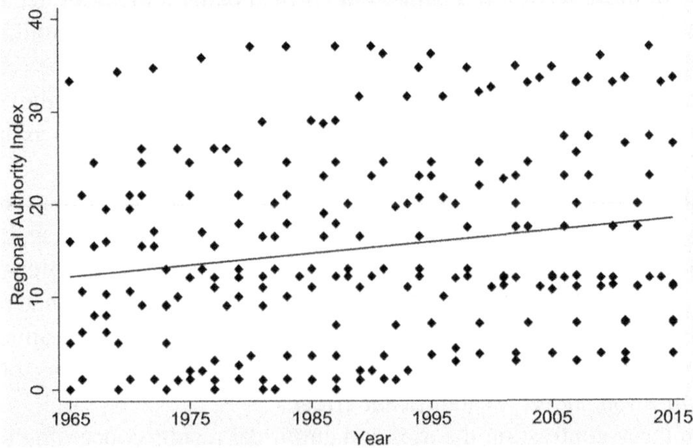

Figure 5.1 Trend of RAI over time, 1965–2015

Figure 5.2 plots the national variations of the RAI over time for the sixteen countries under study. A trend towards increasing decentralisation has taken place in most countries, the exception being Sweden, Denmark, the United Kingdom, Germany and Switzerland. Specifically, the only country that shows a clear decreasing level of decentralisation over time is Sweden, where a decrease of the RAI from 19.5 to 13 occurred after 1970, 'as a result of the abolition in 1971 of the upper chamber of the *Riksdag*, which was composed of regional (*landstinge*) representatives' (Hooghe, Marks and Schakel 2010: 54). In Denmark, the trend towards a strengthening of regional authority has experienced a sharp reversal after 2007, following the reform of the local government that abolished the provinces (*Amter*). In the United Kingdom, the slight decline of the RAI during the 1980s and 1990s is simply due to minor changes occurred in the peripheral regions of the country before the 1999 introduction of an autonomous executive accountable to a directly elected legislature in Scotland and Wales (Hooghe, Marks and Schakel 2010: 100). Finally, in Germany and Switzerland, the level of the RAI is perfectly steady over time. This is because both countries have a functional constraint to decentralisation, the so-called ceiling effect (54): being already federal countries, Germany and Switzerland have little scope for further regionalisation.

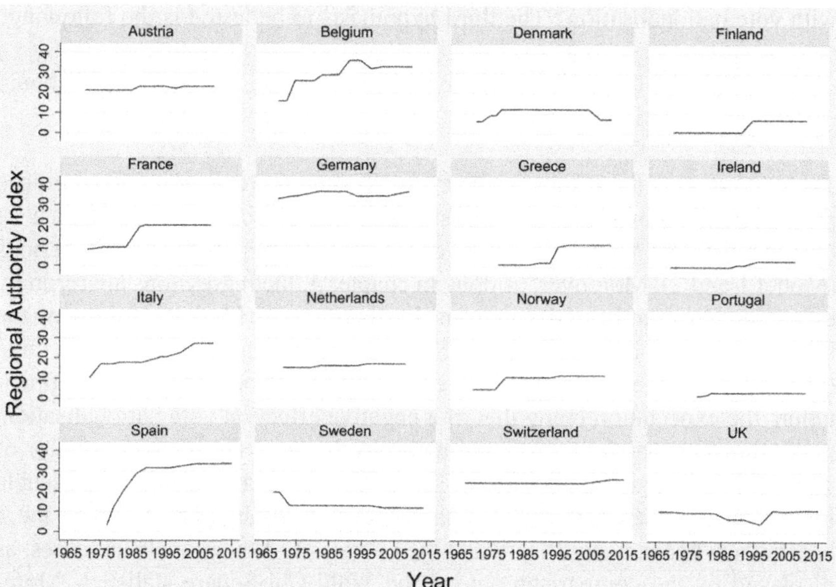

Figure 5.2 National variations of the RAI over time, 1965–2015

All the remaining countries show patterns of decentralisation over time, even if this process is differentiated in terms of strength and timing. In terms of strength, the process of decentralisation has been massive in Belgium, Italy and Spain, while, on the contrary, Austria, Ireland, the Netherlands and Portugal experienced only minor changes compared to the 1960s. In terms of timing, the 1990s emerge as the decade of power devolution in most countries, with France and Spain as early-comers, since the most important steps towards decentralisation occurred during the 1980s, and Italy as a latecomer, given that is only with the constitutional reform of 2001 that regions have been equipped with substantial competencies.

Comparing the mean scores of the RAI, a clear distinction emerges: given the overall mean of 15.3, half of the countries can be considered – even if on different levels – as centralised polities (the four Scandinavian countries, Greece, Ireland, Portugal and the United Kingdom), while the other half belongs to the group of regionalised polities. Two generalisations can be drawn. First, the larger the size of the country, the higher the level of decentralisation. As stressed by Hooghe, Marks and Schakel (2010: 63–64), 'regional authority increases in step with the logarithm of the population'. Second, the higher the level of cultural segmentation in a country, the higher the level of decentralisation. My data confirm these findings.[7]

How are these temporal and national variations reflected in the relation with vote nationalisation? The third hypothesis to be tested is the following:

> H3: As far as the decentralisation increases, vote nationalisation should decrease, and vice versa.

Table 5.1 reports the results of the Prais-Winsten regressions of standardised party system nationalisation score (sPSNS) on RAI[8] across the whole data set of 230 elections (Model 3) as well as the separate results in the two periods (Model 1 and 2). Moreover, as done in chapter 4, the regressions are rerun by excluding Belgium from the analysis. Furthermore, in Model 4, following the hypothesis raised by Morgenstern, Swindle and Castagnola (2009) and Lago (2011), we add the interaction between decentralisation and cultural segmentation, the expectation being that of a negative effect on vote nationalisation.

As shown in Model 3, regional authority is not a significant predictor of vote nationalisation in the whole set of elections. However, a noticeable improvement is reached in the separate regressions by period, where the *b* coefficients become significant and the overall fit of the models increases, as displayed by the comparison among the Wald Chi-Square statistics. Moreover, by excluding Belgium from the analysis, just as in the case of the class cleavage, the picture slightly changes: in the whole set of elections, regional

Table 5.1 Regressions of vote nationalisation on decentralisation

	Model 1	*Model 2*	*Model 3*	*Model 4*
Full data set	*1965–1990*	*1991–2015*	*All elections*	*All elections*
$RAI_{(t-1)}$	−0.002* (0.001)	−0.004** (0.001)	−0.001 (0.001)	−0.000 (0.001)
Cultural segmentation				−0.065** (0.021)
$RAI_{(t-1)}$*Cult. seg.				−0.001 (0.001)
Constant	0.842*** (0.016)	0.872*** (0.018)	0.832*** (0.016)	0.819*** (0.014)
Wald $\chi2$	4.28*	10.07***	1.90	29.74***
N elections	121	109	230	230
N countries	16	16	16	16
Belgium excluded				
$RAI_{(t-1)}$	−0.002* (0.001)	−0.002* (0.001)	−0.001* (0.001)	−0.000 (0.001)
Cultural segmentation				−0.051*** (0.014)
$RAI_{(t-1)}$*Cult. seg.				0.000 (0.001)
Constant	0.850*** (0.011)	0.868*** (0.014)	0.849*** (0.010)	0.828*** (0.011)
Wald $\chi2$	5.90*	6.28**	4.33*	26.82***
N elections	112	102	214	214
N countries	15	15	15	15

Note: Prais-Winsten AR1 regression. Panel-corrected standard errors in parentheses.

† $p < 0.1$; * $p < 0.05$; ** $p < 0.01$; *** $p < 0.001$.

authority becomes statistically significant at the 0.05 level when Belgian elections are not considered. The *b* coefficients are identical in both regressions of Model 3 (with and without Belgium), but the goodness-of-fit statistic reveals a better performance of the latter (the Wald Chi-Square raises from 1.90 to 4.33). Furthermore, the analyses in table 5.1 reveal that – unlike the trend shown by the class cleavage – the impact of decentralisation on vote nationalisation has increased over time: the strength and the statistical significance of the RAI coefficient are higher in Model 2 (1991–2015) compared with Model 1 (1965–1990).

To sum up, decentralisation seems to play a role in reducing vote nationalisation, but this role becomes not trivial only by splitting the sample into 'slides of synchronic comparisons through time' (Bartolini 1993: 159), or by excluding an outlier as Belgium. How can this evidence be explained? Obviously, it will be necessary to wait for the results of the multivariate analysis in order to assess more accurately the effect of the RAI on the sPSNS. Yet some preliminary insights can be drawn.

As regards the improvement in the models when Belgium is left out, something very similar has occurred in the case of class and cultural segmentation (*see* tables 4.2 and 4.3). As shown in the previous chapter, Belgium is an outlier as far as vote nationalisation is concerned. Moreover, for some predictors, Belgian elections are also observations with particular leverage. This was true for cultural segmentation (the country had the second-most culturally segmented polity after Spain), and it is true even now, given that Belgium is, on average, the second-most decentralised country after Germany (*see* the next section). Consequently, Belgian observations are highly influential on the overall results and a most confident estimation is achieved by leaving them out.

Turning to the temporal variability of the results, as shown in the next section, regional authority has risen over time in Western Europe. This may explain why the RAI is a stronger predictor of the sPSNS in the last period than in the pre-1990 period when countries were generally more centralised, and the cross-country variance in the predictor was also more limited. In this context, the non-significant effect of the RAI in the overall set of elections, apparently inconsistent with the significant coefficients of the two separate periods, may have a trend-related explanation: by pooling together all the elections, the positive trend over time of the RAI is at odds with that of the sPSNS which is overall steady over time (*see* figures 3.4 and 3.5). Indeed, by including time (operationalised as in previous chapters) as a control variable (results not shown), the RAI coefficient gets slightly stronger and significant at the 0.1 level, even if the Wald Chi-Square remains not significant.

Finally, Model 4 tests the effect of the interaction between regional authority and cultural segmentation. Though the overall fit of the model greatly

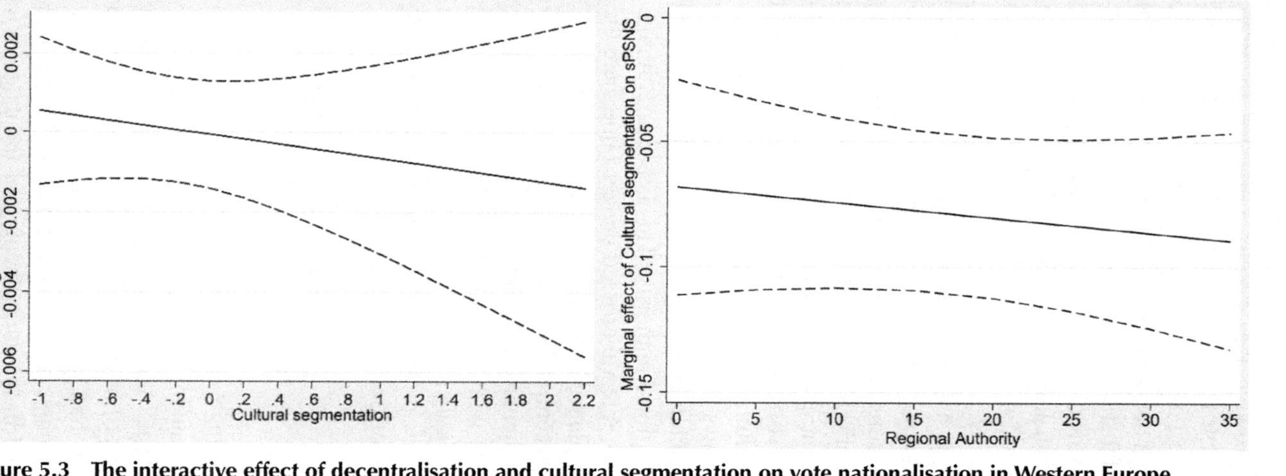

Figure 5.3 The interactive effect of decentralisation and cultural segmentation on vote nationalisation in Western Europe

increases, the effect of the interaction term is negative, as expected, but not significant. Yet, following the strategy suggested by Brambor, Clark and Golder (2006), I assess the statistical significance of the interaction by plotting the marginal effect of the variable of interest on vote nationalisation (with a confidence interval set at 0.05) at different levels of the intervening variable. Indeed, 'the statistical significance of the coefficient of a multiplicative interaction term is considered as neither necessary nor sufficient for determining whether X has an important or statistically distinguishable relationship with Y' (Maggini and Emanuele 2015: 124). Given that the existing literature simply argues that, by combining decentralisation and cultural cleavages, their impact on vote nationalisation 'should be magnified' (Morgenstern, Swindle and Castagnola 2009: 1329), without specifying which of the two variables should be considered the predictor and which the intervening variable, I test both situations in figure 5.3. An interesting finding emerges.

As displayed by the plot in the left part of figure 5.3, the negative marginal effect of the RAI on the sPSNS is not statistically significant across the observed range of cultural segmentation. On the contrary, the plot in the right part of figure 5.3 shows that the negative marginal effect of cultural segmentation on sPSNS – although the slope is rather flat – is significant across the observed range of regional authority. This is because, unlike in the left pane, where the confidence interval crossed the zero line, here the upper bound of the 95 per cent confidence interval is far from the zero line. This means that, while the effect of decentralisation on vote nationalisation is indifferent to the level of cultural segmentation, the effect of this latter on vote nationalisation is higher in contexts with higher decentralisation. In other words, cultural cleavages are more likely to affect vote nationalisation when the institutional setting of the country provides more power and autonomy to the regions where territorial minorities are located.

EU INTEGRATION

On the other side of the 'multi-level governance' (Hooghe and Marks 2001), the process of European integration could affect the levels of vote nationalisation in Western Europe. According to some scholars (Keating 1998; Bartolini 2005), the devolution of powers from nation-states to the supranational European institutions has had a direct impact on the structuring of the political space of the old nation-states. The creation and the consolidation of modern nation-states resulted in the strengthening of the external territorial borders of the state and in the consequent reduction of the exit options. Conversely, the process of European integration has weakened the external territorial boundaries of the nation-states, and, in turn, it has built new external boundaries and new internal functional areas, thus structuring a new European political space that has challenged national political structures. This process seems to foster the resurgence of territorial politics (Bartolini 2005: 251) as well as the strengthening of the historical centre-periphery cleavage that translates into the increasing remobilisation of local actors claiming for the redefinition of the relationship between the old national centres and the peripheries inside them (256–57). Therefore, European integration seems to have offered new opportunities for Western European substate areas and for the processes developed inside them, such as territorial differentiation, competition for the resources, and the reinforcement of local identities.[9]

An alternative argument is offered by Caramani (2015: 30), who – transposing the nationalisation theory to the process of European integration – argues that the structuring of a European political space causes the 'weakening of internal (territorial) boundaries' of the old nation-states and the consequent replacement of territorial cleavages by functional cleavages cutting across territory. Here Europeanisation means the creation of a new 'centre' at the European level, while the old nation-states become the new 'peripheries' that – just as in the nation-building process – try to resist the effort of centralisation and standardisation carried out by the European elite. Moreover, the European integration imposes a new functional and nonterritorial dimension of contestation, namely, the pro-/anti-European Union dimension, opposing mainstream national parties against new anti-establishment populist political forces (Kriesi et al. 2012), and shifts towards the European institutions the arena where the most important issues are dealt with. Therefore, these processes are likely to weaken the saliency of within-country territorial conflicts, since the nation-state as a whole is the new peripheral entity.[10] In other words, Europeanisation would be a homogenising factor of party support.

Given these contrasting assumptions, it is important to control for the process of European integration as a factor potentially affecting the level of vote nationalisation in Western Europe. This dimension has been overlooked so far by scholars dealing specifically with vote nationalisation. Yet, it is still unclear whether European integration can directly affect vote nationalisation (and in which direction) or whether its effect is indirect, mediated by the process of decentralisation. Indeed, following the above-mentioned literature, it seems plausible that the European integration affects vote nationalisation by providing new opportunities to European peripheries and their regional authorities to claim for more powers, competencies and resources. In other words, the European integration fosters the rise of regional authority which in turn affects vote nationalisation. In the absence of existing empirical evidence about the effect of European integration on vote nationalisation, I test both the direct and the indirect effects of this potential predictor on sPSNS, without assuming a specific expectation about this relation.

In order to measure the level of European integration, the index of *European institutional integration* (EURII) (Dorrucci et al. 2002; Mongelli, Dorrucci and Agur 2005) proves useful. It ranges from 0 to 100 according to 4 subsequent stages of integration, originally identified by Balassa (1961), each of which assigns 25 points to the index.[11] The first stage is Free Trade Area/ Custom Union (jointly considered): the *Free Trade Area* is achieved when internal tariffs and quotas among member countries are abolished, while the *Custom Union* is realised when common external tariffs and quotas are set up; the second step, *Common Market*, is achieved when restrictions on internal movements are abolished; the next stage is *Economic Union* that is realised when a significant degree of policy coordination and law harmonisation is achieved; finally, the last stage is *Total Economic Integration*, reached when economic policies are conducted at a supranational level.

The EURII was originally built to account for the six founding members of the Union (Dorrucci et al. 2002) and later supplemented to include scores for all countries acceding to the European Union (EU) in 1973–1995 (Mongelli, Dorrucci and Agur 2005). I use a slightly modified version of this index developed by Krieger-Boden and Soltwedel (2013), who integrate the original index by taking into account a collection of events that have caused acceleration or drawbacks in the process of European integration. Following this rationale, and consistent with the criteria developed by the authors, I also assign scores to Norway and Switzerland, which, despite not being members of the EU, share a certain degree of integration with the other EU members.[12]

As shown in table 5.2, which reports the results of the Prais-Winsten regression of sPSNS on the EURII,[13] the hypothesis of a direct impact of European integration on vote nationalisation has to be rejected: the coefficient of the EURII is never significant at the 0.05 level, regardless of the set of elections taken into consideration (full data set, the separate models for each period, the model excluding Belgium). This means that neither of the two hypotheses advanced by scholars so far seems to take place: European integration is not a factor favouring the resurgence of territorial politics (Bartolini 2005) and not even a homogenising factor of party support, as argued by Caramani (2015). The only barely significant associations emerging from Models 1 to 3 in table 5.2 are those concerning the separate regressions by period with the exclusion of Belgium: in those cases, the EURII is positive and significant even if only at the 0.1 level. This result is not surprising, given that Belgium is one of the founding members of the EU and holds the highest levels of the EURII throughout the period: as we know, this high level of European integration is accompanied by the lowest level of vote nationalisation in Western Europe. Then, by excluding Belgium and its strongly negative association between EURII and sPSNS, the coefficient improves its positive relation.

Table 5.2 Regressions of vote nationalisation on European integration

	Model 1	*Model 2*	*Model 3*	*Model 4*
Full data set	*1965–1990*	*1991–2015*	*All elections*	*All elections*
$EURII_{(t-1)}$	0.000 (0.000)	0.000 (0.000)	0.000 (0.000)	0.000 (0.000)
$RAI_{(t-1)}$				−0.001 (0.001)
$RAI_{(t-1)}$*$EURII_{(t-1)}$				−0.000 (0.000)
Constant	0.808*** (0.017)	0.800*** (0.021)	0.808*** (0.015)	0.815*** (0.018)
Wald $\chi 2$	0.20	0.44	0.40	3.09
N elections	121	109	230	230
N countries	16	16	16	16
Belgium excluded				
$EURII_{(t-1)}$	$0.000^{\dagger}$ (0.000)	$0.000^{\dagger}$ (0.000)	0.000 (0.000)	0.000* (0.000)
$RAI_{(t-1)}$				−0.001 (0.001)
$RAI_{(t-1)}$*$EURII_{(t-1)}$				−0.000 (0.000)
Constant	0.817*** (0.011)	0.804*** (0.020)	0.820*** (0.011)	0.834*** (0.013)
Wald $\chi 2$	$3.18^{\dagger}$	$3.30^{\dagger}$	2.62	11.28*
N elections	112	102	214	214
N countries	15	15	15	15

Note: Prais-Winsten AR1 regression. Panel-corrected standard errors in parentheses.

† $p < 0.1$; * $p < 0.05$; ** $p < 0.01$; *** $p < 0.001$.

In Model 4, I have tested the alternative hypothesis of an indirect effect of the EURII as a contextual effect moderating the impact of regional authority on sPSNS. As shown in table 5.2, there is no empirical evidence of such an effect in the full data set, while in the regression excluding Belgium, a significant effect can be detected, although the coefficient of the interaction is not statistically significant. Indeed, the plot of the marginal effect of the RAI on the sPSNS at different values of the EURII reported in figure 5.4 shows that, as European integration increases, the negative effect of the RAI on the sPSNS increases as well, and this relation becomes significant at the 0.05 level for values of the EURII higher than 15 (i.e., a very low level, given that the average EURII in Western Europe is 49.2). In other words, when the distorting effect of Belgian elections is omitted, European integration plays a (little) role in enhancing the effect of regional authority on vote nationalisation.

The lack of a direct effect of the EURII on the sPSNS can also be explained by looking at the evolution of the EURII over time. The values of the index reflect the incremental nature of the process of European integration. According to the scores assigned by Krieger-Boden and Soltwedel (2013), the countries that are members of the EU have reached, during the past fifty years, three out of four stages identified by Balassa (1961) and, after the achievement of the Monetary Union (1999), are today placed in an intermediate position between the Economic Union and the last possible stage of

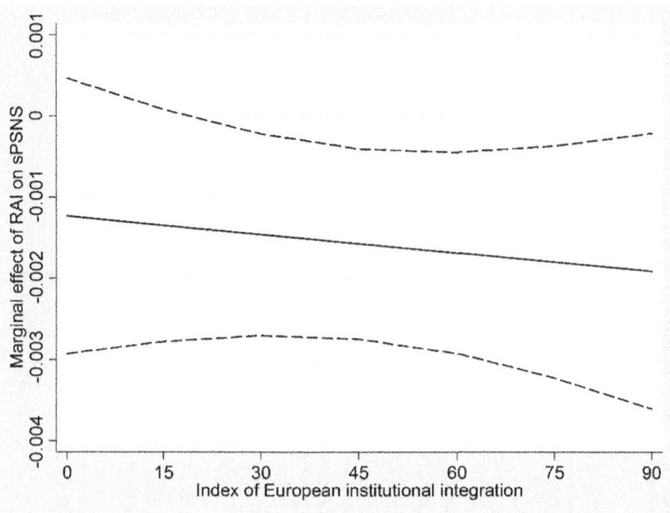

Figure 5.4 The interactive effect of decentralisation and European integration on vote nationalisation in Western Europe (Belgium excluded)

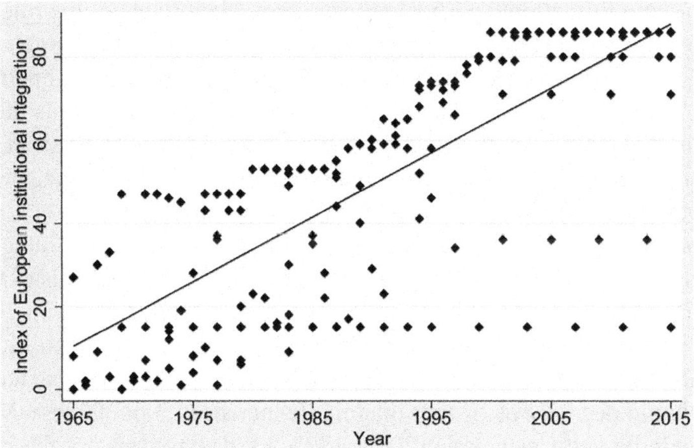

Figure 5.5 Trend of EURII over time, 1965–2015

Total Economic Integration. As stated by Dorrucci et al. (2002: 9–10), it is possible to distinguish three subperiods in the process of European integration. The first period, characterised by a fast integration, proceeds from the sign of the Treaty of Rome (1957) to the completion of the Customs Union (1968). The second period can be identified between the start of the 1970s and the mid-1980s and is characterised by sluggish integration, with the noteworthy exception of the European Monetary System (EMS) which started in March 1979. Finally, in the third, most recent period, a new, considerable acceleration in regional integration can be observed towards the achievement of the Monetary Union. Taking the whole period into consideration, the correlation between EURII and time (*see* figure 5.5) is of course positive and very strong ($r = 0.769$, $p < 0.001$), and this may explain why the EURII seems uncorrelated to sPSNS: while the first indicator outlines an almost linear growth path, the latter shows an enduring stability through time (*see* figure 3.4).

ELECTORAL SYSTEMS AND VOTE NATIONALISATION: AN UNSOLVED PUZZLE

Among the institutional determinants, another key factor to be considered is the 'electoral system', a synthetic wording defining a set of institutional rules providing constraints and opportunities to both parties and voters. These constraints and opportunities can potentially influence the level of nationalisation of a given party system since certain features of the electoral systems are expected to produce incentives both for parties to compete nationally and for voters to vote for national parties, or vice versa. Nevertheless, the role played by the electoral systems as predictors of the territorial structuring of party support has not been fully disentangled yet, thus remaining an open puzzle so far. Among the three fundamental features of electoral systems identified by Lijphart (1999), namely, the formula, the threshold and the district magnitude, the literature has mainly focused on the role of the latter one, even if its effect on vote nationalisation is, still today, not entirely clear.

According to Cox and Knoll (2003: 6), 'the larger the district magnitudes in the system, the fewer wasted votes there will be in each district'. This means that in single-member plurality systems (SMD), there will be more wasted votes and, consequently, a much greater incentive for politicians to link with others and combine votes across districts. Therefore, vote nationalisation should decrease as district magnitude increases. Nonetheless, Morgenstern, Swindle and Castagnola (2009: 1327–1328) have exactly the opposite expectation: SMD systems should decrease nationalisation relative to proportional systems (PR). According to the authors, 'since a plurality is required to win the seat in SMD systems, parties may avoid spending the resources to compete where they have little chance of winning. In PR system, by contrast, wasted votes winning opportunities are costly, because it takes far fewer votes to win a legislative seat'.[14] These contrasting opinions lead Lago (2011) to hypothesise that district magnitude is not related to nationalisation.[15]

However, it can be argued that other aspects of the electoral system matter. First, the presence of a considerable portion of seats allocated at the national level fosters the formation of a nationalised party system, since it provides an obvious incentive to parties to ally across districts and to compete nationally (Cox and Knoll 2003; Simón and Gunjoan 2017); moreover, such framework gives more potential vote surplus to those parties which compete in several districts (Cox 1999: 157). This argument has usually been proposed to account for upper-tier seats, namely, secondary electoral levels where 'unused votes from the primary electoral districts are aggregated and distributed' (Simón 2013: 32). However, from a more general viewpoint, the presence of a national electoral tier may provide incentives for party linkage, regardless of the fact that a given electoral system is single-tier or multi-tier. Therefore, the expectation is that the higher the number of seats allocated at the national level, the higher the level of vote nationalisation.

Second, the degree to which an electoral system provides incentives for cultivating personal vote (Carey and Shugart 1995) can be negatively related with vote nationalisation. The rationale is straightforward: the more personalised the electoral competition, the higher the role played by local factors – such as local candidates' personality traits, support for individual candidates or patronage – on the variability of party support across districts. Some authors have raised this expectation (Lago 2011; Simón 2013; Golosov

2016b), even if the empirical evidence is mixed. Specifically, Golosov (2016b) finds a negative effect of personal vote's incentives. Nonetheless, this latter is not tested as an independent variable but only in combination with district magnitude. Lago (2011) finds no significant effects, and Simón (2013), as previously mentioned, shows that personal vote's incentives moderate the effect of decentralisation on vote nationalisation, but their direct effect is never significant.

Following the above-mentioned literature, three aspects of the electoral system as a potential determinant of vote nationalisation have to be tested: the average district magnitude, the percentage of seats allocated at the national level and the incentives for cultivating personal vote. I do not have a particular expectation about the impact of district magnitude, since there are two opposing schools of thought on the topic and empirically verifying which one of the two is right can be a fruitful exercise to perform. Conversely, regarding the other two aspects, I raise the following hypotheses:

> H4: As far as the percentage of seats allocated at the national level increases, vote nationalisation should increase, and vice versa.
> H5: As far as the incentives for cultivating personal vote increase, vote nationalisation should decrease, and vice versa.

In order to operationalise district magnitude and the percentage of seats allocated at the national level, data have been taken from Bormann and Golder's Democratic Electoral System data set (Bormann and Golder 2013). Average district magnitude (ADM) is calculated by dividing the total number of seats to be allocated by the total number of districts.[16] Following previous empirical research (Taagepera and Shugart 1989; Lago 2011; Simón 2013), I expect a nonlinear effect of the variable, since 'the impact of any marginal seat in the proportionality of the electoral system will tend to be lower than the previous one' (Simón 2013: 42). Given this underlining assumption, I have transformed the variable into its natural logarithm. Moreover, the *percentage of seats at the national level* is measured as the percentage of all legislative seats allocated at the national level.[17]

The measurement of the degree to which a given electoral system incentivises personal vote is less straightforward and more arbitrary. Departing from the original classification provided by Carey and Shugart, Johnson and Wallack (2012) develop an ordinal measure of personal vote, ranging from 1 (lowest incentives possible for personal vote) to 13 (highest incentives possible for personal vote). The index is based on three elements of the electoral law: the level of candidate control over access to and rank on ballots ('Ballot'); the degree to which votes are shared among candidates from a particular party ('Pool'); and finally 'Vote', which focuses on the distinction between casting votes for either parties or individual candidates. I integrate Johnson and Wallack's (2012) index with some specifications provided by Floridia (2008) and Renwick and Pilet (2016).[18] As a result, the index scores its minimum (1) for a PR with closed lists (e.g., Portugal); 2 for a PR with flexible lists (e.g., the Netherlands); 3 for a PR with open lists (e.g., Italy before 1993); 4 for single transferable vote (e.g., Ireland); 7 for a PR with open lists and panachage (e.g., Switzerland); 9, as in Finland, for a PR with open lists and open endorsement, where voters vote only for candidates and 'parties do not have any formal role in nominations' (Carey and Shugart 1995: 428); and eventually 10 for single-member districts (e.g., France and the United Kingdom). Mixed systems' scores (e.g., Germany and Italy between 1994 and 2001) are the result of an average between majoritarian and proportional components, weighted by the respective number of seats allocated to each component.

Table 5.3 presents the results of the regression of sPSNS on the three aspects of electoral systems introduced before. The three predictors are first tested separately (Models 1–3) and then, in Model 4, included together in the same regression. As done for the other potential explanatory factors so far, separate regressions excluding Belgium have been run.

All the regression models consistently show the irrelevance of ADM and the percentage of seats allocated at the national level in the explanation of vote nationalisation, regardless of the presence or the absence of Belgium in the sample. Therefore, data seem to reject both the perspective of a positive effect of district magnitude (emphasised by several authors among which Morgenstern, Swindle and Castagnola (2009)) and that of a negative effect, as stressed by Cox and Knoll (2003). As regards the percentage of seats allocated at the national level, my literature-driven hypothesis (H4) seems to be discarded as well. Here, the substantial presence of observations with a value of 0 (138 out of 230, the 60 per cent of the overall sample) and the very limited variability of the measure over time may have contributed to weaken this relation and make the model completely insignificant (as testified by the quasi-zero value of the Wald Chi-Square). Yet, the third aspect of the electoral system that has been taken into account, namely, the incentive for cultivating personal vote, does appear to play a role. In the full data set, the coefficient of personal vote is negative, as expected, and significant at the 0.05 level. By disentangling the model over time, data show that the impact of such factor has increased in the past decades: during the period 1965–1990, personal vote does not play any role, while afterwards the coefficient appears significant at the 0.05 level.[19] The exclusion of Belgium – where the denationalisation process occurs between the 1960s and the 1970s during which the electoral system remains an unchanged poorly personalised PR with flexible list – improves, as easily imaginable, the strength of the coefficient and its

Table 5.3 Regressions of vote nationalisation on different aspects of electoral systems

Full data set	*Model 1*	*Model 2*	*Model 3*	*Model 4*
ADM (ln)	0.005 (0.004)			−0.001 (0.007)
Perc. of seats at nat. level		0.000 (0.000)		0.000 (0.000)
Personal vote			−0.003* (0.002)	−0.003 (0.002)
Constant	0.802*** (0.015)	0.811*** (0.013)	0.826*** (0.015)	0.829*** (0.023)
Wald $\chi 2$	1.78	0.23	4.22*	4.61
N elections	230	230	230	230
N countries	16	16	16	16
Belgium excluded				
ADM (ln)	0.006 (0.004)			−0.002 (0.006)
Perc. of seats at nat. level		0.000 (0.000)		−0.000 (0.000)
Personal vote			−0.004** (0.001)	−0.005** (0.002)
Constant	0.819*** (0.012)	0.829*** (0.010)	0.851*** (0.009)	0.861*** (0.017)
Wald $\chi 2$	2.20	0.02	9.66**	12.07*
N elections	214	214	214	214
N countries	15	15	15	15

Note: Prais-Winsten AR1 regression. Panel-corrected standard errors in parentheses.

† $p < 0.1$; * $p < 0.05$; ** $p < 0.01$; *** $p < 0.001$.

statistical significance ($p < 0.01$). This effect also persists in Model 4, when all the three aspects are included in the same regression: the exclusion of Belgium is decisive here since in the full data set even personal vote appears irrelevant for vote nationalisation.

Notwithstanding the intriguing effect of personal vote's incentives that need to be put under further scrutiny, these results are rather disappointing. Indeed, both ADM and the percentage of seats allocated at the national level have shown to be unrelated to the territorial configuration of party support in Western Europe, thus disproving the existing literature on the topic.

THE INSTITUTIONAL MODEL

After having shown the relation between each selected institutional constraint and vote nationalisation, this last section aims at achieving a broader overview of the role played by such factors. As a result, by pooling together the index of regional authority, that of European integration and the three measures related to the electoral systems, it is possible to unfold any spurious effect and understand which factors really matter once all the others are taken under control. Furthermore, by putting together RAI and personal vote's incentives in a single regression model, I am able to verify Simón's (2013) finding about the moderating effect played by personal vote in the relation between decentralisation and vote nationalisation. Finally, by comparing the Wald Chi-Square of the institutional model with that of the macro-sociological model reported in table 4.4, I will assess which constellation of factors plays the largest role in the story.

Table 5.4 reports the results of the pooled regression with all the institutional constraints.[20] Model 1 tests the plain institutional model, while Model 2 introduces the interaction between RAI and personal vote. Not surprisingly, and consistent with what found in the separate regressions presented throughout the chapter, in the plain model with the whole set of elections, the two most important institutional determinants of vote nationalisation are the level of decentralisation and the incentives for cultivating personal vote. Both are negatively related with sPSNS, as expected. This means that vote nationalisation is lower in decentralised contexts and in systems with higher incentives to cultivate personal vote. These effects are confirmed also when Belgium is left out from the analysis, and this evidence represents a robust confirmation of such findings. Moreover, when Belgium is omitted, the EURII turns out to be significant, with a positive relationship with sPSNS. This kind of effect has been already noted in table 5.2 and is consistent with Caramani's (2015) hypothesis of European integration as a homogenising factor in the within-country territorial distribution of party support. Yet, here its impact is larger than in the simple bivariate model,

Table 5.4 Regressions of vote nationalisation on the institutional variables

Full data set	*Model 1*	*Model 2*
RAI	−0.004*** (0.001)	−0.004* (0.001)
EURII	0.000† (0.000)	0.000† (0.000)
ADM (ln)	−0.009 (0.007)	−0.008 (0.008)
Perc. of seats at nat. level	0.001† (0.000)	0.001† (0.000)
Personal vote	−0.006** (0.002)	−0.006† (0.003)
RAI*Personal vote		−0.000 (0.000)
Constant	0.894*** (0.027)	0.886*** (0.027)
Wald χ2	34.65***	29.77***
N elections	230	230
N countries	16	16
Belgium excluded		
RAI	−0.002*** (0.001)	−0.001 (0.001)
EURII	0.000** (0.000)	0.000** (0.000)
ADM (ln)	−0.003 (0.006)	−0.005 (0.006)
Perc. of seats at nat. level	0.000 (0.000)	0.000 (0.000)
Personal vote	−0.006** (0.002)	−0.004 (0.003)
RAI*Personal vote		−0.000 (0.000)
Constant	0.875*** (0.020)	0.871*** (0.021)
Wald χ2	29.74***	28.86***
N elections	214	214
N countries	15	15

Note: Prais-Winsten AR1 regression. Panel-corrected standard errors in parentheses.

† $p < 0.1$; * $p < 0.05$; ** $p < 0.01$; *** $p < 0.001$.

and it follows that, all else being equal, the process of European integration triggers vote nationalisation once decentralisation and the features of the electoral system are controlled for.

Model 2 adds to the institutional model the interaction between RAI and personal vote's incentives. Adding the interaction term decreases the main effect of both variables, both in the full model and in that without Belgium, where the coefficients of the RAI and personal vote become insignificant. Yet, a graphical representation of the interaction models clarifies that in the model including all the elections, the effect of decentralisation on the sPSNS is completely indifferent to the level of personal vote provided by the electoral system (and, vice versa, the effect of personal vote's incentives on the sPSNS is independent of the level of decentralisation of the polity), while the interaction in the model excluding Belgium is clearly significant. As figure 5.6 shows,[21] with the confidence interval set at 95 per cent, the negative effect of the RAI on the sPSNS increases as the incentives for cultivating personal vote grow, and this is a confirmation of Simón's (2013) findings.

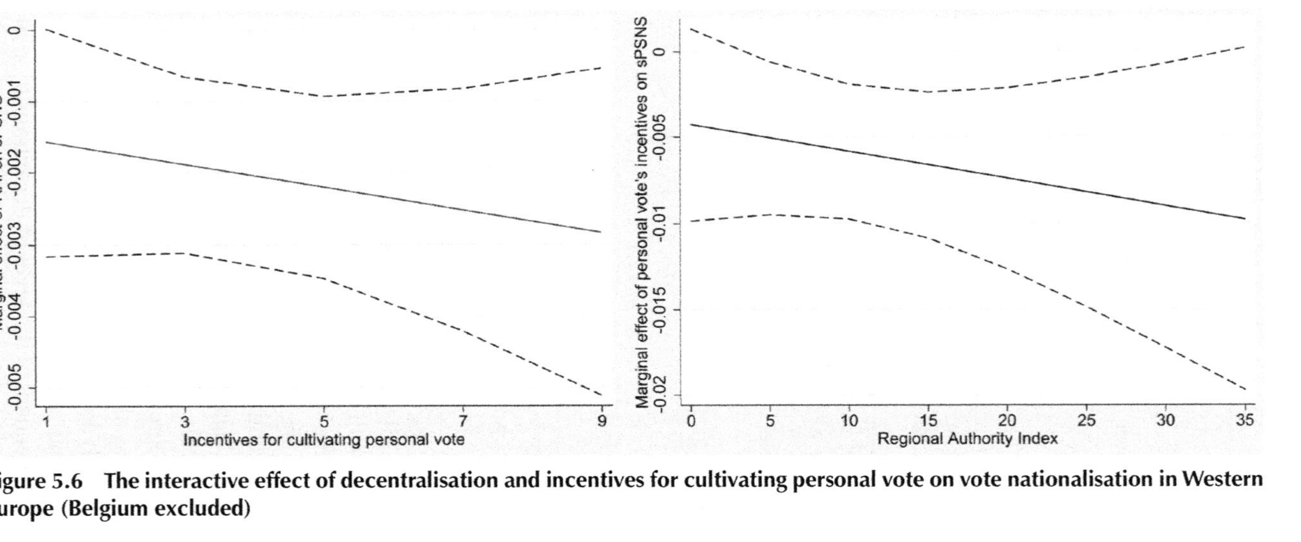

Figure 5.6 The interactive effect of decentralisation and incentives for cultivating personal vote on vote nationalisation in Western Europe (Belgium excluded)

Furthermore, by inverting the direction of the interaction, the relation is significant too, since the marginal effect of personal vote's incentives on sPSNS is stronger in decentralised contexts. Germany and Switzerland are the two most prominent examples of countries where the institutional setting provides incentives to vote denationalisation. Both countries are federal polities with an electoral system offering high incentives for cultivating personal vote: in Germany the majoritarian quota provides a personalisation of the competition (50 per cent of the seats in the Bundestag are allocated in single-member districts); in Switzerland the competition in each canton is instead based on the preferential vote with open lists and panachage allowed to voters. Given these institutional incentives, it is not surprising that these two countries display the most territorially heterogeneous party support in Western Europe after Belgium.

Finally, by comparing the goodness-of-fit of the plain institutional model (Model 1 of table 5.4) with that of the macro-sociological model (Model 3 of table 4.4), the result is extremely similar: the Wald Chi-Square of the institutional model is slightly larger than that of the macro-sociological model (34.65 against 29.65) if the whole set of elections is considered, while the situation is reversed if Belgium is excluded (29.74 against 31.15).

From this evidence, two conclusions can be drawn. First, the deviating effect of Belgium is more remarkable as far as cleavage structures are concerned: the leverage of this country makes the estimation of the macro-sociological model less robust when it is included in the analysis; conversely, as regards the institutional setting, the bias induced by Belgium is less prominent and – also given the higher number of observations and, consequently, the higher number of degrees of freedom – the goodness-of-fit is higher when Belgium is part of the estimation.

Second, contrary to what is claimed by the existing literature, which usually emphasises the role played by the institutional factors in the explanation of vote nationalisation, the overall strength of the institutional model is essentially the same of the macro-sociological model, whose limited explanatory capacity has been already discussed at the end of chapter 4.

Chapter 6

The competition factors

This chapter introduces the last set of potential explanatory factors, those related to the political context. In the previous two chapters, I have tested the impact of two sets of determinants which can be considered external – even if closely related – to the political and, in particular, to the electoral arena. Specifically, the macro-sociological factors derive from the society and refer to the structure of cleavages; the institutional determinants are linked to the external framework of the state (the set of rules, procedures and structures). It is now time to focus on the internal structure of the political setting.

Curiously, the main literature that has dealt with vote nationalisation in Europe has emphasised the role of social cleavages or the impact of some institutional constraints, but the effects of political factors and the structure of the competition have been widely neglected.[1] Yet, it is easy to imagine that those factors closer to the act of voting, or stemming from electoral results, may affect the level of vote nationalisation in a country, given that this latter is, of course, a product of the same electoral arena. Therefore, it is worthwhile to fill this gap.

The structure of the chapter is as follows: the first section, 'Party system fragmentation', introduces the first potential explanatory factor, party system fragmentation, while the second section, 'The mediated effect of electoral volatility on vote nationalisation', tries to disentangle the puzzle about the impact of electoral volatility on vote nationalisation; the third and the fourth sections, 'The "decisiveness" of elections' and 'The territorial concentration of turnout', respectively, deal with other two potentially relevant factors (the decisiveness of elections for the future government formation and the territorial homogeneity of turnout); finally, the last section, 'The "competition" model', pools together these variables and shows the results of the 'political' model, comparing it with the macro-sociological and institutional models presented, respectively, in chapters 4 and 5.

PARTY SYSTEM FRAGMENTATION

As far as the factors linked to the structure of the competition are concerned, the bulk of literature on Western European party systems has often emphasised that the main changes since the 1970s have been the increase in the levels of electoral volatility (Drummond 2006; Chiaramonte and Emanuele 2015; Dassonneville and Hooghe 2015) and the emergence of new parties with the subsequent growth of party system fragmentation (Dalton, Flanagan and Beck 1984; Emanuele and Chiaramonte 2016). The demise of mass parties as agencies of mobilisation, the decomposition of electoral alignments and the decline of party identification have weakened the relationship between parties and voters which is now less stable and predictable and also less anchored to long-term social factors. Parties have become increasingly exposed to the risks of the electoral market, which in turn has become more competitive due to the entrance of new political forces. In this context of growing uncertainty,[2] it is likely that more and more parties develop strategies of territorial concentration of their electoral support.

To fully understand this point, a purely systemic perspective is not sufficient, and one needs to resort to parties' competitive strategies and specifically to focus on how parties adapt and react to the changing political context around them. As acknowledged by Caramani (1994: 278–79; 2004: 231), a parallelism with the Downsian spatial model (1957) proves suitable. According to Downs, in a two-party system, the two parties tend to converge towards the centre of the ideological space to achieve the support of the median voter. An increase in the number of parties and the transition to a multiparty system cause a reduction of the political space available for each party so that they lose the incentive to move towards the centre. If, for instance, a centre-left party moves towards the centre to gain moderate voters, it immediately loses a portion of its leftist voters that moves towards the extreme-left party. In multiparty systems, therefore, no party has a huge incentive to enlarge its ideological space; rather, each party will be more likely to be anchored to a specific ideological position.

Turning this logic from the ideological to the territorial side, it could be hypothesised that, as the number of parties increases and the political space for each party diminishes, the established parties, threatened by the new challengers, are encouraged to develop strategies of territorial concentration of their support, aiming at reinforcing their electoral strongholds, instead of spreading across the country with the risk of losing votes in their historic bastions. At the same time, new parties – especially the small sized ones – could have a great incentive to pursue a territorial focus, in order to build their own electoral strongholds. This strategy can prove very convenient at least in a first phase when the new parties aim at overcoming the threshold of representation and need to find districts ensuring them some safe seats.

Based on the above considerations, I expect that party system fragmentation would affect vote nationalisation as follows:

> H6: The higher the number of parties, the lower the level of vote nationalisation, and vice versa.

The number of parties and the consequent level of party system fragmentation are calculated through the well-known measure developed by Laakso and Taagepera (1979), the effective number of electoral parties[3] (ENEP). The index counts the parties by weighting them for their relative electoral strength so that larger parties count more than smaller ones in the computation of party system fragmentation.[4] In the theoretical case of a system made up of two parties with 50 per cent of the vote each, the score of the index is 2.[5] Despite some critiques,[6] the ENEP is today widely used in most of the articles and books concerning the study of party systems, elections and voting behaviour.

As mentioned earlier, a great bulk of scholars has underlined that, during the past decades, party systems in Western Europe have become more fragmented than in the past: data clearly confirm this widely accepted statement. The positive slope of the regression line in figure 6.1 points out that the effective number of parties has grown over time. The correlation between the standardised party system nationalisation score (sPSNS) and time is positive

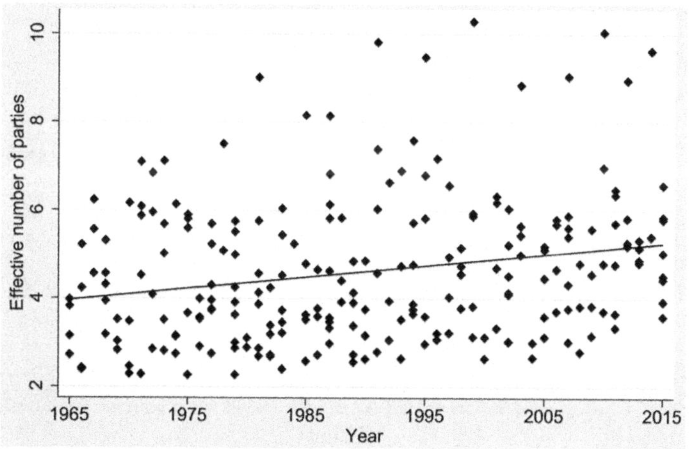

Figure 6.1 Trend of ENEP over time, 1965–2015

and significant at the 0.001 level. The overall average number of parties in Western Europe is 4.61, with an increase from the first (4.22) to the second period (5.04).

Nevertheless, the strength of the correlation coefficient (r = 0.230) is weaker than expected based on the emphasis given by the literature. This suggests that some countries do not respect the hypothesised pattern, thus showing a steady trend through time or even a decrease in the number of parties.

Figure 6.2 plots the national variations of the ENEP over time. Some countries show a fairly constant increase of party system fragmentation since 1965 (Austria, Belgium, Germany, Ireland, Sweden and the United Kingdom). In Greece and Italy, the growth in the number of parties has occurred abruptly on the occasion of critical elections (respectively, in the elections of May 2012 and 1994), following long periods of stability.

Moreover, in Greece, Spain and Portugal – the three countries which experienced the so-called third wave of democratisation (Huntington 1991) – the number of parties has decreased just after the first democratic elections: this trend is typical of young democracies where, in the first elections after the end of the authoritarian regime, there is a flourishing of small parties and a subsequent fragmented system. Then, after some years, the party system consolidates, many small parties disappear and the structure of the competition stabilises around a less fragmented party system. This kind of trend has

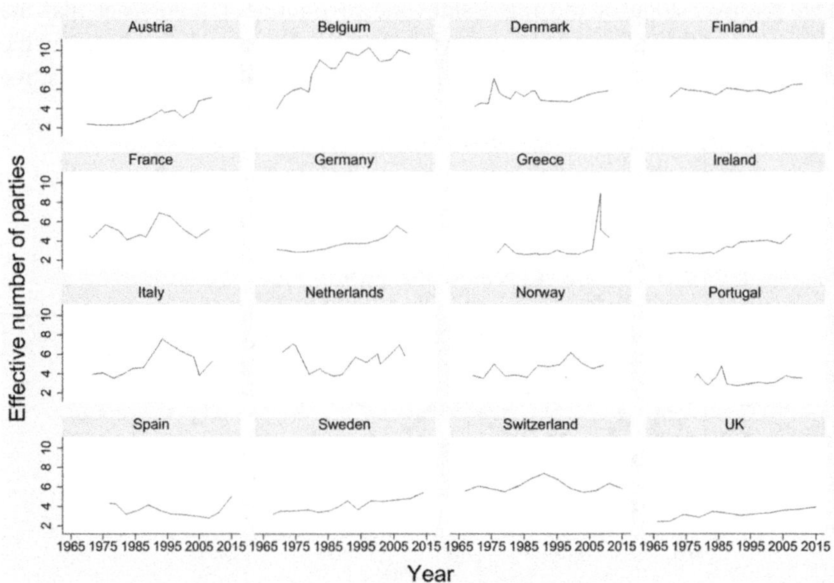

Figure 6.2 National variations of the ENEP over time, 1965–2015

continued to take place in Portugal until now, while in Greece and Spain, it has been interrupted by the dramatic changes occurred during the past few years (the collapse of the PASOK and the rise of Syriza and Golden Dawn in Greece; the emergence of new challengers such as *Podemos* and *Ciudadanos* in Spain). The remaining countries do not exhibit clear trends over time (Denmark, Finland, France, the Netherlands, Norway and Switzerland). Overall, only two countries show a more limited party system format today compared to the beginning of the period under analysis: the Netherlands and Portugal, where, not by chance, the most prominent process of vote nationalisation has occurred (*see* figure 3.8), thus reinforcing the idea that the ENEP gives account of the within country temporal variation of sPSNS.

Beyond the temporal variations experienced by each party system, the country-by-country comparison reveals interesting findings. First of all, by taking into account the whole universe of 230 elections, the effective number of parties ranges from a minimum level of 2.26 (Austria 1975) to a maximum level of 10.28 (Belgium 1999). Rather surprisingly, the more limited party system format is not the British one, for a long time considered the homeland of the two-party format, but instead the Austrian one (3.18).

Second, as mentioned before, the highest fragmentation is detectable in Belgium (7.93), which appears more and more as a really exceptional system in the Western European context, being characterised at the same time by the highest level of cultural diversity, regional authority, European integration, party system fragmentation and by the lowest levels of vote nationalisation.

Third, the other two countries with the most pronounced party system fragmentation are two polities showing a heterogeneous configuration of party support, namely, Switzerland (6.08) and Finland (5.92), while the more limited party system format after Austria and the United Kingdom can be found in Ireland, Germany and in the three Southern European democracies of the third wave (Spain, Portugal and Greece). The Scandinavian countries, France and Italy retain an intermediate position, falling around the general mean of 4.61.

In order to test H6, table 6.1 reports the results obtained by regressing the sPSNS on the ENEP. As usual, besides the full model, the table also reports the separate regressions by period and those excluding Belgium from the analysis.

The results are remarkable. As expected, the effective number of parties is negatively associated with vote nationalisation. This relation is statistically significant at the highest level of confidence ($p < 0.001$) in all the models.[7] By comparing the models, it is possible to note a decrease in the coefficients of the ENEP when Belgium is omitted. This is because, as will be shown in the next section, the leverage of Belgium is notable even as concerns this factor: the country is the most fragmented one in Western Europe, and this

Table 6.1 Regressions of vote nationalisation on the effective number of parties

	Model 1	*Model 2*	*Model 3*
Full data set	*1965–1990*	*1991–2015*	*All elections*
ENEP	−0.026*** (0.005)	−0.021*** (0.005)	−0.016*** (0.003)
Constant	0.921*** (0.020)	0.920*** (0.021)	0.888*** (0.013)
Wald χ2	28.61***	20.22***	40.89***
N elections	121	109	230
N countries	16	16	16
Belgium excluded			
ENEP	−0.019*** (0.003)	−0.009*** (0.002)	−0.011*** (0.002)
Constant	0.905*** (0.014)	0.881*** (0.014)	0.880*** (0.011)
Wald χ2	31.39***	14.39***	50.09***
N elections	112	102	214
N countries	15	15	15

Note: Prais-Winsten AR1 regression. Panel-corrected standard errors in parentheses.

† $p < 0.1$; * $p < 0.05$; ** $p < 0.01$; *** $p < 0.001$.

explains why its exclusion induces a reduction in the strength of the coefficients. Conversely, the Wald Chi-Square increases (an evidence of a higher accuracy in the estimation without Belgium).

Generally speaking, an increase in the number of parties fosters vote denationalisation or, in other words, as the party system gets more fragmented, the territoriality of party support increases. This evidence provides a strong confirmation of H6. The effect of the ENEP is – together with that of cultural segmentation – the most powerful obtained so far among the various possible determinants of vote nationalisation assessed in this study. Moreover, by comparing the regression models concerning cultural segmentation (*see* table 4.3) with those about the ENEP, the latter ones show a better goodness-of-fit,[8] probably because the number of parties accounts not only for cross-country variation (as in the case of cultural segmentation) but also for temporal variation.

Note that from a purely theoretical point of view, the number of parties could be completely independent of the level of homogeneity of party support: a party system could be very fragmented but composed of highly nationalised parties or, conversely, it could be made up of only two parties showing a marked territorial configuration of their support, each of the two parties representing the territorial claims of one part of the country. On this point, Jones and Mainwaring (2003), who note a negative correlation between vote nationalisation and the number of parties in Latin American countries, argue that 'the two issues are obviously conceptually and operationally discrete' (159).[9] The result in table 6.1 is a fascinating and innovative empirical finding since the literature has so far primarily focused on societal and institutional factors, with the only exceptions of the very quick hint suggested by Jones and Mainwaring (2003) and the recent study by Golosov (2016b). Nevertheless, the results of these previous studies can hardly be compared with the present ones: Jones and Mainwaring focus on Latin America and do not expect such a large impact of the number of parties in Western Europe: in their own words, 'this correlation would most likely be lower in Western Europe, where despite considerable variance in the effective number of parties variance in nationalization is lower than in the Americas' (2003: 164). On the other hand, Golosov's (2016b) study is a worldwide cross-section analysis, since it covers eighty countries without accounting for temporal variation within countries, and, furthermore, it operationalises in a slightly different way both vote nationalisation and the number of parties.

Finally, it is useful to understand how the overall negative association between the ENEP and the sPSNS is reflected as far as national variations are concerned. The chart presented in figure 6.3 shows which countries follow the detected pattern and which others deviate from it. The figure is built by plotting the countries' averages on the ENEP and the sPSNS and then by dividing the chart into four quadrants according to the respective overall mean values of the two indices (4.61 for the ENEP and 0.816 for the sPSNS). Given the negative association between the two variables, the average scores of the countries are expected to fall especially in the upper-left and the lower-right quadrants. This is the case for ten countries, while six others fall in the two deviant quadrants. On one side, four countries fall in the upper-right quadrant, thus showing a higher level of vote nationalisation than what expected by their mean level of party system fragmentation. In these countries (Denmark,

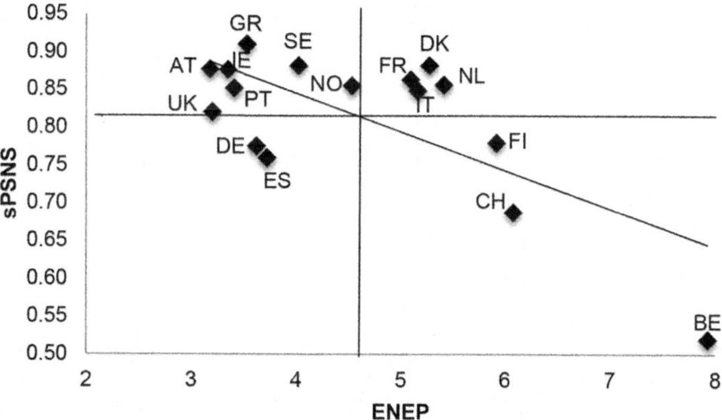

Figure 6.3 Party system fragmentation and vote nationalisation in Western Europe, mean values by country

France, Italy and the Netherlands), territorial homogeneity occurs in spite of the high number of parties running for the elections.

On the other side, in the lower-left quadrant, Germany and Spain show a limited party system format together with a regionalised configuration of party support. In these national contexts, the low level of vote nationalisation has to be explained by looking elsewhere. In sum, there should be some other factors explaining why a nationalised outcome is produced in countries with a highly fragmented party system and, conversely, why a denationalised outcome occurs despite the presence of a limited party system format. This evidence strengthens the idea that vote nationalisation is an outcome whose explanation involves a constellation of factors and that looking only at the impact of individual determinants proves inadequate for reaching a comprehensive explanation.

THE MEDIATED EFFECT OF ELECTORAL VOLATILITY ON VOTE NATIONALISATION

In the previous section, the increase in the levels of electoral instability has been mentioned as one of the most relevant changes occurred in Western European democracies during the past decades. As widely emphasised (Dalton, Flanagan and Beck 1984; Franklin, Mackie and Valen 1992), since the 1970s there has been a remarkable decline in the tie between social divisions and individual voting choice, with the former ones that were no longer able to structure the vote choice as they did in the past. It follows that Western European voters have shown a growing and unexpected unpredictability of their voting decisions[10] that have translated into higher rates of interelectoral change (*see* chapter 2 on this point). This growing 'availability', namely, the propensity of voters to change voting choice between two subsequent elections, is considered by Bartolini (1999) as one of the four fundamental dimensions of party competition.[11]

The most appropriate indicator to measure this concept is certainly that of electoral volatility,[12] that is, the net aggregate change between two subsequent elections (Pedersen 1979). It is calculated by summing the absolute values of the differences between the percentage of valid votes cast by each party contesting an election and the percentage that the parties themselves obtain in the following election. The result is then divided by two to avoid double counting. The variable ranges from 0 to 100, where 0 indicates the lack of vote changes and 100 indicates the opposite situation (where any possible change takes place). Data on electoral volatility have been taken from the 'Dataset of electoral volatility and its internal components in Western Europe' (Emanuele 2015b).

As stated earlier, total volatility (from now on, TV)[13] has tended to increase in Western Europe during the past decades. The empirical analysis confirms the expectation: the correlation between TV and time is positive (as depicted in figure 6.4) and significant ($r = 0.333$; $p < 0.001$). The mean score of TV since 1965 has been 11.23. The amount of change has been more limited during the first period (9.13), while after 1990 it has increased to an average of 13.51. As figure 6.4 shows, the great bulk of the Western European elections since 1965 displays a TV lower than 20, a score that Mair (2011) identifies as the reference point beyond which an election can be considered highly volatile. However, there are some remarkable exceptions, such as the earthquake elections of 1982 and 2015 in Spain, the 1994 and 2013 elections in Italy and the dramatic Greek election of May 2012, where TV flew up to an astonishing 48.50.[14]

More into detail, figure 6.5 plots the trend of TV over time in the sixteen countries under study. A somewhat linear increase of the index is detectable in Austria, Belgium, France, Germany, the Netherlands, Sweden and the United Kingdom. In some cases, there is only a slight increase while in some others, like Austria, the electoral availability increases three times between the first and the last period. In a number of countries, there has been a neat discontinuity between a first phase of stability and a second turbulent period (Italy), while in others (Greece, Ireland and Spain) a shocking electoral instability has been the result of a deep restructuring of the party system following the economic crisis started in 2008 (Casal Bértoa 2014b; Chiaramonte and Emanuele 2015; Hernández and Kriesi 2016).

Notwithstanding the straightforward trend towards a more open and fluid electoral market, some countries deviate from this main pattern, showing

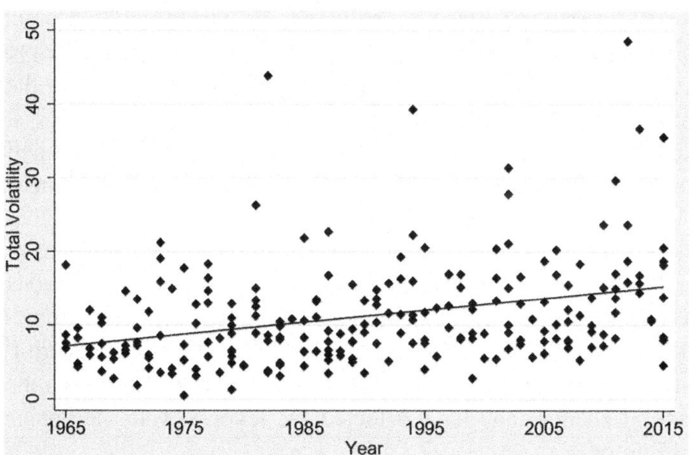

Figure 6.4 Trend of total volatility over time, 1965–2015

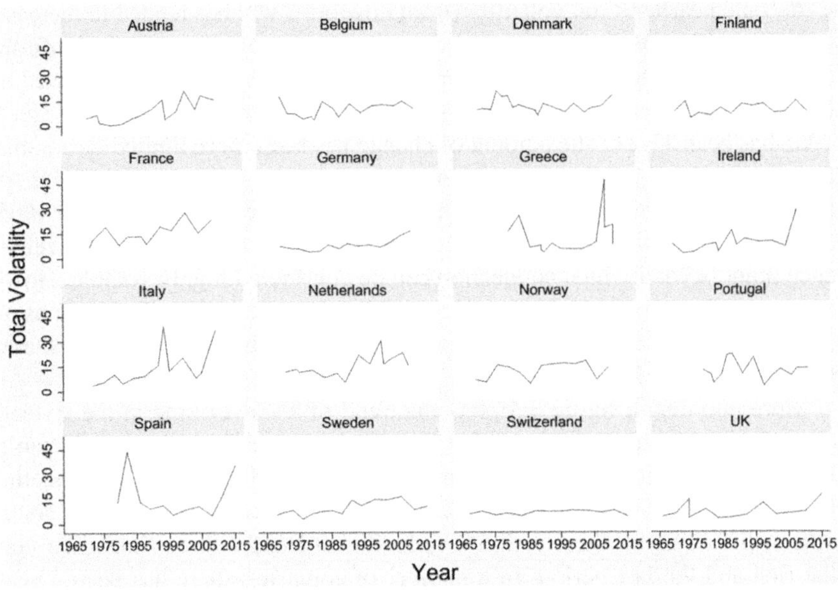

Figure 6.5 National variations of total volatility over time, 1965–2015

a steady trend over time (Finland, Norway and Switzerland) or a general decline (as in Portugal or in Denmark, although one notices the notable level of TV reached in the last election of 2015).

As far as national variations are concerned, two Scandinavian countries like Denmark and Norway belong to the subset of the most volatile countries. This result is quite surprising, since Scandinavian countries are often described as very stable polities, and, according to most of the indicators I have previously implemented, they show a lower amount of change compared to the rest of Europe. In Denmark and Norway, the relative stability of the party system as a whole and the high predictability of its consolidated pattern of competition are counterbalanced by a rather high level of interelectoral shifts among the party labels. Moreover, Spain, the Netherlands and France show the highest levels of volatility, followed by the rest of Southern Europe (Italy, Greece and Portugal). On the opposite side, the United Kingdom and Switzerland, two countries characterised by very different institutional frameworks and structures of party competition, share the highest levels of electoral stability in Western Europe.

Following these preliminary findings, the question is how this increasing interelectoral change may have affected the level of vote nationalisation in Western Europe.

I do not expect a direct linkage between electoral instability and the territorial configuration of party support. Indeed, the rise in electoral volatility only means that the fluidity of the electoral market increases and that a new window of opportunity for parties opens. This window of opportunity may have different sources and may be used by different types of parties, thus leading to very different outcomes. Therefore, there will not be any automatic result implying an increase of territorial homogeneity or, on the contrary, a decrease towards a denationalisation of party support. Table 6.2 reports the results of the Prais-Winsten regression of the sPSNS on total volatility.[15] The regression models seem to show the presence of a negative effect of electoral volatility on vote nationalisation, but this relation is barely significant at the 0.1 level in the general model and increases to the 0.01 level only as far as Belgium is omitted. This country has a positive association between TV and the sPSNS that contrasts with the negative association detected in the whole set of elections. This explains why the coefficient of TV gets stronger and the goodness-of-fit improves as Belgium is excluded. Moreover, by running separate regressions for each period, we notice that the effect of TV was insignificant during the first period, while since the 1990s it has become significant. This evidence seems to bring us to the conclusion that, when the electoral market was very narrow and stable, volatility did not affect the territorial structuring of party support; conversely, as electoral availability of voters has increased in the past decades (as shown in figures 6.4 and 6.5), volatility has started to play a role in the explanation of vote nationalisation, by fostering a territorialisation of party support.

The negative relation between electoral volatility and vote nationalisation has been already highlighted by Jones and Mainwaring (2003: 160), but the

Table 6.2 Regressions of vote nationalisation on total volatility

	Model 1	*Model 2*	*Model 3*
Full data set	*1965–1990*	*1991–2015*	*All elections*
TV	0.000 (0.000)	−0.001* (0.000)	−0.000† (0.000)
Constant	0.809*** (0.015)	0.821*** (0.013)	0.818*** (0.013)
Wald $\chi 2$	0.95	4.64*	2.72†
N elections	118	109	227
N countries	16	16	16
Belgium excluded			
TV	−0.000 (0.000)	−0.001* (0.000)	−0.001** (0.000)
Constant	0.831*** (0.010)	0.845*** (0.009)	0.838*** (0.010)
Wald $\chi 2$	0.14	5.41*	8.78**
N elections	109	102	211
N countries	15	15	15

Note: Prais-Winsten AR1 regression. Panel-corrected standard errors in parentheses.

† $p < 0.1$; * $p < 0.05$; ** $p < 0.01$; *** $p < 0.001$.

authors state that 'the driving force behind this relationship is most likely the previously noted correlation between fragmentation and nationalization'. Indeed, the literature on vote nationalisation has extensively stressed the importance of the number of parties as a factor that triggers electoral volatility (Bartolini and Mair 1990; Roberts and Wibbels 1999; Mainwaring and Zoco 2007; Chiaramonte and Emanuele 2017). Therefore, the negative association detected in table 6.2 is likely to be a spurious effect due to the omission of the number of parties, which is an important determinant of both TV and sPSNS.[16] Not surprisingly, once the effective number of parties is taken under control (results not reported), the negative effect of TV disappears.

Indeed, it can be hypothesised that volatility does exert a certain influence on the territorial configuration of party support, but this effect is not a direct one. It is conceivable that this effect is mediated by the specific structure of cleavages that shape a given party system. If volatility represents the sign of an increasingly open and fluid electoral market, one has to consider the former structure of the party system, with its constraints and opportunities, in order to predict which territorial pattern of party support will be developed once electoral change occurs. When does volatility produce increasing territorial homogeneity? And when, instead, does it lead to a progressive denationalisation of the vote?

To answer these questions, one needs to refer to the theory concerning the process of nationalisation experienced by Western European countries between the end of the nineteenth century and the beginning of the twentieth century, which has been discussed in chapter 1, as well as to the empirical findings concerning the 'macro-sociological' factors discussed in chapter 4. Starting from the Rokkanian framework, Caramani (2004) stresses both the importance of class as a homogenising cleavage and the role of ethnolinguistic and religious cleavages as the primary sources of within-country territorial differentiation. The empirical analyses carried out in chapter 4 have confirmed the strong and negative impact of cultural segmentation on vote nationalisation, while Caramani's assumption about class has been downsized: as a result of the notable decrease of its salience in Western European societies over the past fifty years, the class cleavage has played only a marginal role in the explanation of vote nationalisation in the past decades. Yet, leaving aside for a moment my own empirical results and resorting once again to Caramani's theory, one would expect to identify two opposite cleavage configurations where volatility may affect vote nationalisation. The first configuration can be found in culturally segmented contexts. Here an increase in volatility is likely to witness a defreezing of the former structure of competition, characterised by a high degree of territoriality of party support. The opening of the electoral market will probably produce a more fluid and competitive party environment, reducing the importance of the old cultural cleavages and thus increasing the likelihood of a more nationalised outcome. The second configuration, instead, can be found in contexts where the electoral alignments are structured along a class-based left-right dimension that, in turn, has produced nationalised patterns of party competition. In such contexts, an increase in electoral volatility is likely to be the result of a class cleavage decline, and, consequently, it is likely to open new opportunities for the (re-)emergence of territorial factors. In short, the expectations are the following:

> H7: The effect of total volatility on vote nationalisation is expected to be mediated by the specific cleavage structure of a given country.
> In countries characterised by a high degree of cultural segmentation, volatility is expected to be positively associated with vote nationalisation (H7a).
> Conversely, in countries characterised by a strong class cleavage, volatility is expected to be negatively associated with vote nationalisation (H7b).

The empirical evidence presented in table 6.3 provides only partial support for this expectation. Model 1 presents the interaction between TV and class,

Table 6.3 Regressions of vote nationalisation on total volatility in interaction with the cleavage structure of the polity

Full data set	*Model 1*	*Model 2*
TV	−0.000 (0.000)	−0.000 (0.000)
Class	0.004 (0.006)	
TV*Class	0.000 (0.000)	
Cultural segmentation		−0.089*** (0.016)
TV*Cult. Seg.		0.001* (0.000)
Constant	0.817*** (0.011)	0.817*** (0.009)
Wald $\chi2$	6.44†	39.97***
N elections	227	227
N countries	16	16
Belgium excluded		
TV	−0.000† (0.000)	−0.001** (0.000)
Class	0.010* (0.005)	
TV*Class	0.000 (0.000)	
Cultural segmentation		−0.059*** (0.010)
TV*Cult. Seg.		0.000 (0.000)
Constant	0.839*** (0.008)	0.831*** (0.007)
Wald $\chi2$	14.94***	42.25***
N elections	211	211
N countries	15	15

Note: Prais-Winsten AR1 regression. Panel-corrected standard errors in parentheses.

† $p < 0.1$; * $p < 0.05$; ** $p < 0.01$; *** $p < 0.001$.

while Model 2 shows the interaction between TV and cultural segmentation. The analyses are replicated by excluding Belgium from the regression models.

The hypothesised relation between electoral volatility and cultural segmentation (H7a) is confirmed. The interaction term is positive in both models and significant at the 0.05 level in the model including the whole set of elections. This means that as far as cultural segmentation increases, electoral volatility has a positive effect on vote nationalisation. In other words, in contexts characterised by strong territorial cleavages, the increase in electoral volatility is associated with a defreezing of the old territorial alignments and, consequently, with a homogenisation of party support.

On the other side, the opposite hypothesis does not hold true for the interaction between electoral volatility and class cleavage (H7b). Contrary to what expected based on the aforementioned literature, there is not a negative interaction between TV and class. Interestingly, while the main effect of class is positive (and significant in the model excluding Belgium, consistent with the results shown in chapter 4), the interaction is positive too (albeit never significant), which means that in contexts of strong class cleavage, an increase in electoral volatility does not foster a denationalisation process. In other words, in interaction with the two types of cleavages, the effect of electoral volatility is similar: as far as the cleavage structure becomes stronger, electoral volatility has a positive impact on vote nationalisation.

This apparently counter-intuitive result is in contrast with Caramani's claims about the importance of class as a homogenising factor for the territorial distribution of party support, but it is consistent with the evidence detected in chapter 4, where data clearly showed the decline of class cleavage salience over the past fifty years and its limited effect on vote nationalisation, especially in the past decades. One possible explanation relies on the idea that, as a result of this long-term process of decline, the class cleavage has also become more territorialised than in the past, thus becoming similar to cultural cleavages as regards its effect on vote nationalisation. This hypothesis has been recently empirically verified by Maggini and Emanuele (2015: 23), who find that 'the class cleavage in Europe has undergone a progressive territorialisation, thus losing to some extent, its original nature as a nationwide and functional cleavage'.

THE 'DECISIVENESS' OF ELECTIONS

In their study on constitutional design and electoral dynamics, Carey and Shugart (1992) develop the index of 'identifiability of future governments'. It is a measure that tries to estimate the extent to which voters influence, through elections, the future government composition. For example, in a multiparty system, a coalition government will be the most likely postelectoral outcome. The coalition can derive from an explicit pre-election agreement or, instead, it can be the result of postelection negotiations among parties. In the first case, voters are key actors to determine which pre-electoral coalition will form the government. In the second case, voters are by far less important: negotiations among parties will take election results into account but only to a certain extent since the involvement of a given party in the government will not exclusively depend upon elections. The index of identifiability is, therefore, a measure that gives account of how elections are decisive for government formation. The index has been later used by Powell (2000: 71–76) in his study on elections and democracy.

It is built by assigning to each election a score ranging from 0 to 1[17] according to the extent to which a certain government majority can be predicted before the elections. As it can be seen by looking at table 6.4, the variable has only five possible scores, each corresponding to a specific situation. The higher the score, the higher the likelihood that the election will be decisive for determining the future government. With respect to the original index of identifiability of future governments introduced by Carey and Shugart (1992), I prefer to rename the variable as *decisiveness of elections* since it seems more consistent with what the index actually captures. Indeed, in the case of Switzerland, where the four major parties are steadily represented in the government coalition through the long-standing 'magic formula', the score of the index is 0, since the expectation before each election is that of a continuation of this long-term agreement that is almost completely independent of election results (*see* table 6.4). Here, the 'identifiability' of the future government is very high, but the decisiveness of elections is almost nothing.

I have taken data from Powell as regards the elections that occurred between 1970 and 1995 (the temporal span covered by his research). For previous and later elections, scores are the result of my own assignment according to the situation described in table 6.4. I have proceeded to assign

Table 6.4 Decisiveness of the election for the future government formation: Scores of the index

Score	*Expectation about the prospective government*
0	Long-range agreement apparently independent of elections
0.25	Negotiations among parties after the elections
0.5	Implicit/asymmetric (i.e., on the left but not on the right) pre-election coalition
0.75	Explicit pre-election coalition
1	Single-party majority

Source: Adapted from Powell (2000: 74).

the score of the index to each election by looking at the country's long-term government experience and tradition, the pre-electoral context (presence of pre-electoral implicit or explicit coalitions)[18] and, when available, to opinion polls (fundamental to influence the voters' expectations about the future government formation).

Compared with the other variables presented before, decisiveness shows lower variability, especially across time. This is not only because it is an ordinal variable instead of a continuous one, with only five possible values. The variability of the index is also limited because in some countries the dynamics of government formation has not changed over time.

As figure 6.6 shows, four countries maintain an unchanged level of decisiveness of elections over the period under study. Beyond the aforementioned case of Switzerland, in Finland no party is expected to win the election, and coalitions are formed only after the vote: then, the score of the country is always 0.25, since the government is expected to be the result of negotiations among parties. In France and Germany, the competition is instead based on pre-election coalitions: the coalition that wins a general election is expected to form the government (0.75).

The remaining twelve countries show some variability, with a general pattern of change towards a slight decrease of decisiveness of elections over time.[19]

Some countries display a clear trend of decline, which means that the composition of the government has become increasingly less predictable before

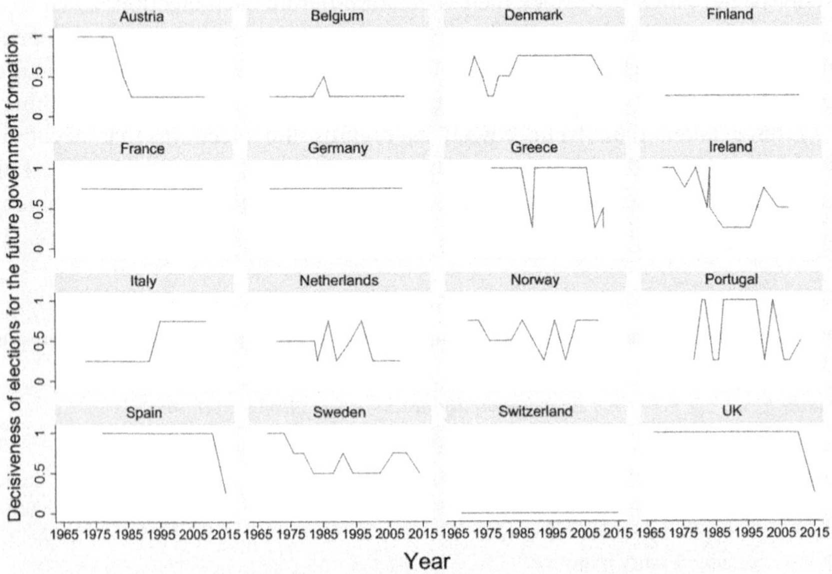

Figure 6.6 National variations of decisiveness of elections over time, 1965–2015

the elections. The latest cases are Spain and the United Kingdom, where a single-party majority government was the rule until the general elections of 2015 when, in both countries, due to the presence of new challengers (*Podemos* and *Ciudadanos* on one side, UKIP on the other), the expectation was a hung Parliament and postelectoral coalitions.[20] In Austria, Greece, Ireland and Sweden, a single-party majority government was usually expected during the first decades. Then, due to the electoral decline of the major parties (as for the former predominant Social Democratic party in Sweden) and the progressive increase of the challengers (as the Liberal FPÖ in Austria), the index has progressively decreased in these countries. Austria has experienced the most valuable change, shifting from the score of 1 to 0.25 during the last period (the government is today the result of postelection negotiations); Greece has remained over high values because, apart from few isolated periods of institutional gridlock (as in 1989 and, more importantly, in 2012), the country has continued to produce single-party majority governments until the dramatic collapse of the old party system in 2012; Ireland, instead, ranges today between the presence of postelection coalitions and implicit or asymmetric pre-election coalitions; this latter situation often occurs also in Sweden, alternating with explicit pre-election coalitions. Even in the Netherlands, a declining trend is detectable, with the country moving from asymmetric or implicit pre-election coalitions towards an expected formation of the government based on postelection negotiations among the competing parties. This latter arrangement has usually been the rule in another consensual country, Belgium: here negotiations among parties take into account not only the electoral results and the respective party size but also the ethnic composition of the executive, thus securing a balance between Wallonia and Flanders.

The opposing trend, namely, an increase in the index over time, is visible in Denmark and Italy: the former country has shifted from a first period characterised by the predominance of asymmetric coalitions to a later period based on explicit pre-election coalitions. Coalitions formed before general elections are also the expected result in Italy's so-called Second Republic, after a long previous phase where government was formed after postelection negotiations. Finally, in Norway and Portugal, the index has always fluctuated between 0.5 and 0.75 without a straightforward temporal trend.

Beyond national and temporal variations in the individual countries, what I need to assess is how this variable can affect the configuration of party support in Western Europe. As emphasised by some scholars (Cox 1997; Lago 2011), the presence of a national prize is a strong incentive for parties to ally across districts, thus producing a nationalisation of the competition and of the electoral results. The national government in a parliamentary or in a semipresidential system can be certainly considered an important national prize. Consequently, it can be hypothesised that, as far as elections get more decisive for the future government formation, voters will have an incentive to vote for those parties and electoral alignments that have a real chance to win. On the contrary, if the composition of the government is difficult to predict or it is the result of negotiations among parties after the elections, electoral coordination will be more likely to fail, and voters will feel freer to vote for their favourite party, regardless of its chances to win the election and enter the government. The expectation concerning the impact of decisiveness on vote nationalisation is therefore as follows:

> H8: The higher the decisiveness of elections, the higher the level of vote nationalisation.

By looking at table 6.5, the expectation about a positive association between decisiveness and the sPSNS seems to be confirmed.

The empirical analysis shows a rather high impact of decisiveness in the overall set of elections. The coefficient (0.019, significant at the 0.01 level) reveals that as far as the decisiveness moves from 0 to 1, the sPSNS increases by 0.019. Notice that the association between the two variables improves over time: the coefficient is stronger in the last period compared to the first one, and the former also shows a better goodness-of-fit. Not surprisingly, the exclusion of Belgium worsens the relation which remains significant but only at the 0.05 level.[21] This is because Belgium positively contributes to the tight association between the two variables, given that its government is the result

Table 6.5 Regressions of vote nationalisation on decisiveness of elections

	Model 1	*Model 2*	*Model 3*
Full data set	*1965–1990*	*1991–2015*	*All elections*
Decisiveness	0.022† (0.012)	0.032** (0.012)	0.019** (0.007)
Constant	0.800*** (0.016)	0.796*** (0.014)	0.804*** (0.011)
Wald χ2	3.74†	6.99**	6.79**
N elections	120	109	229
N countries	16	16	16
Belgium excluded			
Decisiveness	0.018† (0.010)	0.017† (0.009)	0.013* (0.006)
Constant	0.818*** (0.012)	0.827*** (0.010)	0.824*** (0.010)
Wald χ2	3.41†	3.29†	4.77*
N elections	111	102	213
N countries	15	15	15

Note: Prais-Winsten AR1 regression. Panel-corrected standard errors in parentheses.

† $p < 0.1$; * $p < 0.05$; ** $p < 0.01$; *** $p < 0.001$.

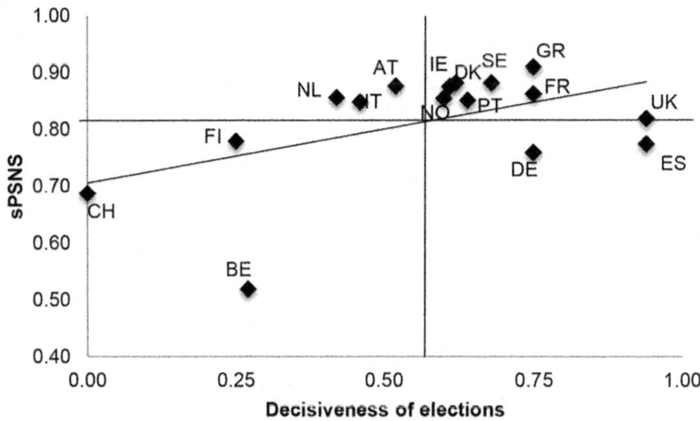

Figure 6.7 Decisiveness of elections and vote nationalisation in Western Europe, mean values by country

of postelectoral negotiations and its level of vote nationalisation is the lowest in Western Europe.

The link between decisiveness and sPSNS is also clearly detectable in figure 6.7, which plots the mean values of the two variables for each country. Most of the country-points are very close to the regression line, which shows a positive slope. Only Belgium and, to a lesser extent, Germany, Spain and the United Kingdom fall quite far from their predicted location, being characterised by a territorial configuration of party support that is more heterogeneous than what expected on the basis of their degree of decisiveness. Yet, this variable – like electoral volatility – is highly related to the effective number of parties. Indeed, as far as the number of parties increases, elections become less decisive for the future government formation. The correlation between ENEP and decisiveness is very strong ($r = -0.558$) and significant ($p < 0.001$). Controlling for the number of parties, the statistically significant effects of decisiveness detected in table 6.5 disappear from the regression models, while the ENEP is still significant at the 0.001 level (results not reported). This evidence not only reduces the emphasis on the importance of this variable in the explanation of vote nationalisation but also warns us, as recently noted by Golosov (2016b), that the strong impact of the effective number of parties comes partly at the expense of some other factors.

THE TERRITORIAL CONCENTRATION OF TURNOUT

The last 'political' factor that deserves to be taken into account concerns the electoral participation. In the past decades, Western European democracies have undergone increasing rates of abstention (Delwit 2013).[22] There are many possible explanations of turnout decline (see Franklin 2004). Yet, what is important here is not turnout per se but its territorial homogeneity. In other words, in order to affect the territorial configuration of the vote in a given election, it does not matter if turnout is low or high, but rather if it is homogeneous within a country.

In his broad historical comparison concerning the evolution of territorial homogeneity of voting behaviour in Western Europe, Caramani (2004: 73–81) focuses not only on party support but also on turnout levels. He considers party support and turnout levels two dimensions of a unique process of nationalisation of the electorates occurred in Europe between the 1850s and World War I, followed by a pattern of stable territorial configurations of both party support and voter turnout after the 1920s. This process is confirmed by his empirical results showing 'a clear trend toward increasing nationally integrated electorates and homogeneous party system over the past 150 years' (73). Therefore, according to Caramani, the two processes of nationalisation of party support and homogenisation of turnout levels are closely related. If we have a high territorial disparity in turnout levels, this could indicate the survival of marginal areas in terms of cultural or socioeconomic development and the persistence of a certain degree of peripherality in some areas. These conditions are generally associated with high levels of territorial disparity in party support. Conversely, homogeneous turnout rates may indicate how these marginal groups have been mobilised and integrated into the national political system, and such a context is expected to be associated with homogeneous patterns of party support.

Following these considerations, the hypothesis to be tested is the following:

> H9: The higher the homogeneity of turnout levels, the higher the level of vote nationalisation.

The homogeneity of turnout levels is measured through the coefficient of variation (CV)[23] – one of the indicators employed by Caramani himself (2004: 79) – across the same territorial units used to measure the sPSNS (*see* table 2.1). Since the CV takes higher values as homogeneity decreases, a negative relation with the sPSNS is expected.

The results of the Prais-Winsten regressions are reported in table 6.6: across the entire universe of 228 elections,[24] the overall association is negative, as expected, but not significant. As far as the full data set is concerned, an appreciable relationship is detectable only in Model 1, namely, between 1965 and 1990. Therefore, until 1990, as far as turnout homogeneity increases, nationalisation increases, consistent with H9. Since then this relation disappears and the two variables seem to vary quite independently of one another.[25]

Why does this kind of pattern occur? Probably this is due to the particular evolution of the two variables over time. While vote nationalisation, as pointed out in chapter 3, follows a trend of enduring stability over time, turnout heterogeneity, as figure 6.8 shows, slightly tends to increase. The correlation between CV turnout and time is positive and significant ($r = 0.148$; $p < 0.05$). The whole set of 228 elections shows a mean CV turnout of 5.53,[26] increasing from 4.93 of the first period to 6.18 of the second one. This finding is rather inconsistent with Caramani's statement of a 'fundamental stability of territorial configurations' of turnout levels after World War II (2004: 80).

The increase in CV turnout over time lowers the strength of the relation with the sPSNS since 1990. Moreover, data show that the decline of turnout levels and the increase of its heterogeneity are closely related:[27] the lower the levels of turnout, the lower the territorial homogeneity of electoral participation within a given country.

These results dramatically change if Belgium is omitted from the analysis. Belgium combines the well-known tremendous level of territorialisation of party support with a very low level of CV turnout, thus its exclusion boosts the regression coefficient of CV turnout. After dropping the fifteen Belgian elections, the association between turnout homogeneity and vote nationalisation is tremendously enhanced, as table 6.6 shows. The coefficient of CV turnout is now significant at the highest possible level of confidence. In the current analysis, a similar outcome has taken place only in the case of cultural segmentation and party system fragmentation, although in those circumstances the effect occurred regardless of the presence of Belgium. Furthermore, Model 2 maintains a significant difference vis-à-vis Model 1: this

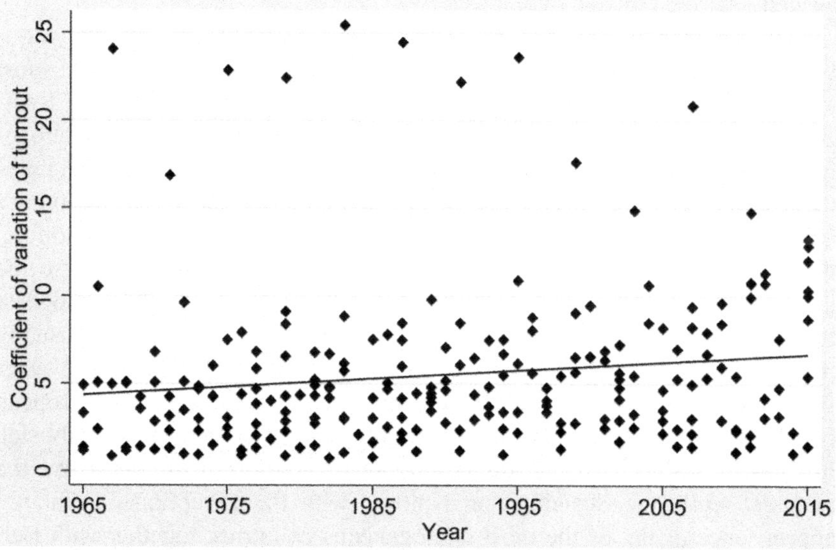

Figure 6.8 Trend of CV turnout over time, 1965–2015

Table 6.6 Regressions of vote nationalisation on turnout homogeneity

	Model 1	*Model 2*	*Model 3*
Full data set	*1965–1990*	*1991–2015*	*All elections*
CV turnout	−0.004* (0.001)	−0.001 (0.001)	−0.001 (0.001)
Constant	0.833*** (0.016)	0.818*** (0.016)	0.822*** (0.013)
Wald $\chi 2$	6.56*	0.53	2.53
N elections	119	109	228
N countries	16	16	16
Belgium excluded			
CV turnout	−0.006*** (0.001)	−0.005** (0.001)	−0.004*** (0.001)
Constant	0.867*** (0.009)	0.866*** (0.010)	0.855*** (0.008)
Wald $\chi 2$	21.63***	9.48**	12.64***
N elections	110	102	212
N countries	15	15	15

Note: Prais-Winsten AR1 regression. Panel-corrected standard errors in parentheses.

† $p < 0.1$; * $p < 0.05$; ** $p < 0.01$; *** $p < 0.001$.

means that, as detected earlier, the impact of turnout homogeneity on vote nationalisation declines over time.

The results displayed in table 6.6 sounds like a confirmation of H9 once Belgium is omitted: as far as electoral participation gets more territorially heterogeneous, the configuration of party support gets more denationalised as well.

This evidence can be furtherly assessed by looking at how national variations of turnout homogeneity are related to vote nationalisation. The most striking evidence emerging from figure 6.9 concerns the position of Switzerland vis-à-vis the other countries. Switzerland has an extremely heterogeneous turnout across its cantons: its mean CV of 20.23 is more than 3.5 times the overall mean and more than two times the average score of the country with the second-most heterogeneous turnout levels (Finland). Furthermore, the country shows the lowest turnout rate in Western Europe and also the largest internal variation, with a gap between the canton with the highest turnout (usually *Schaffhausen*) and the canton with the lowest one (usually *Appenzell Inner-Rhoden*) often reaching fifty percentage points. The other fifteen countries display by far a more limited variation. Southern European countries (Greece, Spain, Portugal and Italy) are all located on the right side of figure 6.9, thus showing a within-country variation of turnout above the average, while the Scandinavian nations (with the exception of Finland) appear, once again, as the most homogeneous countries, together with Belgium, Germany and the Netherlands.

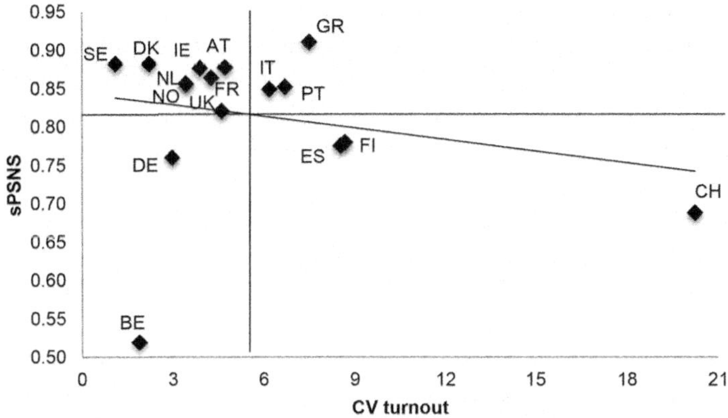

Figure 6.9 Turnout homogeneity and vote nationalisation in Western Europe, mean values by country

Beyond national variations, figure 6.9 reveals which countries deviate from the negative regression slope. Besides the well-documented position of Belgium, two other countries fall away from their expected position: Germany, where party support is more regionalised than what expected based on its high turnout homogeneity, and Greece, showing the opposite situation, namely, a heterogeneous turnout that goes hand in hand with the highest level of vote nationalisation in Western Europe.

The remaining countries fall pretty close to the regression line, including Switzerland. Yet, the powerful leverage of this country is likely to heavily influence the overall association detected between turnout homogeneity and sPSNS. Regression analyses (results not reported) obtained by taking into account the effect of Switzerland (through a dichotomous variable or by excluding it from the sample) show that the effect of turnout homogeneity on vote nationalisation remains negative, but the previously noted significant effect disappears, both in the full data set and in the separate regressions by period. This means that H9 surely needs to be reassessed in a multivariate model, but from this preliminary evidence, it seems that its validity is conditioned by the opposite effects exerted by Belgium (whose inclusion decreases the association) and Switzerland (whose inclusion strengthens the association).

THE 'COMPETITION' MODEL

As previously done in chapters 4 and 5, this section is devoted to both explore the overall impact of the factors linked to the structure of the competition and also to see which of them maintains a significant effect once the others are taken under control. Moreover, the purpose of this section is also that of comparing the 'competition' model with the other two sets of explanatory variables introduced in the previous two chapters (*see* tables 4.4 and 5.4, respectively). This will allow me to verify whether, notwithstanding the large emphasis put by scholars on the macro-sociological factors and the institutional constraints, the most important role in the story is played by factors stemming from the electoral arena.

Table 6.7 presents the results obtained by regressing the sPSNS on the 'political' variables. Given that, as underlined in the previous sections, the number of parties exerts a strong effect not only on the dependent variable but also on some of the other factors presented previously (specifically, on volatility and decisiveness of elections), following Golosov's (2016b) method, table 6.7 firstly presents the regression with the other three political factors (Model 1) and then adds the ENEP (Model 2).[28] The analysis is also replicated by omitting Belgian elections.

In the full data set, Model 1 confirms the positive and significant effect of decisiveness and the negative and significant effect of the CV turnout on sPSNS. Vote nationalisation is, therefore, a positive function of the degree to which elections are decisive for the future government formation and a negative function of the territoriality of voters' participation. Interestingly,

Table 6.7 Regressions of vote nationalisation on the political variables

Full data set	*Model 1*	*Model 2*
TV	−0.000 (0.000)	0.001* (0.000)
Decisiveness	0.018* (0.008)	0.000 (0.001)
CV turnout	−0.002* (0.001)	−0.001 (0.001)
ENEP		−0.023*** (0.004)
Constant	0.820*** (0.014)	0.920*** (0.018)
Wald χ2	14.72**	58.70***
N elections	225	225
N countries	16	16
Belgium excluded		
TV	−0.001* (0.000)	0.000 (0.000)
Decisiveness	0.011 (0.007)	−0.000 (0.007)
CV turnout	−0.004*** (0.001)	−0.004*** (0.001)
ENEP		−0.011*** (0.002)
Constant	0.858*** (0.010)	0.907*** (0.014)
Wald χ2	26.50***	53.32***
N elections	209	209
N countries	15	15

Note: Prais-Winsten AR1 regression. Panel-corrected standard errors in parentheses.

† $p < 0.1$; * $p < 0.05$; ** $p < 0.01$; *** $p < 0.001$.

by excluding Belgium from the analysis, decisiveness becomes not significant, while the role of turnout homogeneity largely improves, consistent with what is shown in the previous sections. Moreover, electoral volatility becomes significant once Belgium is left out, displaying a negative effect on the sPSNS (as in table 6.2). Overall, the regression excluding Belgium shows a better goodness-of-fit, mainly due to the different impact exerted by the CV turnout on sPSNS.

Model 2 adds the effective number of parties which is significant with a confidence of 99.9 per cent in both analyses, even if the *b* coefficient is halved as Belgium is omitted. As expected, the inclusion of the ENEP affects, to different extents, the other variables: in the full data set, TV becomes positive, with a significant effect at the 0.05 level, while the impact of decisiveness and CV turnout disappears; in the regression without Belgium, the effect of volatility fades, while turnout homogeneity maintains its strong and negative influence. Overall, the accuracy of the models largely improves with the addition of the ENEP, with the Wald Chi-Square jumping to 58.70 and 53.32, respectively. This finding is very important since it reveals that, by comparing the factors related to the structure of the competition with the other two sets of explanatory variables presented in chapters 4 and 5, the former ones are by far the most relevant, given that they grant the better performance of the model. Indeed, the Wald Chi-Squares of the macro-sociological model were 29.65 and 31.15 (with and without Belgium, respectively), while those of the institutional model – despite being obtained with the employment of five variables – were 34.65 and 29.74.

Therefore, the factors linked to the structure of the competition appear as the most important determinants of vote nationalisation, and, among them, party system fragmentation clearly emerges as the key factor. Yet, one still needs to understand how the ENEP interacts with the two other factors that are largely affected by its inclusion in the models, TV and decisiveness. In this regard, table 6.8 presents the 'competition' model, with the addition of the interaction between the ENEP and TV (Model 1) and with that between the ENEP and decisiveness (Model 2).

As witnessed by the increase of the Wald Chi-Square, the addition of the interactions improves the goodness-of-fit and offers new elements in the explanation compared to the plain model in table 6.7: both the interactions with the ENEP are indeed positive and significant. The graphical representation of figure 6.10 provides clarification of these relationships. The positive slope of the line in both charts means that the marginal effect of the effective number of parties on the sPSNS decreases as far as, respectively, electoral volatility and decisiveness increase. More specifically, in contexts of low electoral volatility (say, 5 per cent), an increase in the number of parties by one unit induces a decrease of the sPSNS of 0.029, while in highly volatile

Table 6.8 Regressions of vote nationalisation on the political variables, models with interactions

Full data set	*Model 1*	*Model 2*
TV	−0.001* (0.001)	0.001** (0.000)
Decisiveness	−0.002 (0.008)	−0.087* (0.035)
CV turnout	−0.001 (0.001)	−0.001 (0.001)
ENEP	−0.031*** (0.005)	−0.035*** (0.006)
ENEP*TV	0.000** (0.000)	
ENEP*Decisiveness		0.023* (0.009)
Constant	0.958*** (0.023)	0.969*** (0.026)
Wald χ2	64.93***	68.68***
N elections	225	225
N countries	16	16

Note: Prais-Winsten AR1 regression. Panel-corrected standard errors in parentheses.

† $p < 0.1$; * $p < 0.05$; ** $p < 0.01$; *** $p < 0.001$.

contexts (say, 40 per cent) the reduction in vote nationalisation following the marginal increase in the number of parties is more than halved (0.013). A similar trend is displayed as far as decisiveness is taken into consideration: in contexts of nondecisive elections, where, for instance, the government is the result of postelectoral negotiations (decisiveness = 0.25), an increase of the ENEP by one unit produces a decrease in the sPSNS by 0.029; conversely, when elections are actually decisive, and a single-party majority government is expected, the impact of the ENEP is largely lower and causes a reduction in the sPSNS by only 0.012.

The interpretation of these results is fascinating: the effect of the number of parties in stimulating patterns of territorialisation of party support is stronger in contexts of consensual politics, namely, wherever elections are not decisive for government formation (in other words, where postelectoral multiparty coalitions or long-term agreements among parties are expected) and electoral stability is the rule (TV is low). Here, as hypothesised in the first section of this chapter, a new party needs to develop strategies of territorial concentration of its support to create its own niche and improve its chances to gain parliamentary representation. Conversely, when the government represents a prize at stake for voters at each election and/or when voters are available to change frequently their previous vote choice, party system fragmentation is less related to the territorial homogeneity of party support. Here, a strategy of territorial concentration could be less fruitful for a new party, since the electoral context is unstable and there are no safe strongholds, and, conversely, the context structurally favours parties that are able to compete for the 'prize' of the government.

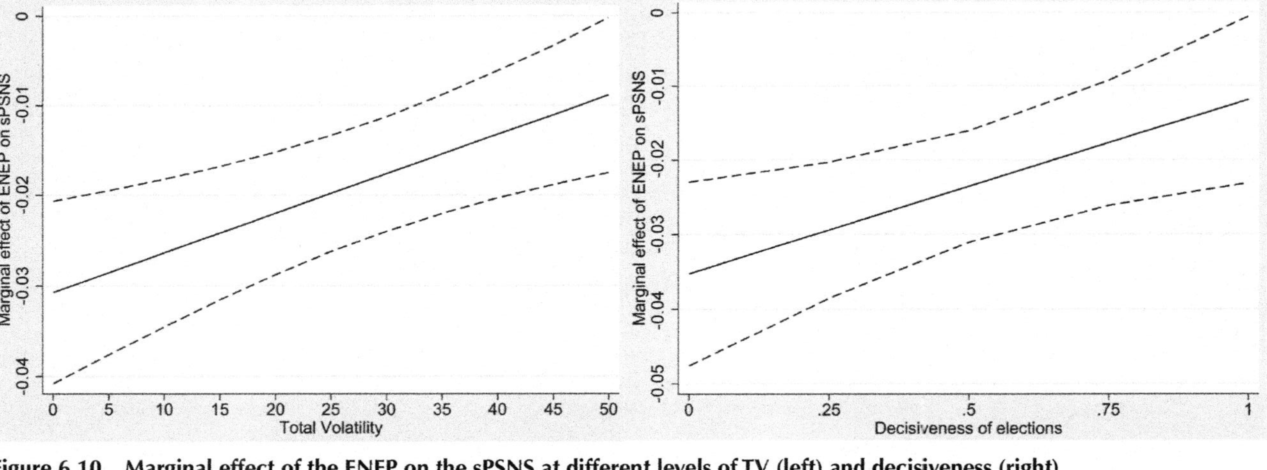

Figure 6.10 Marginal effect of the ENEP on the sPSNS at different levels of TV (left) and decisiveness (right)

Chapter 7

Towards an explanation

The last three chapters have presented many empirical factors that may help to explain the level of vote nationalisation in Western Europe in the past fifty years. So far, these possible determinants have been introduced following specific underlying assumptions on the expected impact of these variables. Many hypotheses have been formulated, either following the existing literature on the topic or starting from compelling theoretical assumptions. Then, in chapters 4, 5 and 6, the hypotheses have been preliminarily tested, by assessing the independent impact of three variables' clusters (the macro-sociological one, the institutional one and the competition-related one) over time and across countries. The first pieces of evidence have shown some important substantive results. Nonetheless, these findings tell us only a part of the story. To better understand what explains the territorial configuration of party support in Western Europe, a general explanatory model is needed. This is the task of the present chapter. In the following pages, I assess the combined influence of the independent variables on vote nationalisation, as well as the contribution of each single factor once the other predictors are taken under control. Therefore, the purpose of this final analysis is to build an overall explanatory model to reach a comprehensive understanding of the macro-constellation of factors underlying vote nationalisation. This analysis is performed by using a particular model specification, which is suitable to deal with the issues deriving from a time-series-cross-section data structure. Moreover, after having clarified the general explanatory model, a further concern is devoted to the temporal variations of such model. In other words, by resorting to the two temporal slices (1965–1990; 1991–2015) – as done in the previous chapters – a specific model for each period is run, in order to assess the extent to which the relative impact of the independent variables changes over time or, conversely, proves time-resistant. Finally, the chapter focuses on country-related variations to detect the possible presence of national deviations from the general model.

The structure of the chapter is as follows: the first section, 'The macro-constellation', briefly reviews the hypotheses and the related independent variables employed in the empirical analysis, discusses some potential alternative explanation and summarises the features of the statistical model used to test the hypotheses; the second section, 'The general model', presents the general model, that is, the macro-constellation of factors explaining vote nationalisation in the overall universe of elections; the third section, 'Temporal variations', explores the temporal variations, looking for the presence of changes over time in the factors explaining vote nationalisation; finally, the fourth section, 'National variations', gives an account of evidence related to national variations.

THE MACRO-CONSTELLATION

Hypotheses and data

Before moving to the regression models and the comprehensive explanation of the macro-constellation of factors underlying vote nationalisation, it is useful to resort to the hypotheses raised and preliminarily tested in the previous three chapters. Table 7.1 summarises the nine hypotheses presented so far, the related variables, and also the control variables hitherto implemented.

To begin with, chapter 4, where the 'macro-sociological determinants' are discussed, has shown that overall the class cleavage (H1) is not a powerful predictor of vote nationalisation over the past fifty years. Indeed, its effect is constrained by the distorting presence of Belgium and also by the declining salience of this factor over time. As a result, the class cleavage has displayed the expected positive and significant effect only by excluding Belgium from the analysis and by just considering the first period under study (1965–1990). On the other side, cultural conflicts, summarised through the index of cultural segmentation (H2), have played a major role in the explanation of vote nationalisation. Data are unequivocal in showing that, as far as cultural segmentation increases, the territorial homogeneity of party support decreases.

Passing to the analysis of the institutional constraints, examined in chapter 5, some important findings have emerged. First, the effect of decentralisation (H3) on vote nationalisation is negative, as expected, but not so strong as the literature usually emphasises (Chhibber and Kollman 1998; 2004; Cox and Knoll 2003; Jones and Mainwaring 2003; Harbers 2010; Golosov 2016b). Moreover, the evidence carried out to test the effect of the European integration – for which I did not raise a specific hypothesis, instead testing two rival expectations – seems to show that European integration is neither

Table 7.1 Hypotheses, factors, measures and expected effect on vote nationalisation (sPSNS) in Western Europe (1965–2015): A general scheme

Hypothesis	*Factor*	*Measures*	*Expected effect on sPSNS*
H1	Class cleavage	Left partisan density (LPD) and trade union density (TUD), then combined in a standardised index (Class)	+
H2	Cultural segmentation	Fractionalisation and segregation index, then combined in a standardised index (cultural segmentation)	-
H3	Decentralisation	Regional Authority Index (RAI)	-
H4	Electoral system	Percentage of seats allocated at the national level	+
H5	Electoral system	Incentives for cultivating personal vote	-
H6	Party system fragmentation	Effective number of electoral parties (ENEP)	-
H7	Electoral volatility	Pedersen index of electoral volatility (total volatility, TV)	mediated by cleavages
H8	Decisiveness of the elections	Index of decisiveness	+
H9	Territorial concentration of turnout	Coefficient of variation turnout (CV turnout)	-
	Control variables		
	European integration	Index of European institutional integration (EURII)	
	Electoral system	Average district magnitude (ADM)	

a factor favouring the resurgence of territorial politics (Bartolini 2005) nor a homogenising factor of party support as argued by Caramani (2015). Finally, as regards the role played by the features of the electoral system, only the incentives for cultivating personal vote (H5) exert a nontrivial explanatory capacity, while the percentage of seats allocated at the national level (H4) as well as the average district magnitude – for which I did not raise a specific assumption, also given the contrasting opinions among scholars on its effect – do not play any significant influence on vote nationalisation.

The last set of explanatory factors taken into consideration has been that related to the structure of the electoral competition. The analysis performed in chapter 6 has shown, first, the powerful effect of party system fragmentation in fostering vote denationalisation (H6). Second, the assumption according to which the effect of electoral volatility is mediated by the specific cleavage

Table 7.2 Descriptive statistics

	N	*Mean*	*Std. Dev.*	*Min.*	*Max.*
sPSNS	230	0.816	0.105	0.441	0.935
Class index	230	0.00	0.85	−1.20	3.09
Cultural segmentation index	230	0.00	0.90	−0.91	2.13
RAI(*t*–*1*)	230	15.31	10.50	0	37
EURII(*t*–*1*)	230	49.22	29.27	0	86
Average district magnitude (ln)	230	2.04	1.23	0	5.73
Perc. of seats at the nat. level	230	14.29	28.22	0	100
Personal vote	230	4.09	2.91	1	10
ENEP	230	4.61	1.64	2.26	10.28
Total volatility	227	11.23	7.06	0.45	48.50
Decisiveness	229	0.57	0.32	0	1
CV turnout	228	5.53	4.59	0.75	25.43

structure of a given country (H7) has been rejected, given that only a part of the story seems true: more specifically, electoral volatility fosters an increase in vote nationalisation in culturally segmented contexts, but it does not foster denationalisation in contexts characterised by a strong class cleavage. Third, the decisiveness of elections for the future government formation (H8) is a positive predictor of vote nationalisation, but its effect disappears once the effective number of parties is taken under control. Finally, the territorial concentration of turnout (H9) is negatively associated with vote nationalisation, but this effect is significant only when Belgium is omitted.

Furthermore, beyond the direct effect exerted by each determinant on vote nationalisation, the use of interaction models has allowed disentangling the relationship among certain independent variables[1] and to see how they interact in the explanation of the outcome.

Finally, the comparison of the regression models among the three sets of determinants has revealed that overall the set of factors linked to the structure of the competition – widely neglected by the existing literature so far – appears as the most important determinant of vote nationalisation. Moreover, these factors also show a better goodness-of-fit than the macro-sociological and the institutional ones.

Table 7.2 provides the descriptive statistics of the dependent variable (sPSNS) and of the eleven independent variables that enter the models. Each election in a country corresponds to one observation.

Potential alternative explanations

The employment of these eleven independent variables, derived from nine hypotheses and two controls, is expected to depict a clear map of the macro-constellation of factors underlying the *explanandum* and of their interplay. I have excluded from this analysis other factors that have previously been taken into account by other scholars focusing on different regions or a different set of countries.

For instance, I have omitted the nature of the executive (Morgenstern, Swindle and Castagnola 2009; Lago 2011; Golosov 2016b) and the degree of democracy (Golosov 2016b) since none of my national cases is a presidential regime or a nondemocratic one. Concerning other aspects of democracy, Lago and Lago (2016) have recently argued that the number of years after the inauguration of democracy may affect vote nationalisation. Indeed, following Caramani (2004), as time goes by, parties become more nationalised. This assumption directly derives from the literature on party system institutionalisation (Mainwaring and Zoco 2007; Mainwaring, Gervasoni and España-Najera 2016) and follows the idea that the patterns of interparty competition become more stable over time. In this respect, it might be hypothesised that, by considering nationalisation as a dimension of party system institutionalisation,[2] the higher the number of years since the inauguration of democracy, the higher the level of vote nationalisation. I have preliminarily tested this potential determinant, by drawing data on the inauguration of democracy from Mainwaring, Gervasoni and España-Najera (2016), but I have not found the expected positive association with sPSNS.[3]

Moreover, I have also excluded from the analysis the size of the polity, a factor that Golosov (2016b: 4) finds to be negatively related to vote nationalisation. He posits 'large countries are more likely to develop sub-national bases of party politics than small polities, partly because the populations of large countries exhibit higher levels of diversity, and partly because the territorial structures of large countries tend to be complex'. The underlying idea is that the size of the polity is a proxy for the peripherality of the voters, and in turns, this latter is expected to be negatively associated with vote nationalisation. Yet, preliminary tests have found no impact of the size of the polity on vote nationalisation in my data set, regardless of the measure employed to operationalise this predictor.[4] This reinforces the idea that the 'peripherality' that matters for vote nationalisation is not determined by size or geographical distance, but, instead, by the territorial distinctiveness in terms of cultural cleavages expressed by the peripheral regions of each country (and well captured by the index of cultural segmentation). This explains why large countries in terms of voting population, such as France or Italy, and in terms of physical extension, such as Sweden or Norway, show highly nationalised patterns of electoral support, while small and scarcely populated (but culturally segmented) countries such as Belgium or Switzerland show very denationalised outcomes.

Finally, another factor recently claimed as a potential determinant of vote nationalisation is the economic performance of the country (Lago and Lago 2016; Jurado and Leon 2017). Lago and Lago (2016) argue that the two major groups of determinants emphasised by the literature so far, namely, the institutional characteristics and the structure of cleavages, succeed in accounting for cross-national variations but fail in accounting for the non-negligible short-term variations in the levels of vote nationalisation in a given country. They find evidence of a positive impact of economic performance on vote nationalisation. In their conceptualisation, 'economic hardship increases electoral support for small parties. As small parties are less nationalized than large parties, the consequence is a tendency towards less nationalization of the party system' (Lago and Lago 2016: 413). In other words, the effect of the economy on vote nationalisation is not direct but mediated by party system fragmentation, a factor that I explicitly take into account (H6) and that, according to preliminary evidence in chapter 6, seems to be one of the most important determinants of sPSNS. Yet, surprisingly, they do not include a control for the number of parties in their models, thus what they actually find is a spurious effect. Nonetheless, I have tested the impact of economic performance on vote nationalisation, and I have not found any significant effect.[5]

Still linked to the idea of a role played by the economic factors, De Miguel (2016) argues that the territorial concentration of income, just like that of ethnicity, language or religion, fosters the territorialisation of the party system. I have tested this hypothesis by relying on the same source for the collection of data about the territorial concentration of income in each country[6] and, just as in De Miguel's analysis, I have not found any significant relation with vote nationalisation.

Method

As far as the model specification is concerned, I have provided a detailed discussion in chapter 2, to which I refer now. In a nutshell, I deal with pooled time-series-cross-section (TSCS) data (Beck and Katz 1995; Beck 2001; 2008) with repeated observations over time (elections) on the same fixed units (countries) and specifically with a so-called cross-sectional dominant pool (Stimson 1985), where cross-section units are more numerous than temporal units ($N > T$). In this context, the best method to tackle issues of panel-heteroskedasticity and autocorrelation[7] is the panel-corrected standard errors method (PCSE) with a first-order autoregressive parameter (AR1), namely, the so-called Prais-Winsten regression[8] (Beck and Katz 1995). The PCSE method has already been used by other scholars dealing with the issue of vote nationalisation and faced with a similar data matrix (Harbers 2010; Lago and Lago 2010; Schakel 2012; Su 2017). Moreover, to increase the robustness of the results, the analyses have been replicated by using different models, and the results substantively confirm the findings of the Prais-Winsten regression.[9]

THE GENERAL MODEL

After having excluded potential alternative explanations and having summarised the main methodological issues, by resorting to the general scheme of table 7.1, we are finally ready to discuss the findings of the explanatory analysis. The general model to be estimated is the following:

$$\begin{aligned} \text{sPSNS} = \alpha &+ \beta(\text{Class}) + \beta(\text{Cultural segmentation}) \\ &+ \beta(\text{RAI}_{t-1}) + \beta(\text{EURII}_{t-1}) + \beta(\text{ADM}_{\text{ln}}) \\ &+ \beta(\text{Perc. seats nat.}) + \beta(\text{Personal vote}) \\ &+ \beta(\text{ENEP}) + \beta(\text{TV}) + \beta(\text{Decisiveness}) \\ &+ \beta(\text{CV turnout}) + \text{e}. \end{aligned}$$

Table 7.3 presents the general model (Model 1) and, for the sake of reliability, other six slightly different model specifications. Model 2 adds – as done in previous chapters – a trend variable ('time', operationalised as the number of days elapsed since 1 January 1965) as a control. Model 3 excludes the average district magnitude from the analysis. This variable presents the higher level of multicollinearity in the model, so it is useful to control whether its presence alters the results. Moreover, Models 4 and 5 exclude, one at a time, the other two factors related to the electoral system (i.e., the percentage of seats allocated at the national level and the incentives for cultivating personal vote) that present the highest correlations with the average district magnitude (*see* the previous section). Finally, Models 6 and 7 show the results of the regression obtained by excluding, respectively, the ENEP and decisiveness, whose high level of correlation has been documented in chapter 6.

The results of the general model are simple and clear: out of the eleven potential predictors separately tested in the previous chapters and included in Model 1 of table 7.3, two are by far the most important determinants of sPSNS: cultural segmentation (H2) and party system fragmentation (H6). Both are significant at the highest level of confidence, and this result confirms the preliminary findings obtained in the previous chapters. Both factors exert a constraining effect on the sPSNS, thus fostering a reduction of vote nationalisation as far as they increase. Specifically, cultural segmentation is a

Table 7.3 Vote nationalisation in Western Europe (1965–2015): The general explanatory model

Full data set	*Model 1*	*Model 2*	*Model 3*	*Model 4*	*Model 5*	*Model 6*	*Model 7*
Class	−0.006 (0.005)	−0.005 (0.005)	−0.005 (0.005)	−0.007 (0.005)	−0.007 (0.005)	−0.007 (0.006)	−0.006 (0.005)
Cultural segmentation	−0.065*** (0.012)	−0.063*** (0.011)	−0.064*** (0.012)	−0.066*** (0.011)	−0.066*** (0.011)	−0.074*** (0.015)	−0.065*** (0.011)
RAI	−0.001 (0.001)	−0.001 (0.001)	−0.001 (0.001)	−0.001 (0.001)	−0.001 (0.001)	−0.001 (0.001)	−0.001 (0.001)
EURII	0.000 (0.000)	−0.000 (0.000)	0.000 (0.000)	0.000 (0.000)	0.000 (0.000)	0.000 (0.000)	0.000 (0.000)
ADM (ln)	0.006 (0.006)	0.004 (0.006)		0.007 (0.004)	0.008* (0.004)	0.001 (0.007)	0.006 (0.006)
Perc. seats nat.	0.000 (0.000)	0.000 (0.000)	0.000 (0.000)		−0.000 (0.000)	0.000 (0.000)	0.000 (0.000)
Personal vote	−0.001 (0.002)	−0.001 (0.002)	−0.003* (0.001)	−0.001 (0.002)		−0.002 (0.002)	−0.001 (0.002)
ENEP	−0.020*** (0.003)	−0.021*** (0.003)	−0.019*** (0.003)	−0.020*** (0.003)	−0.020*** (0.003)		−0.021*** (0.003)
TV	0.001* (0.000)	0.001* (0.000)	0.001* (0.000)	0.001* (0.000)	0.001* (0.000)	0.000 (0.000)	0.001* (0.000)
Decisiveness	0.001 (0.008)	0.002 (0.009)	−0.001 (0.008)	0.002 (0.008)	0.001 (0.008)	0.019* (0.008)	
CV turnout	0.000 (0.001)	0.000 (0.001)	0.000 (0.001)	0.000 (0.001)	0.000 (0.001)	−0.000 (0.001)	0.000 (0.001)
Time		0.000 (0.000)					
Constant	0.893*** (0.029)	0.894*** (0.029)	0.909*** (0.022)	0.891*** (0.026)	0.881*** (0.021)	0.828*** (0.033)	0.895*** (0.026)
Wald χ2	206.15***	232.32***	181.83***	204.26***	173.88***	111.10***	210.30***
N elections	225	225	225	225	225	225	225
N countries	16	16	16	16	16	16	16

Note: Prais-Winsten AR1 regression. Panel-corrected standard errors in parentheses.

† $p < 0.1$; * $p < 0.05$; ** $p < 0.01$; *** $p < 0.001$.

standardised variable, and its *b* coefficient of 0.065 means that as far as cultural segmentation increases by one standard deviation, the sPSNS decreases by 0.065, that is, more than half of its standard deviation (0.105). The interpretation of the effect of the ENEP is instead the following: as far as the number of parties increases by one unit, the sPSNS decreases by 0.020. By replicating the analysis by using standardised coefficients (beta), the effect of the ENEP appears powerful, though lower than that of cultural segmentation: an increase of the ENEP by one standard deviation reduces the sPSNS by 0.31 standard deviations.

All the other independent variables turn out to be unrelated to vote nationalisation, except electoral volatility (TV), which shows a positive sign and a statistical significance at the 0.05 level. Indeed, all else being equal, an increase in electoral volatility is associated with a homogenisation process. The analyses performed in chapter 6 have revealed that the effect of volatility is mediated by the cleavage structure of the polity and, more specifically, by the level of cultural segmentation: the more a national context is culturally segmented, the more electoral volatility is associated with a defreezing of the old territorial alignments and, consequently, electoral volatility fosters a homogenisation of party support (H7). Yet, not only is the positive effect of TV very weak, but its impact is also strongly affected by the presence of the ENEP in the regression. As already detected in chapter 6, if the ENEP is excluded (Model 6 in table 7.3), the effect of TV disappears.

The fact that, with the exception of cultural segmentation and ENEP, all the other potential explanatory factors do not significantly affect vote nationalisation should bring us to debunk what has been emphasised so far by the existing literature on the topic. Nonetheless, a careful look at the other model specifications is necessary to obtain a comprehensive picture.

The results of Model 1 are perfectly confirmed by Model 2, where the linear effect of time is taken into account. As expected, time is not related to sPSNS, given that overall vote nationalisation has undergone a steady trend during the past fifty years, without significant patterns of homogenisation or territorialisation.[10] Moreover, the inclusion of this control does not alter the other coefficients. All the other model specifications confirm the robustness of the findings related to both the impact of cultural segmentation and party system fragmentation (that remain significant with a confidence of 99.9 per cent across all the models) and also to the absence of any other explanatory factor with a comparable strength and significance.

In addition, other interesting findings emerge. In Model 3, with the omission of average district magnitude (ADM), the incentives for cultivating personal vote gain a significant predictive power. The direction of this effect is consistent with its related hypothesis (H5): the higher the incentives for cultivating personal vote, the lower the level of vote nationalisation.

Symmetrically, in Model 5, the exclusion of personal vote brings ADM to reach the statistical significance at the 0.05 level. Given the negative correlation between ADM and personal vote ($r = -0.56$), the interplay of these two factors at stake is straightforward: vote nationalisation is higher in countries with high district magnitude and low incentives for cultivating personal vote, and vice versa. Typically, the two extreme poles of an ideal continuum are PR systems with closed lists and majoritarian systems with single-member district (SMD): the former ones provide the highest incentives for parties to ally across districts and for voters to vote according to national stimuli; conversely, the latter ones discourage parties from 'going national' (De Miguel 2016) and increase the incentives for voters to vote according to local factors. Yet, the fact that both variables become significant only when one of the two is omitted is a clear sign that their effect is not robust and that they are associated with each other more than with the *explanandum*.[11]

Finally, Models 6 and 7 control for the collinearity between ENEP and decisiveness ($r = -0.56$). As already shown in chapter 6, the explanatory power of a strong predictor like the effective number of parties comes partly at the expense of other factors related to the structure of the competition. Model 6 confirms this preliminary finding: as the ENEP is omitted, the effect of volatility vanishes and decisiveness becomes significant, showing a remarkable positive impact. Specifically, the sPSNS increases by 0.019 as decisiveness shifts from 0 to 1, that is, when elections become decisive for the future government formation. Conversely, in Model 7, the exclusion of decisiveness does not imply any relevant change for the general model. Contrary to the factors related to the electoral system, here the primacy of the effective number of parties over decisiveness is not questioned: when both factors are taken under control, only the ENEP has a meaningful impact, while decisiveness turns out to be significant only when the ENEP is omitted.

Table 7.4 reports the results of the general model and the other specifications after having replicated the analyses without Belgian elections.

First of all, the omission of Belgium drastically reduces the goodness-of-fit of the model: the Wald Chi-Square decreases from 206.15 to 164.71. This can be partly due to the reduction in the number of degrees of freedom that negatively affects this statistic, but this decrease is also influenced by the impoverishment of the predictors' explanatory capacity once Belgium is excluded.[12]

Second, the two powerful predictors highlighted before, cultural segmentation and ENEP, are still the most important factors in the explanation even if Belgium is omitted. Yet, the macro-constellation becomes more complex, and other factors seem to play a role. In particular, the negative influence of personal vote on the sPSNS is significant across all the different specifications and even when ADM is taken under control. Moreover, other factors

Table 7.4 Vote nationalisation in Western Europe (1965–2015): The general explanatory model (Belgium excluded)

Belgium excluded	*Model 1*	*Model 2*	*Model 3*	*Model 4*	*Model 5*	*Model 6*	*Model 7*
Class	0.004 (0.004)	0.005 (0.004)	0.004 (0.004)	0.005 (0.004)	0.003 (0.004)	0.006 (0.005)	0.004 (0.004)
Cultural segmentation	−0.032*** (0.008)	−0.032*** (0.008)	−0.032*** (0.009)	−0.031*** (0.008)	−0.036*** (0.008)	−0.031*** (0.009)	−0.032*** (0.008)
RAI	−0.001† (0.001)	−0.001* (0.001)	−0.001† (0.001)	−0.001* (0.001)	−0.001 (0.001)	−0.001† (0.001)	−0.001† (0.001)
EURII	0.000*** (0.000)	0.000*** (0.000)	0.000*** (0.000)	0.000*** (0.000)	0.000*** (0.000)	0.000** (0.000)	0.000*** (0.000)
ADM (ln)	0.001 (0.005)	0.001 (0.005)		−0.000 (0.004)	0.010** (0.004)	−0.000 (0.005)	0.002 (0.005)
Perc. seats nat.	−0.000 (0.000)	0.000 (0.000)	−0.000 (0.000)		−0.000 (0.000)	−0.000 (0.000)	−0.000 (0.000)
Personal vote	−0.004* (0.002)	−0.004* (0.002)	−0.004** (0.001)	−0.004** (0.001)		−0.004* (0.002)	−0.004* (0.002)
ENEP	−0.011*** (0.002)	−0.011*** (0.002)	−0.011*** (0.002)	−0.011*** (0.002)	−0.011*** (0.002)		−0.011*** (0.002)
TV	−0.000 (0.000)	−0.000 (0.000)	−0.000 (0.000)	−0.000 (0.000)	0.000 (0.000)	−0.001* (0.000)	−0.000 (0.000)
Decisiveness	0.001 (0.006)	0.002 (0.006)	0.000 (0.006)	0.001 (0.006)	0.004 (0.006)	0.011† (0.006)	
CV turnout	−0.002† (0.001)	−0.001† (0.001)	−0.001 (0.001)	−0.001† (0.001)	−0.002* (0.001)	−0.002* (0.001)	−0.002† (0.001)
Time		0.000 (0.000)					
Constant	0.894*** (0.021)	0.892*** (0.022)	0.899*** (0.016)	0.900*** (0.020)	0.863*** (0.016)	0.857*** (0.022)	0.897*** (0.019)
Wald $\chi 2$	164.71***	175.57***	146.26***	156.75***	159.84***	106.31***	165.35***
N elections	209	209	209	209	209	209	209
N countries	15	15	15	15	15	15	15

Note: Prais-Winsten AR1 regression. Panel-corrected standard errors in parentheses.

† $p < 0.1$; * $p < 0.05$; ** $p < 0.01$; *** $p < 0.001$.

that were irrelevant in the full data set enter the story. Conversely, electoral volatility is irrelevant now, although it shows a negative sign that becomes statistically significant in Model 6 when the ENEP is omitted (as in the bivariate regression in table 7.2).

The effect of European integration shows a positive and statistically significant effect in all the models that exclude Belgium. The size of the *b* coefficient (0.000) must not deceive since it is due to the different range of the EURII (ranging from 0 to 86) compared to that of the sPSNS (0–1). By replicating the analysis with the beta coefficients (not reported), the EURII shows a noticeable size (0.21). This means that, after the exclusion of Belgium, an increase in the European integration is associated with a homogenisation of the territorial patterns of party support. This finding is opposite to the expectation raised by Bartolini (2005) and consistent with Caramani's recently developed theory of the 'Europeanisation of politics' (*see* chapter 5). Another institutional factor, the RAI, and a competition factor, the CV of turnout, become barely significant at the 0.1 level[13] in the data set without the Belgian elections. The sign is negative for both variables, as expected (H3 and H9): on the one side, the more decentralised the country, the more territorialised the party support; on the other side, the higher the territorial variation of turnout levels, the higher the territorial variation of party support. While the link between territorial homogeneity in the levels of electoral participation and in the voting choice has been somewhat neglected by scholars so far (the only exception is Caramani (2004)), the effect of decentralisation has been highly emphasised by the recent literature (Chhibber and Kollman 1998; 2004; Cox and Knoll 2003; Jones and Mainwaring 2003; Brancati 2007; Thorlakson 2007; Harbers 2010; Golosov 2016b). Yet, the result for both variables is modest, and this is another reason to carefully reconsider what has been shown so far by scholars on the topic.

The other factors, class (H1) and the percentage of seats allocated at the national level (H4), are never significant, regardless of model specification and the inclusion of Belgium. Thus, at least regarding Western Europe in the past fifty years, these results reject the emphasis put by scholars on the importance of the class cleavage (Caramani 2004), or, more generally, on social structure (Ersson, Janda and Lane 1985; Knutsen 2010) in the account of vote nationalisation's variance. These results also clearly reject the emphasis on the institutional constraints: not only does regional authority – as stated before – exerts only a modest effect, but also the electoral system's features play a marginal role in the story, unlike what stated by a large strand of literature (Cox 1999; Cox and Knoll 2003; Morgenstern, Swindle and Castagnola 2009; Simón 2013).

In sum, the results of the general model can be synthesised in a formal way through the following regression equation:

$$\begin{aligned} \text{sPSNS} = 0.893 &- 0.065(\text{Cultural segmentation}) \\ &- 0.020(\text{ENEP}) + 0.001(\text{TV}) + \text{e.} \end{aligned}$$

This equation refers to the results presented in Model 1 of table 7.3, concerning the overall universe of elections. By resorting to the model performed with the exclusion of Belgium (Model 1 in table 7.4), the equation is instead a bit more composite:

$$\begin{aligned} \text{sPSNS} = 0.894 &- 0.032(\text{Cultural segmentation}) \\ &- 0.001(\text{RAI}_{t-1}) + 0.000(\text{EURII}_{t-1}) \\ &- 0.004(\text{Personal vote}) - 0.011(\text{ENEP}) \\ &- 0.002(\text{CV turnout}) + \text{e.} \end{aligned}$$

The two equations show a similar value of the constant (0.893–0.894), and this value is by far higher than the overall mean of the sPSNS in the full data set (0.816) or the mean obtained after the exclusion of Belgium (0.839). Given that the constant represents the value of the dependent variable when all the predictors are 0, this is a very important piece of information: the higher level of the constant vis-à-vis the mean value of the sPSNS is a consequence of the fact that the most important explanatory factors of vote nationalisation are negatively related with it. In other words, this information reveals that the model predicts better when vote nationalisation fails rather than when it succeeds. In both equations, the two most important predictors (cultural segmentation and ENEP) are negatively related with sPSNS. This means that the constant of 0.893 (in the full data set) decreases by 0.065 points as cultural segmentation increases by one unit and further by 0.020 for a unitary increase of the ENEP. Moreover, in the model without Belgium, even RAI, personal vote and CV turnout push towards a decrease in sPSNS. Only the feeble effect of electoral volatility in the first equation and that of the EURII in the second equation[14] exerts a positive effect, pushing towards an increase of sPSNS. Another way to interpret the same data is that the residual error in the model (e), including all the latent factors accounting for the portion of unexplained variance, contains some 'homogenising' predictors of territorial party support that have not been considered yet. For instance, within this error term, one may find factors that are difficult to be measured at the systemic level, such as the effect of the information technology revolution on the individual voting choice (Bimber 2001), the increasing personalisation of politics (Karvonen 2010; Garzia 2014) and the role of the media (and especially social media) in electoral campaigns (West 2013), all pushing towards a nationalisation of the electoral competition.

TEMPORAL VARIATIONS

So far the empirical analysis has focused on the identification of the determinants of vote nationalisation in Western Europe over the whole temporal span (1965–2015), regardless of the possible changes occurred over time. It is now time to shed some light on the temporal variations that may have concerned the determinants of vote nationalisation and their relative impact over the past fifty years.

Table 7.5 summarises the results of the Prais-Winsten regressions including, for each period, the general model (Models 1 and 3) and the models with the addition of time as a control (Models 2 and 4).

The first thing to be noticed is that, although the number of cases is definitely lower compared to the general model (it is now equal to 116 observations and 109 observations for, respectively, the first and the second periods), the overall significance is not endangered, and the Wald Chi-Square statistic continues to be significant with a confidence of 99.9 per cent. Yet, a comparison of the models reveals a sharp decrease in the goodness-of-fit of the models between the first and the second period. Moreover, the Wooldridge test of autocorrelation (Drukker 2003) performed on both periods shows that concerns of serial correlation are less serious for the second period.[15]

The lower significance of the models in the last electoral period and the lower serial correlation affecting the past twenty-five years are clear signs that the patterns of vote nationalisation since the 1990s have become less predictable: on the one side, data are somewhat more scattered and less dependent from their own past (as suggested by the lower serial correlation detected by the Wooldridge test); on the other side, the macro-constellation of factors introduced in this book, despite representing a step forward compared to the existing studies (especially because they consider not only societal and institutional predictors but also factors linked to the structure of the competition), left something to be explained yet (as certified by the sharp reduction of the Wald Chi-Square). In other words, as suggested in the previous section, one can infer that there may be some omitted variables in the model that were broadly irrelevant in the past but that have got increasing importance in the last period. Furthermore, on this point, the increase in the value of the constant (from 0.871 in Model 1 to 0.914 in Model 3) witnesses that the ability of the model in explaining why nationalisation fails increases over time, but

Table 7.5 Vote nationalisation in Western Europe (1965–2015): Temporal variations

	Model 1 (1965–1990)	*Model 2 (1965–1990)*	*Model 3 (1991–2015)*	*Model 4 (1991–2015)*
Class	0.002 (0.007)	0.000 (0.007)	−0.024* (0.011)	−0.021† (0.011)
Cultural segmentation	−0.057*** (0.013)	−0.057*** (0.013)	−0.067*** (0.014)	−0.066*** (0.013)
RAI	−0.001 (0.001)	−0.001† (0.001)	−0.001 (0.001)	−0.001 (0.001)
EURII	0.000† (0.000)	0.000† (0.000)	−0.000 (0.000)	−0.000 (0.000)
ADM (ln)	0.025** (0.008)	0.024** (0.008)	0.003 (0.009)	0.003 (0.009)
Perc. seats nat.	−0.000 (0.000)	−0.000 (0.000)	0.000 (0.000)	0.000 (0.000)
Personal vote	0.005* (0.002)	0.005* (0.002)	−0.003 (0.003)	−0.002 (0.003)
ENEP	−0.033*** (0.005)	−0.033*** (0.005)	−0.018*** (0.004)	−0.020*** (0.004)
TV	0.001 (0.001)	0.001 (0.001)	0.001 (0.000)	0.001† (0.000)
Decisiveness	0.016 (0.018)	0.015 (0.018)	0.001 (0.011)	0.003 (0.012)
CV turnout	−0.001 (0.001)	−0.001 (0.001)	0.001 (0.001)	0.001 (0.001)
Time		0.000 (0.000)		0.000 (0.000)
Constant	0.871*** (0.045)	0.871*** (0.045)	0.914*** (0.038)	0.910*** (0.041)
Wald $\chi 2$	342.58***	414.01***	172.14***	188.97***
N elections	116	116	109	109
N countries	16	16	16	16

Note: Prais-Winsten AR1 regression. Panel-corrected standard errors in parentheses.

† $p < 0.1$; * $p < 0.05$; ** $p < 0.01$; *** $p < 0.001$.

at the same time, the model is increasingly unsuccessful in explaining why nationalisation succeeds.

Besides these pieces of evidence, it can be noted that the two fundamental determinants of vote nationalisation, cultural segmentation and party system fragmentation, maintain their explanatory power over time at the highest level of confidence. Notwithstanding this continuity, some elements of change emerge.

During the first period, beyond cultural segmentation and ENEP, other factors show a noticeable effect. In particular, two features of the electoral system, the ADM and the incentives for cultivating personal vote, which were irrelevant in the general model (*see* Models 1 and 2 in table 7.3), are now significant. Contrary to the expectation, personal vote shows a counterintuitive positive sign, which means that the territorial homogeneity of party support is higher in countries with higher incentives for cultivating personal vote. By controlling for the distorting effect of Belgian elections (results not reported), this effect disappears. The pronounced positive effect of district magnitude suggests that, consistent with Morgenstern, Swindle and Castagnola (2009), but contrary to Cox and Knoll (2003), all else being equal, the more proportional the system, the more nationalised the electoral competition. The effect may be partly reinforced by the weak influence exerted by Greece during this period (the country enters the data set for the first time in 1974). Indeed, Greece shows the highest level of nationalisation in Western Europe and a rather disproportional PR system (its unlogged ADM is 5.26 during the 1965–1990 period, more than three times lower than the Western European average). Both the effects of the two electoral systems' variables vanish during the second period and personal vote turns to its expected negative sign. It is plausible to hypothesise that the ADM has increased in certain countries during the past twenty-five years without being accompanied by an increase in nationalisation levels (e.g., Belgium since 2003), or it has decreased in others without fostering a process of denationalisation (e.g., Greece since 2007). At the same time, the increase in the levels of personal vote in countries, such as Austria and Sweden, witnessing a denationalisation process in the last period, or in Belgium, characterised by the lowest level of territorial homogeneity in Western Europe, may account for the negative influence exerted by this variable since the 1990s.

Still, among the institutional constraints, European integration is positively associated with vote nationalisation during the first period, even if only at the 0.1 level. This is because countries that were not members of the European Economic Community (EEC) tended to show lower levels of nationalisation compared to the EEC members. This finding is not surprising if one recalls that some of the most regionalised countries, such as the United Kingdom, Spain and Finland, were not members of the community at the beginning of the period. Then this positive effect reverses since the 1990s, when these countries had already joined the union.

Overall, the institutional factors have undergone a noticeable decline in their explanatory capacity: while almost all of them showed some effects until 1990,[16] none of them is significant from then on. Yet, this decline has not been replaced by other remarkable determinants, and this is a further evidence of the lower explanatory capacity of the model in the past decade. Partial exceptions are represented by electoral volatility, whose positive effect slightly improves over time, and the class cleavage. This latter shifts from positive to negative between the first and the second period. While its positive impact is not significant until 1990, its negative effect becomes significant at the 0.05 level since the 1990s, being eventually reduced once time is taken under control. As we have already noted throughout the book, due to the remarkable decline of its salience in the Western European societies experienced over the past decades, the class cleavage has no longer represented a homogenising factor for the territoriality of party support. The negative relation that appears in Models 3 and 4 can be explained by resorting to Maggini and Emanuele (2015), who argue that as a result of this long-term process of decline, the class cleavage has also become more territorialised, thus ceasing to create functional alignments and to trigger a nationwide electoral competition.

Finally, I have replicated the analysis by period by excluding the Belgian elections. Substantive results are confirmed, including the remarkable reduction of the significance of the models since the 1990s. The main changes concern, consistent with what already shown for the general model in table 7.4, a stronger effect of European integration, RAI and CV turnout during the first period and the significance of the negative effect of personal vote during the second period. Furthermore, for the sake of reliability, I have also replicated the analysis by running five separate regressions, one for each ten-year period.[17] Once again, evidence shows a linear decrease in the significance of the models from the first to the fifth ten-year period, together with an almost linear increase in the value of the constant. As in all the previous models, cultural segmentation and party system fragmentation are the only continuously significant variables throughout the periods. Moreover, as in the separate regressions by period, it is possible to observe a decline over time in the explanatory capacity of the institutional constraints. However, the disaggregation of the data into five periods instead of two obviously brings about a more nuanced and varied picture. First, consistent with Caramani (2004), the effect of class is positive and significant before 1985. Second, cultural segmentation loses strength in the past decade, when its negative effect on the sPSNS is significant only at the 0.05 level. By putting together these two pieces of evidence, we can infer the presence of a decline in the macro-sociological factors that has deep roots in the case of class, while it is a product of the past decade in the case of cultural segmentation. Finally, the effective number of parties, despite the halving of its *b* coefficient (from 0.044 during the period 1965–1974 to 0.022 after 2004), remains the only predictor that stays significant at least at the 0.01 level throughout the fifty-year period.

NATIONAL VARIATIONS

The results discussed so far concern the pooled model and therefore apply to Western Europe as a whole. It would be interesting to focus also on national variations and check if these findings are replicated in each country or whether some countries deviate from the common pattern by showing different factors as important predictors of vote nationalisation. Unfortunately, the number of temporal observations per country (14.4 on average) is too small to run separate regressions for each country. However, something interesting can be said by running separate regressions of the general pooled model (Model 1 in table 7.3) with the adding of a dummy for each country (one country at a time, for a total of sixteen separate regressions). Table 7.6 reports the results of these analyses.

By doing this, it is possible to have a general idea about the consequence for vote nationalisation obtained by taking into account, each time, the effect of being elections occurred in a specific country against of being elections occurred in the rest of Europe. Moreover, the variation in the Wald Chi-Square compared to the general model (Model 1 in table 7.3) tells us how much each country dummy adds to the overall significance of the model. From another perspective, the larger this statistic, the lower the ability of the general model to explain the variance in vote nationalisation in that particular country. Finally, table 7.6 reports also the sign and the level of significance of all the independent variables. By comparing these effects with those of the general model devoid of countries' fixed effects, one can make inferences about the role of individual countries in contributing to the overall significance of a certain predictor or in preventing a factor to reach statistical significance.

Starting from the *b* coefficients of the country dummies, for five countries (Greece, Italy, Norway, Switzerland and the United Kingdom), the respective dummy is not significant, which means that controlling for the specific effect of that country does not add anything to the explanation. Not by chance, even the Wald Chi-Square of these regressions only shows a small increase compared to the general model. Conversely, the dummies for each of the remaining countries, to different extents, all show some influence. For

Table 7.6 Vote nationalisation in Western Europe (1965–2015): National variations

Country	Class	Cult. Seg.	RAI(t–1)	EURII(t–1)	ADM(ln)	% seats nat.	Pers. vote	ENEP	TV	Decis	CV turnout	Country dummy	Δ Constant	Δ Wald χ2
Austria		–***						–***	+*			+**	+0.001	+5.82
Belgium		–***	–†	+**			–*	–***	+†		–†	–***	+0.023	+19.28
Denmark	–†	–***						–***	+**			+***	–0.008	+63.28
Finland		–***						–***	+*			–†	–0.013	+42.35
France		–***						–***	+**			+**	+0.060	+30.65
Germany	–†	–***				+*		–***	+*			–***	+0.016	+150.80
Greece		–***						–***	+*				–0.002	+26.35
Ireland		–***						–***	+*			–*	+0.011	+9.55
Italy		–***						–***	+*				+0.005	–6.86
Netherlands		–***						–***	+**			+†	–0.006	+23.79
Norway		–***						–***	+*				+0.002	+0.26
Portugal	–†	–***						–***	+*			–***	+0.017	+53.50
Spain		–***						–***	+†			+***	–0.037	+13.10
Sweden	–†	–***						–***	+*			+**	–0.000	+33.72
Switzerland		–***						–***	+*				–0.001	+9.84
UK		–***						–***	+*				–0.003	+4.07

Note: Prais-Winsten AR1 regressions performed by running Model 1 in table 7.3 sixteen different times, with the addition of a different country dummy at a time. Variations in the value of the constant and in the Wald Chi-Square with respect to the general model are reported.

† $p < 0.1$; * $p < 0.05$; ** $p < 0.01$; *** $p < 0.001$.

Austria, Denmark, France, the Netherlands, Spain and Sweden, the country dummy has a positive and significant effect, which means that, for instance, by taking into account the effect of being Austrian elections against of being elections occurred in the rest of Europe, the sPSNS increases. Conversely, for Belgium, Finland, Germany, Ireland and Portugal, the country dummy has a negative and significant effect. In this case, by taking into account the effect of, say, being Belgian elections against of being elections occurred in the rest of Europe, the sPSNS decreases. One could be surprised to find a positive effect in the case of a territorialised country (Spain) and vice versa a negative effect in a rather nationalised one (Portugal). This evidence tells us that Spain is more nationalised than what one should expect based on the independent variables in the model: indeed, given that Spain is the most culturally segmented country in Western Europe, with a particularly weak class cleavage and powerful regional authorities, one would have expected a much lower level of sPSNS. Consequently, when the effect of being Spanish elections is taking into account, all else equal, vote nationalisation increases. On the contrary, Portugal, the most culturally homogeneous country in Western Europe, with very weak regional authorities and a limited party system format, should be more nationalised than it actually is. Consequently, when the effect of being Portuguese elections is taken into account, all else equal, vote nationalisation decreases.

Moving to the variation in the Wald Chi-Square, a large variation strikingly emerges when the effect of Germany is taken into account (+150.80). This means that this is the country for which the model provides the worst explanation. Indeed, even more than in the Portuguese case, Germany shows a level of the sPSNS that is lower than what expected based on the predictors considered. As documented in the typology presented in figure 4.4, Germany belongs to the type of nonterritorial heterogeneity, since it shows a high level of cultural heterogeneity without a territorial concentration of the main cultural groups. Consequently, cultural segmentation is on average for the country. Moreover, although the presence of half of the seats in the Bundestag allocated through SMD provides incentives for cultivating personal vote, the distribution of seats to parties occurs at the national level, and this is a factor that should foster a more nationalised competition. Furthermore, as regards the 'political' factors, Germany shows a limited party system format (the ENEP is 3.72 against the average of 4.61 in Western Europe), a homogeneous turnout throughout the country (the CV turnout is 2.97 against the overall mean of 5.53) and elections that are usually decisive for government formation, given that explicit pre-electoral alliances among parties are frequent (decisiveness is 0.75 against a Western European average of 0.57). Yet, Germany shows the third most territorialised party system in Western Europe, and this cannot be entirely explained by the presence of the strongest regional authorities in Western Europe (the *Länder*). These are the reasons why the overall significance of the model largely benefits from the adding of the dummy for Germany.

Finally, some words can be spent by looking at the independent variables in table 7.6. The first thing to say is the robustness of the two most important predictors of sPSNS. Indeed, cultural segmentation and ENEP remain significant at the highest level of confidence in all the sixteen regressions. Conversely, some changes can be noted by looking at electoral volatility. In the general model (table 7.3), TV was significant at the 0.05 level. Here, the models including a dummy for Denmark, France and the Netherlands show a coefficient that is significant at the 0.01 level. These results are interpretable as follows: the effect of volatility is significant at the 0.01 level when the observations of, respectively, Denmark, France and the Netherlands are set at 0. In other words, the increased significance of TV means that in these three countries, electoral volatility is less associated with vote nationalisation compared to the rest of Western Europe. Conversely, an opposite effect is detectable in Belgium and Spain, where, instead, volatility exerts a larger effect on vote nationalisation compared to the rest of Western Europe.

Beyond the differences produced by taking into account the Belgian case, whose effects have been extensively documented elsewhere (*see* in particular table 7.4), very few significant changes compared to the general model can be noted. This is a remarkable indication of the fundamental homogeneity of Western Europe and a further validation of the choice to perform a pooled analysis. The most relevant change vis-à-vis the general model concerns the percentage of seats allocated at the national level (H4) that becomes significant at the 0.05 level once the dummy for Germany is added. In other words, it is the presence of the German case (with its national distribution of seats associated with a markedly regionalised party support) that prevents this variable from playing its positive effect on vote nationalisation. Finally, Denmark, Germany, Portugal and Sweden prevent the class cleavage to be negatively associated with vote nationalisation in the general model. This means that, in these four countries, the class cleavage works in the expected positive direction, thus counterbalancing the negative effect (although significant only at the 0.1 level) observable in the rest of Western Europe.

Chapter 8

Vote (de)nationalisation in Western Europe: Main findings and implications

This book has provided a comprehensive understanding and explanation of the territorial structuring of party support in Western Europe over the past fifty years. The object of this study has been vote nationalisation, conceived as the level of territorial homogeneity of party support and measured through the standardised party system nationalisation score (sPSNS). As emphasised in the Preface, the level of vote nationalisation in a given country has implications that go beyond the mere electoral point of view, involving the representative process, the scope of public policies, the stability of the democratic regime and the unity of the nation-state.

The book has moved from two main research questions. The first investigates the evolution of the vote nationalisation process during the past fifty years. I have tested two rival assumptions: the first derives from Caramani (2004) who assumes that Western European countries have been characterised by a continuing homogenising process of electoral behaviour; the opposite hypothesis, advocated by other scholars (Broughton and Donovan 1999; Hopkin 2003), suggests the idea of a reverse of this historical trend of nationalisation and the resurgence of some territorial distinctiveness leading to the opening of a denationalisation process.

The second research question is connected to an overall explanation of the phenomenon under study. In other words, I have tried to detect the macro-constellation of factors that gives account of the territorial structuring of party support in Western Europe, as well as of its national and temporal variations.

In order to answer the two main research questions, I have carried out a comparative study focusing on the 230 general elections occurred in sixteen Western European countries during the 1965–2015 period. Following a 'macro' perspective, the book has focused on the structural features of the political systems, in the belief that the systemic level of analysis is the best viewpoint to understand structural changes like those related to the territorial configurations of party support.

Empirical evidence has shown that the territorial structuring of party support in Western Europe has been characterised by an enduring stability through time. A steady trend over time is detectable if one considers the entire universe of elections and even dividing them into two meaningful periods (1965–1990; 1991–2015) or five ten-year periods. This finding addresses the first research question, concerning the kind of pattern over time followed by vote nationalisation. Curiously, the two patterns of evolution hypothesised before have not taken place: in the aggregate, neither the pattern of increasing homogeneity nor a reversal trend towards a denationalisation process have occurred.

Yet, this long-lasting stability over time hides a lot of variability in the levels of vote nationalisation both among countries and within them. As far as the first aspect is concerned, some countries show a very high level of vote nationalisation (Greece, Sweden, Denmark and Austria), while some others display markedly regionalised territorial configurations (Switzerland, Germany, Spain and Finland), or even a territorially disintegrated system (Belgium). As regards the national trends over time, some countries, notably Norway, Portugal and Switzerland, have experienced a substantial increase in the territorial homogeneity of party support; some others, such as Belgium, Ireland and the United Kingdom, have shown exactly the opposite trend, that is, a sharp decline in territorial homogeneity since the mid-1960s. Overall, by comparing the beginning and the end of the fifty-year period, the sample of countries is perfectly split into two subgroups: half of them show a higher level of vote nationalisation in 2015 compared to 1965 (or the respective year when the first democratic or postauthoritarian election occurred), while the other half displayed a higher level fifty years ago than today. Chapter 3 has provided a detailed account of these variations (and a detailed country-by-country analysis can be found in the appendix).

The last part of the book (from chapter 4 to chapter 7) has been devoted to answering the second aforementioned research question, namely, to the quest for an explanation of vote nationalisation's variance. Three sets of potential explanatory factors have been identified and empirically tested: macro-sociological determinants (class and cultural cleavages), institutional constraints (decentralisation, European integration and the electoral system's features) and factors related to the structure of the competition (party system fragmentation, electoral volatility, decisiveness of elections and the territorial homogeneity of turnout). Following the existing literature and my own assumptions, I have raised nine hypotheses concerning the impact of these factors on vote nationalisation. By using an estimation method (Prais-Winsten regression with panel-corrected standard errors) able to tackle the usual problems arising with a time-series-cross-section data structure, I have run several analyses to assess the impact of each factor and also its interplay with the other assumed determinants. I have also provided detailed accounts of cross-national and cross-time variations of each explanatory factor, and, by resorting to typologies, I have offered qualitative insights about the relationship at stake between each factor and vote nationalisation.

All these analyses, and especially the regression models, have allowed for a comprehensive understanding of the phenomenon under study and for a satisfactory detection of the determinants that play a significant role in this story against those that have nothing to do with it. A number of remarkable findings have emerged.

First, this study has highlighted the distorting influence exerted over the universe of elections by Belgium, a real outlier whose configuration of party support is by far the most territorialised in Western Europe and whose impact has been accurately taken into account.

Second, the analyses have shown the overall primacy of competition factors in explaining vote nationalisation at the expense of both macro-sociological determinants and institutional constraints. This is a very innovative finding achieved by this work compared to a consolidated literature that has instead emphasised for a long time the impact of social cleavages (Ersson, Janda and Lane 1985; Caramani 2004; Knutsen 2010), or the role of the institutional constraints (Chhibber and Kollman 1998; Cox and Knoll 2003; Morgenstern, Swindle and Castagnola 2009; Simón 2013), widely neglecting the effect of competition factors.

Third, as far as the individual determinants are concerned, the book has primarily clarified which factors are *not* related with vote nationalisation (or play a role only under specific conditions), sometimes disproving long-term consolidated assumptions emphasised by the existing literature on the topic. To begin with, the class cleavage, based on the functional division between the interests of the working class and those of the employers, is no longer a 'homogenising cleavage' (Caramani 2004: 196) as it was in the past, when it created nonterritorial nationwide left-right alignments that translated in nationalised party families (the Social Democratic family and, on the opposite side, the Conservative and the Liberal families). Over the past decades, its hold on the Western European societies has massively declined (Franklin, Mackie and Valen 1992), and the expected positive association between this predictor and vote nationalisation has disappeared.

Moreover, all the institutional factors, the area of research to which scholars focusing on vote nationalisation have paid the larger attention so far, have not proved to be strong predictors of the territorial configuration of party support. In particular, the extent to which a country is decentralised is substantially unrelated to vote nationalisation once the other predictors are taken into account, notwithstanding the emphasis of certain literature (Chhibber and Kollman 1998; 2004; Cox and Knoll 2003; Jones and Mainwaring 2003; Harbers 2010; Golosov 2016b) but consistent with the empirical findings of other scholars (Deschouwer 2009; Lago and Lago 2010; Schakel 2012). Yet, as further analyses carried out in chapter 5 have shown, decentralisation acts as a moderating factor on the impact of cultural cleavages, in the sense that the negative impact of cultural segmentation on vote nationalisation is stronger in decentralised countries. In other words, even if decentralisation does not exert a direct impact on vote nationalisation, it creates a favourable institutional setting for the political expression of culturally heterogeneous minorities. The other institutional constraints play a significant role only under specific conditions. Thus, they should not be considered robust predictors of vote nationalisation. The process of European integration seems to foster the homogenisation of territorial support, consistent with the theory of the 'Europeanisation of politics' (Caramani 2015), but contrasting with Bartolini's expectation of a resurgence of territorial politics fostered by the weakening of the old national centres and the new opportunities granted to the peripheries inside them by the process of European integration. The incentives for cultivating personal vote are instead negatively related with vote nationalisation, following the straightforward idea according to which the higher the incentives for cultivating personal vote, the higher the role played by local stimuli at the expense of national incentives (Simón 2013; Golosov 2016b). However, both the process of European integration and the incentives for cultivating personal vote are associated with vote nationalisation only insofar Belgium is left out from the analysis. Similarly, a large percentage of seats allocated at the national level should provide parties with an obvious incentive to ally across districts in order to become competitive at the national level, where those seats are at stake (Cox 1999; Cox and Knoll 2003). Yet, evidence suggests that the presence of Germany – whose national distribution of seats is associated with a markedly regionalised party support – prevents this variable from playing its positive effect in the pooled model. Additionally, another largely debated institutional constraint, district magnitude – for which I did not raise a specific assumption, given the contrasting opinions among scholars – shows a positive sign. Therefore, as suggested by Morgenstern, Swindle and Castagnola (2009) and others, but contrary to Cox and Knoll (2003), the more proportional the system, the more nationalised the electoral competition. Nonetheless, this effect is significant only during the first period taken into consideration (1965–1990); it disappears in the past decades as well as in the general model including all the elections.

Regarding the factors linked to the structure of the competition, evidence indicates that electoral volatility is positively associated with vote nationalisation, and this effect is reinforced in interaction with cultural cleavages.

Indeed, in contexts characterised by a strong cultural segmentation, the increase in electoral volatility is associated with a defreezing of the old territorial alignments and, consequently, with a homogenisation of party support. Yet, once again, this finding is not very robust, since it is influenced by the presence of Belgium in the models, where a massive denationalisation process is associated with a decrease in the levels of electoral volatility. Once this country is omitted, the detected positive association disappears. Further analyses on the political factors have also clarified that electoral volatility moderates the effect of party system fragmentation on vote nationalisation. As shown in chapter 6, the negative impact of the number of parties on the territoriality of party support becomes lower as far as electoral volatility increases. A similar effect is shown by the interaction between party system fragmentation and the decisiveness of elections for the future government formation. This latter variable was expected to trigger a homogenisation of party support as far as elections become more decisive for government formation. Although a direct effect of this variable is not detected,[1] the decisiveness of elections works as a contextual factor, by lowering the impact of party system fragmentation on vote nationalisation as elections become more decisive for government formation. Finally, the territoriality of voter turnout has largely increased over the past fifty years, but, contrary to what was hypothesised, this has not led to a generalised process of vote denationalisation observable in Western Europe. Therefore, the two processes are not directly associated.

The last remarkable finding is that, over the great bulk of empirical analyses carried out throughout the book, two factors strikingly emerge as the most important determinants of vote nationalisation, showing a powerful impact across different specifications of the models, regardless of temporal and national variations: cultural segmentation and party system fragmentation.

Cultural segmentation refers to two elements: the extent to which a given society is culturally heterogeneous (i.e., formed by different ethnic, linguistic and religious groups) and the extent to which this heterogeneity is territorially concentrated throughout the country. Since Rokkan's path-breaking contribution (1970), cultural cleavages have been considered the main long-term source of deviation from a nationwide electoral competition. More recently, many authors have underlined the persistence of cultural cleavages in shaping a territorially based electoral competition in Western Europe (Caramani 2004; Lago and Lago 2010; Lago 2011; Simón 2013). This book has successfully demonstrated that it is not merely cultural heterogeneity to trigger the territorialisation of party support but the territorial distinctiveness of such heterogeneity. A clear example of this point is provided by the Dutch case: in the Netherlands, the high level of cultural heterogeneity does not translate into a territorially heterogeneous electoral competition, since this heterogeneity is not territorially distinct, that is, each cultural group is dispersed throughout the country (and functionally organised into the respective *zuilen* or pillar). As mentioned earlier, the effect of cultural segmentation is even stronger in contexts of decentralisation with powerful regional authorities. More generally, across all the analyses, cultural segmentation has shown to be the most powerful predictor of the cross-country variation of vote nationalisation: in other words, most of the variance *among* countries in Western Europe is explained by just looking at the extent to which those countries are culturally segmented. Indeed, all the countries with the highest levels of vote nationalisation (Greece, Sweden, Denmark, Austria, Ireland and France) are culturally homogeneous polities; conversely, the two countries with the highest territorial heterogeneity of party support, Belgium and Switzerland, are culturally segmented polities.

Nevertheless, cultural segmentation is a time-invariant factor[2] and cannot account for the variance *within* countries, namely, for the patterns of variation over time in the levels of vote nationalisation followed by each country. This second source of variation is mainly accounted for by party system fragmentation. This factor has been neglected by scholars studying vote nationalisation for a long time, with the only exceptions of the very quick hint suggested by Jones and Mainwaring (2003) and by the recent study by Golosov (2016b), both referring to a different set of cases. The hypothesis concerning party system fragmentation has resorted to a parallelism with the Downsian (1957) spatial model, which has been translated from the ideological to the territorial side, assuming that, as the number of parties in a system increases and the political space for each competitor diminishes, political parties are encouraged to develop strategies of territorial concentration of their support. Specifically, new parties – especially if they are small sized ones – would have a great incentive to pursue a territorial specialisation, in order to build their own electoral strongholds, overcome the threshold of representation and secure some seats. At the same time, established parties, threatened by the new challengers, would aim at reinforcing their electoral strongholds, instead of spreading across the country with the risk of losing votes in their historic bastions. This hypothesis finds strong evidence in the Italian case (Emanuele 2015a), where, after a long period of stability in the territorial patterns of party support, at the end of First Republic the level of fragmentation in the system increases due to the rise of new markedly territorialised parties (above all, the Northern League). In order to fend off the threat carried on by these new parties, the main established political forces develop strategies of territorial concentration of their support. In particular, Christian Democracy, challenged by the Northern League's expansion in its former strongholds (Lombardy and Veneto), undergoes a process of 'southernisation' of its electoral support; similarly, the Communist Party withdraws towards its historic bastions of the so-called Red Belt (Emilia-Romagna, Tuscany, Umbria and Marche).

Beyond the specificity of the Italian case, this hypothesis concerning the negative effect of party system fragmentation finds confirmation in the empirical analysis, since this factor is one of the two most important determinants of vote nationalisation and, more specifically, is a powerful predictor of vote nationalisation trends within each country. Not by chance, the Netherlands and Portugal, showing the strongest increase in vote nationalisation between 1965 and 2015 (respectively, from a sPSNS of 0.725 to 0.881 and from 0.755 to 0.888), are the only two systems where party system fragmentation has decreased over the past fifty years. Conversely, Belgium, where the most spectacular denationalisation process has occurred (from a sPSNS of 0.791 to 0.465 between 1965 and 2014), has experienced a dramatic increase in party system fragmentation (from 4 to 9.6 effective parties). To a lesser extent, in all the other countries undergoing a marked territorialisation of party support in the past fifty years (such as Germany, Ireland and the United Kingdom), the party system has become more fragmented.

As a result, the two most important predictors of vote nationalisation, that is, cultural segmentation and party system fragmentation, are negatively related with the *explanandum*. This means that the general explanatory model is more able to predict when vote nationalisation fails rather than when it succeeds. After the demise of the class cleavage, other powerful structural predictors fostering a nationalisation process have not emerged yet. Neither the process of European integration nor the percentage of seats allocated at the national level and nor the decisiveness of election for the future government formation have proved to be important triggers of the homogenisation of party support. Moreover, party system fragmentation has increased over time. And so do other factors negatively (though significantly only under certain conditions) associated with the outcome, such as decentralisation, incentives for cultivating personal vote and territorial concentration of turnout.

These processes tell us that, during the past decades, most of the factors potentially able to determine a failure of the vote nationalisation process and a resurgence of the territoriality in party support have increased their importance.

Nonetheless, a process of denationalisation has taken place only in some countries so far. This evidence has a possible twofold implication. On the one hand, one can imagine that, if these factors – and especially party system fragmentation – continue to follow this increasing trend also in the next future, the possibility of an overall denationalisation process will be far from unlikely. This outcome, in turn, would be fraught with negative consequences for Western European democracies. The absence of political parties able to represent voters' interests and preferences on a nationwide basis may have implications on the circuit of representation and the policy outcomes (Jones and Mainwaring 2003: 144–45) and eventually on the maintenance of the state (Rose and Urwin 1975: 46). Indeed, recent empirical evidence shows that in denationalised systems, the central government is more likely to focus on targeted and locally oriented expenditures (Castañeda-Angarita 2013; Crisp, Olivella and Potter 2013), to provide worse health services (Hicken, Kollman and Simmons 2016) and to attract lower foreign direct investments (Simmons et al. 2016). Finally, and even more importantly, a denationalised party system may hinder the preservation of democracy (Diamond 1988; Stepan 2001) and may put the unity of the state at serious risk, as shown by the virtual disintegration of the Belgian nation-state (de Winter and Dumont 1999) and by the increasingly supported claims of independence carried out by Scottish and Catalan governments vis-à-vis London and Madrid.

On the other hand, and despite these potential threats, the presence of nationalised electorates and party systems is still the rule in Western Europe. The absence of a generalised trend towards vote denationalisation occurred so far seems to suggest that there may be some homogenising predictors of territorial party support that have not been considered yet. It is plausible that these factors specifically act at the individual level, by pushing voters towards a homogenisation of their demands and preferences, thus determining a nationalisation of the electoral competition that counterbalances the opposite process fostered by the increase in party system fragmentation. The meticulous search for these 'hidden' determinants and a careful analysis of the role played by individual-level factors shall characterise the future research on this topic.

Appendix: Vote nationalisation trends (1965–2015): National variations

This appendix analyses the different patterns of vote nationalisation for each of the sixteen Western European countries included in this study. This country-by-country analysis aims at determining the historical evolution of nationalisation for both the party system as a whole and the main parties of each country.[1] It combines, on the one hand, the macro-level analysis on the territorial configuration of electoral support for each party system and, on the other hand, the party-level analysis on the territorial distribution of votes for each party of the system. Hence, I present a short outline for each country that includes a brief account of the historical roots of the party system and the cleavage constellation by which it has been shaped. Afterwards, I proceed with the evolution of vote nationalisation based on Bochsler's index, in order to discover the specific trends towards either more homogeneous or more heterogeneous territorial configuration followed by each party system over time. Finally, I report the level of territorial homogeneity of each party by reporting in summary tables the sPNS scores for the whole time span and for the two periods in which the temporal span has been divided (1965–1990; 1991–2015).

AUSTRIA

The origins of the postwar Austrian party system are rooted in the constitution of two extra-parliamentary movements at the end of the nineteenth century, under the former Austro-Hungarian Empire. They were both organised around a distinct political subculture or *Lager* (Luther 1999: 119): the Christian Social Party and the Social Democratic and Workers Party, respectively, forerunners of today's Austrian People's Party (henceforward ÖVP) and

Social Democratic Party of Austria (SPÖ), the two main parties of the whole postwar period.

The Austrian party system is based on cross-cutting cleavages, not directly linked to a territorial dimension: the state-church one and the capital-labour one, with the Catholic subculture representing the clerical side and the socialist *Lager* being the expression of workers' claims and a secular vision of politics. However, the structuring of these cleavages contains a certain degree of territoriality because of a clear urban-rural conflict that did not give origin to specific parties for the defence of agrarian interests, as it happened in Scandinavian countries or Switzerland. The urban-rural cleavage was instead subsumed under the main cultural and socioeconomic opposition between ÖVP, supported by the rural peasantry, farmers and landowners, with a territorially concentrated backing in the Catholic regions of Tyrol and Vorarlberg and rural Lower Austria, and SPÖ, particularly strong among the secular urban proletariat of Vienna.[2] The two parties established mass organisations and a myriad of *Lager*-specific occupational, educational and cultural associations to mobilise their electorate and develop partisan attachment and specific '*Lager* mentalities' (Plasser, Ulram and Grausgruber 1992). That is why many authors talk about the 'pillarisation'[3] of the Austrian society. ÖVP and SPÖ soon developed as successful mass membership parties, with the highest levels of party membership of the entire Western World (Beyme 1985; Müller 1992), with an organisational density (members of a party as a proportion of the total electorate) which was between 25 and 30 per cent until 1990. The two parties together received more than 90 per cent of the votes until the mid-1980s, thus narrowing the electoral market and leaving very little room to third parties and challengers. Even if the Austrian party system has often been classified as an example of two-party system (Blondel 1968: 184), the 'politics of accommodation'[4] by the two parties and their propensity to share the power and govern together in oversized coalitions (from 1949 to 1966 and again, after a decade of Socialist's absolute majority during the 1970s, from 1986 to 1999) led Sartori (1976: 189) to conclude that the country was 'the very negation of the "spirit" of twopartism', being rarely characterised by single-party government and alternation, typical elements of a two-party competition. Austria was instead a classic case of consensual democracy (Lijphart 1999).

Sartori's intuition is also particularly suitable to explain the party system evolution that started in the mid-1980s. The party system witnessed growing dealignment, the emergence of new parties and, since the beginning of the 1990s, the dramatic rise of the former liberal Freedom Party of Austria (FPÖ) that shifted to right-wing populist positions under the leadership of Jörg Haider. The FPÖ has been the third Austrian party for the whole postwar period, the only one besides ÖVP and SPÖ contesting all the fifteen elections falling into the temporal span of this analysis (1965–2015). It formed the so-called third *Lager*, with an appeal to the liberal urban bourgeoisie and those not incorporated into the Socialist and Catholic-Conservative subcultures. However, it only obtained a minority support until the 1983 elections. Then, since 1986, under Haider's new leadership, the party has sharply increased its electoral strength, gaining more than 20 per cent of the votes between 1994 and 1999 (and again in 2013). The formation of the black-blue coalition in 1999 (from the distinctive colours of the two parties, respectively ÖVP and FPÖ) is generally considered a remarkable turning point in the history of Austrian party system (Müller and Fallend 2006: 288): for the first time since World War II, a new party entered the government and structured a bipolar competition, based on the opposition between the centre-right government (ÖVP and FPÖ) and the centre-left minority (SPÖ and the Green party, born in 1986).

During the past years, SPÖ and ÖVP have declined (for the first time in the 2008 general election they jointly collected less than 30 per cent of the votes) and new relevant political forces have emerged: among them we find the centrist Liberal Forum (LIF, NEOS since 2013), the Alliance for the Future of Austria (BZÖ), founded in 2005 as a moderate splinter from the FPÖ by Haider himself, and finally the Team Stronach, a populist personal party launched in view of the 2013 election by the businessman Franck Stronach.

Figure A.1 plots the values of vote nationalisation for the fifteen Austrian general elections occurred from 1965 to 2015. Austria belongs to the group of highly nationalised systems, with a mean sPSNS value of 0.877, well above the average of the entire data set (0.816). As long as the party system has been structured around the opposition between SPÖ and ÖVP, the differences in the territorial configurations of support among the various regions of the country have not substantially affected the systemic values of vote

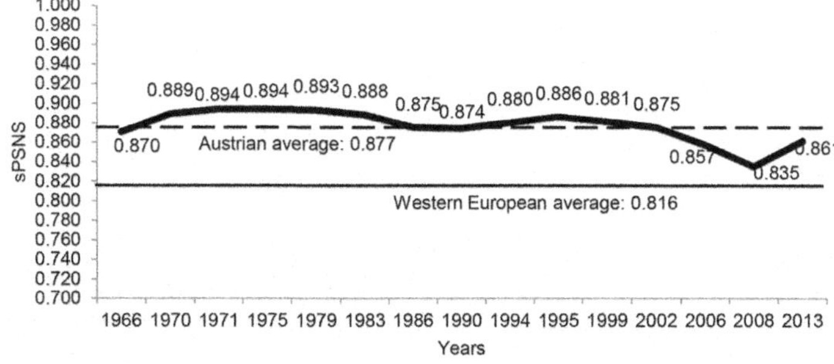

Figure A.1 Evolution of vote nationalisation over time, Austria 1966–2013

nationalisation so that the level of vote nationalisation until 1999 has been noticeably stable.

During the 2000s, Austria has experienced a sharp denationalisation of the vote, with the coefficients of Bochsler's index that have dropped up to 0.835 in 2008, with a small upward reversal in 2013. The decrease in the homogeneity of party support has been simultaneous to the electoral decline of the two main parties and the entry of new parties into the electoral arena.

Moving down to the level of individual parties, the biggest political force of the Austrian party system, the SPÖ (averaging a vote share of 40.7 per cent between 1966 and 2013) is also the most nationalised party, with a mean sPNS of 0.906 (*see* table A.1), which remains perfectly constant over time in spite of its electoral decline (the Socialists halved their vote share between 1979 and 2013). The second-largest party, the Catholic ÖVP, is also quite nationalised (mean 0.873), even if it has been faced with a slight decrease of homogeneity of the electoral support since the beginning of the 1980s.

Table A.1 Austrian parties: Mean share of votes and mean sPNS by electoral period, 1966–2013

	1965–1990		*1991–2015*		*1965–2015*		
*Party**	*% Votes*	*sPNS*	*% Votes*	*sPNS*	*% Votes*	*sPNS*	*N*
Social Democratic Party of Austria (SPÖ)	47.0	0.908	33.4	0.903	**40.7**	**0.906**	**15**
Austrian People's Party (ÖVP)	42.2	0.886	29.9	0.859	**36.5**	**0.873**	**15**
Freedom Party of Austria (FPÖ)	7.4	0.729	18.6	0.888	**12.6**	**0.803**	**15**
The Greens (GRÜNE)	4.8	0.799	9.0	0.819	**8.1**	**0.814**	**9**
Liberal Forum (LIF)			4.4	0.767	**4.4**	**0.767**	**5**
Alliance for the Future of Austria (BZÖ)			6.1	0.629	**6.1**	**0.629**	**3**
Tot. Austria	_	**0.885**	_	**0.868**	_	**0.877**	**15**

Note: In 2013 LIF joined the NEOS (The New Austria and Liberal Forum) electoral alliance, whose score is computed in the LIF's row.

* Other five parties fit the criteria only in one election.

During the same years, the third-largest party, the FPÖ, shifted from liberal to right-wing populist positions and started to increase its electoral strength, spreading throughout the country and going from a markedly regionalised distribution (0.651 in 1966) – with strong backings in Carinthia and Salzburg – to the most homogeneous configuration in the country (0.938 in 2013), thus becoming even more nationalised than SPÖ and ÖVP.

The other parties show lower levels of sPNS. The Greens is a quite homogeneous party, with a significant concentration in Vienna and the small region of Vorarlberg, a former ÖVP's stronghold. All the other minor parties show a mean vote nationalisation lower than 0.800, with the BZÖ particularly supported in Carinthia (a former liberal stronghold) and the LIF receiving most of its support in Vienna and Vorarlberg.

BELGIUM

Belgium is certainly the Western European country where territory plays the most important role in shaping the party system so that Caramani (2004: 121) describes it as having 'two party systems', since all the Belgian political forces are split along the linguistic division between a Flemish and a Walloon part. A Walloon voter and a Flemish voter find two entirely different electoral supplies on the ballot paper for the same election,[5] thus configuring a perfect example of what Marsh (2002: 207) calls 'global effect'.[6]

Nevertheless, the linguistic cleavage, which has become so relevant in the past decades, was not the founding cleavage from which the first Belgian parties originated at the end of the nineteenth century.

Since 1830, when Belgium gained independence from the Netherlands, the central core of nation-builders has been an alliance between different groups of the French-speaking upper classes: the francophone elite of Flanders and the urban bourgeoisie of Wallonia. The Dutch-speaking Flemish region was poor and agricultural, while the French-speaking Wallonia was rich and highly industrialised. French became the official language of the state, and Brussels, a former Flemish city situated inside the Flemish territory, was chosen as the new administrative and political capital and gradually became a French-speaking city. Since the political elites were all French speakers, the 'centre' of the system was identified with the Walloon region and with Brussels, while Flanders remained politically, economically and culturally peripheral. Therefore, the oldest cleavages in Belgian politics developed inside the alliance of urban nation-builders, divided between the Catholic and the anticlerical and Liberal sides, represented, respectively, by the Christian Social Party (PSC) and by the Liberal Party, later renamed Party for Freedom and Progress (PLP).[7] 'This denominational confrontation also had a regional flavour, with a very Catholic Flanders, and a Wallonia and Brussels in which anti-clerical tendencies had more success' (de Winter and Dumont 1999: 186–87).

The third historical party of Belgium, the Socialist Party (PS), stemmed from the class cleavage and originated in Wallonia, one of the most industrialised regions of Europe. The PS was particularly rooted among the Walloon industrial districts of Hainaut and Liege, the so-called industrial furrow (Frognier, Quevit and Stenbock 1982: 261), while the Catholic Flanders remained dominated by the Catholic Party. Both the Socialists and the Catholics were able to organise by creating a wide spectrum of sociocultural collateral organisations, thus developing two densely organised subcultures or 'pillars'[8] (de Winter and Dumont 1999: 191). This process was conducted at the expense of the Liberals, which lacked a structured organisation and started to experience an electoral decline. Therefore, traditional Belgian parties are so deeply rooted in the society that scholars define Belgian politics as a case of *particracie*, just like the Italian *partitocrazia* (Dewachter 1987: 285).

Since the end of the nineteenth century, and until the emergence of the regional cleavage, the Belgian party system was organised along mainly functional lines of opposition (the state-church and the class conflict). There was a stable three-party system[9] with the three core parties collecting together about 90 per cent of the national votes in the lower chamber, elected with a PR system.

The situation radically changed during the 1950s, when the centre-periphery cleavage found political expression. The political changes were preceded by radical socioeconomic ones: from 1945, Flanders started a sharp economic growth, attracting new small and medium-sized enterprises and multinationals, whereas Wallonia, whose economy was based on heavy industry, slowly began to deindustrialise and decline (de Winter and Dumont 1999: 196). As a consequence, the historical 'regional imbalance' (Frognier, Quevit and Stenbock 1982: 274) was completely reversed, with the former peripheral Flemish region gaining a stronger economic position. Even from a cultural point of view, the Flemish language, spoken by the overall majority of Belgian citizens (about 58 per cent, against 42 per cent of French speakers), became the current language of the Flanders elites, and the 'frenchification' of the region was stopped by the linguistic laws of 1963.

This reversal in the centre-periphery relations provided the basis for some dramatic changes in the party system. First, the emergence (1954) and the first electoral breakthrough (1961) of a Flemish nationalist party, People's Union (VU); second, the emergence of Walloon (Walloon Rally, RW) and Brussels francophone (Democratic Front of the Francophones, FDF) regionalist parties, born as a 'reaction of the francophone population to the growing grip of the Flemish on the Belgian state' (de Winter and Dumont 1999: 188);

third, the break-up of the three traditional parties along linguistic lines. In 1968, the Catholics split between the Flemish and Walloon wing, followed by the Liberals in 1974 and by the Socialists in 1978.

Since the beginning of the 1980s, some new parties have entered into the electoral arena: the ecologist issues found political expression through the rise of two green parties (the Flemish *Agalev*, renamed *Groen!* since 2003, and the Walloon *Ecolo*); on the Flemish side, there has been the emergence of a new, far-right ethnic and nationalist party, the Flemish Interest, later renamed Flemish Block (VB), that has further contributed to widening the ideological polarisation of the system. In Belgium, like in some other segmented societies (like Switzerland and the Netherlands), but with some additional problems of accommodation, all these potential disruptive divisions are composed through a prevalent consensual style of politics and the search for compromises in surplus coalition governments including an equal number of Dutch-speaking and francophone ministers. The 1993 constitutional reform created a federal state, which consists of three regions (the Flemish, the Walloon and the Brussels ones) and three language communities (the Dutch, the French and the German-speaking[10] ones) (Fabbrini 2008: 183; Hooghe, Marks and Schakel 2010: 135). Despite all these formal and informal tools to mitigate contrasts, the system still seems 'on the eve of disintegration' (de Winter and Dumont 1999), and the new record-breaking 541 days occurred to form a new government after the 2010 election witnesses the growing problems of coexistence among the different, segmented parts of Belgian politics.

As shown in chapter 3, the territorial configuration of Belgium represents a real outlier in the Western European landscape. With a mean sPSNS of 0.519, Belgium is by far the less nationalised country in Western Europe. Furthermore, it also shows the greater level of instability through time (*see* figure 3.3). The period covered starts in 1965, the last election with the three major parties still united. The overall level of nationalisation was that of a normal regionalised polity (0.791), higher than the mean score of Germany, Spain and Finland. The split of the Christian Democrats in 1968 marks the beginning of a ten-year period of dramatic denationalisation: Belgium shifts from 0.791 to 0.441 (1978), nearly halving its former level of territorial homogeneity. The following period, from 1978 to 2014, is instead characterised by a substantive stability of the index, with a slight tendency towards homogenisation (*see* figure A.2).

Table A.2 summarises the mean vote share and the mean nationalisation score, by period. All parties fitting the two criteria for inclusion (3 per cent nationwide or 4 per cent in at least one territorial unit) show an average level of nationalisation lower than 0.570, with the obvious exception of the three main parties before the linguistic split. Paradoxically, the most nationalised party appears the ethnoregionalist People's Union (VU) (0.570) and its

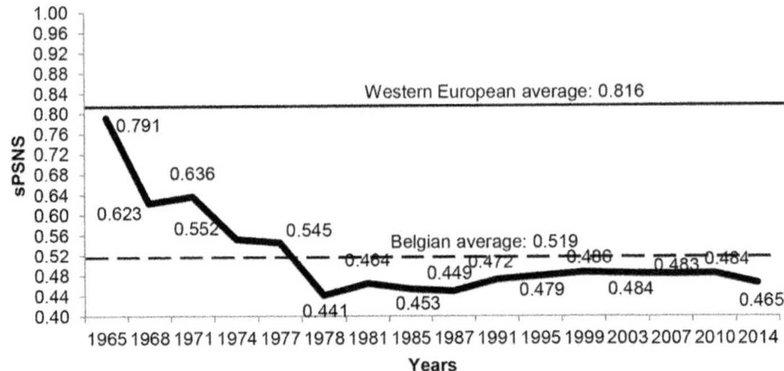

Figure A.2 Evolution of vote nationalisation over time, Belgium 1965–2014

Table A.2 Belgian parties: Mean share of votes and mean sPNS by electoral period, 1965–2014

	1965–1990		*1991–2015*		*1965–2015*		
*Party**	*% Votes*	*sPNS*	*% Votes*	*sPNS*	*% Votes*	*sPNS*	*N*
Catholic Party (Flanders)	20.3	0.490	14.6	0.572	**17.6**	**0.528**	**15**
Catholic Party (Wallonia)	10.3	0.379	6.2	0.318	**8.4**	**0.351**	**15**
Unified Catholic Party	34.5	0.798			**34.5**	**0.798**	**1**
Socialist Party (Flanders)	12.5	0.506	11.0	0.555	**11.6**	**0.538**	**11**
Socialist Party (Wallonia)	14.8	0.346	12.1	0.318	**13.1**	**0.328**	**11**
Unified Socialist Party	27.3	0.847			**27.3**	**0.847**	**5**
Liberal Party (Flanders)	9.6	0.457	12.1	0.563	**11.0**	**0.514**	**13**
Liberal Party (Wallonia)	8.7	0.372	10.3	0.368	**9.5**	**0.370**	**13**
Unified Liberal Party	19.6	0.835			**19.6**	**0.835**	**3**
People's Union (VU)	9.0	0.562	5.4	0.593	**8.1**	**0.570**	**12**
Agalev/Groen!	3.3	0.461	4.6	0.555	**4.2**	**0.527**	**10**
Ecolo	2.8	0.396	4.7	0.356	**4.1**	**0.368**	**10**
FDF/RW	6.1	0.281	1.6	0.226	**5.2**	**0.270**	**10**
Flemish Interest (VB)			8.5	0.549	**8.5**	**0.549**	**7**
Communist Party (PCB)	3.2	0.555			**3.2**	**0.555**	**6**
National Front (FN)			1.9	0.308	**1.9**	**0.308**	**4**
New Flemish Alliance (N-VA)			13.6	0.572	**13.6**	**0.572**	**2**
List Dedecker (LDD)			3.2	0.472	**3.2**	**0.472**	**2**
Belgium	_	**0.550**	_	**0.479**	_	**0.519**	**16**

* Other seven parties fit the criteria only in one election.

successor, New Flemish Alliance (N-VA), the largest party in the last two elections (0.572). In general, Flemish parties, which contest seats in the five provinces of Flanders and the capital, display a Bochsler's index around 0.510–0.570, while the Walloon parties, contesting seats in the five provinces of Wallonia and Brussels, show much lower results (around 0.310–0.370).

The Catholic Party was the largest political force before the split and also the less nationalised among the traditional parties (34.5 per cent and 0.791 in the sole election included here, that of 1965). Its electoral strength was higher in Flanders, as the results after the split reveal: the Flemish wing continued to be the largest party of the segmented party system, although it experienced a sharp decline through time (from 20.3 per cent to 14.6 per cent between the first and the second periods). A similar decline has been undergone by the French-speaking Catholic wing, whose electoral strength is less than half of the Flemish counterpart: the Walloon wing has strong roots only in the province of Luxembourg, while the Flemish one is more homogeneously distributed (except the Brussels area, where the party is very weak).

The Socialist Party was the second-largest party before the split, and its Walloon wing has remained the largest force in the French-speaking region, with a national mean of 13.1 per cent, even higher than that of its Flemish counterpart (11.6 per cent). This is a unique case among the Belgian parties, since the Walloon parties can be voted only by about 40 per cent of the Belgian population. Today the Walloon Socialist party has still been dominant in the former heavily industrialised districts of Liege, Hainaut and Namur, while the Flemish wing is rooted in Leuven (the Dutch-speaking part of Brussels region) and Limburg.

The Liberals are the only traditional force that has increased its electoral strength through time. Moreover, the Walloon wing is the dominant force in the Brabant Walloon (the French-speaking area of the Brussels region), while in the capital, the two parties considered together often get the relative majority.

Finally, the Flemish nationalist parties (VU, VB and N-VA) show a relatively high level of homogeneity. The core of the regionalist claims is Antwerp.

DENMARK

Denmark can be defined as a homogeneous country: no significant ethnic, religious, regional or linguistic differences exist (Bille 1992: 199). Thus, the first political parties, appeared during the second part of the nineteenth century, stemmed from the two cleavages of the Industrial Revolution: primarily the socioeconomic opposition between owners and workers and, to a lesser extent, the urban-rural cleavage. This latter consisted in the struggle by the strong and organised association of the Danish farmers against the process of urbanisation of the country and the policy of incentives to free trade of primary commodities granted by the urban ruling elites.

Like other Scandinavian countries, the Danish party system that emerged at the end of the nineteenth century was based on the opposition between the Liberals (the Left or *Venstre*) and the Conservatives (*Hojre*, since 1915 renamed Conservative People's Party, DKF). They both were bourgeois parties but with different connotations. The *Venstre* grew up as the representative of the farmers' interests and was rooted in the rural areas of West and North Jutland. However, until 1905, it also maintained a significant urban support among the radical and secularised petty bourgeoisie. Conversely, the Conservatives represented the party of the ruling classes, with a concentrated support in Copenhagen and the other urban districts of the country (Bille 1992).

The emergence of the Social Democratic Party (SD) changed the original structure of the competition, pushing the Liberals to cooperate with the Conservatives to restrain the socialist advance. Supported by the strong labour movement, the Social Democratic Party soon became the predominant party of the system, with a highly nationalised territorial configuration. Nevertheless, it never obtained an absolute majority in the *Folketing* (the Danish unicameral Parliament), unlike its Norwegian and Swedish counterparts. For this reason, since the 1920s, it has often formed single-party minority governments, with the external support of other parties, or coalition minority governments, usually in cooperation with the Social-Liberal Party (RV) (Bille 1992). This latter was founded in 1905 by a splinter group from the Liberal party. As reported by Rokkan (1970: 128), it consisted of urban radicals that came into conflict with the predominantly agrarian-based *Venstre*.[11] The Social-Liberal Party represented the smaller of the four 'old parties' of the original Danish party system that stabilised at the beginning of the 1920s, according to the Lipset and Rokkan's (1967) freezing hypothesis.

At the left of the Social Democrats, since 1919 the small Communist Party (DKP) remained a minor and antisystem force, always excluded from the government. In 1959, the chairman of the party, advocating a third road to socialism and looking for a cooperation with the Social Democrats, founded the Socialist People's Party (SF) that soon received a significant share of the popular vote (10.9 per cent in 1966), thus becoming an important actor of the party system.[12] From then on, a clear alignment of the parties into a socialist and a nonsocialist bloc can be discerned (Borre 1992: 145).

The party system underwent a dramatic change in the earthquake election of 1973. In the wake of a heated debate about the country's accession to the European Economic Community (EEC), the four old parties dropped their electoral support from 84 per cent to 58 per cent. The number of parties gaining seats in the Folketing increased from five to ten, and since then, it has not been less than eight. Three new parties emerged: the Christian Democrats (KD), founded in 1970 among the revivalist and nonconformist churches' adherents of North and West Jutland as a reaction to the general moral decay and disintegration of traditional Christian norms emanating from the '1968 rebellion' (Karvonen 1993); the Centre Democrats (CD), a rightist splinter of the Social Democrats which soon became a genuine centre party, open to alliances and agreements with both blocs; and, eventually, the Progress Party (FRP), an extreme-right-wing populist party with a charismatic leadership, risen as the second-largest party in 1973 and later declined during the 1980s.

After these notable changes, the ideological space of the party system has expanded, and the traditional party cooperation has been shaken (Bille 1992: 200–201). Yet, Danish politics has remained quite predictable: the party system has continued to be oriented on a one-dimensional line of competition based on the bipolar opposition between the Social Democrats-led bloc and the Liberals-led bloc.[13] In this context, all parties, including the new ones,[14] can be located on the left-right spectrum; moreover, both 'the socialist and the bourgeois side have succeeded in maintaining so a stable balance over the long run in the face of important changes in social structure as well as in political values' (Borre 1992: 146).

From the territorial point of view, Denmark is a highly homogeneous country, confirming Caramani's findings (2004: 136). With a mean sPSNS of 0.883, Denmark is the third-most nationalised country after Greece and Sweden. Figure A.3 plots the evolution of vote nationalisation over the eighteen elections included into the time span covered by the current research. An irregular but continuous path of increasing homogenisation can be clearly distinguished: the Bochsler's index goes from 0.856 in the first election under study (1966) to the highest peak of 0.909 in the 2001 election. Hence,

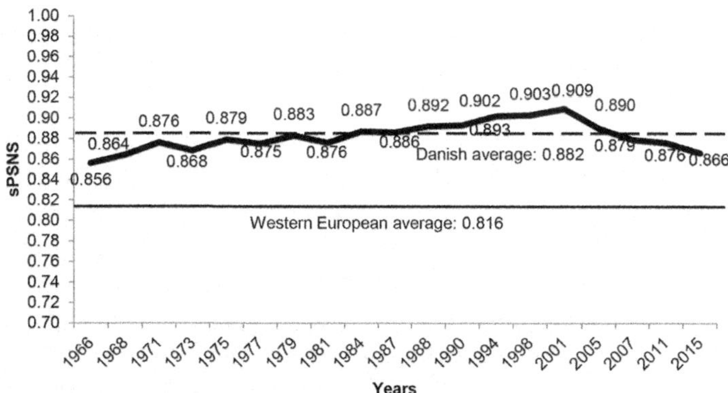

Figure A.3 Evolution of vote nationalisation over time, Denmark 1966–2015

the nationalisation trend has seemingly not been affected by the earthquake election of 1973. Finally, during the past decade, the country has started an inverse process of vote reterritorialisation, as the nationalisation index has gone down for the last four consecutive elections, up to the 0.866 score of the 2015 election, the lowest level since 1968.

The Social Democratic Party is by far the most nationalised one, with a mean sPNS of 0.940, that remains virtually constant over time, in spite of its slight electoral decline. Due to the almost perfect territorial homogeneity, it is hard to identify areas of relative strength or weakness, except Copenhagen and the neighbouring province of North Zealand, where the party receives many fewer votes than its national mean.

Unlike the other Scandinavian countries, in Denmark the largest party of the bourgeois bloc is not the Conservative but the Liberal *Venstre*. Its mean sPNS is very low compared with the other national parties, since it reflects the agrarian origins of the party, which were clearly visible during the first decades under study: the electoral strongholds of *Venstre* were the predominantly rural districts of North and West Jutland (*Ribe, Ringkoebing, Viborg* and *Nordjyllands*), while in the capital as well as in the urban districts surrounding it (*Soendre, Oestre, Vestre*) the party was virtually irrelevant. During the last period, in the wake of its electoral upsurge, the party has undergone a sharp process of nationalisation (from 0.774 to 0.879), thereby losing much of its former heterogeneity.

The historical bourgeois party, the Conservative People's Party (DKF), appears as extremely homogeneous (mean sPNS of 0.889) during the whole time span, with only a slight decline in the last period, where it has experienced an electoral collapse (from 23.4 per cent in 1984 to 3.4 per cent in 2015). According to its origins as a party of the urban ruling classes, the DKF receives the largest support from the Copenhagen district.

The last two parties contesting each of the nineteen elections of the period are the highly nationalised Social-Liberal Party (DK) (a mean of 0.878) that receives relatively more support from the capital and the Socialist People's Party (SF) that instead shows a much more regionalised territorial configuration (a mean of 0.823) but with the same bias towards Copenhagen and the surrounding urban region. However, these two parties have experienced two opposite trends: while DK has undergone a process of denationalisation since the end of the 1990s, the Socialist People's Party has followed a continuous trend of homogenisation since the 1960s so that today the former party has by far a more heterogeneous territorial configuration than the latter one.

All the other parties included in table A.3 appeared in 1973 or later. Among them, the Centre Democrats (0.890) and the Liberal Alliance (0.870) as well as the extreme-right parties like the Progress Party (with the exception of the 1995 election) and especially the Danish People's Party are very

Table A.3 Danish parties: Mean share of votes and mean sPNS by electoral period, 1966–2015

	1965–1990		*1991–2015*		*1965–2015*		
Party	*% Votes*	*sPNS*	*% Votes*	*sPNS*	*% Votes*	*sPNS*	*N*
Social Democratic Party (SD)	33.5	0.945	28.9	0.941	**31.8**	**0.940**	**19**
Liberal Party (*Venstre*)	14.6	0.774	25.7	0.879	**18.7**	**0.812**	**19**
Conservative People's Party (DKF)	15.4	0.899	8.9	0.871	**13.0**	**0.889**	**19**
Socialist People's Party (SF)	8.8	0.796	7.7	0.870	**8.4**	**0.823**	**19**
Social-Liberal Party (RV)	7.5	0.904	6.0	0.833	**6.9**	**0.878**	**19**
Progress Party (FRP)	9.8	0.882	4.4	0.776	**8.8**	**0.863**	**11**
Christian Democrats (KD)	3.2	0.736	2.0	0.779	**3.0**	**0.745**	**9**
Centre Democrats (CD)	5.9	0.886	4.3	0.921	**5.7**	**0.890**	**8**
Red-Green United List	1.7	0.674	4.0	0.719	**3.7**	**0.714**	**8**
Danish People's Party (DF)			13.3	0.908	**13.3**	**0.908**	**6**
Left Socialists (VS)	2.6	0.684			**2.6**	**0.684**	**5**
Communist Party (DKP)	3.3	0.738			**3.3**	**0.738**	**4**
Liberal Alliance			5.1	0.870	**5.1**	**0.870**	**3**
Schleswig Party	0.2	0.061			**0.2**	**0.061**	**2**
The Alternative			4.8	0.716	**4.8**	**0.716**	**1**
Denmark	_	**0.878**	_	**0.889**	_	**0.882**	**19**

homogeneously distributed (the latter one is indeed the second-most nationalised party after the Social Democrats). Some others show more regionalised configurations: the leftist Communist Party (0.738), Left Socialists (0.684) and Red-Green United List (0.714) as well as the newly emerged green party (The Alternative) display a particularly concentrated support around the urban area of Copenhagen, while the Christian Democrats (0.745) receives most of its votes from the provinces of western and northern Jutland (*Ringkoebing* and, to a lesser extent, *Viborg* and *Ribe*) and in the small island of Bornholm.

Finally, table A.3 reports the scores of the ethnoregionalist Schleswig Party, the party of the German-speaking minority concentrated in the province of South Jutland, the only one where it contested seats. It succeeded to reach 4 per cent in that constituency twice, in the 1968 and the 1971 elections. Obviously, its mean score approaches the lower limit of the index (0.061).

FINLAND

The genesis of the Finnish party system has been strongly affected by the initial condition of Finland as 'an interface periphery' (Alapuro 1982: 113) influenced by two dominant external centres of power, Sweden and Russia.

The heritage of the Swedish domination created the most divisive cleavage of Finnish politics until the rise of the Industrial Revolution: the linguistic division between the Swedish-speaking minority, predominant among the ruling classes and in general in the southwestern urban areas, and the Finnish-speaking majority. This cleavage gave rise to the Swedish People's Party (RKP), an ethnolinguistic force with a liberal-conservative ideology, whose support declined during the twentieth century together with the decrease of the Swedish-speaking share of population (from 14.3 per cent in 1880 to 7.4 per cent in 1960, as reported by Allardt and Pesonen (1967: 332)).

The other two major cleavages (capital-labour and urban-rural ones) developed during the nineteenth century, as Finland experienced a sharp process of industrialisation linked to the lumber trade and the internal migration from the northern and eastern rural peripheries (Lapland, Oulu, Karelia) to the urbanised areas of the Southwest, where the most populated cities are located (Helsinki, Turku, Tampere). A Social Democratic Party (SDP) emerged in 1899 and soon spread its support across the country, becoming the largest party of the system. It faced the opposition of two other important parties: the Agrarian Party (renamed Centre party, KESK, in 1965), deeply rooted among the farmers of the North and East, and the Conservative National Coalition Party (KOK), whose support was (and is still today) concentrated among the ruling classes and the white collars in the urban areas of the Southwest (particularly in Uusimaa, the province surrounding Helsinki) and in Ostrobothnia. The latter was a region characterised by a strong conservative subculture, and it assumed an active role under the Civil War of 1918, becoming the stronghold of the 'Whites', the antirevolutionary movement that opposed the pro-Russian Communists called 'Reds'.[15]

Compared to the other Scandinavian party systems, the Finnish one holds two main peculiarities. The first is the linguistic division, virtually absent from the other Scandinavian countries (with the partial exception of Norway); the second and most important one is the presence of a strong Communist Party (SKDL). The rise of the Communist Party provoked a division inside the workers' movement and prevented the Social Democratic Party from assuming a predominant role in the electoral arena, unlike in Denmark, Norway and, primarily, Sweden. In Finland the Communists emerged as an antisystem party, and, since 1948, they have been continuously in opposition since no other party has been willing to cooperate with them. From a territorial point of view, the Communists gathered support mainly from the rural working class of the North and East and the peasants that did not support the Agrarian party, while the Social Democrats managed to retain the majority of urban working-class votes in the Southwest. The peculiarity of Finnish communism was indeed its strong rural character.

With its multiple and criss-crossing cleavages (linguistic, class-based, urban-rural and workers' movement divisions), Finland belongs to the Sartori's (1976) type of pluralised polarism. Moreover, the politics of accommodation carried out by the ruling elites through the continuing formation of governments supported by overwhelming parliamentary majorities[16] brings the country to the consensual side of Lijphart's classification of democracies (1999).

For a long time after World War II, the Finnish party system had four major parties (SDP, SKDL, KOK and KESK) and four minor parties, relevant to form the coalition governments. Besides the Swedish People's Party, there have been the Liberal People's Party (LKP), the Christian League (SKL, since 2001 Christian Democrats, KD) – which emerged in the 1970s as a protest against the existing parties' indifference towards Christian values and morale (Suhonen 1980: 239) – and the Finnish Rural Party (SMP), born in 1959 as a breakaway faction of the Agrarian League. While the Liberals and the Christian Democrats represented only small portions of the electorate (the former one had mainly Helsinki-centred support, with the latter one concentrated in western Finland, particularly in the province of Vaasa), the Finnish Rural Party obtained around 10 per cent votes at the beginning of the 1970s (with peaks of more than 20 per cent in the eastern rural provinces of Karelia and Kuopio), thus representing a third major deviation of the Finnish party system from that of the other Scandinavian countries, all of them structured without a second Agrarian party. The Finnish Rural Party disappeared in 1995. In that year, its leader Timo Soimi launched the Finns Party (PS), a right-wing nationalist and Eurosceptic party, very similar to those that appeared during the same years in other Nordic countries (e.g., the Danish and Norwegian Progress Parties or the Swedish Democrats). It has maintained the populist appeal of the Finnish Rural Party but has left the original rural claims by nationalising its programmatic platform. After having remained a minor party for the first three elections, the Finns Party achieved sensational success in the last two general elections (2011 and 2015), thus stabilising as the third-largest party in Finland.

Figure A.4 displays the evolution of vote nationalisation over time in Finland. As stated in chapter 3, Finland belongs to the group of regionalised and stable countries. This is not surprising, given that the party system is structured on multiple and cross-cutting cleavages and marked territorial differences. The black trend line of the chart points out three main contrasting variations through time: an initial pattern of nationalisation between 1970 and 1983, where the Bochsler's index reaches the highest point (0.808); a following trend of slight denationalisation between 1983 and 1999 (0.761); and eventually a new slight increase of the index up to the 2011 election (0.794), probably due to a nonstructural factor such as the sudden rise of the Finns Party,

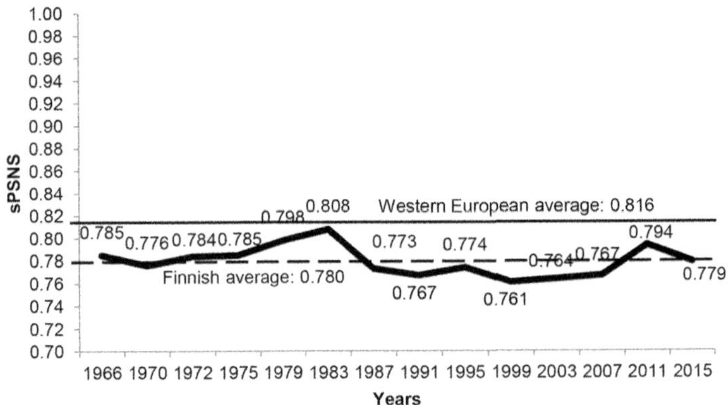

Figure A.4 Evolution of vote nationalisation over time, Finland 1966–2015

which strongly contributed to nationalise the electoral competition, having the highest sPSNS of all Finnish parties.

By moving to the individual parties, no political formation appears to be highly nationalised. The two most homogeneous parties are the SDP and the KOK (*see* table A.4), although they show a mean level of vote nationalisation that is far lower than that of other parties of the two traditional families (0.863 and 0.847, respectively).

Despite the growing process of migration from the rural Northeast to the urbanised Southwest, the Centre Party has retained its old support and is the second-largest party of the system, with a trend of slight increase through time. With a mean value of nationalisation around 0.700, the Centre Party is clearly a marked regionalised political force, with a distinctive electoral geography: it is by far the first party in the scarcely populated northern regions of Lapland and Oulu (where it obtains about one-third of the votes) and in the mainly agricultural North Karelia, while it receives less than 5 per cent in Helsinki.

The fourth-largest party in Finland during the period 1965–2015 is the SKDL (Left Alliance, VAS, since 1990). After having been the second-most voted party until the 1970s, it has experienced a progressive electoral decline since the 1980s, and in the past fifteen years, it has been reduced to fewer than 10 per cent of the votes nationwide, thus losing much of its relevance. Although it has never been characterised by a homogeneous support, its territorial distinctiveness has increased over time, as long as the party reduced its electoral strength and retired into its traditional bastions in the far northern periphery (Lapland and Oulu).

Apart from these four major parties, all the other smaller political forces show a mean sPNS below 0.800, thus outlining heterogeneous territorial

Table A.4 Finnish parties: Mean share of votes and mean sPNS by electoral period, 1966–2015

	1965–1990		*1991–2015*		*1965–2015*		
*Party**	*% Votes*	*sPNS*	*% Votes*	*sPNS*	*% Votes*	*sPNS*	*N*
Social Democratic Party (SDP)	25.0	0.859	22.1	0.867	**23.6**	**0.863**	**14**
Centre Party (KESK)	17.8	0.703	21.7	0.710	**19.7**	**0.707**	**14**
National Coalition Party (KOK)	19.2	0.859	19.7	0.836	**19.4**	**0.847**	**14**
SKDL/VAS	16.3	0.828	9.4	0.768	**12.9**	**0.798**	**14**
Swedish People's Party (SFP)	5.3	0.342	5.2	0.346	**5.3**	**0.344**	**14**
Christian Democrats (KD)	3.7	0.833	4.0	0.762	**3.9**	**0.784**	**10**
Green League (VIHR)	4.0	0.740	7.5	0.723	**7.1**	**0.725**	**8**
Finnish Rural Party (SMP)	7.3	0.782	4.8	0.742	**6.9**	**0.776**	**7**
Liberal People's Party (LKP)	5.1	0.799			**5.1**	**0.799**	**5**
Finns Party (PS)			10.6	0.778	**10.6**	**0.778**	**4**
Finland	_	**0.787**	_	**0.772**	_	**0.780**	**14**

* Other four parties fit the criteria only in one election.

configurations. The main factor accounting for the regionalised score of the index at the systemic level is the ethnoregionalist Swedish People's Party: it contests only about a half of the fifteen electoral districts, but it indeed succeeds to gain seats in the *Eduskunta* (the Finnish unicameral Parliament), thanks to the support of the Swedish speakers in the provinces of Vaasa, Uusimaa, Helsinki and the Aaland Islands, which are inhabited only by the Swedish minority. In this tiny district (just 27,000 registered electors in 2015), the Swedish People's Party always receives at least 90 per cent of the votes, and it is often the only party contesting the election. Its electoral support proves very stable through time, as well as its level of homogeneity (very close to the mean of 0.344).

Among the more recently born parties, the electoral success of the Green League (VIHR) is noticeable. The party contested the election for the first time in 1987, and since then it has become one of the largest green parties in Europe (it has a mean vote share of 7.5 per cent in the last electoral period). Its territorial distribution of votes seems not very homogeneous, with a mean sPNS similar to that of the Centre Party (0.725). Its support is markedly urban-oriented (in Helsinki it is the third-largest party after Conservatives and Social Democrats). Nonetheless, the most interesting case is certainly that of the right-wing Finns Party. As mentioned earlier, the party was created in 1995, but it has been able to fit the criteria of this analysis (3 per cent nationwide or 4 per cent in at least one constituency) only since 2003. Its sPNS was similar to that of a regionalist party (0.486 in 2003). In the following election (2007), the party grew up to 4.1 per cent and significantly homogenised its electoral geography (0.802). Finally, in the last two elections, the dramatic upsurge of the party was accompanied by the final transformation of its territorial configuration; today this party is the most nationalised actor of the system (0.919 and 0.905 in the last two elections). Moreover, its electoral geography is now completely reversed compared to that of 2003: its former stronghold of Helsinki is currently the district where it receives the lowest support (11 per cent in 2015), while in the other districts it ranges between 16 and 25 per cent.

FRANCE

The genesis of the actual French party system can be traced back to the split between democrats and authoritarians at the time of the Revolution (Hanley 1999: 49). Two cleavages emerged from the French Revolution: state-church, probably the most important line of conflict up to the rise of class politics, and centre-periphery.

Religion has played a central role in the state- and nation-building (Guillorel 1981): France is today a homogeneously Catholic country, but Catholic dominance was brought into question during the sixteenth century by the spread of Protestantism (the so-called Huguenots) and finally reaffirmed during the Counterreformation through the use of force in a tough religious conflict. The Protestants are today only a tiny minority (about 2.5 per cent of the population), territorially concentrated in some peripheral regions (Occitan, Alsace-Lorraine), but the old religious cleavage is reflected in the very different political behaviour of the Protestants compared to the Catholics: while the latter are traditional conservative voters with a mainly centre-right orientation, the former have always supported secular ideas and are characterised by a centre-left political orientation (Dargent 2005).

The church was a loser of the French Revolution: the Jacobins introduced the concept of the lay state, a core idea of modern political systems. Not surprisingly, Rokkan (1970: 115–18) places France in type VI of his typology of basic political oppositions in Europe: the central core of nation-builders has a secular posture and is predominantly urban. The alignment of the opposition sees the rural landowners allied with the Roman Church and with the movements of resistance in the subject peripheries. Nonetheless, the church, even after 1789, continued to command the loyalty not just of the aristocratic losers but of large parts of rural France and of peripheral areas,[17] particularly in the East (Alsace-Lorraine), the Northwest (Brittany, Vendee), the Southwest (the French Basque Country) and the areas south of the Massif Central, 'where even today it is possible to speak of a "Catholic vote"' (Hanley 1999: 50).

The second cleavage stemming from the French Revolution is the centre-periphery one. The Revolution saw the victory of the centraliser Jacobins over the decentraliser Girondins. As stated by Rokkan (1970: 118), 'In France the distinction between "centre" and "periphery" was far more than a matter of geography; it reflected long-standing historical commitments for or against the Revolution . . . the *Droite* had most stubbornly resisted the revolutionary drive for centralisation and equalization'. However, as just seen, the centre-periphery cleavage was partly subsumed into the religious cleavage. Those peripheral parts of France with the strongest regional identities (Alsace, Brittany or the Basque Country) were precisely the same ones where Catholicism was the dominant culture. 'This is probably the main reason why regional parties were never more than of marginal importance'[18] (Hanley 1999: 50).

The most important cleavage of French politics has been certainly the class conflict. It was politicised at the end of World War I when the first recognisable party system began to be formalised. As in many other European countries, the Left split into two parties, following the outcome of the Russian Revolution: the socialist SFIO (French Section of the Workers International, since 1969 renamed Socialist Party, PS) and the French Communist Party (PCF), which shortly became one of strongest Communist parties in Europe. On the opposite side, the Right consisted in electoral cartels of notables with very weak party organisations.

In general, the weak organisational structure is one of the common features of French parties, with the notable exception of the Communist Party, the only real mass party of the country (Ventura 2007: 83). From the 1930s to the 1980s, the Communists were dominant among the workers of the large factories in the industrial suburbs around Paris, where they organised a deep and rooted 'red' subculture,[19] up to the rapid deindustrialisation that invested that area accelerating the decline of that subculture and the PCF[20] in general. Even the Socialist Party has maintained a predominantly electoral character and has been dominated by factions of notables, without close territorial ties, except that in the region of Nord-Pas-de-Calais, where an enduring socialist subculture can be detected (Caciagli 2006: 143).

To sum up, two main cleavages structured the modern French party system, an older one (the state-church conflict, with the subsumed centre-periphery one) and a more recent one, produced by the industrial revolution (the class conflict). They are not cross-cutting and tend to reinforce each other, thus orientating French politics towards a left-right pattern of competition: 'the aged, the rich, the religious and the rural tend to vote on the Right, whereas the irreligious, the urban and the lower classes vote on the Left' (Hanley 1999: 65).

French politics has been very unstable through time: 'in each election one observes new parties appearing and old parties disappearing, or perhaps reappearing in another guise' (Lewis-Beck and Skalaban 1992: 167). Since the beginning of the Fifth Republic (1958), the system has stabilised mainly through the introduction of the direct election of the president and the two-round majority system with single-member districts for the election of the National Assembly. These radical changes provided the establishment of a moderate pluralism format and of a stable bipolar pattern of competition opposing the two blocs (centre-left and centre-right).

While the centre-left camp was represented by PS and PCF, on the centre-right President De Gaulle (and, since 1969, his successor Pompidou) succeeded in unifying the different liberal-conservative components under one political organisation (UNR, since 1976 renamed RPR, after 2002 UMP, and after 2015 LR), that is, the Gaullist right. On the centre of the political spectrum, some other components existed especially radical, liberal and Christian Democratic groups, heirs of the Christian Democratic Party of the Fourth Republic (MRP). In 1978 these groups of the non-Gaullist centre-right formed, under the leadership of the then president Giscard d'Estaing, the Union for French Democracy (UDF), electoral cartel persisted until the 2007 election. This change created the so-called *quadrille bipolaire*, that is, a party system with four relevant forces, two for each bloc, with similar electoral strength: the PCF and the PS on the left, the RPR (and its successors) and the UDF on the right. This stable model gradually eroded in the following elections, as the PS and the RPR became the dominant parties in their respective sides. In the same years, new parties appeared in the electoral arena: the populist extreme-right-wing National Front (FN), systematically excluded from electoral alliances and coalition governments by mainstream parties (the so-called *cordon sanitaire*) and The Greens (LV), a centre-left partner of the PS.

The line chart of figure A.5 plots the evolution of vote nationalisation over time in the twelve legislative elections occurred in the country since 1965. A pattern of homogenisation of the territorial structure of voting behaviour is

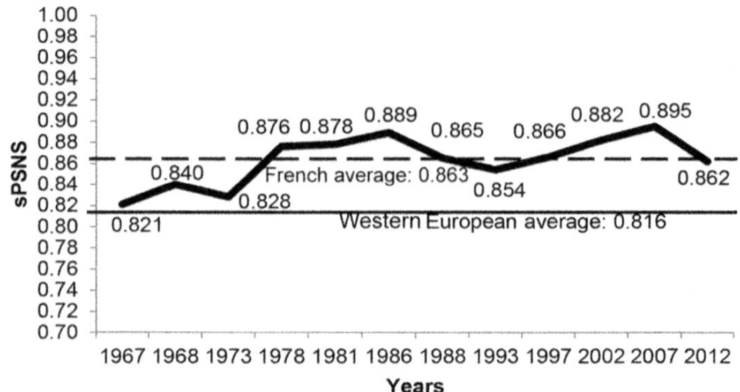

Figure A.5 Evolution of vote nationalisation over time, France 1967–2012

clearly detectable,[21] with a sharp rise of the Bochsler's index until the 1978 election, at the onset of the *quadrille bipolaire*. Then a thirty-year period of fluctuating stability on quite high values follows, up to the peak of nationalisation in the 2007 election.

If before 1978 the French system could be labelled as a regionalised polity, since then it has shifted towards the group of nationalised countries while maintaining a certain instability of the interelection indices (*see* figure 3.6).

Surprisingly enough, the PS is not (unlike most European countries) the most nationalised political force of the country (*see* Table A.5). On the contrary, this primacy belongs to the Gaullist Party. The Gaullists show the highest national share and the most homogeneous territorial configuration (0.907) over time. They have their strongholds in the Northeast (*Alsace*, *Lorraine* and *Champagne-Ardenne*) and the Southeast (*Provence-Alpes-Côte d'Azur* and *Rhône-Alpes*) and they are weaker in the North and the Southwest.

The Socialists are the second-largest party, and, as the Gaullists, they are also homogeneously distributed (0.897). Their electoral geography shows an opposite configuration compared to that of the Gaullists: the PS is strongest in the West-central part of the Hexagon, west of the line Le Havre-Valence-Perpignan and specifically in *Bretagne*, *Poitou-Charentes*, *Limousin*, *Aquitaine* and *Midi-Pyrénées* as well as in the northern region of *Nord-Pas-de-Calais*, legacy of the above-mentioned rooted socialist subculture. The French electoral geography has therefore changed very much over time: as reported by Caramani (2004: 146), at the beginning of the Third Republic, the configuration was completely reversed: 'the Right (conservatives) was stronger in the western regions of France, whereas the Left (the Republicans and, later, the Radicals and Socialists) dominated in the eastern half'.

The PCF has undergone a steady decline over time: until the end of the 1970s it was the largest party of the Left; today it has lost much of its relevance, falling to single-digit percentages. Its territorial distribution displays a higher heterogeneity compared with that of the Gaullist and the PS (a mean of 0.847, slightly declining through time). Communist bastions are located, aside from the Paris suburbs, in the *Midi* (the southern regions of the country), *Limousin* and *Nord-Pas-de-Calais*.

The centre-right electoral cartel of UDF shows a regionalised territorial configuration, which becomes increasingly heterogeneous in the last period (0.792), in correspondence with the electoral decline of the party. The UDF was territorially concentrated around the *Massif Central* (a former Catholic stronghold) and particularly in *Auvergne* and *Poitou-Charentes*, and in the historic bastions of the traditional Right: the Northwest (*Bretagne* and *Pays de la Loire*) and *Alsace*.

Notwithstanding its populist discourse and its ability in winning the support of different social groups by leveraging on the anti-immigrant appeal, the

Table A.5 French parties: Mean share of votes and mean sPNS by electoral period, 1967–2012

	1965–1990		*1991–2015*		*1965–2015*		
*Party**	*% Votes*	*sPNS*	*% Votes*	*sPNS*	*% Votes*	*sPNS*	*N*
Gaullists (UDR-RPR-UMP)	25.6	0.901	27.4	0.915	**26.4**	**0.907**	**12**
Socialist Party (PS)	25.9	0.893	24.0	0.904	**25.1**	**0.897**	**12**
Communist Party (PCF)	17.3	0.853	7.1	0.840	**13.0**	**0.847**	**12**
Union for French Democracy (UDF)	18.9	0.856	9.8	0.792	**13.8**	**0.820**	**9**
National Front (FN)	9.8	0.819	11.6	0.848	**11.1**	**0.840**	**7**
Greens (LV)			4.3	0.884	**4.3**	**0.884**	**5**
Radical Party of the Left (MRG/PRG)	1.2	0.328	1.8	0.410	**1.3**	**0.345**	**5**
Corsican regionalists	0.1	0.011	0.1	0.010	**0.1**	**0.011**	**4**
Democratic Centre (CD)	9.4	0.737			**9.4**	**0.737**	**3**
Independents Republicans (RI)	6.4	0.621			**6.4**	**0.621**	**3**
Unified Socialist Party (PSU)	2.7	0.662			**2.7**	**0.662**	**3**
France	_	**0.857**	_	**0.872**	_	**0.863**	**12**

* Other fourteen parties fit the criteria only in one election. Other fifteen cases are represented by Miscellaneous Right, Miscellaneous Left and Extreme Left: these labels refer to candidates running for the elections but who are not members of any large party. Moreover, the PCF contested the 2012 under a wider electoral cartel (the Left Front, FDG), but it has been computed in PCF's row of the table; the same applies to the Democratic Movement (MoDem), successor of the UDF in 2012, whose score is computed in the UDF's row of the table.

FN shows a quite heterogeneous territorial distribution (0.840), with support concentrated in both former communist strongholds (*Nord-Pas-de-Calais*) and traditional areas of conservative strength (*Provence*, *Alsace*).

The ecologist party is instead very homogeneously distributed (0.884), showing in Paris, *Alsace*, *Bretagne* and *Pays-de-la-Loire* a relative larger strength. Finally, among the minor parties, it is noteworthy the presence of the Corsican regionalists, able to gain about 21 per cent of the regional share in 1993 legislative election (albeit only corresponding to 0.1 per cent nationwide).

GERMANY

The territorial features of the contemporary German party system reflect the legacy of an unparalleled institutional and political discontinuity, as well as the historical roots of the old political subcultures. The actual federal unitary state stemmed from the ruins of World War II, but the origins of the German state date back to the Wilhelmine era, when the Second Reich was built through the centralising and standardising action of the

Conservative and Protestant bureaucracy of the former Prussian Kingdom.[22] The eastern and rural German provinces of Prussia were the first core of the new German Empire, in a context of important socioeconomic and political changes occurred between the unification (1871) and the defeat in the World War I (1918).

On the socioeconomic side, a massive process of industrialisation took place by the end of the nineteenth century in the western regions of the country, followed by large-scale migrations from the predominantly rural Northeast to the urbanised Southwest (Urwin 1982b: 182). This led to the development of a state without a dominating centre, because Berlin failed to assume this role apart from a merely administrative viewpoint, and because the economic and demographic development of the West reinvigorated the well-established city polycephality inherited from the Middle Ages.

From the political viewpoint, the imperial party system saw the rise of new political parties representing the losers of the two main cleavage lines of German politics: the Social Democratic Party (SPD), rooted among the industrial and urban working class, and the Centre Party (*Zentrum*), supported by the substantive Catholic minority (about one-third of the population at the beginning of twentieth century).[23] Both parties opposed the political domination of the Liberal-Conservative Prussian centre-builders, a ruling class made up mostly of large landowners and aristocrats (the so-called *Junkers*). However, since these parties, as well as most of the smaller parties, 'had regional sources of strength, it follows that the imperial party system was not a national system' (Urwin 1982b: 191).

The heterogeneous territorial configuration of the German party system started to decline during the years of the fragile and fragmented Weimar Republic (1919–1933): new parties emerged, and the introduction of proportional representation with large electoral magnitudes encouraged parties to spread nationwide, thus contributing to nationalise the competition. Nevertheless, the regional political subcultures maintained their strength and this is of crucial importance to understand the German electoral geography also after the re-establishment of a democratic rule (1949).

In the Federal Republic of Germany (which consisted in the ten western *Landër* occupied by the allies after the end of World War II, while the remaining six eastern *Landër* remained under Soviet influence and formed the German Democratic Republic), the partisan alignments continued to be structured on the cross-cutting influence of the socioeconomic and religious cleavages, which in turn 'tend to overlap considerably less than in some of the Catholic Latin countries' (Linz 1967b: 286).

The politicisation of these two functional cleavages led to the emergence of a marked regional distinctiveness, enhanced by the presence of older regional political cultures. As a result, red and black[24] political subcultures can be clearly distinguished: the Socialists had their strongholds in Berlin and in the Hanseatic cities of Hamburg and Bremen (Caciagli 2006: 140–41), while the Christian Democratic Party (CDU) and its Catholic Bavarian ally, the Christian Social Union (CSU), represented the overwhelming majority in the southern and western *Landër* of Bavaria, *Baden-Württemberg* and Saarland and also in the highly industrialised and urbanised areas of *North Rhine-Westfalia* and Rhineland-Palatinate.

The two properly territorial cleavages, the centre-periphery and the urban-rural ones, were not decisive in the development of the German party system, except a form of romantic regionalism in Bavaria. Nonetheless, the legacy of its peripheral claims for independence against the centralising action of the Prussian nation-builders was first dealt with the extensive self-government granted during the Weimar Republic and, later, with the federal structure of the state after 1949. The remaining claim for autonomy has been politicised by the CSU, the dominant party of the region as well as the biggest European regionalist party.

In the Federal Republic, the initial fragmentation of the first postwar election in 1949 soon disappeared through the effects of the 5 per cent nationwide electoral thresholds introduced in 1953. Since the early 1960s, the German party system has been characterised by the so-called two-and-a-half format (Blondel 1968: 184–87), where the 'half' was the Liberal Party (FDP), which played a pivotal role in the system allying from time to time with the CDU (1961–1966) or with the SPD (1969–1982), thus determining the composition of the governments. This 'politics of centrality' (Smith 1976) endured until the early 1980s where a new political actor entered the electoral arena and changed the structure of the competition: the Green Party. The party system continued to belong to the Sartori's limited and moderate pluralism (1976), but the competition shifted towards a bipolar form, with The Greens aligned with the SPD against the centre-right coalition of CDU and FDP.

The reunification of West Germany and East Germany involved the inclusion into the Federal Republic of about a quarter of new voters. Yet, the party system did not suffer a great transformation except for the emergence of a new party on the far left of the political spectrum, the Party of Democratic Socialism (PDS, since 2005 named The Left, DL), the heir of the ruling Communist Party of the German Democratic Republic.[25] During the past years, the three traditional parties, and especially the SPD and the FDP, suffered from a substantive loss of votes (the latter in the 2013 election failed to access the Bundestag for the first time). Conversely, other minor parties emerged, particularly on the right, most of them with a negligible electoral support, except the Eurosceptic Alternative for Germany (AFD), which has been able to get 4.7 per cent of the national share in 2013.

The chart in figure A.6 plots the evolution of German vote nationalisation over time. With a mean sPSNS of 0.760, Germany appears as one of the less nationalised polities in Western Europe (*see* also figure 3.2). The levels of

Bochsler's index prove quite stable through time, both before and after the reunification. This evidence is rather unexpected, since the inclusion of the East, with its social and political peculiarities, could have increased the level of territorial heterogeneity of the country. Yet, a notable downward peak of 0.717 in the last election is noted, maybe the beginning of a denationalisation trend in the years to come.

As far as the individual parties are concerned, the SPD appears as the more homogeneous party of the system, and this evidence is not surprising since in most countries the Social Democrats show the highest coefficients. Its sPNS remains stable despite the electoral decline of the party in the past decade (*see* table A.6). The SPD has retained the historical features of its electoral geography, showing still today some electoral bastions (Northwest Germany: Schleswig-Holstein, Hamburg, Bremen, Lower Saxony) and some areas of relative weakness (Bavaria, Saxony and in general the eastern Landër).

Compared with many other Conservative or Christian Democratic parties in Europe, the CDU shows a very low level of nationalisation (0.762). The regionalised territorial configuration of the party is mainly due to the presence of the long-term allied CSU in Bavaria, where the CDU does not contest seats. The trend of nationalisation over time shows a homogenisation pattern. The support for the CDU primarily comes from southwestern Germany (Baden-Württemberg, Rhineland-Palatinate and North Rhine-Westphalia) while it is particularly weak in Berlin and the Hanseatic cities of the North. The aforementioned CSU, here considered as an independent party,[26] is the biggest European regionalist party with a mean share of 8.8 per cent. Since the presence of CSU is limited to Bavaria (where it usually receives more than 50 per cent of the votes), it is not surprising that it shows an extremely low level of nationalisation (0.119).

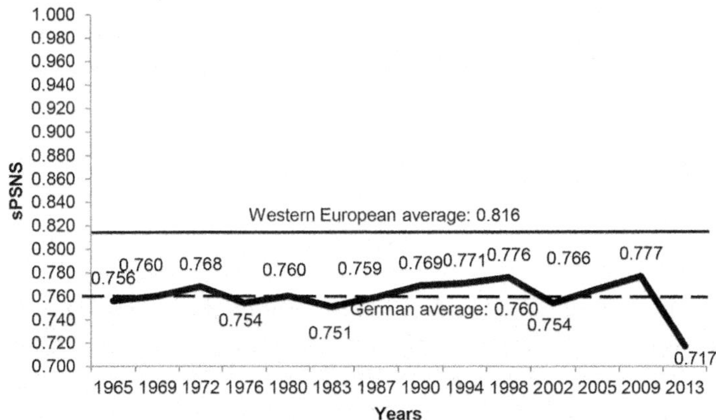

Figure A.6 Evolution of vote nationalisation over time, Germany 1965–2013

Table A.6 German parties: Mean share of votes and mean sPNS by electoral period, 1965–2013

	1965–1990		*1991–2015*		*1965–2015*		
*Party**	*% Votes*	*sPNS*	*% Votes*	*sPNS*	*% Votes*	*sPNS*	*N*
Social Democratic Party of Germany (SPD)	40.2	0.899	33.1	0.887	**37.2**	**0.894**	**14**
Christian Democratic Union (CDU)	36.4	0.744	30.2	0.787	**33.7**	**0.762**	**14**
Christian Social Union (CSU)	9.6	0.109	7.4	0.133	**8.7**	**0.119**	**14**
Free Democratic Party (FDP)	8.6	0.89	8.3	0.872	**8.5**	**0.882**	**14**
Alliance 90/The Greens	5.9	0.848	8.3	0.837	**7.5**	**0.840**	**9**
PDS-*Die Linke*	2.4	0.274	7.1	0.485	**6.4**	**0.455**	**7**
National Democratic Party of Germany (NPD)	4.3	0.854	1.5	0.719	**2.5**	**0.764**	**3**
Germany	_	**0.760**	_	**0.760**	_	**0.760**	**14**

Note: Since the 1994 election, Alliance 90 and The Greens contested elections as a merged list: votes and scores are reported in The Greens' row of the table.

* Other four parties fit the criteria only in one election.

The Liberal FDP is the only other party of the system that contested all the fourteen elections of the period. Its level of territorial homogeneity is very high, not far from that of the SPD (0.882): just like the other two founding parties of the former West Germany (SPD and CDU), its electoral support is concentrated in the western Landër. The Greens, instead, shows a more heterogeneous configuration (a mean of 0.840 in the nine elections contested). The relative weakness in the eastern regions can be found even here, but with the significant exception of Berlin, the land where The Greens receives the highest support. Finally, the postcommunist PDS-DL has a Bochsler's index of barely 0.455, such a low level that makes it similar to other European regionalist parties, even if it is formally a national party. By observing the electoral performance of the party across the country, a marked concentration of support in the eastern Landër is noted. However, there is a clear trend of nationalisation over time, which goes hand in hand with the increase of its electoral support.

GREECE

In this country, during the hundred years between the beginning of the independence war against the Ottoman Empire (1821) and the last conflict against Turkey after World War I (1919–1922), a proindependence bourgeoisie emerged and opposed the old aristocracy, tied to the Turkish regime. From this first cleavage line, the Greek political system was divided along the opposition between a liberal Centre and a conservative Right. The 'Left' emerged only during the 1946–1949 civil war opposing the bourgeois forces (liberal Centre and Right), supported by the United States, and the Communist-led National Liberation Front. From 1951 to the coup d'état of 1967, Greek politics was dominated by the liberal Centre, contrasted by a bipolar opposition. The breakdown of the military dictatorship (the so-called Regimes of the Colonels) in 1974 and the promulgation of a republican constitution led to the restoration of the democratic rule (*Metapolitefsi*) celebrated with the first multiparty elections since 1964.

The current analysis covers the forty-two years of democratic experience between 1974 and 2015, where three main periods could be distinguished.

The first period (until 1981) was characterised by the electoral dominance of the new conservative party, New Democracy (ND) with its leader Konstantinos Karamanlis. The old liberal Centre Democratic Union (EDK) was still relevant, although declining, while the new left party, the Socialist PASOK (Panhellenic Socialist Movement), founded in 1974 by Andreas Papandreou, was growing but remained a minority among the Greek electorate. On the far left, the filo-soviet Communist party (KKE), legalised since 1974, represented a substantive portion of the electorate, but it was overcome by the PASOK as the main left force. These four main parties were surrounded by many other small groups, mainly located at the extremes of the political spectrum. In general, during this first period, the party system was characterised by a high degree of ideological polarisation and political fragmentation, thus belonging to the Sartori's type of 'polarised pluralism'[27] (Pappas 2003).

The second period (1981–2012) opened with the alternation in power between the conservatives and the progressives. The PASOK obtained a landslide victory in 1981[28] and formed a single-party majority government until 1989, from 1993 to 2004 and eventually from 2009 to 2012. In the remaining years (1989–1993 and 2004–2009), there were conservative governments held by New Democracy, thus establishing a quasi-two-party system[29] (with the two main parties holding together more than 80 per cent of the votes) and a bipolar structure of the competition: the liberal Centre disappeared, while the extreme Right became a small minority. The Communist Party was the only resilient 'third' force, and it allied with many other small leftist groups, forming in 1989 the Coalition of the Left and Progress (*Synaspismos*) which lasted until 1993, when the alliance broke up and both the KKE and the left coalition (renamed SYN) contested the election with their own label.

Finally, the third period has opened with the dramatic 2012. In the wake of the harshest economic crisis of the country, the party system has undergone an unprecedented breakdown with some radical changes in the historical balance of powers among the established parties and with the emergence of new relevant political organisations. The PASOK has collapsed and has lost its status as the largest left-wing party, being overtaken by SYRIZA, a coalition of the radical left movements and groups, successor of SYN. New Democracy has also suffered major losses, but it has still retained its key role on the right of the political spectrum. In general, fragmentation has increased to its highest levels and some new parties have won seats in the *Vulì* – the Greek unicameral Parliament – such as the centre-right Independent Greeks (ANEL), the neo-Nazi Golden Dawn (XA), the PASOK's splinter group Democratic Left (DIMAR) and the centrist, pro-European, The River (*To Potami*).

Although the Greek party system appears very similar to that of many other European countries, the applicability of the 'freezing hypothesis' and the related articulation of the cleavage system becomes problematic. Indeed, Greece's class stratification earned a distinct dimension compared to the other Western democracies, due to the country's poor industrial production. Since 1974, 'the majority of the Greek citizens were poor, uneducated farmers, and only a small proportion of Greece's total population . . . could be conceived as typical proletariats. Correspondingly, only a small proportion of large cities dwellers could be conceived as bourgeois strata' (Pierides 2009: 5). Another cleavage seems to have more salience, the urban-rural one, due to the importance of the agricultural production, and the rapid urbanisation in the past decades, with the Greater Athens area housing one-third of the country's total population (Dimitras 1992: 207). Moreover, the Greek Orthodox Church designates another peculiarity of Greece, compared to the other Western European democracies. Here, the entire population is homogeneously Orthodox,[30] and although the Greek Church sometimes acquires an essential political role, a religious cleavage has never been established,[31] and even the KKE sustains an ideology that appreciates Greek religious customs (Pierides 2009: 6–7). For these reasons, the predominant left-right axis[32] of competition is neither entirely the result of a class cleavage nor a clear religious cleavage (Voulgaris 2007: 51).

As a consequence, the territorial configuration of support for the main parties is highly homogeneous, and Greece is the most nationalised country in Western Europe, with a mean sPSNS of 0.910 (*see* figure 3.2). Figure A.7 plots the evolution of vote nationalisation in Greece over time. The chart displays a clear path of growing nationalisation during the first years of the postdictatorship period (1974–1985). Between 1985 and 2004, during the years of the consolidated quasi-two-party system, Greece shows a pattern of prolonged stability on impressively high levels of territorial homogeneity. Finally, the last period of increasing fragmentation and destructuring of the formerly stable party system format is associated with the beginning of a denationalisation process that reaches its peak in the dramatic May 2012 general election.

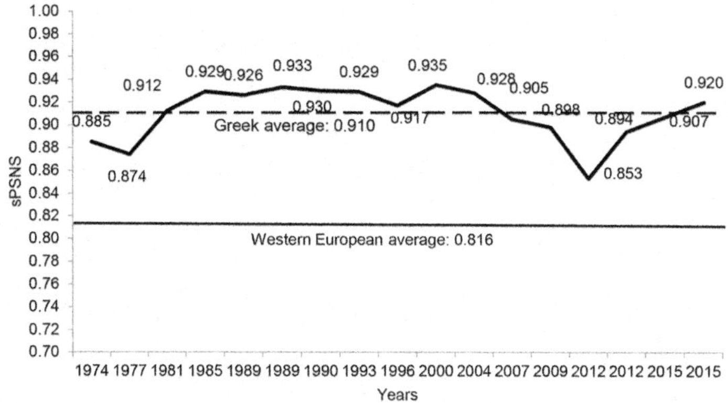

Figure A.7 Evolution of vote nationalisation over time, Greece 1974–2015

By turning to the individual parties, the electoral geography does not substantially play the essential role it has in other countries. In other words, in Greece is difficult to talk about 'electoral strongholds', 'bastions' or 'safe constituencies' regarding parties (Bolgherini 2002: 70). This is because, except a very small number of relatively stable areas, most of the fifty-six electoral constituencies (*Nomoí*), as well as the thirteen regions (*Peripheries*) in which they are grouped, tend to swing between the two main parties in every election, according to the national result.

Table A.7 shows the mean share of votes and the mean sPNS for the major Greek parties. The level of territorial homogeneity of the two main parties, ND and PASOK, is absolutely striking. They both show a mean Bochsler's index higher than 0.900 along the seventeen elections of the postdictatorship period. Furthermore, they both experienced a slight decrease of homogeneity in the past years, in the wake of their electoral decline. During the period of their maximum electoral strength, they both often exceeded the sPNS of 0.950 reaching some of the highest scores of the whole data set concerning the party cases ($N = 1789$).

According to Caramani (2004: 149), the country is characterised 'by a clear geographical segmentation based on the scheme of old versus new provinces'. *Nea Demokratia* is indeed stronger in the 'new provinces' (Epirus, Macedonia and Thrace) as well as in the southeastern peninsula of Peloponnese (*Argolis, Laconia, Messenia*) and, more generally, in most of the rural areas. On the other side, PASOK is rooted in the islands like Crete (a former liberal stronghold that became the most prominent socialist bastion since the 1980s), the Dodecanese, the Ionian Corfu and Zakynthos and in the northwestern Peloponnese (*Achaea, Elis*).

The two big urban areas of Athens and Thessaloniki are characterised by a balance of power between the two main parties: specifically, in Athens, a

Table A.7 Greek parties: Mean share of votes and mean sPNS by period, 1974–2015

	1965–1990		*1991–2015*		*1965–2015*		
*Party**	*% Votes*	*sPNS*	*% Votes*	*sPNS*	*% Votes*	*sPNS*	*N*
New Democracy	44.3	0.933	34.5	0.920	**38.6**	**0.925**	**17**
PASOK	35.9	0.937	29.1	0.899	**31.9**	**0.915**	**17**
KKE	10.1	0.771	6.1	0.812	**7.0**	**0.803**	**13**
SYN/SYRIZA			14	0.833	**14.0**	**0.833**	**10**
Golden Dawn (XA)			6.8	0.890	**6.8**	**0.890**	**4**
ANEL			6.6	0.912	**6.6**	**0.912**	**4**
Coalition of the Left (*Synaspismos*)	11.5	0.798			**11.5**	**0.798**	**3**
Centre Union (EK)	16.2	0.871			**16.2**	**0.871**	**2**
DIMAR			6.2	0.922	**6.2**	**0.922**	**2**
The River (*To Potami*)			5.1	0.849	**5.1**	**0.849**	**2**
LAOS			4.7	0.790	**4.7**	**0.790**	**2**
POLA			3.9	0.844	**3.9**	**0.844**	**2**
Union of Centrists (EK)			2.6	0.795	**2.6**	**0.795**	**2**
Greece	_	**0.913**	_	**0.909**	_	**0.910**	**17**

* Other ten parties fit the criteria only in one election.

conservative prevalence can be noted in the centre of the municipality, while PASOK receives the majority in the great suburban area of Piraeus. The electoral behaviour in the islands is instead more left-oriented than the rest of the country, with the significant exception of the Cyclades.

All the other parties included in table A.7 show lower sPNS. However, they have a mean value around or higher than 0.800; thus they can all be considered national parties. Specifically, the KKE relies on the support of urban agglomerations and of the region of Thessaly and in the islands (both Ionian and Aegean). SYRIZA (before 2004, SYN) retained a similar electoral geography and an even more regionalised territorial configuration compared to the KKE (with an average sPSNS of 0.786), up to the 2012 elections. Since then, the party has become much more nationalised, reaching a sPSNS of 0.951 in the September 2015 election, showing a much similar territorial configuration to that of the once-in-power PASOK. Finally, the extreme-right parties, like Political Spring (POLA) and the Popular Orthodox Rally (LAOS), show their best results in the same areas of ND, while all the relevant parties emerged after the two consecutive elections held in 2012 (Golden Dawn, ANEL and DIMAR) display very high homogeneous territorial configurations.

IRELAND

The literature on comparative political studies has often labelled the Irish party system as a *sui generis* one, mainly due to the idiosyncratic features of the Irish party system that make it difficult a comparison with the other Western European countries, as well as the application of Lipset and Rokkan's (1967) genetic theory.

The origins of the contemporary Irish party system date back to 1921, when the signing of the Anglo-Irish Treaty established the Irish Free State[33] and granted commonwealth status to twenty-six of the Island's thirty-two counties (the six Ulster counties remained under the British rule). This solution caused a brief, but bloody, civil war in 1922–1923 and a break into the nationalist movement, the *Sinn Féin* ('We ourselves') between those who supported the treaty and those who opposed it, judging it as a downward compromise. The civil war and the 1922 election were fundamental events to crystallise the opposition between these two sides and to form the basis of the party system. The forces that were favourable to the treaty were in office from 1922 to 1932 and in 1933 created the *Fine Gael* ('Tribe of the Irish'); on the other side, the more pragmatic elements of the antitreaty forces dropped their early policy of abstention and founded the *Fianna Fáil* ('Warriors of Destiny'), and in 1932 they won the majority in the *Dáil Éireann* (the Irish Parliament) and formed their first government. Since that moment, *Fianna Fáil* has always been Ireland's major party, until the resounding defeat in the 2011 general election.

The main cleavage of the Irish party system, therefore, concerns the position about the treaty. Out of this opposition line, there is a third political force, the Irish Labour Party. Following the pattern of its British counterpart, the Labour was launched in 1912 as a trade union party, representative of the industrial labour force. This latter has been very small since 1922, when the signing of the treaty left out from the new Irish State most of the industrial base, primarily located in Belfast and its hinterlands. However, this is not the only reason of the Left's weakness[34] and the uniqueness of the Irish party system. The absence of class politics in Ireland is also explained by the behaviour of the Labour Party in the key election of 1918, the first with a suffrage extension that increased the electorate to 75 per cent of the population aged twenty and over (Sinnott 1995: 25). In this crucial 'crystallizing election', in which the main issue was the secession from the United Kingdom, the Labour Party decided not to field any candidate, unwilling to distract attention from the National Question (Farrell 1970). Therefore, voters were not given the option of voting on the class issue.

As I mentioned at the beginning, Lipset and Rokkan's theory of social cleavages does not apply well in Ireland.[35] Indeed, not only is the socioeconomic conflict very weak, but even the other historical cleavages are virtually absent. Ireland is a predominantly rural, agricultural, peasant-based economy with an almost totality of practising Catholics. That is why the urban-rural and the religious cleavages seem not to apply to this country. Furthermore, the state-church conflict has never emerged, since the church was a fundamental actor in the struggle for the national independence and therefore, just as in the Protestant countries of Northern Europe, an important ally of the state (Rokkan 1970: 125). All these factors led Whyte (1974) to conclude that Ireland is characterised by 'politics without social bases'.[36] It is nevertheless true that some regional differences in the electoral geography of the country exist: as Gallagher (1998: 83–94) shows, the forty-one electoral constituencies of the country can be grouped into four distinct regions. A clear dichotomy between two of them can be identified: the Anglicised, more secularised and predominantly urban district of Dublin, and the Connacht-Ulster, located on the western border and characterised by a weak urbanisation, a high proportion of Gaelic-speaking population and the domain of the small peasant property. The other two areas of Munster and Leinster are in an intermediate position, primarily based on rural farms but with bigger urban centres than the Connacht-Ulster. *Fianna Fáil* and *Fine Gael* are both stronger in the rural regions than in Dublin, with the former showing larger differences between the votes usually obtained in Connacht-Ulster (very often close or even above the absolute majority) and those received in the capital. The Labour Party shows an opposite territorial configuration instead, since it is stronger in the urban areas, particularly in Dublin, and particularly weak in Connacht-Ulster, where the two major parties have an undisputed predominance.

In spite of these interesting variations, the two main parties rely on a quite heterogeneous social support, with small differences among them: *Fianna Fáil* is a typical 'catch-all party' (Kirchheimer 1966). It received votes among the working class as well as the middle class, and it is particularly strong among the small farmers and the Irish speakers.[37] *Fine Gael* is supported by the large farmers, the business community and, more generally, people with higher incomes (Carey 1980).

Generally described – following Blondel's analysis – as a 'two-and-a-half' party system[38] (Farrell 1970), with Labour representing the 'half' party, the Irish party system has experienced great changes since the mid-1980s, with the emergence of new parties and a dramatic rise in the levels of electoral instability, in the wake of a rising process of secularisation and a declining role of Catholic Church, particularly among the younger, better educated, urban sector of the electorate (Marsh 1992: 226). On the centre-right, the Progressive Democrats (PDs) emerges in 1987, attracting the support of secularised middle-class voters; on the centre-left, we find the Greens, the Workers' Party (a *Sinn Féin* splinter), the Democratic Left (a Workers' Party splinter) and the Socialist Party (a Labour splinter). Moreover, *Sinn Féin* has significantly increased its votes during the past decade, thus becoming the fourth-largest party in the election of 2011.

Figure A.8 plots the evolution of Ireland's vote nationalisation over time. After about twenty years of stability, with a further increase of nationalisation

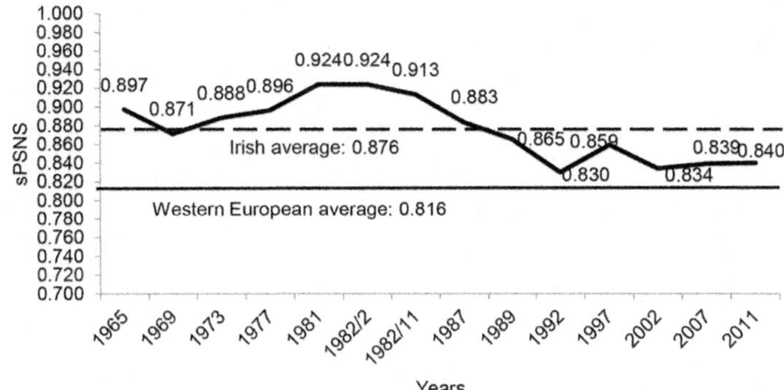

Figure A.8 Evolution of vote nationalisation over time, Ireland 1965–2011

between the mid-1960s and the mid-1980s, territorial homogeneity has significantly decreased since the election of 1987, reaching the point of maximum denationalisation of the vote in the 1992 election (0.830). In the past two decades, vote nationalisation has remained quite stable, settling on much lower levels than in the first electoral period. In general, Ireland has experienced a pattern of vote denationalisation, moving from a pattern of homogeneous support until the mid-1980s to a regionalised territorial configuration since the early 1990s.[39]

Having regard to the preceding considerations about the 'catch-all' nature of *Fianna Fáil*, its extraordinarily high level of vote nationalisation (0.936) is not surprising (*see* table A.8).[40] Its sPNS is one of the highest in the whole Western Europe (the score of 0.968 in the 1965 election is actually the highest recorded in the data set), witnessing a marked territorial homogeneity across the eight regions of the country (*see* table 2.1). However, its values of Bochsler's index declines over time, together with its mean share of votes. *Fianna Fáil* has always been the largest party until the electoral upheaval occurred in 2011, an election labelled 'not only as the most volatile in Irish democratic history, but also as one of the most volatile elections in postwar Europe' (Mair 2011).

Similarly, *Fine Gael* displays a high degree of homogeneity of its electoral support (0.907), with a pattern of stability until the end of the 1980s, followed by a slight decrease in the index since 1992 (0.880).

The incomplete territorial coverage (the party does not contest seats in every constituency of the country) and the distinctly urban-oriented support led the Irish Labour Party to have a lower level of vote nationalisation compared to the other two major parties.

The other parties contest less than half of the total elections held in Ireland between 1965 and 2011. All of them show incomplete territorial coverage

Table A.8 Irish parties: Mean share of votes and mean sPNS by electoral period, 1965–2011

	1965–1990		*1991–2015*		*1965–2015*		
*Party**	*% Votes*	*sPNS*	*% Votes*	*sPNS*	*% Votes*	*sPNS*	*N*
Fianna Fáil	46.3	0.942	35.8	0.926	**42.5**	**0.936**	**14**
Fine Gael	33.7	0.923	27.7	0.880	**31.5**	**0.907**	**14**
Irish Labour Party	11.3	0.685	14.1	0.773	**12.3**	**0.716**	**14**
Progres. Dem. Party	8.7	0.760	4.0	0.604	**5.6**	**0.656**	**6**
Sinn Féin			6.5	0.613	**6.5**	**0.613**	**4**
Green Party			3.3	0.649	**3.3**	**0.649**	**4**
Workers' Party	4.4	0.487			**4.4**	**0.487**	**2**
Democratic Left			2.6	0.348	**2.6**	**0.348**	**2**
Ireland	_	**0.896**	_	**0.840**	_	**0.876**	**14**

* Other seven parties fit the criteria only in one election.

and a heterogeneous territorial configuration. With the exception of *Sinn Féin*, particularly concentrated in southern districts, all the other relevant parties (PDs, Greens, Workers' Party) have in Dublin's constituencies their strongholds.

ITALY[41]

The origins of the postwar Italian party system can be traced during the period going from the formation of the new unitary and independent state (1861) to the advent of the Fascist regime (1922). The emerging parliamentary system was dominated by the Liberal Party, which was internally divided into many wings and factions. As stated by Rokkan (1970: 118), Italy belongs to type VI of its alliance-opposition model: the nation-building effort was achieved by the secularist and urban Liberal bourgeoisie, and the resistance to this process was mainly carried out by the Catholic Church, allied with conservative and peripheral rural interests. After a long period during which the pope prohibited Italian Catholics from taking part in the political life (the famous *non expedit*), in 1919 they formed the Italian People's Party (PPI), thus politicising the long-time established state-church conflict, the oldest cleavage of the Italian system.

The class cleavage found political organisation since 1892, when, in the wake of the rising industrialisation of the country, the Italian Socialist Party (PSI) was founded, opposing the bourgeois interests represented by the Liberals. Therefore, just after the end of World War I and on the eve of fascism, the Italian party system was structured on the opposition between three main parties stemmed from the two functional cleavages (state-church and capital-labour). The two territorial cleavages did not find political representation but were mainly absorbed into the functional ones: the presence of the church, deeply rooted in rural areas, prevented the creation of a rural party, and the peripheral resistance to the new Piedmontese administration did not produce direct expression in the party system. Despite the absence of rooted territorial conflicts, the two functional cleavages translated into marked regional variations in the electoral support of each camp: the PPI emerged as the largest party in the rural and staunchly Catholic Northeast; the PSI was largely dominant in the industrial districts of the North as well as in the Apennine regions, where it had established a rooted 'red' subculture; finally, the old Liberals dominated in the economically poor and culturally backward South (Zuffo 2001).

A competitive party system was re-established with the election of the Constituent Assembly in 1946, following more than twenty years of fascism and wartime occupation. The system was still structured along the two same cleavages that were relevant in the previous period, but the class conflict became the most important dimension and orientated the political space along a left-right continuum (Bardi and Morlino 1992: 461).

The new party system was by far more fragmented and polarised than before. On the left, there was the largest Communist party of the Western world as well as the most structured mass party in Europe, the Italian Communist Party (PCI).[42] It replaced the PSI as the main opposition party; the Socialists split between the largest and maximalist wing (PSI) and the Social Democratic one (PSDI), which from the outset entered in the centrist coalition governments. The centre of the political spectrum was occupied by the Christian Democracy (DC), the largest Christian Democratic party of Western Europe. It was an interclass mass party, supported by the Catholic Church and, in foreign policy, a guarantor of the Italian positioning in the Western camp. Being the largest party of the system from 1948 to 1992, the DC ruled the country during its whole lifetime (1945–1993), for some periods through single-party governments and other times in broad coalitions. It consolidated its hold on the electorate through pervasive penetration into civil society (the so-called *partitocrazia*) and the use of state resources for patronage and clientelism[43] (Daniels 1999: 72). Still in the centre, and usually allied with the DC, there were other smaller parties, like the Italian Liberal Party (PLI) and the Italian Republican Party (PRI), both with a predominantly bourgeois support and a secular attitude. On the far right, there was the postfascist Italian Social Movement (MSI), systematically excluded from government.

This multiparty structure has been classified by Sartori (1976: 146), as a case of 'extreme and polarised pluralism', characterised by the presence of more than five relevant parties, and high ideological polarisation with a centrifugal mechanics (due to the existence of two 'anti-system' parties at the edge of the ideological spectrum, the PCI on the Left and the MSI on the Right).[44]

The territorial basis of support[45] for the main parties denoted a durable continuity and remained more or less the same of the prefascist era: the DC dominated in the Northeast as well as in many areas of the South, especially the rural ones; the Apennine regions and the industrial cities of the Northwest continued to display a marked communist and socialist prevalence; the MSI had its strongholds in the South and the small centrist parties were relevant in urban settings.

After a long period of stability, since the beginning of the 1990s, Italian politics experienced profound changes, with the complete transformation of its relevant political actors (that is why the literature often refers to the period since 1994 as the 'Second Republic'). The core parties of the First Republic entered into a deep crisis and disappeared (PSDI, PLI, PRI), changed their names and underwent processes of internal self-reform (PCI, MSI),[46] splintered into many smaller wings (DC)[47] or became electorally irrelevant (PSI). They were replaced by some new parties, the most important ones being the Liberal-Conservative *Forza Italia* (FI) and the ethnoregionalist Northern League (LN). The former, founded by the TV tycoon Silvio Berlusconi, soon became the largest party of the centre-right, with a populist and charismatic leadership and an effective appeal to the former DC and conservative voters. The latter emerged in the late 1980s, politicised the long-time existing centre-periphery conflict between the industrialised, rich and 'virtuous' North and the poor, corrupted and 'backward' South of the country.

Even the party system radically changed its internal dynamics: a new bipolar pattern of competition emerged, based on the alternation between a centre-left and a centre-right, each of them consisting in broad and internally fragmented blocs.[48] This new pattern was favoured by the electoral system change: the former pure PR system was replaced in 1993 by a new mixed electoral system,[49] with 75 per cent of the seats allocated to single-member districts and 25 per cent with PR corrected by a 4 per cent threshold at the national level. The new party system suffered from a congenital lack of structuring, and, prior to the emergence of an almost two-party format after the 2008 general election,[50] there was a continuing rise of new political parties and a sharp increase in the levels of party fragmentation and volatility (Chiaramonte 2010). Finally, the election of 2013 brought about an unprecedented transformation in the structure of the party system. The former bipolar format was replaced by an unstable system with three relevant poles, with the presence of a new leading actor, the Five Star Movement (M5S), a populist and anti-establishment party led by the former comedian Beppe Grillo, emerged as the most voted list in the country with 25.6 per cent of the votes. There was also a sudden shift of many of the party-system indicators, especially electoral volatility, which rocketed to almost unprecedented levels (Chiaramonte and Emanuele 2013; Emanuele 2015a).

Notwithstanding these radical changes, the electoral geography of the Second Republic has been marked by substantive continuity with the past: the conservative predominance in the South and the supremacy of the Left in the so-called red zone have been maintained. One major change has occurred: the North became an area of centre-right prevalence, with *Forza Italia* stronger in the former industrial triangle and the Northern League replacing the DC in its former strongholds of the Northeast (which has shifted from 'white' to 'green').[51]

In a comparative perspective, Italy occupies an intermediate position regarding the level of vote nationalisation. As shown in chapter 3, the mean Bochsler's index during the period under analysis is 0.848, slightly lower than the median (0.858).

Moreover, the standard deviation and even more the mean absolute inter-electoral change are remarkable (*see* figures 3.2 and 3.6), primarily due to the instability occurred in the past two decades. Figure A.9 plots the values of vote nationalisation in Italy through time. The trend of the Bochsler's index follows a nonlinear path during the thirteen elections included into this analysis. The values of the sPSNS tend to grow during the first decade, reaching the highest peak in the 1976 election. After this, they start to decline, with a sharp decrease at the end of the First Republic, reaching the lowest point in 1994 (0.758), the election marking the start of the transition towards the Second Republic. Since 1994, vote nationalisation has risen again, reaching a new peak in 2006 (0.873), although remaining, on average, at lower levels than before. Despite being an 'earthquake' election (Chiaramonte and De Sio

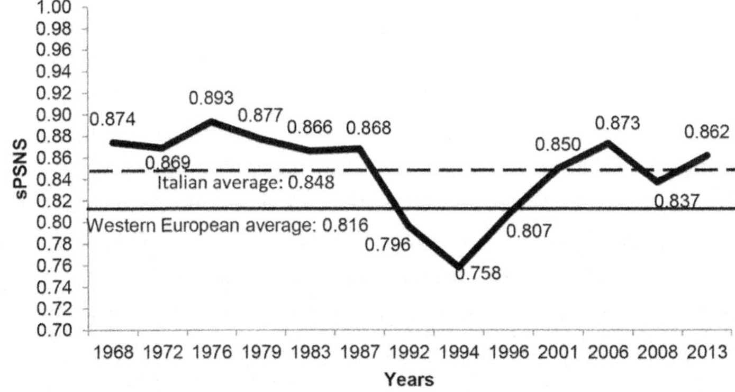

Figure A.9 Evolution of vote nationalisation over time, Italy 1968–2013

2014), in 2013 vote nationalisation only slightly increases. In general, during the whole time span, there is a quite constant level of vote nationalisation, except the denationalisation trend during the destructuration and restructuration years (1992–1996).

In contrast with the emphasis on the within-country territorial diversity put by the literature on the Italian electoral geography (Galli et al. 1968; Corbetta, Parisi and Schadee 1988; Diamanti 2009; Emanuele 2011), the three parties of the First Republic score high sPNS. Christian Democracy records a mean sPNS of 0.905 and the PSI of 0.907, which is the highest during the First Republic. The Communist Party (PCI) scores 0.863, a coefficient that reflects greater heterogeneity as compared to the DC and the PSI, but is still lower than expected (*see* table A.9). All the other small parties contesting the elections in the period 1948–1992 have lower scores. In particular, the PLI gathers most of its votes in Northwest Italy (Piedmont, Liguria and the city of Milan); the support for the PRI is territorially concentrated in certain areas of Romagna and Tuscany, while that for the extreme-right parties (the MSI and the Monarchists) is concentrated mainly in the South.

By the end of the 1970s, the mean level of vote nationalisation for Italian parties decreases, and this is partly due to the emergence of new political forces whose support is very unevenly distributed. They include not only regionalist parties – such as the Venetian League (LV) (0.100), Association for Trieste (0.207), the Sardinian Action Party (PSd'Az) (0.124) and the main responsible for the country's vote denationalisation, the Northern League (0.432) – but also formally 'national' parties having distinct regional support bases, like *La Rete* (0.516), whose votes come especially from Sicily.

As these new parties enter the electoral arena, the main established political forces of the system undergo a process of denationalisation of their vote: all the five largest parties except one (the MSI) show a decrease of the sPNS over time. In particular, the DC, threatened by the LN's expansion in its former stronghold of the Northeast, experiences a process of 'southernisation', shifting its centre of gravity southbound, while the PCI sees an increase in the extent to which its support is concentrated in the so-called Red Belt (Emilia-Romagna, Tuscany, Umbria and Marche).[52]

Turning to Second Republic's parties, their support is less evenly distributed than the support for their predecessors: both the PPI and the United Christian Democrats (CCD-CDU) have sPNS quite far from those of the DC, while support for the PDS-DS is less evenly distributed than was support for the old PCI. The parties with the highest vote nationalisation scores in the most recent phase are the two new large parties created shortly before the 2008 election, the Democratic Party (PD) and the People of Freedom (PDL) (0.895 and 0.897, respectively). Immediately below them there is Berlusconi's party, *Forza Italia* (0.888) – a media-oriented political force which was so unrelated

Table A.9 Italian parties: Mean share of votes and mean sPNS by electoral period, 1968–2013

	1965–1990		*1991–2015*		*1965–2015*		
*Party**	*% Votes*	*sPNS*	*% Votes*	*sPNS*	*% Votes*	*sPNS*	*N*
DC	36.9	0.912	29.7	0.862	**35.9**	**0.905**	**7**
PCI	29.2	0.863			**29.2**	**0.863**	**6**
PSI	11.5	0.924	7.9	0.856	**10.6**	**0.907**	**8**
MSI/AN	6.2	0.780	5.4	0.815	**6.1**	**0.785**	**7**
PSDI	3.9	0.871	2.7	0.714	**3.7**	**0.845**	**6**
Radical Party	3.4	0.850	3.5	0.747	**3.5**	**0.798**	**2**
PRI	3.3	0.849	4.4	0.899	**3.4**	**0.857**	**7**
PLI	3.3	0.782	2.9	0.838	**3.2**	**0.791**	**6**
Greens	2.5	0.774	2.7	0.874	**2.6**	**0.849**	**4**
SVP	0.5	0.023	0.5	0.023	**0.5**	**0.023**	**12**
Venetian League	0.4	0.100			**0.4**	**0.100**	**2**
PSd'Az	0.3	0.124			**0.3**	**0.124**	**2**
Associazione per Trieste	0.2	0.207			**0.2**	**0.207**	**2**
UV	0.1	0.003	0.1	0.003	**0.1**	**0.003**	**13**
Olive Tree/PD			29.9	0.895	**29.9**	**0.895**	**3**
PDL			29.4	0.897	**29.4**	**0.897**	**2**
Forza Italia			23.7	0.888	**23.7**	**0.888**	**4**
PDS-DS			18.5	0.804	**18.5**	**0.804**	**4**
AN			13.4	0.824	**13.4**	**0.824**	**4**
Ppi/*La Margherita*			10.8	0.898	**10.8**	**0.898**	**3**
Northern League			6.9	0.432	**6.9**	**0.432**	**7**
Communist Refoundation			5.7	0.872	**5.7**	**0.872**	**6**
CCD-CDU/UDC			4.6	0.836	**4.6**	**0.836**	**5**
IDV			3.5	0.884	**3.5**	**0.884**	**3**
La Rete			1.9	0.516	**1.9**	**0.516**	**2**
Italy	_	**0.875**	_	**0.826**	_	**0.848**	**13**

Note: In 1968 PSI and PSDI formed a joint list (Unified Socialist Party, PSU), whose score is reported in the PSI's row of the table. Similarly, the 2008 score of the joint list, The Left-The Rainbow (SA), is reported in the Communist Refoundation's row of the table.

* Other nineteen parties fit the criteria only in one election.

to a specific territory that Diamanti called it a 'party without territory' (2009: 91) – as well as another personal party with a populist appeal, Italy of Values (IDV), led by the former public prosecutor Antonio Di Pietro (0.884).

However, none of the parties that have contested elections since the early 1990s has mean vote nationalisation levels that match the score (0.912) achieved by the M5S in 2013.[53] The party led by Beppe Grillo emerges as the political force with the most evenly distributed support in Italy, equalling the mean score for the DC. Just like *Forza Italia*, the M5S is based on the populist appeal of its charismatic leader and seems to be unanchored to specific parts of the Italian territory. Evidence of this can be drawn from the unprecedented electoral geography of the party: the M5S is the strongest party in regions with very different electoral traditions, like the conservative Sicily, the 'red' Marche and even Veneto, formerly core 'white zone' and later became a Northern League stronghold.

Finally, as one might expect, the small ethnoregionalist parties like the South Tyrolean People's Party (SVP) and the Valdostan Union (UV), given their minimal territorial coverage, have mean sPNS that approach 0 (with 0.023 and 0.003, respectively).

THE NETHERLANDS

The Dutch party system stemmed from the structuring of three subcultures, usually known as *zuilen* or pillars:[54] the Roman Catholic, the orthodox Protestant, and the secular or humanist, which was in turn divided into a socialist pro-working-class side and a liberal-conservative pro-middle-class side (Daalder and Koole 1988). These four subcultures originated from two cleavages: the religious one and the socioeconomic one. The oldest and probably the most important one was the religious cleavage. Since the sixteenth century, the Dutch state consisted of three main religious groups (Catholics, Protestants and a secular minority). According to Rokkan (1970: 115), the Dutch case belongs to the fourth type of his typology on the nation-building process in the European countries: the secular liberal elite, allied with the urban interests, was the central core of the nation-builders, facing resistance of the other two groups, the Catholics in the South[55] and the orthodox Protestants in the North, both allied with the landowners and the agrarian interests. The second cleavage – the social-class-related one – did not become important until about 1880 since industrialisation in the Netherlands took place later than in other Western European countries. Moreover, 'because of the binding force that religion constituted within both the Catholic and the Protestant segments of the population, only the secular or humanist group was actually divided into two parts – socialists and liberal-conservatives – as a result of this cleavage' (Ten Napel 1999: 164).

These four pillars gave rise to a wide array of cultural, social and economic institutions organised along denominational and class lines, thus creating four cohesive segments of society. So, from 1918 to the late 1960s, most people voted according to the subculture to which they belonged,[56] even if the overlapping between social and political membership was never complete (van der Eijk and Niemöller 1992: 257–58).

According to the structure of the society, the Dutch party system was based on five major political forces: in the secular pillar there were the Labour Party (PvdA) and the People's Party for Freedom and Democracy (VVD);

the followers of the Roman Church supported the Catholic People's Party (KVP), while the Protestant side was divided between Christian Historical Union (CHU) and the Anti-Revolutionary Party (ARP).[57] Together, these five parties used to win between 86 and 92 per cent of the national vote during the first two decades after 1945.

Since the end of the 1960s, the pillars started to crumble and melt down (*ontzuiling*), weakened by the process of secularisation and challenged by the emergence of new parties such as Democrats 66 (D66), a progressive liberal party whose original purpose was to 'explode' the pillarised party system (Irwin 1980: 173; Ten Napel 1999: 175), claiming for new 'post-materialists' issues (Inglehart 1977) and rejecting religion as a basis for parties. The remarkable electoral stability of the Dutch party system faced a major breakdown in the parliamentary election of 1967 when the three religious parties lost their combined majority in the *Tweede Kamer* (the lower house) for the first time after World War I. In the following elections, secularisation continued eroding the religious vote share, and in particular the Catholic side (the KVP lost almost half of its votes between 1963 and 1972). In order to avoid losing their pivotal role in Dutch politics, in 1977 the three religious parties merged into the Christian Democratic Appeal (CDA): as a result, until 1994, it was impossible to form a national coalition without the Christian Democrats. The 1994 election is the second breakthrough in Dutch electoral history: CDA lost thirteen percentage points, together with its pivotal position in government formation. Since then, the confessional party has never returned to its previous strength, and in the last decade, its electoral decline has dramatically increased. During the past years, the eclipse of the Christian Democrats has altered the long-term consolidated pattern of party competition, now based on an increasingly left-right distinction between the PvdA and the VVD.[58] Moreover, new parties have entered the electoral arena during the past twenty years, in a context of increasing aggregate volatility and fragmentation; on the left, the ecologist GreenLeft (GL), which resulted from the merging of the Communist Party (CPN) with other small leftist parties, and the Socialist Party (SP). On the right, two Eurosceptic and right-wing populist parties have arisen: the demised Pim Fortuyn List, from the name of a charismatic political columnist, winning 17 per cent of the votes in 2002, in the wake of the assassination of Fortuyn himself the day before the election, and the Party for Freedom (PVV), the third-largest party since the 2010 election.

As argued by Caramani (2004: 142), the Dutch case combines a high level of social segmentation with a low level of territorial heterogeneity. As it can be noted by looking at figure A.10, this is true only after the 1977 general election, when the merging of three main religious parties into the interconfessional CDA suddenly contributed to homogenise the aggregate level of

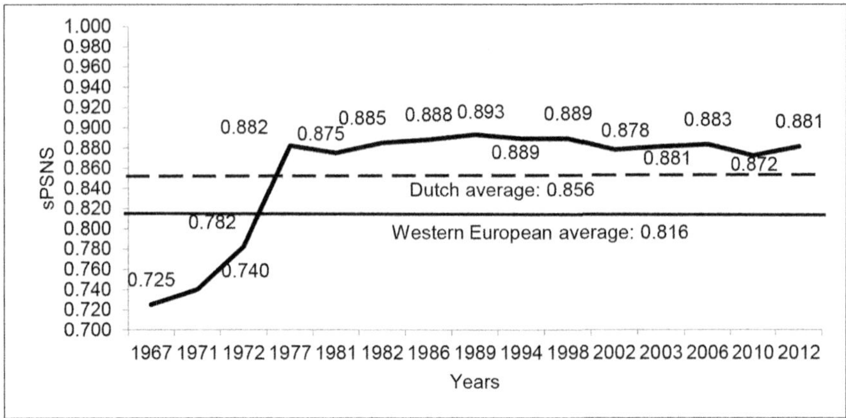

Figure A.10 Evolution of vote nationalisation over time, the Netherlands 1967–2012

vote nationalisation. Until 1977, the overall nationalisation of the vote in the Netherlands portrayed a regionalised territorial configuration. Since then, instead, the vote nationalisation has stabilised on very homogeneous levels till date.

Turning to individual parties, the main actors of the system rely on a quite homogeneous support (*see* table A.10).

The PvdA is the largest and the most nationalised party, and it shows two areas of particular strength: the northern provinces (Groningen, Drenthe) and the big urban areas of Amsterdam and Rotterdam. The other party representing the secular pillar, the VVD, has followed a similar pattern, with an increasing nationalisation between the two periods, which has been accompanied by an electoral growth over time that has made it the largest party in the Netherlands in the last two elections. As noted by Daalder (1966b: 204), the Liberals were (and still are) overrepresented in the international, commercially oriented Northwest (particularly in Flevoland, North Holland and Utrecht).

The most significant contribution to the regional distinctiveness of the country is given by the parties belonging to the religious pillar. Before merging into the CDA, the Catholic KVP was one of the most territorialised parties among the major European political forces. Its regional distinctiveness was very pronounced: for instance, in the 1967 parliamentary election, the KVP received only between 5 and 7 per cent of the votes in the Protestant and northern provinces of Groningen, Drenthe and Friesland; around 12 per cent in the urbanised areas of Amsterdam and Rotterdam; and exceeded the absolute majority of votes in the southern provinces of North Brabant (56.6 per cent) and Limburg (63.7 per cent). Looking at the Protestant parties, the territorial distribution of support for both the ARP and the CHU was very similar:

Table A.10 Dutch parties: Mean share of votes and mean sPNS by electoral period, 1967–2012

	1965–1990		*1991–2015*		*1965–2015*		
*Party**	*% Votes*	*sPNS*	*% Votes*	*sPNS*	*% Votes*	*sPNS*	*N*
PvdA	29.1	0.893	23.0	0.917	**26.3**	**0.904**	**15**
VVD	15.7	0.878	20.0	0.907	**17.7**	**0.892**	**15**
Democrats 66 (D66)	6.6	0.868	8.1	0.894	**7.3**	**0.880**	**13**
CDA	32.4	0.855	20.8	0.866	**25.6**	**0.861**	**12**
Reformed Political Party (SGP)	2.1	0.507	1.7	0.499	**1.9**	**0.502**	**12**
Socialist Party (SP)			8.6	0.879	**8.6**	**0.879**	**6**
GreenLeft (GL)			6.1	0.881	**6.1**	**0.881**	**5**
ChristianUnion (CU)			3.0	0.666	**3.0**	**0.666**	**5**
KVP	22.0	0.618			**22.0**	**0.618**	**3**
PVV			10.5	0.849	**10.5**	**0.849**	**3**
ARP	9.1	0.724			**9.1**	**0.724**	**3**
CHU	6.4	0.657			**6.4**	**0.657**	**3**
CPN	4.0	0.590			**4.0**	**0.590**	**3**
Reformed Political League (GPV)	1.7	0.602	1.3	0.550	**1.5**	**0.585**	**3**
Pim Fortuyn List			11.3	0.842	**11.3**	**0.842**	**2**
Democratic Socialists '70 (DS'70)	4.7	0.821			**4.7**	**0.821**	**2**
Netherlands	_	**0.834**	_	**0.882**	_	**0.856**	**15**

* Other five parties fit the criteria only in one election.

in the three elections contested before the merging with the KVP, they showed a regionalised configuration, with the constituencies of Friesland, Groningen and Drenthe as their electoral bastions. Among the small Protestant parties, the orthodox Calvinist Reformed Political Party (SGP) party is the least nationalised party of the system. Even if it receives only around 2 per cent of the national vote, it relies on a very concentrated support from a strip of land called *De Bijbelgordel* (the Dutch Bible Belt), mainly corresponding to the province of Zealand, where it receives about seven times more votes than in the other provinces.

All the new parties that entered the electoral arena during the 1990s display a homogeneous distribution of support, except the new Protestant party (ChristianUnion, CU) that is evenly distributed apart from the Catholic provinces of Limburg and North Brabant and the secularised North Holland where it is virtually nonexistent. The other new parties, the SP, the GL, the PVV and the Pim Fortuyn List, show high levels of vote nationalisation. The Socialist Party is stronger in the Catholic provinces; the GreenLeft in the urbanised and secularised areas of Utrecht and North Holland; conversely, the populist Pim Fortuyn List relied on a quite evenly distributed support, while the extreme-right-wing Party for Freedom has its major stronghold in the Catholic Limburg.

NORWAY

With its peripheral location on the fringe of the European continent and its demographic marginality, Norway has been extensively studied as a paradigmatic example of the structuring of the centre-periphery cleavage, a foundation of the Rokkanian theory on the genesis of party systems in Europe (Rokkan 1967; Rokkan and Valen 1970; Aarebrot 1982).

The main line of opposition began to take shape during the long Danish domination (1376–1814). At that time, the political-administrative elite started its effort to achieve a cultural and legal standardisation of the country's peripheries to impose the authority of the centre and realise a national political integration. This process of centralisation led by the pro-Danish ruling classes continued during the Swedish rule (1814–1905), when the first political parties emerged: the political conflict was centred around the polarity of Conservatives (*Høire*) and Liberals (*Venstre*). The former ones were expression of the urban and secularised ruling classes of Oslo and gained most of their support from the cities, particularly in the East, and in the coastal communes around *Oslofjord* (Aarebrot 1982: 94). The latter ones, instead, represented the agrarian interests, the farmers, and, in general, they supported the peripheral struggle against the centre's harmonisation efforts. The Conservative support has remained stable through time, while the Liberal consent rapidly declined after the emergence of the Labour Party (A) and the introduction of a proportional electoral system in 1920. By that time, the party system stabilised around two main cleavage lines and became frozen up to the end of the 1960s.

The first cleavage is the historical centre-periphery conflict. Three 'countercultures' stemmed from the peripheral regions during the nineteenth century: the religious movement of Lutheran orthodoxy – spread in many localities in western Norway (the so-called Bible Belt) – that gave rise to the Christian People's Party (KRF), which since 1945 has become an important actor in the party system (Nilson 1980), with a territorially concentrated support in the provinces (*Fylker*) of the West and the South (Karvonen 1993); the linguistic division, with the emergence of the 'Nynorsk' movement, created in the 1850s as an attempt to combine traits of oral Norwegian dialects into a written standard, grown out in opposition to the official Norwegian written language (*bokmål*) and spoken in the nonurban and nonindustrialised communes of the South, West and East inland regions (Aarebrot 1982: 83); and, finally, the temperance movement (*teetotalism*), which spread in the 1840s along the southern seaboard with the attempt to limit the consumption of spirits. These three movements mobilised the peripheral population of the western and southern provinces, becoming relevant actors in Norwegian politics: still, in the 1972 referendum to enter the EEC, they played a decisive role in the organisation of the Front against the Norwegian EEC membership. The peripheral western and southern provinces are also the territorial strongholds of the Centre Party (SP, before 1959 called Farmers' Party, BP), a former agrarian party, supporting farmers' interests and decentralisation. The urban and secularised 'centre' (which mainly means Oslo and the other communes of the eastern seaboard) is instead represented by both the Conservative and the Labour parties.

The second important cleavage that structured the Norwegian party system is the socioeconomic conflict between industrial workers and employers. Being mainly a functional cleavage, with a weak territorial specificity, such conflict contributed to nationalise the political competition by dividing the party system into two blocs: the socialist and the nonsocialist one. The socialist bloc consists of the Labour, the predominant party in the system, continuously holding power between 1945 and 1963, and the Labour-splinter Socialist People's Party (SF, today Socialist Left Party, SV), while the non-socialist bloc is composed by the so-called bourgeois parties, namely, the Conservatives, the Liberals, the Christian Democrats and the Agrarians. The two blocs compete to gain the majority of seats in the Norwegian Parliament (*Storting*) and alternate in government. From the mid-1960s, the party system has experienced a remarkable stability in the electoral results of the individual parties and an overall balance between the two blocs,[59] with just a major change: the emergence and rise of the right-wing Progress party (FRP), founded in 1973 on the model of its Danish counterpart. In the last decade, this party has increased its electoral support, becoming the second-largest party in 2009 and supplanting the Conservatives as the first party of the non-socialist bloc for the first time since 1945.

As emphasised in chapter 3, Norway belongs to the group of nationalised and stable polities. Yet, by looking at figure A.11, plotting the evolution of vote nationalisation in Norway, a general trend towards increasing nationalisation can be detected: in 1965 the Norwegian party system could be considered a rather regionalised one, with a sPSNS of 0.822, well below the overall median value of 0.858 (*see also* figure 3.1). Since the mid-1970s, the system slightly increased its level of territorial homogeneity at each election. The constant process of vote nationalisation is due to the increasing weight held by the functional, socioeconomic left-right cleavage in the structuring of the electoral competition in Norway, to the detriment of the old, territorial, centre-periphery conflict that gave rise to the three countercultures whose importance has declined in the past decades.

As table A.11 shows, the Labour Party (A) is the largest and most nationalised party of the system during the 1965–2013 period. However, to a certain extent, it maintains 'a regionally uneven pattern of support' (Aarebrot 1982: 95), being stronger in the industrial districts of the North and in the East, with

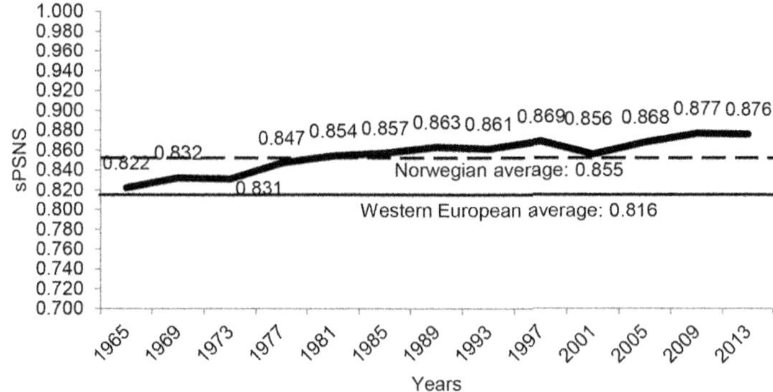

Figure A.11 Evolution of vote nationalisation over time, Norway 1965–2013

Table A.11 Norwegian parties: Mean share of votes and mean sPNS by electoral period, 1965–2013

	1965–1990		*1991–2015*		*1965–2015*		
*Party**	*% Votes*	*sPNS*	*% Votes*	*sPNS*	*% Votes*	*sPNS*	*N*
Norwegian Labour Party (DNA)	39.9	0.907	32.5	0.916	**36.5**	**0.911**	**13**
Conservative Party (H)	23.9	0.831	18.5	0.859	**21.4**	**0.845**	**13**
Christian People's Party (KRF)	9.7	0.744	8.6	0.765	**9.2**	**0.754**	**13**
Centre Party (SP)	8.5	0.724	8.1	0.728	**8.3**	**0.726**	**13**
Socialist Left Party (SV)	6.5	0.843	7.6	0.868	**7.0**	**0.855**	**13**
Liberal Party (V)	5.3	0.783	4.5	0.848	**4.9**	**0.813**	**13**
Progress Party (FRP)	6.6	0.827	16.3	0.899	**12.4**	**0.870**	**10**
Red Electoral Alliance/Red Party			1.3	0.624	**1.3**	**0.624**	**4**
Coastal Party (KP)			1.3	0.450	**1.3**	**0.450**	**2**
Norway	–	**0.844**	–	**0.868**	–	**0.855**	**13**

* Other four parties fit the criteria only in one election.

the exception of Oslo – which has always remained a Conservative stronghold – while it is underrepresented in southwestern Norway, where the three countercultures are more deeply rooted.

Besides the Labour, other five parties contested all the thirteen elections of the period 1965–2013: among them, the Socialist Left Alliance is the more territorially homogeneous one, followed by the Conservative Party. The other traditional bourgeois parties show a clear regionalised support: the Liberal Party has lost much of its old electoral strength and now relies on a more homogeneous support than in the past, while the former agrarian Centre Party and the orthodox Protestant Christian People's Party have a marked regional distinctiveness, which is a legacy of the old centre-periphery conflict.

If the overall evolution of vote nationalisation of Norway shows a pattern of increasing homogeneity, this is also due to the emergence of the Progress

Party (FRP) as a fundamental actor in the party system by the mid-1990s: its electoral growth goes hand in hand with the homogenisation of the territorial distribution of its support. It has moved from an average of 4.5 per cent until the mid-1980s to an average of 19 per cent since the 2000s, during which its sPNS has averaged 0.914, a level comparable only to that of the Labour and understandable in light of the populist, non-territorial-based appeal of the party.

The other parties included into the analysis are minor and territorially heterogeneous parties, some of them with explicit regional or local claims: the regionalist Future for Finnmark was a regional splinter of the Labour Party, and it contested the 1989 election only in the northern province of Finnmark (Caramani 2004: 141). Finally, in 2001 and 2005, the Coastal Party (KP) was able to obtain votes in the coastal communes of three provinces of the northern periphery: *Nordland, Troms* and *Finnmark.*

PORTUGAL

Portugal is a late-coming democratic country since it belongs to the so-called third wave of democratisation (Huntington 1991). After about fifty years of authoritarian regime (the so-called organic democracy of the *Estado Novo*) under the dictator Salazar (1926–1968) and, after his death, under his son Caetano (1968–1974), the 'Carnation Revolution' of 1974 inaugurated the transition to democracy, encouraging a process similar to those occurred in other authoritarian regimes of Southern Europe, like Spain and Greece (Pridham 1984).

As far as the social structure is concerned, Portugal is one of the most homogeneous European countries, being devoid of either a linguistic divide (everyone speaks Portuguese) or a religious divide (almost everyone is a Roman Catholic). As stated by Mendes, Camões and McDonald (2001: 6), there are essentially three cleavages that deserve to be mentioned: the Catholic/anticlergy divide, the North-South regional cleavage and the urban-rural cleavage. These cleavages have ancient origins, traceable in the period preceding the establishment of the authoritarian regime. They contributed to shaping the actual Portuguese party system, even though this latter has also been influenced by some other features of the Portuguese historical development, which are not directly related to the cleavage constellation. Among these latter features, the most important ones are the semiperipheral nature of the polity (Mouzelis 1986: 74), the late and vertical incorporation of the masses into the democratic life, the clientelistic relationship between the electorate and political parties (a legacy of the nineteenth-century Portuguese political system based on a clientelistic system known as *Caciquismo*),[60] the relative weakness of the associations and interest groups and, in general, the low involvement of the population into the democratic experience (declining turnout rates over time and low membership rates for the most important parties, with the possible exception of the Communists).[61]

By going back to the cleavages, there is a wide degree of overlapping between the church/anti-clergy divide and the regional cleavage, since the former has a marked territorial distinctiveness. Indeed, the main territorial cleavage lies between a conservative and Catholic North, largely comprising small farmers and predominantly voting for the centre-right parties (and previously representing the social base of Salazar's support) and a more lay, socialist-communist South. In particular, it was the Communist party (PCP) that politicised the state-church cleavage against the Salazar clerical regime, becoming the leading actor during the Carnation Revolution and the first period of the democratic transition, before being downsized in the first democratic election of 1975. The PCP was hegemonic among the lesser-skilled strata of the industrial working class in the southern urban centres, as well as among the rural wage earners in the provinces of Alentejo (Wiarda 1980: 317), a region dominated by the presence of large landowners and which is still today the most secularised and left-leaning region of the country.

The urban-rural cleavage divides between the rich, western coastal fringe were 70 per cent of the population, and the most important cities are located (Lisbon, Porto, Braga) from the poor eastern provinces bordering Spain (*Beja, Évora, Portalegre, Castelo Branco, Guarda* and *Bragança*) and subjected to a process of internal migration of young people towards the larger towns of the West, which is further reinforcing this cleavage (Magone 1999: 246). From a political viewpoint, western regions tend to concentrate their support on the two most important parties[62] of the system, located near to the centre of the political spectrum: the centre-left Socialist Party (PS) and the centre-right Social Democratic Party (PSD). Conversely, the rural eastern areas are supportive of the most extremist parties of the system, the PCP and the Social Democratic Centre (CDS, since 1995 Popular Party). The latter one is a Conservative and Catholic rightist party, initially comprising many politicians from the former authoritarian regime, whose strongholds are the northeastern provinces of *Viseu, Guarda* and *Bragança.*

Since 1975, the Portuguese party system has always been characterised by a format of moderate pluralism (Sartori 1976), with four relevant parties lying of a left-right pattern of competition (PCP, PS, PSD and CDS). The Communists have been the only party excluded from power during the entire postauthoritarian period so far. The alternation in government has concerned the two major parties, the PS and the PSD.[63]

The PS was founded in 1973 in Germany by some exiled socialists among which the first leader (and then prime minister) was Mário Soares. During the revolution, the party moved away from the Marxist ideas, becoming closer to the other Social Democratic parties of Western Europe. Relying on a passive membership, mainly mobilised during elections, the PS has never been a mass party, but it seems rather characterised by a catch-all nature. The party is indeed dominant not only among the industrial proletariat in the North and the farmers of central Portugal but also among the new middle classes (Magone 1999: 241, 246).

The PSD (originally PPD, *Partido popular democrático*) was founded in 1974 by some former members of the liberal wing of the prerevolution National Assembly. The ideology of the party was flexible to the outset, placing the modernisation and democratisation of the country as its core. Later on, during the leadership of Cavaco Silva, the party moved towards more liberal-conservative positions. The PSD is mainly the party of the small rural and urban petty bourgeoisie, and it also has strong affinities with the business organisations as well as the small farmer's associations.

The party system has always been characterised by a high degree of fluidity due to the low level of partisanship of the electorate, which tends to be available to change vote from one election to the next one. Despite the quite high levels of volatility (see Emanuele 2015b), the Portuguese party system has been labelled as an 'ultra-stable' system (Aguiar 1985; Lisi 2007) where the same partisan alternatives are offered to the electorate at every election and where the trend since the mid-1980s has been one of further simplification towards an almost two-party format.

Figure A.12 plots the aggregate trend of vote nationalisation in Portugal since 1975. A sharp nationalisation process is detectable. It is especially the first half of the democratic period that deserves particular attention: in the first democratic election of 1975, Portugal appears as a regionalised country (0.755), while sixteen years later, in the 1991 election, it has become a highly nationalised polity (0.885) also compared to Western Europe.

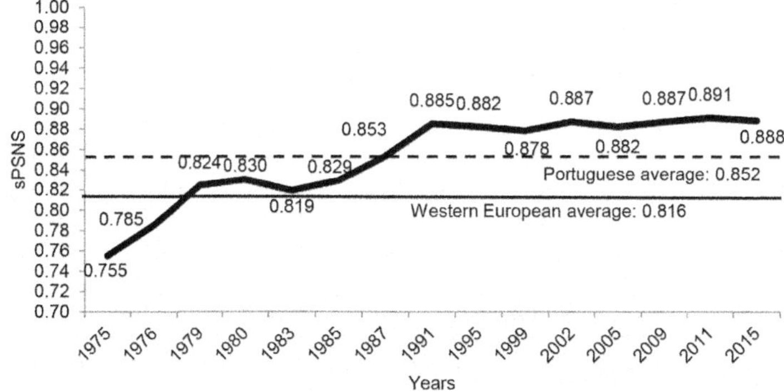

Figure A.12 Evolution of vote nationalisation over time, Portugal 1975–2015

This sharp pattern of nationalisation is consistent with Caramani's theory (2004) according to which nationalisation of politics is a historical process that occurred in Europe during the first period of the democratic experience. With the obvious differences related to the dissimilar timing of the Portuguese democratisation process, vote nationalisation seems to follow an almost identical path. After 1991, the sPSNS has stabilised, in perfect continuity with the stabilisation of the party system, and even this evidence is consistent with Caramani's finding of a long pattern of stability of territorial configurations in Western Europe after World War II (2004: 80).

Table A.12 summarises the mean share of votes and the mean nationalisation scores by period for the Portuguese parties. The PSD appears as the largest party even if, as reported in the note at the foot of the table, in the 1979, the 1980 and the 2015 elections, it formed a joint list with the CDS. All the four main parties show some kind of trend towards nationalisation over time. This trend is particularly sharp for PSD and the CDS. The former is dominant in the two autonomous regions of Azores and Madeira (where it usually reaches the absolute majority) and, to a lesser extent, in the mainland district of *Leiria, Viseu, Vila Real* and *Bragança.*

The most homogeneous party is the PS, which was highly nationalised even during the first democratic period. This finding is consistent with the European context, where the Social Democratic parties are the most homogeneous parties almost everywhere. During the past years, the sPNS of the PS shows an impressively high level. As mentioned earlier, the strongest support for the party comes from the western urban district of the country (Lisbon, Porto, Santarem, Setubal and Coimbra). The PCP is the only party that has continued to show a very high level of regionalisation: the electoral

Table A.12 Portuguese parties: Mean share of votes and mean sPNS by period, 1975–2015

	1965–1990		*1991–2015*		*1965–2015*		
*Party**	*% Votes*	*sPNS*	*% Votes*	*sPNS*	*% Votes*	*sPNS*	*N*
PPD/PSD	36.8	0.821	37.5	0.881	**37.2**	**0.853**	**15**
PS	30.8	0.906	38.1	0.942	**34.7**	**0.925**	**15**
PCP/CDU	16.1	0.612	8.4	0.643	**12.0**	**0.628**	**15**
CDS/PP	10.4	0.758	8.8	0.883	**9.5**	**0.831**	**12**
Left Bloc (BE)			6.4	0.817	**6.4**	**0.817**	**6**
PRD	11.8	0.815			**11.8**	**0.815**	**2**
Portugal	_	**0.814**	_	**0.885**	_	**0.852**	**15**

Note: In the 1979, 1980 and 2015 elections, PPD/PSD and CDS/PP formed electoral alliances whose scores are reported in the PPD/PSD's row of the table.

*Other two parties fit the criteria only in one election.

strongholds of the party are still today the provinces of Alentejo (*Beja, Evora, Setubal*) and, to a lesser extent, Lisbon.

Finally, two other parties deserve to be mentioned: the Democratic Renewal Party (PRD), a moderate left-wing party reaching a great success in the 1985 election (18 per cent) before disappearing after 1987, and the Left Bloc (BE), a coalition of extreme-left-wing movements with a libertarian and postmaterialist ideology that have run since 1999. Although it is a minor party, it has increased over time its share of votes, thus replacing the CDU as the main party left to the PS both in 2009 and in the 2015 elections.

SPAIN

The Spanish party system is relatively new compared to the other European ones. After about forty years of authoritarian regime, Franco's death in 1975 gave start to a process of peaceful transition (the *ruptura pactada*) that first led to the founding democratic election of 1977 and then to the draft of the new constitution in 1978.

According to Linz and Montero (1999: 14), the newness of Spanish democracy marks its very modernity, because 'Spanish democracy has skipped many of the stages of development that older party systems have passed through', thus creating a party system in a modern society. Moreover, the re-emergence of political parties in post-Franco Spain is marked by a high degree of organisational discontinuity with the former democratic experience of the Second Republic (1931–1936) (Linz 1980: 102): most of the Second Republic parties simply did not reconstitute themselves after the end of the dictatorship, or, if they survived, they were often led by figures which were too young to have been involved in the previous party system (Hopkin 1999: 211).

Nonetheless, the main cleavages that gave rise to the modern Spanish party system are the same that were relevant during the 1930s (and that led to the civil war between Republicans and Nationalists in 1936).[64] There are three main sources of political conflict.

The most explosive cleavage is the one between the subject and the dominant culture (Hopkin 1999: 208). The centre-periphery conflict is deeply rooted in Spanish history, and it could be dated back to the state-building process with the unification of the kingdoms of Castile and Aragon. The economic decline of Castile and the ascendancy of Aragon-Catalonia created a disjunction between the economic power of the Catalan region and the institutional power set in Madrid. Catalan nationalism emerged to defend Catalan economic interests and also to protect Catalonia's distinctive cultural and linguistic heritage. A similar movement emerged in the rich and industrialised

Basque Country.[65] In other words, as Blondel states, 'Centralisation did not succeed . . . in part because feelings of separatism were higher, in part because Madrid was not until recently a dynamic centre of economic activity' (1981: 319). Catalan and Basque historical national movements arose during the nineteenth century and rapidly found political expression with the birth of nationalist parties. The repressive action during Franco's dictatorship led to their powerful re-emergence in the new democratic system.

Regional claims for greater autonomy from the centre[66] and the protection of the historical, cultural and linguistic distinctiveness now concern Catalonia and the Basque Country and also Galicia,[67] Andalusia, Navarra, Valencia and Canary Islands. In each of these regions, specific regional parties ranging from the extreme left to the centre-right emerged, thus creating quite distinct party subsystems in all these regions. That is why most of the scholars distinguish Spanish political parties between *partidos de ámbito estatal* (Pae) and *partidos de ámbito no estatal* (Pane) (Lanza 2007: 118). Even Linz and Montero (1999: 3) prefer to speak about Spanish *party systems* rather than *a party system*, to highlight the fact that the national party system coexists with a number of regional party systems where distinct patterns of competition operate.[68]

While the centre-periphery conflict determines the features of the regional party systems, the other two main cleavages, the class one and the religious one, have a nationwide scope, and they both cross-cut the territorial conflict.

The class cleavage opposed large landowners – allied with the secular liberal-conservative centre-builders[69] – and landless peasants organised into socialist and anarchist trade unions, establishing a radical left-wing tradition in areas such as Andalusia and Estremadura that still today remain a bedrock for the Left. In the areas where industrialisation took hold (Catalonia, the Basque Country, Asturias and Madrid), the capital-labour cleavage was an important source of conflict (Hopkin 1999: 209), and still today, even if in a context of weakening class divisions, the left-right conflict structures Spanish national politics.

Finally, the state-church cleavage was a fundamental source of conflict during the Second Republic, based upon an anticlerical constitution, and during the civil war and the initial stages of the authoritarian regime, where Franco presented the church as a guardian of Spanish values. However, this cleavage did not give rise to any relevant political party in post-Franco Spain. Unlike what happened in other Catholic countries like Italy and France, a confessional party did not emerge in Spain,[70] and the religious cleavage has been absorbed by the prominent class conflict, losing importance due to a growing secularisation.

Since 1977, the Spanish party system has experienced some notable changes concerning the number of the relevant actors and the patterns of competition. Most scholars identify three main periods.

The first period (1977–1982) is characterised by a format of moderate pluralism and by a centripetal direction of party competition. In both the 1977 and the 1979 elections, the Union of the Democratic Centre (UCD) – a coalition of thirteen small centre or centre-right groups ranging from Liberals to Christian Democrats and Social Democrats – emerges as the leading force of the system and as the main guarantor of a smooth transition to democracy, with its leader Adolfo Suárez serving as prime minister (Blondel 1981; Lancaster 1992). The main opposition party is the socialist PSOE (*Partido Socialista Obrero Espanol*). These two parties establish a classic left-right pattern of competition and get together the vote of about two-thirds of the electorate. The other relevant national parties are, on the extreme Left, the Communist Party (PCE) and, on the extreme Right, the Popular Alliance (AP, later Popular Party, PP), founded by Manuel Fraga along with other former prominent figures of Francoism.

The second period (1982–1996) opens with the 'cataclysmic' (Caciagli 1986) election of 1982: the UCD collapsed from 35 to 6 per cent and the PSOE gained a massive 48 per cent, thus emerging as the new dominant actor of Spanish politics. On the right wing of the system, a realignment occurs, with many former UCD voters shifting towards the AP, which hereafter becomes the main party of the centre-right, and total volatility reaches the unprecedented level of 43.8 per cent (Emanuele 2015b), the highest ever detected in Western Europe until the Greek election of May 2012. During the 1982–1993 period, the PSOE wins four consecutive elections, thus fitting the features identified by Sartori to detect the presence of a 'predominant party system' (1976: 199).

The third period (since 1996) has been characterised by an alternation in power, with the PP replacing PSOE as the ruling party from 1996 to 2004 and again from 2011 to 2015. Moreover, the number and the electoral strength of the so-called PANE have increased since the 1980s, while the small national parties have lost ground (aside from PSOE and PP, only the leftist *Izquierda Unida* is able to gain seats).

Finally, the 2015 election is likely to have opened a fresh period in Spanish politics: the previous quasi-two party system has been wiped out by the rise of two new national parties, the leftist *Podemos* and the centrist *Ciudadanos* (Orriols and Cordero 2016). The consequence has been a hung Parliament for the first time in the Spanish postauthoritarian history and a prolonged political crisis.

As shown in chapter 3 (*see* figure 3.3), Spain belongs to the regionalised and stable polities. Its mean sPSNS of 0.775 is lower than the overall mean value of 0.816, and its internal dispersion among the eleven general elections occurred since 1977 is limited. Figure A.13 plots the evolution of vote nationalisation over time. The Bochsler's index follows an irregular path, reaching its lowest point in the 1989 election. From then on, the party system starts a

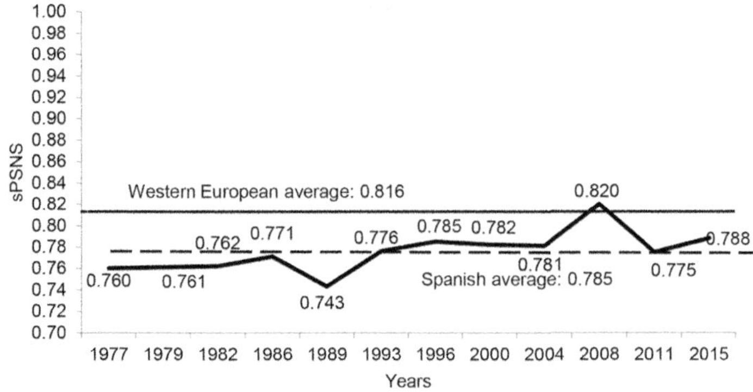

Figure A.13 Evolution of vote nationalisation over time, Spain 1977–2015

process of increasing homogenisation. In general, we note the apparent discrepancy, underlined by Caramani (2004: 112), between the overall level of nationalisation of the country and the degree of territorial coverage for Spanish parties. The latter one is indeed the lowest in Western Europe, due to the high number of regionalist parties that contest only one or a few provinces. However, the overall level of nationalisation is not so low in a comparative perspective (*see* figure 3.2), no matter which index of homogeneity is taken into account (both Caramani's indices and Bochsler's one provide similar results). This is because, as parties are weighted by size, the large number of small regionalist parties has only a limited impact on the systemic level of homogeneity, while the few big national (and indeed more nationalised) parties play a major role.[71]

As far as the individual parties are concerned, the two groups of PAE and PANE are clearly distinguishable according to their mean level of nationalisation. Starting with the PAE, the PSOE is by far the bigger and most nationalised party of the system. It was the predominant party during the period 1982–1996, and it has always been the leading party of the Left. Like many other European Social Democratic parties, PSOE's homogeneity is very high, but the party also displays a certain variability of support, retaining its own strongholds in urban and industrial centres (and, more generally, in Andalusia and Estremadura) and, to a lesser extent, in Catalonia, where it is the only national party which is able to overcome the support of the Catalan nationalist parties. It is, instead, relatively weak in Madrid, *Castilla-León*, *Región de Murcia* and Galicia, and in rural areas with a rooted Catholic-Conservative tradition, which are a stronghold of the Popular Party. This latter has progressively increased its share of votes eventually overcoming the PSOE in the second electoral period. Its level of homogeneity is significantly lower than that of PSOE, in line with other Conservative parties in Europe. Nonetheless, it has undergone an intense process of nationalisation over time. The discrepancy of the index between PP and PSOE is mainly due to the historic distrust of the electorate of some autonomous regions towards the PP: in particular, in the Basque Country and Catalonia, the PP is particularly weak because the electorate of these regions still suffers from the legacy of the Francoist past and the centralising and repressive policies carried out by the *Caudillo*.

The third-largest party among those contesting all the twelve Spanish general elections is the United Left (IU, until 1982 PCE). Its territorial configuration appears as more regionalised than that of the other two nationwide parties. The party is particularly rooted in the industrial and urban areas of Madrid, Asturias, Andalusia and Barcelona.

As said before, the UCD, disappeared after 1982, showed a territorial distribution of its support that was not far from that of the Nationalists during the 1930s or that of the PP from the 1980s onwards. This pattern of support is similar to the one of another nationwide party appeared for three elections during the 1980s, the Democratic and Social Centre (CDS), founded in 1982 by Adolfo Suárez after having abandoned the UCD. The CDS showed a mean Bochsler's index very close to that of the UCD, with a territorially concentrated support in the region of *Castilla-León* and the Canary and Baleares Islands.

Most of the table A.13 is occupied by the statistics of many ethnoregionalist parties that are the most important specificity of Spanish party system. Among them, the most relevant one is certainly Convergence and Union (CiU), the Christian Democratic Catalan nationalist party. It has a very low

Table A.13 Spanish parties: Mean share of votes and mean sPNS by electoral period, 1977–2015

	1965–1990		*1991–2015*		*1965–2015*		
*Party**	*% Votes*	*sPNS*	*% Votes*	*sPNS*	*% Votes*	*sPNS*	*N*
PSOE	38.5	0.893	35.8	0.905	**36.9**	**0.900**	**12**
AP/PP	18.0	0.762	38.9	0.842	**30.2**	**0.809**	**12**
PCE/United Left (IU)	7.6	0.742	6.0	0.668	**6.7**	**0.699**	**12**
UCD	25.5	0.745			**25.5**	**0.745**	**3**
CDS	6.7	0.746			**6.7**	**0.746**	**3**
Convergence and Union (CiU)	3.9	0.161	3.8	1.59	**3.8**	**0.160**	**12**
Basque Nationalist Party (PNV)	1.6	0.056	1.4	0.054	**1.4**	**0.055**	**12**
Republican Left of Catalonia (ERC)	0.7	0.164	1.3	0.148	**1.1**	**0.153**	**10**
Canarian Coalition (CC)	0.3	0.032	0.8	0.042	**0.6**	**0.039**	**10**
Basque Solidarity (EA)	0.7	0.061	0.6	0.072	**0.6**	**0.071**	**8**
Galician Nationalist Bloc (BNG)			0.8	0.780	**0.8**	**0.078**	**6**
Popular Unity (HB)	1.0	0.066	0.8	0.059	**1.0**	**0.063**	**6**
Aragonese Party (PAR)	0.3	0.033	0.3	0.027	**0.3**	**0.030**	**6**
Basque Country Left (EE)	0.5	0.063			**0.5**	**0.063**	**5**

(*Continued*)

Table A.13 (Continued)

	1965–1990		*1991–2015*		*1965–2015*		
*Party**	*% Votes*	*sPNS*	*% Votes*	*sPNS*	*% Votes*	*sPNS*	*N*
Andalusian Party (PA)	1.4	0.165	0.8	0.207	**1.1**	**0.186**	**4**
Aragonese Union (CHA)			0.3	0.038	**0.3**	**0.038**	**4**
Valencian Union (UV)	0.5	0.069	0.5	0.103	**0.5**	**0.080**	**3**
Yes to Navarre (NB)			0.2	0.033	**0.2**	**0.033**	**2**
Yes to the Future (GB)			0.1	0.013	**0.1**	**0.013**	**2**
Spain	_	**0.759**	_	**0.787**	_	**0.775**	**12**

Note: The result of the Democratic Agreement for Catalonia (PDC) in 1977 has been computed in the CiU's row. This latter was a federation of two parties, the Democratic Convergence of Catalonia (CDC) and the Democratic Union of Catalonia (UDC). As it dissolved in 2015, the result of 2015 of its largest counterpart (CDC), under the label of Freedom and Democracy (DL), has been computed in the CiU's row. EA contested the 2011 election under the electoral coalition of Amaiur and the 2015 election under the electoral coalition of Basque Country Unite (EHB).

* Other nineteen parties fit the criteria only in one election.

sPNS, given that it contests only the four constituencies of Catalonia and is stronger in Gerona and Lerida and weaker in Barcelona. The same territorial configuration is shown by the other Catalan parties, like the leftist ERC (*Esquerra Republicana de Catalunya*), which often contest the electoral districts of the neighbouring *Comunidad Valenciana* and Baleares.

The second bigger nationalist party is the Basque Nationalist Party (PNV), while all the other parties are of minor importance at the national level, although they are able to receive a significant portion of the vote share in their province(s).

SWEDEN

As posited by Oskarson (1992: 339), 'taking a long-term view, the most salient trait of the Swedish party system has been its stability'. Unlike other Scandinavian peripheral countries like Norway or Finland, Sweden has never undergone a foreign domination since its independence from Denmark in 1523; Sweden grew up as a politically strong nation-state, embraced the Reformation and became a homogeneously Protestant country. These historical features of the Swedish nation-building process led to the absence of rooted ethnic linguistic or religious conflicts, thus endowing the country with a marked cultural and political homogeneity, reflected in the party system's features since the early 1900s.

The first national party organisations were formed at the beginning of the twentieth century. The original partisan aggregate linked to the agrarian interests (the Party of the Rural People, *Lantmannapartiet*) splits into two opposite factions: a liberal and antiprotectionist wing, which formed the Liberal Party in 1902, and a protectionist wing, made of several agrarian and land-owning groups, which formed the Conservative Party in 1904 (Borioni 2005: 24; Poli 2007: 152). These first two national organisations were parliamentary parties that steered the electoral competition alongside a left-right line of opposition, just like in the United Kingdom and the other Scandinavian countries. The first Swedish party that emerged outside the Parliament (*Riksdag*) was the Social Democratic Party (SAP), founded in 1889 and soon risen as a nationalised mass party organisation with close ties to the emerging Labour Union Federation and the growing industrial labour force. As in many other European countries, a Communist splinter group (SKP) separated from SAP just after the Russian Revolution of 1917. The configuration of the Swedish party system was completed through the formation of the Farmers' League, defending the interests of the agrarian class. This latter was threatened by the uniquely rapid industrialisation of the country and by the consequent internal migration of the population from the rural to the urban areas (Hancock 1980: 186–87; Christensen 1997: 395). The urban-rural axis was the only conflict supplementing and cross-cutting the overwhelmingly predominant economic left-right cleavage that oriented the electoral alignments of Swedish politics (Berglund and Lindström 1978: 18; Bergström 1991: 8–9).

The introduction of the universal suffrage in 1921 stabilised the Swedish party system for almost seventy years, setting a five-party format with the same actors, which were also the only ones to enter the Parliament until the 1988 election. This unprecedented stability and continuity of the party system had no other comparable cases in Europe and contributed to building the so-called Scandinavian '1 vs. 3–4' system (Rokkan 1970) or '2+3 formula' (Berglund and Lindström 1978). This model consisted of a two-bloc system based on the class cleavage and on the dichotomy between two socialists and three nonsocialists or 'bourgeois' parties: on the left there was the powerful SAP, dominating the electoral competition and ruling uninterruptedly between 1932 and 1976,[72] flanked by a relatively weak but stable radical Left; on the opposite bloc there were, from the centre to the right wing, the Agrarian Party (renamed Centre Party in 1957), the Liberal Party (FP) and the conservative Moderate Party (M). The bourgeois bloc succeeded to win a majority of seats and form a coalition government only between 1976 and 1982, 1991 and 1994 and from 2006 to 2014.

At the end of the 1980s, this long-lasting stability was altered by the progressive erosion of the class-cleavage voting[73] and by the emergence of new issue-based divides that vested the party system with a new multidimensionality it had previously lacked. First, there was the growth-ecology divide that led the Greens (MP) to become in 1988 the first new parliamentary party in seventy years; second, a morality versus secular cleavage emerged and led to the formation of a religious party, the Christian Democratic Party (KD), which entered the *Riksdag* in 1991. After these changes, the frozen five-party model evolved in the new seven-party format that lasted until 2010, when the populist right-wing Sweden Democrats (SD) received 5.7 per cent of the votes and twenty seats.

As underlined in chapter 3, Sweden is the second-most nationalised country in Europe (after Greece), with a mean sPSNS of 0.882 between 1968 and 2014. Moreover, the cross-time variation of the index reveals a considerably low variability through time, although, by looking at figure A.14, a steady trend of denationalisation can be detected.

This notable systemic stability on high levels of nationalisation is the consequence of the homogeneous territorial configurations shown by the individual parties. This finding is consistent with the historical backgrounds of the Swedish party system that emerged and consolidated along with a predominant socioeconomic left-right cleavage, while the traditional territorial-based conflicts have always been absent (cultural cleavages) or declining through time (urban-rural cleavage). As a result, the main parties in Sweden appear as nationalised, with fragile territorial ties and without many specific regional strongholds.

As shown by Rose and Urwin (1975: 27), and by Caramani (2004: 141), the Social Democratic Party has always been remarkably homogeneous across the territorial units of the country. Table A.14 confirms this finding: the SAP shows a very nationalised configuration, which is more or less maintained over time, notwithstanding the marked electoral decline of the party. Yet, the party has always retained some areas of particular strength: the SAP is indeed electorally dominant in the industrial and scarcely populated northern counties (*Norrbotten, Västerbotten, Västernorrland, Jämtland*), while it appears largely underrepresented in the most important cities (Stockholm, Gothenburg and Malmö) and, more generally, in the southern and eastern counties.

The three main bourgeois parties underwent significant shifts in their levels of support through time. The Moderate Party became the biggest nonsocialist

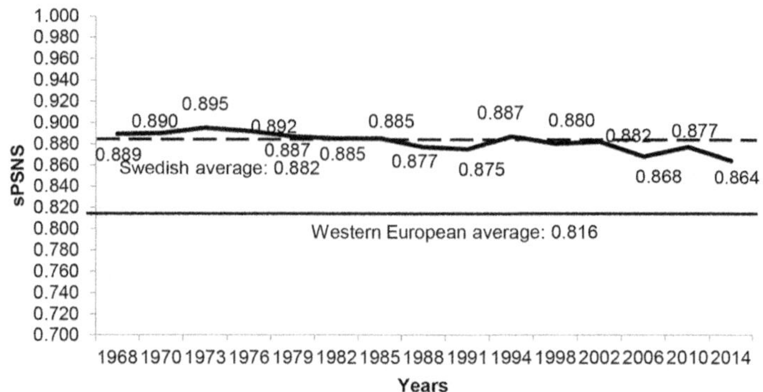

Figure A.14 Evolution of vote nationalisation over time, Sweden 1968–2014

Table A.14 Swedish parties: Mean share of votes and mean sPNS by electoral period, 1968–2014

	1965–1990		*1991–2015*		*1965–2012*		
*Party**	*% Votes*	*sPNS*	*% Votes*	*sPNS*	*% Votes*	*sPNS*	*N*
Social Democratic Party (SAP)	44.3	0.939	36.6	0.911	**40.7**	**0.926**	**15**
Moderate Party (M)	17.1	0.846	23.2	0.862	**19.9**	**0.854**	**15**
Centre Party (SP)	17.5	0.852	6.9	0.816	**12.6**	**0.835**	**15**
Liberal Party (FP)	9.7	0.906	8.2	0.890	**10.1**	**0.890**	**15**
Left Party (V)	5.0	0.797	6.9	0.875	**5.9**	**0.834**	**15**
Christian Democratic Party (KD)	2.4	0.748	7.0	0.869	**6.0**	**0.842**	**9**
Green Party (MP)	5.5	0.918	5.3	0.895	**5.3**	**0.898**	**8**
Sweden Democrats (SD)			7.2	0.826	**7.2**	**0.826**	**3**
Sweden	_	**0.888**	_	**0.876**	_	**0.882**	**15**

Note: In the 1985 election, SP and KD formed an electoral alliance, whose score is reported in the SP's row of the table.

*Other two parties fit the criteria only in one election.

party since the end of the 1970s, and its level of territorial homogeneity proves quite high and slightly increasing over time. Despite emerging from the protectionist and agrarian wing of the *Lantmannapartiet*, the Conservatives show a pronounced urban-oriented support and are particularly strong in the highly populated area surrounding the city of Stockholm (40 per cent in the 2010 election, almost double the SAP).

An opposite trend is shown by the Centre Party, which became the first bourgeois party between 1968 and 1979, before collapsing in the following decades. Being the party that originally politicised the urban-rural cleavage, it is not surprising to discover that the Centre Party is electorally very weak in the cities and receives the strongest support in the rural Northwest (*Västerbotten, Jämtland*) and the island of Gotland. Compared to the other traditional Swedish parties, the Centre Party is (together with the Left Party) the most territorially heterogeneous one, with a notable trend of further regionalisation between the first and the second period.

The third main bourgeois force is the Liberal Party (the first nonsocialist force for a long time before 1968). The Liberals show a very high level of nationalisation that remains quite stable over time despite the ongoing electoral decline of the party. Consistent with their historical roots, the party's support comes primarily from the urban area of Gothenburg and both the city of Stockholm and its surrounding county.

The last party contesting every election of the period 1965–2015 is the Left (former Communist) Party that has a relatively low level of sPSNS, especially during the first period. Its strongholds are somehow similar to those of the SAP (industrial North and *Norrbotten* in particular), but the Left shows a comparatively higher concentration in large cities, such as Gothenburg and Stockholm.

Among the minor parties, the Greens are extremely nationalised, showing a marked urban-oriented support. The Christian Democrats became a relevant party at the beginning of the 1990s and soon increased their support reaching the peak of 11.7 per cent in the 1998 election. After their first elections in the 1980s, when they showed a regionalised territorial configuration, their electoral geography has become quite homogeneous: they have a relative weakness in the urban areas and the North, while they receive a sensational support in the southern county of *Jönköping*. Last, the rising right-wing party, the Swedish Democrats, which succeeded to enter the *Riksdag* for the first time in 2010 and became the third-largest party in the 2014 election, shows a quite heterogeneous territorial configuration, with a strong overrepresentation in the southwestern county of *Skåne*, the area surrounding the city of Malmö.

SWITZERLAND

The Swiss political system has been described as one displaying unusual, if not unique, features (Kerr 1987: 108). The origins of this uniqueness have to be traced in the historical development of the country. According to Rokkan (1970: 118), the nation-building process has been carried out by the Radicals, with the support of the urban and secularised sector of the Swiss society. The drive for national centralisation has been slowed down by the peripheral resistance of the strong Catholic minority, while the Protestant cantons showed little opposition. The Swiss Confederation developed through the unification of highly dispersed political communities. Inside the single communities, cities gained a dominant position in the surrounding countryside, but none of them became a dominant centre for the whole country. Therefore, Switzerland emerged as an independent political society 'without either a strong central government apparatus or an articulate national identity' (Daalder 1971: 358), but with the persistence of an entrenched particularism and a rooted tradition of local government inside the cantons.

The modern federal state was established with the 1848 Constitution at the end of a brief but bitter civil war won by the federal centre against the league of Catholic cantons (the *Sonderbund*). By that time the former 'loose *Staatenbund*, an alliance of independent sovereign units, became an increasingly centralised *Bundesstaat* (federal state)' (Caramani 2004: 261). The new federal and unitary state has been therefore built up on a deeply segmented society, with multiple and cross-cutting cleavages running along class, religious, regional and linguistic lines.

First, there is the linguistic division that cuts the territory along an east-west axis. The overwhelming majority of the eastern cantons' population speaks German, while in the western cantons (the so-called Romandie),[74] French is the first language. Furthermore, the southern canton of Ticino is an Italian-speaking area and the Romansh is a strong minority language in the eastern Grisons canton. The linguistic cleavage did not give birth to specific parties, but it 'cut across all the major partisan groupings with the effect of attenuating ideological conflict' (Kerr 1987: 121).

The second – and the most politically crucial – cleavage is the religious one, cross-cutting the linguistic divide and opposing the Protestants, mainly located in the northern part of the country, and the Catholics of the central and southern cantons.[75] During the last century and a half, processes of secularisation, urbanisation and social mobilisation have caused the reduction in the territoriality of the religious cleavage: as reported by Caramani (2004: 280), the number of religiously homogeneous cantons dropped from nineteen of the 1860s to ten of the 1970s, and these ten cantons are all Catholic ones. The Catholic Christian Democratic People's Party (CVP) dominates in the Catholic cantons, while the Protestant side of the cleavage is represented by the small Evangelical People's Party (EVP).

Aside from the old linguistic and the religious divides, the party system is also segmented along class lines. Although less important than in other European democracies, the class cleavage became relevant during the industrial development of the country, opposing the Radical Democratic Party (FDP), supported by the Protestant bourgeoisie and the Social Democratic Party (SP), backed by the working class. Furthermore, among the bourgeois side of the cleavage, the Liberal Party of Switzerland (LPS) existed until 2009 (when it merged with the FDP), particularly strong in the French-speaking cantons and Basel. Still from Romandie, another class-based party gets a consistent support, the Swiss Party of Labour (PdA).

The fourth major cleavage of the country is the divide between rural and urban areas, 'usually emphasised as one of the crucial factors for the explanation of Swiss politics' (Kübler, Scheuss and Rochat 2013: 199). As mentioned earlier, cities gained a dominant position over the surrounding countryside, but the self-reliant rural communities, based on smallholders (Daalder 1971: 357), succeeded in maintaining their traditions and autonomy. As in the Scandinavian cases, the need for protecting farmers' interests against the urban predominance led to the formation of an agrarian party (Party of Farmers, Traders and Independents, BGB, renamed Swiss People's Party, SVP since 1971).

There are also many other smaller political forces, and some of them are only relevant at the cantonal level, like the Ticino League, a regionalist party contesting seats only in the canton of Ticino. As a consequence, the party system has different power configurations in each of the twenty-six cantons, in such a way that it can be regarded as a party system composed of twenty-six different party systems (Ladner 2001: 124).

Notwithstanding these multiple and cross-cutting cleavages, the potential sources of conflict are taken under control by the consociational style of government,[76] expressed in the long-term consolidated 'magic formula' of representation for the four major parties in the Federal Council. Moreover, in Switzerland, electoral politics is considered only one of the possible channels of 'voice' (Hirschman 1970). Indeed, people's discontent primarily finds expression through the institutions of direct democracy.[77] As a result of the possibility of correcting unfavourable decisions through the popular vote, elections themselves are relatively unimportant. This can explain the considerably weak levels of turnout registered at the federal elections (always lower than 50 per cent in the past decade).

Given the importance of the territory in the shaping of the party system, the very low level of territorial homogeneity of Switzerland is not surprising. With a mean score of 0.688 on the Bochsler's index, the country has the second least nationalised party system after Belgium.

An almost linear trend of growing nationalisation is easily detectable (figure A.15). The overall time span under study is divisible into two distinct periods. During the first period, which goes from 1967 to 1991, the sPSNS is quite stable on very heterogeneous values. The second period opens after 1991 and is characterised by a very intense and fast process of homogenisation that leads the nationalisation score to grow up by about 20 per cent of its original value (from 0.640 in 1991 to 0.768 in 2007). During the last four elections, the sPSNS has stabilised on values greater than 0.750. In other words, Switzerland is becoming 'an ever closer union' (Bochsler, Mueller

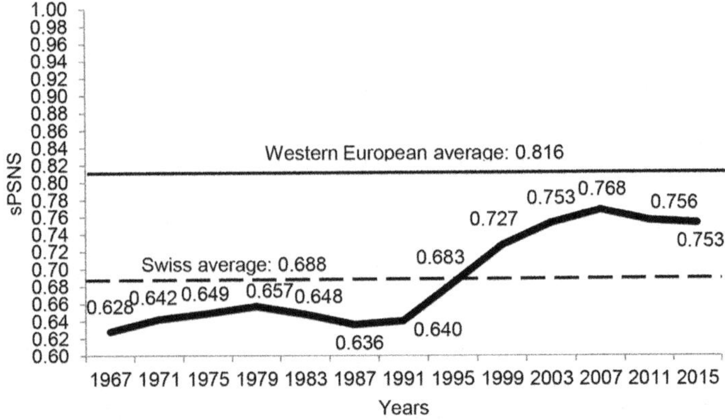

Figure A.15 Evolution of vote nationalisation over time, Switzerland 1967–2015

and Bernauer 2016), mainly due to the reduced importance of the territory-based religious cleavage to the benefit of the less territorially structured GAL-TAN (where GAL stands for Green, Alternative, Libertarian and TAN for Traditional, Authoritarian and Nationalist) cultural conflict, politicised by the Swiss People's Party (Kriesi 2015).

Table A.15 shows the mean share of votes and the mean nationalisation score of the Swiss parties during the thirteen elections falling in the 1967–2015 period.

The two largest parties of the system, the Social Democrats and the Radical-Liberals, are also the most nationalised ones. Not surprisingly, they represent the opposite sides of the former class cleavage. However, they rely on lower levels of nationalisation compared to their European counterparts. The Social Democrats have an average sPNS of 0.846, steadily increased over time. Data show that the SP is relatively stronger in the northern cantons (Jura,

Table A.15 Swiss parties: Mean share of votes and mean sPNS by electoral period, 1967–2015

	1965–1990		*1991–2015*		*1965–2015*		
*Party**	*% Votes*	*sPNS*	*% Votes*	*sPNS*	*% Votes*	*sPNS*	*N*
Social Democratic Party (SP)	22.7	0.829	20.6	0.860	**21.6**	**0.846**	**13**
Radical Democratic Party (FDP)	22.8	0.823	17.8	0.825	**20.1**	**0.824**	**13**
Swiss People's Party (SVP)	10.8	0.472	23.1	0.766	**17.4**	**0.630**	**13**
Christian Democratic People's Party (CVP)	20.8	0.547	14.2	0.541	**17.2**	**0.544**	**13**
Party of Labour (PdA)	1.9	0.212	0.7	0.178	**1.3**	**0.194**	**13**
Liberal Party (LPS)	2.5	0.152	2.4	0.174	**2.5**	**0.162**	**11**
Green Party (GPS)	2.4	0.317	7.0	0.751	**5.6**	**0.621**	**10**
Alliance of Independents (LdU)	5.7	0.505	2.3	0.455	**4.9**	**0.492**	**8**
Christian Social Party (CSP)	0.4	0.051	0.4	0.059	**0.4**	**0.057**	**9**
Swiss Democrats (NA/SD)	2.8	0.570	2.3	0.537	**2.6**	**0.554**	**8**
Evangelical People's Party (EVP)	2.1	0.440	2.4	0.592	**2.2**	**0.516**	**8**
Ticino League			0.8	0.053	**0.8**	**0.053**	**7**
Republican Movement (RB)	1.7	0.272			**1.7**	**0.272**	**5**
Progr. Organ. of Switzerland (POCH)	1.2	0.210			**1.3**	**0.276**	**5**
Autonomous Socialist Party (PSA)	0.4	0.055	0.6	0.053	**0.5**	**0.058**	**5**
Green Alternative (GA)	2.4	0.419	1.1	0.340	**1.4**	**0.359**	**4**
Solidarity			0.4	0.113	**0.4**	**0.113**	**4**
Car Party	2.6	0.582	5.1	0.540	**3.8**	**0.561**	**2**
Green Liberal Party (GLP)			3.4	0.457	**3.4**	**0.457**	**2**
Switzerland	_	**0.643**	_	**0.726**	_	**0.688**	**13**

* Other eleven parties fit the criteria only in one election.

Schaffhausen and Basel) and the non-religious cantons of Swiss Romandie (Vaud, Neuchatel and Geneva), consistent with Kerr (1987: 122).

The FDP shows a slightly lower electoral average and a little more heterogeneity compared to the SP. Challenged on its right by the SVP, the FDP is experiencing an electoral decline, in spite of the merger with the Liberal Party in 2009. The founding party of the Swiss nation-state is still dominant in the canton of Uri and is above average in Jura, Luzern, Solothurn and the Protestant part of *Appenzell* (*Ausserhoden*).

The third historical component of the magic formula, the CVP has been one of the three largest parties for a long time, but in the last period, it has lost much of its original strength, dropping to a mean of 14.2 per cent and even to just 7.6 per cent in the last election. It is by far the most territorially heterogeneous party among the four historical Swiss political forces (a mean of 0.544).

Like all the other Swiss parties, the CVP has an incomplete territorial coverage, and it also shows a regionally concentrated support in the Catholic cantons. The party often wins uncontested in the cantons of Obwalden, Nidwalden and *Appenzell Innerhoden*. Moreover, it is highly supported in the French-speaking Catholic cantons of Valais, Fribourg and Jura as well as in many German-speaking Catholic ones like Luzern, St. Gallen and Zug. It is above the national mean also in the Italian-speaking Ticino. However, the party has lost much ground during the last electoral period, thus resizing in many former dominant positions throughout the country.

The Swiss People's Party is the party that has experienced the most prominent change in the past fifteen years. Originally stemmed from the urban-rural cleavage, it progressively turned into a right-wing populist party, massively increasing its electoral strength since the 1990s, eventually becoming the largest party in Switzerland. At the same time, it has experienced a sharp process of nationalisation of its territorial support: originally being a markedly regionalised party, it has increased both its territorial coverage and its electoral homogeneity. In the last election of 2015, it displayed the highest score among the Swiss parties running for the election after the Social Democrats (0.863). Its territorial configuration has been for a long time biased in favour of the German-speaking Protestant areas of the country (Basel-Landschaft, Schaffhausen, Thurgau) and the rural areas of the Zurich and the Bern cantons (see also Bochsler, Mueller and Bernauer 2016).

Out of the four major parties, all the smaller ones contest less than 50 per cent of the cantons and show a very territorially concentrated support. The only significant exception is the Green Party (GPS): emerged at the end of the 1970s, the party contests most of the districts and its territorial homogeneity has impressively rocketed since the 1980s.

THE UNITED KINGDOM

The United Kingdom represents the archetype of the two-party system. The early development of the parliamentary system, based on the conflict between Tories and Whigs, the basic consensus on the constitutional order emerged after the Glorious Revolution (1688), and the homogeneity of the national political culture were the embryonic conditions for the birth of a two-party system. This system structured during the nineteenth century through the transformation of the parliamentary system into the so-called Cabinet Government (Bagehot 1963) and was reinforced by the presence of the single-member district plurality or 'first-past-the-post' electoral system.

Until the end of World War I, the two-party system was based on the competition between the Conservatives and the Liberals: both were bourgeois parties, but they relied on different electorates. The Conservatives were defenders of the established National Anglican Church and were particularly strong among the economic elite and in rural areas, where they also collected the support of a significant minority of the working class (Pugh 1992: 82). The Conservative party was also a 'Unionist' force, defending the centralisation of power against the pro-independence claims coming from the periphery of the United Kingdom (Ireland, Scotland and Wales). The Liberals, instead, grew up as the party of the petty bourgeoisie, with a support rooted in the urban areas among the artisans and small businessmen, groups that remained 'outsiders' within the British Victorian society (Webb and Fisher 1999: 10). As far as the religious cleavage is concerned, the Liberals were the expression of the secularised-rationalistic side of the state-church conflict, but they also received the support of nonconformist Protestants. As mentioned by Urwin (1982a: 20), religious differences had a territorial component: Scotland, Wales and Northeast Ireland were strongly nonconformist, while England was the land of Anglicanism. This geographical distinction, added to the more favourable attitude of the Liberals towards the peripheries of the United Kingdom, explains the different territorial configuration of support for the two parties.

In the 1918 general election, the Labour Party, born in 1906 as an affiliated organisation of the trade unions, became the second-largest party in the country, overtaking the Liberals and replacing them in the two-party competition. With the rise of the Labour during the 1920s, class replaced religion as the predominant cleavage structuring the party system: as posited by Pulzer (1967), 'class is the basis of British politics, all else is embellishment and detail'. A frequently employed form of shorthand to describe the nature of the British party system was the notion of the 'two-party, two-class' system (Webb and Fisher 1999: 8). Patterns of electoral alignment were overwhelmingly structured by the class cleavage, where the Labour Party obviously represented the working class side and the Conservative Party the employers' one. After World War II, the 1945–1970 period is often described as the 'Golden Age' of two-party politics in Britain: Conservatives and Labour obtained a mean share of votes above the 90 per cent in the eight elections of the period, with an almost perfect alternation in single-party majority governments (thirteen years for the Conservatives, twelve years for the Labour). The Liberal Party obtained less than 10 per cent of the votes and about 1 per cent of the seats in the House of Commons so that it gave serious consideration to the idea of merging with the Conservatives (Cook 1989: 134).

Since the 1970s, the British party system has experienced deep changes: the economic crisis, the process of increasing deindustrialisation and the shift from the Keynesian to the monetarist model[78] first led to a situation of growing electoral instability (the double election of 1974 is emblematic in this regard) and then pushed towards the progressive electoral decline of the Labour Party. From 1979 to 1992, there were four consecutive victories of the Conservatives, and the Labour suffered from a growing process of class dealignment[79] and from a general reduction in the number of industrial workers, its main social base.

Another important factor of change in the British party system was the resurfacing of the centre-periphery cleavage: until the 1980s the United Kingdom was a 'strongly monocephalic state' (Urwin 1982a: 35), and Scottish and Welsh nationalists showed a growing capacity to mobilise electoral support in ways that completely cut across the declining two-class, two-party model of party competition. The rise of the Scottish National Party (SNP) established a format of moderate pluralism and led to the rapid decline of the Conservative support in Scotland.[80] This latter became a Labour stronghold, up to the 2015 general election, when the SNP gathered a historic 50 per cent of the votes and secured fifty-six seats out of fifty-nine, thus replacing the Labour as the dominant force in Scotland. The centre-periphery cleavage has had a smaller impact in Wales, where the *Plaid Cymru* ('The Party of Wales') was able to receive about 9–10 per cent of the votes, but the dominance of the Labour party in the region was not endangered. These changes led Miller (1983) to talk about the 'denationalization' of the British electorate. Therefore, since the 1980s there has been a re-emergence of the territorial basis of British politics, with the Conservatives drawing their parliamentary majorities mainly from the southeast of England and the Labour from the North and West. Conversely, the Conservatives had derisory representation in Scotland and Wales, like the Labour in Southeast England except the city of London.

After eighteen consecutive years of Conservative rule, government alternation came back, as the Labour Party led by Tony Blair managed to win the 1997 election and, subsequently, to be confirmed in power in 2001 and 2005.

During the past years, the two-party equilibrium has been shaken: in the 2010 election, the Conservative Party won the elections but fell short of a parliamentary majority, and they were forced to form, for the first time in British history as an election outcome, a coalition government with the Liberal Democrats. Finally, in the 2015 election, the Tory leader, David Cameron, was confirmed as prime minister, but in a context of growing electoral instability, with the collapse of the Liberal Democrats and the dramatic upsurge of the right-wing Eurosceptic United Kingdom Independence Party (UKIP) and of the SNP.[81]

Figure A.16 plots the evolution of vote nationalisation over time in the United Kingdom. As shown by the solid and the dotted line in the chart, the average UK level of 0.820 is very close to the overall mean (0.816) and also well below the overall median value (0.858; *see* figure 3.1). Consistent with the historical evolution of the party system summarised previously, the trend line of figure A.16 clearly shows a pattern of increasing denationalisation of the vote.

The highest point of vote nationalisation in the period is that of 1966, at the end of the Golden Age of two-party system in Britain. Since the 1970 election, the mean level of territorial homogenisation of the UK party system has started to decline. The crisis of the Labour Party and the rise of Scottish and Welsh nationalist parties have led to the emergence of diversified patterns of party competition throughout the country: the sPSNS fell to 0.811 in the 1987 election, and then it stabilised around 0.805–0.812 during the 1990s and Blair's era, before dropping further to the lowest point of 0.758 in the 2015 general election.

This trend of decline observed at the macro-level could also be identified in the evolution through time of the indices for the two main parties. Table

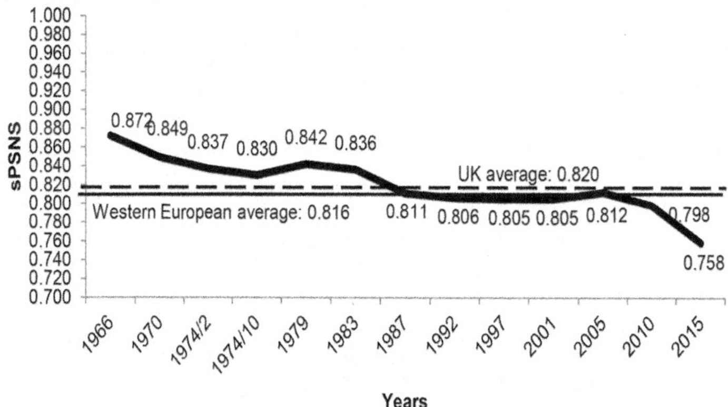

Figure A.16 Evolution of vote nationalisation over time, United Kingdom 1966–2015

A.16 shows that the United Kingdom is one of the very few countries where the party expression of the Social Democratic family is less homogeneous than the one representing the Conservative family. Indeed, the Labour Party shows an overall mean of 0.845, very low compared to its Western European counterparts, while the Conservative Party is the most nationalised of the country (0.864) and also the largest party in the fifty years under study. Both parties have undergone a marked territorialisation of their electoral support over time. It is plausible to hypothesise that, following the emergence of new challengers in the electoral arena, both parties have undertaken a strategy of electoral concentration of their support in their historic bastions (*see* also chapter 6 on this point): the Labour in Wales and in the industrial North of England, the Tories in their strongholds of rural England, particularly the Southeast.

The third-largest party, the Liberals (since 1992 Liberal Democrats), shows an opposite trend, namely, of increasing nationalisation of the vote. Until the 1970s, the Liberal party had a small territorial coverage since it contested seats in little more than half constituencies: in the 1966 election, for example, it was practically absent from the northeast of England (1.5 per cent of votes and just seven seats contested out of thirty-one). In the following periods, the formation of 'The Alliance' with the Labour-splinter Social Democratic Party (1983–1987) and then the merger of the two in the new Liberal Democrats led to a sharp increase in the party's electoral strength and to the spread of the

Table A.16 UK parties: Mean share of votes and mean sPNS by electoral period, 1966–2015

	1965–1990		*1991–2015*		*1965–2015*		
*Party***	*% Votes*	*sPNS*	*% Votes*	*sPNS*	*% Votes*	*sPNS*	*N*
Conservative Party	41.1	0.887	34.9	0.838	**38.3**	**0.864**	**13**
Labour Party	37.5	0.860	35.5	0.828	**36.6**	**0.845**	**13**
Liberal Democratic Party	16.5	0.831	17.6	0.853	**17.0**	**0.841**	**13**
Scottish National Party	1.5	0.085	2.3	0.090	**1.8**	**0.087**	**13**
Plaid Cymru	0.5	0.049	0.6	0.052	**0.5**	**0.051**	**13**
Ulster Unionist Party*	1.0	0.024	0.6	0.034	**0.8**	**0.030**	**13**
Social Dem. and Lab. Party*	0.4	0.024	0.5	0.026	**0.5**	**0.025**	**13**
Democratic Unionist Party*	0.3	0.024	0.6	0.026	**0.4**	**0.025**	**11**
Sinn Fein*	0.3	0.024	0.6	0.027	**0.5**	**0.026**	**8**
Alliance Party*	0.2	0.024	0.2	0.024	**0.2**	**0.024**	**8**
UK Independence Party			7.9	0.806	**7.9**	**0.806**	**2**
Vang. Union. Progr. Party*	0.3	0.024			**0.3**	**0.024**	**2**
UK	_	**0.840**	_	**0.797**	_	**0.820**	**13**

* Northern Ireland party.

** Other seven parties fit the criteria only in one election.

party across all the constituencies of the country, so the Liberal Democrats have become the most nationalised political force of the UK system in the second period of the analysis (1991–2015, *see* table A.16).

Finally, the UKIP, fitting the criteria to be included in the analysis twice (2010 and 2015), shows a pronounced regionalised and English-oriented configuration, being stronger in the east of England, Yorkshire and Midlands.

All the parties marked with an asterisk in table A.16 belong to Northern Ireland. The region shows an entirely autochthonous party system, with two Conservative and Protestant, pro-Britain, Unionist parties, one Social Democratic and Labour Party, and the Catholic and pro-Irish Union *Sinn Féin*, contesting elections both in Eire and Ulster.

Notes

Chapter 1

1 Notice that this interpretation of nationalisation as competitiveness does not seem to be convincing. The territorial homogenisation of electoral support is indeed 'neither sufficient nor a necessary condition for a competitive systemic configuration on the national level' (Caramani 1996: 209). The two processes are distinct: a nationalised configuration means that parties must receive a homogeneously distributed support across the various regions of the country, regardless of the balance of power among parties at the national level; conversely, a competitive configuration means that parties must receive similar support nationwide, but this support may be unevenly distributed throughout the different territorial units of the country. The assimilation between homogeneity and competitiveness has also been made by Urwin (1982a) and is reflected in the adoption of various indices of nationalisation that will be critically discussed in the next chapter.

2 Italics in the original text.

3 Still in the American setting, further empirical contribution on vote nationalisation has been provided, among others, by Kawato (1987) on the US congressional elections, Jones and Mainwaring (2003) and Harbers (2010) on Latin America and Chhibber and Kollman (1998; 2004) on the link between federalism and national party competition in India, the United States, Canada and Great Britain.

4 In the next chapter, I will get deeper into the problem of the operationalisation of the dependent variable (the nationalisation of the vote), also outlining a short critical review of the most common indicators employed in the literature.

5 Following this conceptualisation, Schakel (2012) identifies the 'party-linkage' nationalisation as a third dimension (alternative to dynamic and distributional) of nationalisation, conceived as the extent to which candidates link together under common party labels.

6 According to Hirschman (1970), exit and voice are two alternative mechanisms for an individual's reaction to the performance of organisations. Facing a situation of dissatisfaction, an individual can react by choosing the exit (as in the market economy, where the consumer leaves a product for another one) or the voice, staying within the organisation. In situation of pure monopoly, among which Hirschman includes the state, exit is not a viable option. Belonging, as a citizen or as a subject, to a state is not a choice but a given for each member. Furthermore, the consolidation of membership boundaries makes exit options less likely because the individuals develop a feeling of loyalty to the group.

7 The institutional channels of democratic representation based on the numerical and the territorial principles replaced the old predemocratic Parliaments based on the representation of estates or corporate interests.

8 Similarly, Daalder (1990: 84) states that 'political forces in the centre sought to extend their political bases by mobilising political support over wider geographical areas'. This process resulted in a 'fundamental nationalization of politics (that) led to a far-reaching "homogenization" between politics at the centre and in regional areas; such a movement was facilitated by the absence of strong economic or cultural regional cleavages, by good communications, and by the entry of issues that helped to nationalise politics (e.g. class)' (*ibidem*).

9 The territoriality of political cleavages and of the party families stemming from each of these cleavages varies from country to country and over time. In general, Lipset and Rokkan (1967: 1–64) distinguish between functional cleavages (state-church and class) and territorial ones (centre-periphery and rural-urban), although in some way all four hold a certain degree of territoriality.

10 On the transformation of cleavages from territorial to functional ones, see also Cox (1969) and Taylor and Johnston (1979: 107–63).

11 There are two kinds of exit options: secession (a territorial form of exit) and emigration as well as the refusal to perform fiscal and military duties that are instead nonterritorial forms of exit (Finer 1974). From a historical point of view, functional exit (emigration) replaced territorial exit (secession) through the processes of centre formation and nation building.

12 Sources of deviations from the nationalisation pattern will be presented in the next section. This section deals exclusively with sources of territorial homogenisation (Liberal, Conservative and Social Democratic parties).

13 This generalisation is well suited to countries where the centre-builders were committed to secular interests on the religious front (Italy, France, Spain) or where the Roman Church was dominant (Belgium) or at least played the role of strong and concentrated minority (Switzerland, the Netherlands). However, it is not true in Protestant contexts as Scandinavia, Prussia and Britain. Here, according to Rokkan's eightfold typology of basic political oppositions, the 'N' party, namely, 'a central core of cooperating "nation-builders" controlling major elements of the machinery of the state' (Rokkan 1970: 114), was the Conservative Party, while the Liberals stood in the opposition, sometimes included in broad 'Left' front (as for the *Venstre* parties in Scandinavia).

14 The class cleavage represents a clear example of functional conflict: it is structured on specific interests (the defence of working class rights) and ideology (Socialism) instead of being based on territorial claims. Obviously, in the political expression

of the cleavage, a certain degree of territoriality persisted, due to the uneven development of industrial areas throughout the European countries.

15 Also Aldrich (1995: 291) agrees that 'the nationalization of elections means primarily the spread of two-party competition, as at least always potential, broadly speaking, to all constituencies'.

16 Italics in the original text.

17 Conversely, in another homogeneously Catholic country (Ireland), a specific Catholic party did not emerge. For the historical reasons underpinning this development, *see* the appendix.

18 *See* the previous section on this point.

19 On the ethnoregionalist parties in Europe, see De Winter and Türsan (1998) and Tronconi (2009).

20 See Urwin (1980) about the politics of agrarian defence in Europe.

21 In particular, this was the case of many areas of England and Scotland, in the Prussian regions at the east of the Elbe, in the Reconquista provinces of Spain, in Lower Austria and the Portuguese region of Alentejo. For a detailed analysis on the link between land tenure and voting behaviour in Europe, see Linz (1976).

22 This also applies to the Catholic cantons of Switzerland.

23 On the urban-rural cleavage in the French case, see Tarrow (1971).

24 Moreover, in large areas of France and Italy (especially the South, dominated by the so-called latifondo), the large dimension of land tenure further hindered the rise of agrarian parties. For a comparison of French and Italian agricultural structure, see Dogan (1967).

25 The Roman Catholic parties proved able to cut across the urban-rural cleavage. From this point of view, Ireland is a fascinating case since it is a Catholic country without a distinct Catholic party: here an agrarian party emerged (the Farmer's party) during the 1920s but later disappeared (Rokkan 1970: 129).

26 Even if in Jutland, in southern Sweden and in southwestern Finland, rural society was organised through large estates, the broad masses of the Nordic peasantry could not be brought into any alliance with the established urban elites (Rokkan 1970: 128).

27 Sporadic peasants' parties emerged in the Netherlands, Italy, France, Bavaria and in the more secularised regions of Austria, such as Carinthia and Styria.

28 For a comparison of the evolution of agrarian parties in Norway and Sweden, see Christensen (1997).

29 For further details on this point and in general on country specificities, *see* the country-by-country analysis reported in the appendix.

Chapter 2

1 Furthermore, the thesis of nationalisation of politics has been recently challenged by Sellers et al. (2013) who propose the newsworthy theory of the 'metropolitanization of politics', according to which in the past decades, Western societies have become increasingly urbanised with a growing number of people living in interconnected urban regions. Consequently, the diversity of metropolitan geography

has replaced the long-time rooted divide between urban and rural areas. Instead of producing growing territorial homogeneity, as in the nationalisation thesis, they argue that the metropolitanisation of politics produced new patterns of political cleavages with new intrametropolitan social, cultural and economic divisions (26–27).

2 Bochsler (2010: 156) calls them 'indices of frequency' or 'competition indices'.

3 $E = \sum_{i=1}^{n} v_i * s_i$, where v_i is the proportion of votes received by the party in a given district and s_i is the proportion of seats allocated to that district.

4 See Laakso and Taagepera (1979).

5 The formula is D = ENEP nat. − ENEP avg.

6 I = ((ENEP nat. − ENEP avg.) / ENEP avg.) × 100.

7 For a detailed and comprehensive review of the various indices and their respective shortcomings, see Caramani (2004: 61–70) and Bochsler (2010: 157).

8 The two indices are also affected by the so-called *insensitivity to transfers*. 'In certain situations, when votes are transferred from a district where a party is weaker to another one where it is relatively stronger, the . . . indices are not affected, even if such transfers increase heterogeneity' (Bochsler 2010: 158).

9 PNS = 1−Gini = $\Sigma\ (1-Gi(\mathrm{P}))\mathrm{p}_N = 1-\Sigma\ (Gi(\mathrm{P}))\mathrm{p}_N$.

10 Assuming that the heterogeneity measured at a lower territorial level, that is, PNS(n^2), corresponds to the squared heterogeneity measured at a higher level, that is, PNS(n) – where n is the number of units – we have PNS(n^2) = PNS$(n)^2$. After the introduction of the logarithmic function, the result is the following formula: sPNS = $(1-G_E)^{(\log 10/\log E)} = (1-G_E)^{(1/\log E)}$ = PNS$_E^{(1/\log E)}$. In the formula, G stands for Gini and E stands for the effective number of territorial units.

11 Nevertheless, Bochsler's formula will provide less reliable estimations under particular circumstances. If, for example, there are 'important ethno-cultural divisions that follow (partly) the administrative regions or electoral districts', but party support inside these regions is territorially very homogeneous, 'then, moving from few territorial units to more fine-grained data from a lower level will report only slightly more heterogeneity, so that our standardisation might overdo' (Bochsler 2010: 164–65). Moreover, Morgenstern, Polga-Hecimovich and Siavelis (2014) underline that the Bochsler index has one important problem related to the weighting mechanism concerning the number and size of districts. This may produce misleading results under particular circumstances. Their conclusion is that, despite the advances provided by the sPSNS, a perfect measure of 'static' party system nationalisation does not exist, and each index has its own trade-off.

12 For Greece, Portugal and Spain, the beginning of the study corresponds to the first democratic election after the end of the respective authoritarian regime.

13 Just think about the process of socioeconomic and political modernisation in the West, where almost all the crucial variables affecting it (industrialisation, urbanisation, literacy, enfranchisement, etc.) are different but temporally interrelated factors and therefore strongly correlated with each other.

14 Only general elections for the lower chamber have been considered. In mixed electoral systems such as Germany and Italy (1994–2001), only the proportional vote (*Zweitstimmen*) has been taken into consideration; in France, where there is a two-round majority system (with the significant exception of the 1986 legislative

election when a proportional formula was introduced), only the first-round vote is considered.

15 Data at subnational level have been provided by CLEA (*Constituency-Level Election Archive*) of Kollman, Hicken, Caramani and Baken (www.electiondataarchive.org). For a few number of elections for which CLEA's data were unavailable or particularly troubling (e.g., with too many missing data or with the exclusion of relevant parties), data have been collected from the website www.electionresources.org that in turn is based on Adam Carr's electoral archive (psephos.adam-carr.net).

16 At any rate, as stated previously, Bochsler's (2010) index introduces a specific correction for the number of units.

17 Note that in Ireland since 2014, the eight former regional authorities have been pooled into two new regions.

18 The number of provinces in the Netherlands was eleven until 1986 when the new province of Flevoland was created. Moreover, during the period 1986–1998, a further unit of postal voters (*briefstemmer*) was also created. The same applies to Switzerland, with the creation of the Jura canton, seceding from Berne in 1979.

19 Note that also in Germany the number of *Länder* increased from ten to sixteen in 1990, but this is a direct consequence of the reunification of the country.

20 With the only exception of Denmark since 2007, where, as mentioned earlier, the ten districts do not correspond to any tier of local government.

21 Note that six countries of the selected sample (Denmark, Finland, Greece, Norway, Portugal and Sweden) are actually unicameral Parliaments.

22 Diagnostics test confirmed the presence of heteroscedasticity and autocorrelation in our data. I performed an LR-test for panel-heteroskedasticity ($p = 0.000$) and a Wooldridge test of autocorrelation ($p = 0.000$) (Drukker 2003).

23 The Prais-Winsten transformation has been preferred to the use of the lagged dependent variable, to preserve sample size and degrees of freedom (Harbers 2010). Contemporaneous correlation across panels (one of the assumptions of the PCSE) has been ruled out given noncontemporaneous electoral cycles across countries (unbalanced panels). Consequently, only the correction for panel-level heteroskedasticity has been included. On this latter point, see also Lago and Lago (2010).

Chapter 3

1 Other two, rather residual, groups are the aforementioned extremely regionalised elections (sPSNS < 0.700, $N = 23$) and the extremely nationalised ones (sPSNS > 0.900, $N = 18$).

2 Based on the Gini index, the theoretical minimum of zero is almost impossible to achieve, not only for a party system but also for a single party that should receive, in order to approximate the zero value of the index, all its votes in a single constituency, and this one should be composed by only one voter.

3 Belgium meets the statistical definition of 'outlier'. A usual rule of thumb to identify the presence of outliers in a distribution is the so-called Tukey's test (Tukey 1949). An observation is considered a mild outlier if it is lower than $Q1 - 1.5 \times IQ$ (lower inner fence) or higher than $Q3 + 1.5 \times IQ$ (upper inner fence), where Q1 is

the value of the lower quartile, Q3 is the value of the upper quartile and IQ is the interquartile range. Moreover, an observation is considered an extreme outlier if it is lower than Q1 − 3 × IQ (lower outer fence) or higher than Q3 + 3 × IQ (lower outer fence). In the data set, the lower inner fence is 0.616, while the lower outer fence is 0.455. Thirteen out of sixteen Belgian elections fall below the lower inner fence, and three of them fall even below the lower outer fence.

4 Caramani (2004: 77) states: 'There is a constant decrease in the values of territorial heterogeneity of voting behaviour from the first to the third period'. His research covers a period ranging from the beginning of the nineteenth century to the 1990s.

5 The Pearson's r correlation between time and sPSNS is not significant, $r = 0.037$.

6 However, computing the mean of all the elections in each period leads to virtually identical results.

7 Note that in the case of PCSE with AR(1) the ratio is reversed, with seven countries showing a negative association and nine showing a positive association, since, unlike with Pearson's r coefficients, Germany and Greece display a positive, albeit not significant, association.

8 Note that by moving from the period-average to the individual elections, the shifts are obviously larger, with Switzerland increasing its sPSNS by 0.140 between its two extreme points (1967 and 2007) and Belgium decreasing its sPSNS by 0.350 between 1965 and 1978.

9 The correlation of the mean absolute interelectoral change by country with the Pearson's r coefficients between time and sPSNS (in absolute terms) and the standard deviation of the sPSNS is, respectively, $r = 0.638$ and $r = 0.833$ ($p < 0.001$; $N = 16$).

10 This strategy follows the example of the classification provided by Pedersen (1979; 1983) with regard to the level of electoral volatility in Europe.

11 The only partial exception is represented by the Netherlands which is not among the six most nationalised countries if the mean level of sPSNS is taken into account (*see* figure 3.2).

Chapter 4

1 However, Evans (2000) takes the opposite view, namely, of a persistent significance of class politics in contemporary democracies. Moreover, Knutsen (2010) shows the ongoing importance of structural variables and especially of the class cleavage in the explanation of regional variations of party support.

2 The organisational point of view in the study of cleavage strength has also been emphasised by Rokkan (1990: 141).

3 The other two dimensions are, according to Bartolini and Mair (1990: 225), social homogeneity and cultural distinctiveness.

4 As 'left parties' I have considered the most important Socialist, Social Democratic and Communist parties of each country. Minor parties have not been taken into account. For example, as regards Italy, PCI, PSI and PSDI have been considered during the period 1968–1987. PDS-DS-PD, Communist Refoundation (PRC), Party of Italian Communists (PDCI) and Left, Ecology and Freedom (SEL) have been included for the later period.

5 Bartolini and Mair (1990: 232) use a slightly different indicator, the left parties' membership ratio, which divides the total number of left parties' members by the total number of votes for the left parties. However, this measure is subject to relevant shifts due to the electoral fortunes of the left parties in a given country, and thus, its ability to capture the strength of the class cleavage is very weak (if, for instance, a party loses votes and the number of members remains constant, this will result in an increase of the index only because of the reduction of the denominator). Given that this measure is 'totally inadequate for cross-country or cross-party comparisons' (Bartolini 2000: 263), I prefer to normalise the number of left parties' members by the total electorate of a given country.

6 Data refer to net union membership (students, unemployed or retired members are excluded). Besides Bartolini and Mair (1990), TUD is employed as a proxy for the class cleavage also by Robert and Wibbels (1999) and Mainwaring and Zoco (2007).

7 See www.projectmapp.eu. For Greece, excluded from the MAPP project, I have relied on Mair and Van Biezen (2001) and Van Biezen, Mair and Poguntke (2012).

8 Note that the correlation between LPD and TUD is positive and significant ($p < 0.001$) but far from perfect ($r = 0.442$). This means that the two variables take into account different aspects of the organisational dimension of the class cleavage, namely, partisan and corporate organisation, respectively.

9 In order to deal with the small number of missing data for the two variables (10 and 11 observations for, respectively, LPD and TUD), I have proceeded with a linear interpolation and extrapolation before creating the standardised index of class cleavage strength. This procedure is logically acceptable since the observations on a given country tend to follow a predictable linear trend over time so that each observation is closely linked to the previous and the following ones. At any rate, the results of the regression models are extremely similar if one uses the original variables instead of the interpolated ones.

10 This is shown by the Wald Chi-Square statistic of each model. It tests the hypothesis that the predictors' regression coefficients are not equal to zero. When it is statistically significant, it means that the null hypothesis that the predictors' regression coefficients are simultaneously equal to zero is falsified. In table 4.1, the values of the Wald Chi-Square are larger in the first period than in the second one and in the model with all elections. This evidence is confirmed if the two original variables of class cleavage strength, LPD and TUD, are employed instead of the class index. On the Wald Chi-Square, see Thomas and Rao (1985) and Cameron and Trivedi (2009).

11 A similar result is obtained by running separate regressions of the sPSNS on LPD and TUD. They are never significant, with the partial exception of LPD during the first period (1965–1990), that is significant only at the 0.1 level. Moreover, as a control, the regressions have been rerun by adding a trend variable 'to avoid the problem of spurious correlation arising when the values of the dependent variable and those of more independent variables vary independently but in a consistent direction over time' (Tavits 2005: 290). This trend variable is time, operationalised – as in chapter 3 – as the number of days elapsed since 1 January 1965, namely, since the beginning the period under study. The results (not reported here) do not vary greatly: the standardised class index and TUD remain not significant, while LPD becomes significant at the 0.05 level during the first period.

12 Similarly, the correlation between LPD and time is $r = -0.350$; the correlation between TUD and time is $r = -0.252$. Both are statistically significant 0.001 level.

13 Including the United Kingdom into the subset of countries characterised by a weak strength of the class cleavage may seem strange if one looks at the traditional conceptualisation of British politics as a 'two-party, two-class' system (Webb and Fisher 1999: 8). The reason for the position of the United Kingdom in the figure is that it shows a very low value of left partisan density, while TUD appears close to the Western European average.

14 Indeed, some authors dealing with vote nationalisation and considering Belgium as an outlier include a dummy for Belgium as a control variable in the multivariate regression analysis (Lago and Lago 2010; Simón 2013) or exclude Belgium from the analysis (Lago 2011).

15 An alternative method could have been that of excluding only those particular elections detected as outliers instead of all Belgian elections. I have decided to exclude Belgium since its mean level of sPSNS is itself an outlier. However, the results do not vary so much if one uses this alternative method.

16 Moreover, by comparing the model presented in table 4.2 with those regressing the sPSNS, respectively, on LPD and TUD, the results are similar both in terms of statistical significance of the coefficients and trends over time, but the model with the best goodness-of-fit – as revealed by the Wald Chi-Square statistic – is the one regressing the sPSNS on the class index. This means that the combination of the two original variables in a standardised and synthetic index produces an additive effect on the dependent variable.

17 According to Caramani (2004: 29), 'The territoriality of political cleavages is essentially equivalent to the degree to which (linguistic, religious, economic) groups of individuals are opposed along territorial lines'.

18 *See* chapter 1 for further insights about the conditions accounting for the emergence and the survival of territorial parties in Europe. See also Rokkan and Urwin (1982) for an in-depth cross-country analysis about the centre-periphery conflict in Western Europe.

19 $F = 1 - \sum_{i=}^{n} p_i^2$, where p_i is the population share of ethnic (or linguistic or religious) group in a country.

20 The most important shortcoming of the Alesina et al.'s (2003) archive is that it only provides one score for each country, thus being not able to assess the temporal variance of such indices. Yet, this is not a troubling issue since the dominant assumption is that of a fundamental stability of cultural heterogeneity over time (Bartolini and Mair 1990: 228; Bartolini 2000: 185).

21 Exceptions are the contributions by Morgenstern, Swindle and Castagnola (2009), Lago (2011) and De Miguel (2016).

22 Like the index of fractionalisation, the segregation index is time invariant within countries.

23 Fractionalisation and segregation are highly correlated ($r = 0.633$; $p < 0.001$). The Cronbach's alpha test, measuring the internal consistency of the standardised index of cultural segmentation based on the two items of fractionalisation and segregation, shows a satisfactory result (0.68).

24 I have also tested the separate impact of the two variables used to create the index of cultural segmentation, fractionalisation and segregation (results not reported): the regression coefficients are always significant at least at the 0.01 level.

25 Furthermore, in the models including the full set of elections, class shows a counter-intuitive negative sign (significant in the 1991–2015 model): this unexpected effect may be the result of spurious relations with other omitted variables. Alternatively, it can be an effect of model specification. Indeed, alternative tests with other regression methods, commonly used in time-series-cross-section analyses (generalised estimated equations, feasible generalised least square regression, ordinary least squares (OLS) regression with Huber/White/sandwich robust standard errors within the country clusters), do not show such result, and class always maintains a positive (although not significant) effect on sPSNS.

26 For instance, the most nationalised country of this study, Greece, belongs to the same cleavage setting of a markedly regionalised polity such as Germany; and again, the contrast between Sweden and Finland in the lower-right quadrant or Switzerland and the Netherlands in the upper-left quadrant brings to similar evidence.

Chapter 5

1 According to Chhibber and Kollman (2004: 227), problems of endogeneity between decentralisation and denationalisation do not exist since the former variable always foregoes the latter one: 'It is typically the changing nature of political authority that initiates changes in party systems, not the other way around'.

2 For an accurate review of the existing measures, see Hooghe, Marks and Schakel (2010: 33–37).

3 Specifically, the *Self-rule* consists of Institutional depth, Policy scope, Fiscal autonomy, Borrowing autonomy and Representation. The *Shared rule* consists of Law making, Executive control, Fiscal control, Borrowing control and Constitutional reform.

4 Only regions with more than 150,000 inhabitants are considered.

5 For the single regional authority, the index ranges from 0 to 30, while for the whole country, the score may reach a higher level (as in the case of Belgium, Germany and Spain). This is because the index weights the scores by the population of regional authorities of the same level but not among authorities at different levels (e.g., provinces and regions) which rest on the same population and to which different scores are assigned and then summed. Consequently, the RAI tends to overrepresent the level of decentralisation in countries with many local authorities.

6 Note that Simón (2013), as well as Lago and Lago (2010), consider only the *Self-Rule* and not the whole RAI. Differences in the operationalisation of regional authority – together with differences in the operationalisation of vote nationalisation – may partly explain the diverging results obtained by scholars as far as the relationship between regional authority and vote nationalisation is concerned.

7 The correlation between RAI and voting population of a country is positive and significant ($r = 0.446$), while that between RAI and cultural segmentation is even higher ($r = 0.640$). Both are significant at the 0.001 level. Note that by measuring

country size in square kilometres instead of population, there is no correlation at all. Therefore, regional authority is associated with a large population, not with a vast territory.

8 Since the effect of decentralisation on vote nationalisation may not be contemporary and in order to reduce the risk of inverse causality, the RAI is measured one year before the election (i.e., RAI at *t*–1). Notice that the results are almost identical if the unlagged measure is used.

9 In the same vein, Hooghe, Marks and Schakel (2010: 55) stress that 'European integration has reduced the costs of regionalization and has catalysed reform'.

10 A practical example of this process is offered by the Italian Northern League. As seen in chapter 4, the Northern League is a regionalist party emerged from the centre-periphery conflict. Yet, during the past years, under the new leadership of Matteo Salvini, the party has abandoned its traditional territorial claims and has opted for a nationwide appeal, shifting its focus to the struggle against Europe and the single currency, thus embracing the new 'sovereignty dimension' (Caramani 2015: 29).

11 For further details about the scores given to each event, see Dorrucci et al. (2002: 36–41).

12 Indeed, both countries have been members of the EFTA (European Free Trade Area) since 1960, and Norway has also been member of the EEA (European Economic Area) since 1994. Being members of the EFTA affects the first stage of integration identified by Balassa (1961), that is, *Free Trade Union* (consistent with the other countries that are also EU members today). Moreover, since 1994, Norway has received a higher score due to its accession to the EEA, affecting the *Common Market* dimension of the index.

13 As for the RAI, I take the value of the EURII one year before the election. The results are almost identical if the unlagged measure is used.

14 A different argument is carried out by Nikoleny (2008) and Harbers (2010), who nonetheless come to similar conclusions to that of Morgenstern, Swindle and Castagnola (2009). According to the former authors, party aggregation across districts becomes more challenging as the number of districts increases. Given that SMD systems have a larger number of districts than PR, SMD should decrease nationalisation. Similar evidence is found by Golosov (2016b; 2016c) and by Simón (2013: 38), who argues that 'low district magnitude shrinks the nationalization of party systems because parties do not allocate resources when the representation threshold is very high'.

15 According to Lago (2011: 7), both with PR or majoritarian systems, 'parties face the same incentives to spread their support across district'. What is important here is the presence of only one electoral prize in a democracy, such as the national government or the presidency. However, he finds that the nature of the executive does not affect nationalisation, since both in presidential or in parliamentary systems, the incentive to linkage for parties will be the same. In a similar vein, Morgenstern, Swindle and Castagnola (2009: 1327) stress that, while the nature of the executive has an impact in the 'dynamic' dimension of nationalisation, it does not affect the 'distributional' nationalisation (i.e., the object of the current study). Consistently, Golosov (2016b) finds no statistically significant impact of presidentialism on vote nationalisation. Moreover, this variable shows only a limited variability in Western Europe, since there are no presidential democracies but only parliamentary or

semipresidential ones and none of the sixteen countries under study has experienced a change in the type of regime during the past decades. Therefore, I do not include the nature of the executive as an institutional constraint for nationalisation. Similarly, despite the positive evidence found in recent studies involving cross-national analyses (Golosov 2016b), I do not include the degree of democracy as an explanatory factor of vote nationalisation, since all my national cases are fully democratic countries, and therefore there is a lack of variation on this predictor.

16 In case of mixed electoral systems, following Johnson and Wallack (2012), I divide the total number of seats for the sum of the number of districts in which seats are allocated in each tier. For instance, a country with 300 seats divided between one national district with 200 members and 100 single-member districts will have an average district magnitude of 2.97 (i.e., 300/101).

17 I consider only seats directly allocated at the national level by the electoral law. Therefore, Italy before 1994 is coded as 0 since the number of seats that were allocated in the national electoral constituency depended upon the number of seats that were not assigned at the district level through the Imperiali quota, and potentially this number could even be 0.

18 For instance, I deviate from Carey and Shugart (1995) and Johnson and Wallack (2012), by assigning the same score (1) to one or multiple preference votes (while these authors assign a score of 2 to single and a score of 1 to multiple preference votes).

19 For the sake of simplicity and because of the limited variability over time of the electoral systems' measures, the regression models by period are not reported here. As expected, both the (non-significant) effects of ADM and the percentage of seats allocated at the national level do not change over time.

20 Diagnostics tests show no problem of multicollinearity among the institutional variables: the level of VIF (variance inflation factor) ranges between 1.1 and 2.6, and it is by far lower than the level of 10, usually identified as a spy of a multicollinearity problem.

21 The figure plots the interaction effect of the regression where Belgium has been omitted and does not report the charts concerning the whole set of elections, where the interaction effect was instead not significant.

Chapter 6

1 A partial exception is represented by Caramani's study (1994), even if he only takes into account parties' competitive strategies. More recently, Golosov (2016b) includes the number of parties in his analysis of the determinants of party system nationalisation.

2 This process of increasing unpredictability in the patterns of interparty competition is known as party system deinstitutionalisation (Mainwaring and Scully 1995; Casal Bértoa 2014a; Chiaramonte and Emanuele 2016).

3 ENEP = 1/Σpi2 where *p* is the party's national share of votes. Data have been taken from Gallagher (2016).

4 For this reason, I have preferred this method to other quantitative methods of counting, such as the two used by Bartolini and Mair (1990: 131–32), or the alternative to Laakso and Taagepera's index proposed by Golosov (2010).

5 In the case of three parties with 33.3 per cent each, the score is 3 and so on.

6 One of the harshest critics of the index is Sartori (1994) who claims that the ENEP is not able to assess the systemic relevance of the parties given that it does not distinguish between party systems with a similar format but very different mechanics: the United Kingdom and Germany, for example, will result to have a similar level of the ENEP, but they work in a deeply different way – the former is a two-party system, while the latter is a system of 'limited and moderate pluralism'. However, if one uses the index only with the purpose to get a reliable measure of party system fragmentation (as I do in this analysis), this limit of the index does not matter at all.

7 The results do not change if time is included as a control.

8 The Wald Chi-Squares of, respectively, the full model and the model without Belgium are 40.89 and 50.09 for the ENEP and 24.55 and 27.91 for cultural segmentation.

9 Yet, one cannot exclude problems of endogeneity arising when party system fragmentation is employed as an explanatory factor of vote nationalisation. Golosov (2016b: 5) argues that 'we do not know – and there are no clear theoretical reasons for deciding – whether party systems become fragmented because they sustain sizeable regional parties, or fragmentation as such decreases nationalization because small parties survive because of their local appeal'. I have addressed this issue by running an instrumental variable regression (IVreg) with the ENEP assumed as the endogenous regressor, followed by an ordinary least squares (OLS) regression with the ENEP assumed as a linear exogenous regressor. Then, following Cameron and Trivedi (2009: 182–84), I have performed a Hausman test: the result is that H_0 is not rejected (i.e., the difference in the coefficients is not systematic) and therefore the ENEP is exogenous. The alternative Durbin-Hu-Hausman test of endogeneity has led to the same result.

10 This growing unpredictability is not only exogenous, namely, derived from changes in voters' preferences, but as found by Tavits (2008), partially determined also by the changes occurred in the supply of parties. When the parties contesting the election change, electoral volatility increases even if voters' preferences stay the same, simply because in this case 'the faithful [voter] have no other place to go' (Sikk 2005: 394).

11 The other three are 'contestability', 'decisiveness' and 'vulnerability'.

12 The most important references on aggregate volatility in Western Europe are the classical works by Pedersen (1983) and Bartolini and Mair (1990). More recent studies have been delivered by Drummond (2006), Chiaramonte and Emanuele (2015) and Dassonneville and Hooghe (2015).

13 When I directly address to the measure employed in the analysis, I prefer to use the expression 'total volatility' instead of the more generic 'electoral volatility' since I refer to the whole aggregate electoral change instead of its internal components of volatility by regeneration or volatility by alteration (see Chiaramonte and Emanuele 2015; Emanuele 2015b).

14 *See* the appendix for more insights about these elections.

15 The number of observations is 227 instead of 230 since a measure of TV obviously lacks in the first postauthoritarian elections occurred in Greece, Portugal and Spain, given that the index of electoral volatility implies a comparison between two subsequent elections.

16 Note that in the data set the correlation between the ENEP and TV is positive and significant ($r = 0.302$; $p < 0.001$).

17 Powell only distinguishes between 'low', 'moderate' and 'high' identifiability of prospective governments before the elections. I decided to code the variable as ranging from 0 to 1 to make it usable for the empirical analysis.

18 The references for this collection of information have been the election reports regularly published by West European Politics and the countries' reports in the Political Data Yearbook of the *European Journal of Political Research.*

19 The correlation between decisiveness and time is negative ($r = -0.118$) and significant at the 0.1 level.

20 Note that what matters here is the expectation before the election and not what actually happened after it. Indeed, in the United Kingdom, the general expectation was a hung Parliament with postelectoral negotiations among parties, while the Conservative Party eventually succeeded to gain the absolute majority and to form a single-party government.

21 Moreover, the association significantly decreases in the separate regressions by period. Yet, the significance of all the coefficients improves if time is taken under control.

22 This widely accepted statement is also confirmed by the empirical analysis: the correlation between turnout and time in the whole set of 230 elections occurred in Western Europe since 1965 is $r = -0.419$ ($p < 0.001$).

23 The coefficient of variation is defined as the ratio of the standard deviation to the mean. The CV is more reliable than the simple standard deviation because it takes the size of turnout at the national level into account.

24 The 1966 and 1968 general elections in Denmark have been excluded for the lack of turnout data at the district level.

25 The results are essentially the same if time is taken under control. However, the differences between Models 1 and 2 are even more pronounced, with the coefficient of CV turnout that becomes significant at the 0.01 level during the period 1965–1990.

26 All the scores have been multiplied by 100 to make them more easily readable.

27 The correlation between turnout and CV turnout is strong ($r = -0.761$) and significant at the 0.001 level.

28 Diagnostics tests show no problem of multicollinearity, with the VIF ranging from 1.1 to 1.8.

Chapter 7

1 See, among the others, the interactions between cultural segmentation and RAI, incentives for cultivating personal vote and RAI, and about ENEP and, respectively, electoral volatility and decisiveness.

2 On this point, see Chiaramonte and Emanuele (2014) and Lupu (2015).

3 I have operationalised the effect of age of democracy through different measures: the number of years since the inauguration of democracy until a given election (as in Lago and Lago 2016), the year in which democracy was inaugurated (i.e., a time-invariant variable) and the natural log of both measures to take into account the assumption that the effect of age on party system stability diminishes over time (Mainwaring, Gervasoni and España-Najera 2016: 6). However, similarly to what found by Lago and Lago (2016), and regardless of the measure used, there is not the expected positive association with sPSNS.

4 I have tested three different measures: the voting population size (as done by Golosov 2016b), the physical extension in square kilometres (Lago 2011) and the sum of the geographical distance (expressed in degrees, minutes and seconds) between, respectively, the northernmost and the southernmost points of a country on one side and the westernmost and the easternmost points on the other side.

5 I have operationalised the economic performance by using two different measures: the GDP growth rate at constant prices (i.e., adjusted for inflation) measured one year before the election and the unemployment rate measured one year before the election. Data come from the Total Economy Database (The Conference Board 2015). I have tested the impact of both variables on the sPSNS separately and even controlling for the ENEP, without discovering any significant effect.

6 The data set is the 'Cross-national Indices of Multidimensional Measures of Social Structure' (CIMMSS) by Selway (2011).

7 Diagnostic tests confirm the presence of heteroscedasticity and autocorrelation in my data. I performed an LR-test for panel-heteroskedasticity (p = 0.000) and a Wooldridge test of autocorrelation (p = 0.0001) (Drukker 2003). Conversely, a diagnostic test confirmed that there are no serious problems of multicollinearity among the independent variables: the VIF (variance inflation factor) ranges from 1.3 (total volatility) to 6.1 (the logged average district magnitude). The only rather highly correlated factors are the logged average district magnitude with the other two features of the electoral systems (r = 0.59 with the percentage of seats allocated at the national level and r = −0.56 with the incentives for cultivating personal vote) and the previously documented correlation between ENEP and decisiveness (r = −0.56; *see* chapter 6).

8 The Prais-Winsten transformation has been preferred to the use of the lagged dependent variable to preserve sample size and degrees of freedom (Harbers 2010). Contemporaneous correlation across panels (one of the assumptions of the PCSE method) has been ruled out given noncontemporaneous electoral cycles across countries (unbalanced panels). Consequently, only the correction for panel-level heteroskedasticity has been included. On this latter point, see also Lago and Lago (2010). In addition, given that some covariates in the model are completely or almost time-invariant (cultural segmentation and, to a lower extent, the three variables of the electoral system), the inclusion of country-fixed effects is not recommendable (Beck and Katz 2004; 2007). Moreover, following Beck and Katz (2004: 6), the choice of running separate regressions for Belgium is correct, since that unit shows a large effect, 'that could be taken as an indication that the one unit should not be analyzed with the others'.

9 The general model in table 7.3 has been replicated through many different models. In particular, I have performed an ordinary least squares (OLS) regression with Huber/White/sandwich robust standard errors within the country clusters (as in Cox and Knoll 2003); a feasible generalised least squares (FGLS) regression with a specification for panel heteroscedasticity and an autoregressive parameter (AR1) (Parks 1967); a generalised least squares (GLS) regression with random effects (as in Simón 2013); a generalised estimating equations (GEE) method (Liang and Zeger 1986) with an autoregressive correlation structure (AR1) and semi-robust standard errors; a random-intercept multilevel model, where elections (level 1) are nested in countries (level 2); finally, I have performed the general model by using a PCSE method with the lagged dependent variable as a predictor. The Hausman test confirmed that there is no correlation between the unobserved heterogeneity and the independent variables, a crucial assumption of the random effect model (Treiman 2009: 371). Both the FGLS and the GLS with random effects have shown very similar results to those obtained by the PCSE method. However, in general, this latter method is to be preferred since it produces more conservative estimates with larger standard errors, as shown by Beck and Katz (1995). All these analyses are not reported but are available upon request.

10 Conversely, individual countries have experienced either homogenisation (Norway, Portugal, Switzerland) or territorialisation trends (Belgium, Ireland, the United Kingdom). For more details, see chapter 3 and the appendix.

11 Conversely, the omission of the other variable showing a high correlation with ADM, namely, the percentage of seats allocated at the national level (Model 4), does not produce any significant change in the model.

12 A replication of the model with the exclusion, one at a time, of the other fifteen countries (leave-one-out test) reinforces this idea: the Wald Chi-Square of the model without Belgium is the lowest one after the model excluding Switzerland (146.78). This means that the general model discussed in this chapter is very powerful in the explanation of the variance of Belgium and Switzerland's nationalisation trends. Conversely, Germany and Portugal appear as the most difficult cases to be explained: by excluding them, the model becomes remarkably more efficient, with the Wald Chi-Square that increases, respectively, to 304.81 and 238.61. For more insights on this point, see later in this chapter.

13 Notice that in table 7.4, the RAI becomes significant at the 0.05 level once time is taken under control (Model 2).

14 Both equations consider only those factors that show *b* coefficients significant at the 0.1 level.

15 The hypothesis of no first-order autocorrelation is not rejected at the 0.05 level ($p = 0.0524$). By replicating the analyses for this period without the autocorrelation parameter (AR1), substantive results are confirmed (cultural segmentation and ENEP remains significant at the 0.001 level), but the negative effect of the class cleavage is not significant, contrary to table 7.5.

16 Note that even the RAI is significant at the 0.1 level in Model 2.

17 These tables are not reported but are available upon request. The number of observations is thirty-eight for the period 1965–1974, forty-seven for 1975–1984, forty-nine for 1985–1994, forty for 1995–2004 and finally fifty-one for 2005–2015.

Given that the Wooldridge test shows that serial correlation is not a concern for three of the five ten-year periods, these analyses have been run both with and without the autocorrelation parameter (AR1) and both with and without the linear control for time. The results are almost identical, regardless of the specification used.

Chapter 8

1 More precisely, a direct positive effect of the decisiveness of elections on vote nationalisation is visible only insofar party system fragmentation is omitted from the model.

2 As most of the literature, I have relied on data from Alesina et al. (2003) and Alesina and Zhuravskaya (2011), who do not provide over time variation in the levels of cultural heterogeneity and segregation for countries. However, this shortcoming is not particularly serious since the dominant assumption is that of a fundamental stability of cultural heterogeneity over time (Bartolini and Mair 1990: 228; Bartolini 2000: 185).

Appendix

1 As mentioned in chapter 2, only parties receiving at least 3 per cent of the votes nationwide or 4 per cent in at least one territorial unit are included in the sample. A total of 1,789 cases (the party at a given election) fit at least one of the two criteria.

2 According to some authors (Gerlich 1987; Müller 1992), because of the domination of Vienna by the Socialist, a centre-periphery cleavage, which has become relevant since the interwar period, has to be added to the cleavage structure.

3 The term 'pillarisation' derives from the Dutch *verzuiling*, and it refers to the vertical division of the society into several segments, or pillars, according to different religions or ideologies. The term suggests a nonterritorial differentiation, albeit potentially containing some degree of territoriality depending on the specific strength of each pillar among the different areas of the country.

4 The expression refers to the prevalent consensual decision-making style of the two partisan elites that was reflected in 'practices such as mutual veto and log-rolling, as well as in the high proportion of laws passed unanimously' (Luther 1999: 125). Another widespread expression with the same meaning is that of '*Proporz* democracy' (Mommen-Reindl 1980: 284).

5 The French-speaking parties present candidates only in the five Walloon provinces (Hainaut, Liege, Luxembourg, Namur and Walloon Brabant) and in Brussels, while the Flemish parties run only in the five Flemish provinces (Antwerp, East and West Flanders, Limburg and Flemish Brabant) and Brussels. Therefore, 'real national competition exists only in the capital' (Deschouwer 1992: 121).

6 This is a type of contextual effect, and it occurs when the voter is 'faced with a different practical choice, with different names and possibly different parties on the ballot paper according to the constituency. This difference affects all those in an area' (Marsh 2002: 207).

7 Rokkan (1970: 115) places Belgium in type VIII of its typology of basic political oppositions: the Roman Church is allied with the state, and the nation-builders are predominantly urban, divided into a Liberal and a Christian side. The resistance of the periphery is carried out by the Flemish separatists, allied with the landowners.

8 The grip of the pillars on people's lives has been diminishing since the 1960s. As noted by Deschouwer (1989: 34), 'this de-pillarisation is very obvious in the more urban areas, while in rural areas the social control of the pillars remains quite strong'.

9 There was also a fourth small party, the Communist Party (PCB).

10 The German-speaking community concerns the German minority concentrated in the eastern borders, especially in the province of Liège.

11 Unlike the other Scandinavian countries, a genuine agrarian party has never emerged in Denmark because the Liberal *Venstre* has played for a long time the role of defender of the farmers' interests.

12 Moreover, in 1967, the leftmost members of the party, refusing the collaboration with the Social Democrats, founded a new splinter party, the Left Socialists (VS).

13 The two blocs tend to converge towards the centre. This latter is now almost empty after the electoral decline of both the Centre Democrats and the Christian Democrats, while on the extremes the far left and the far right are increasing their support (Marini 2011: 90).

14 The most important new parties that entered in the *Folketing* are located on the edges of the political space: on the far left side, the Red-Green United List, created in 1990 by the merger of Left Socialists with the Communist Party; on the far right, the Danish People's Party (DF) – founded in 1995 by some of the most prominent members of the Progress Party – has become the second-largest party in Denmark after the 2015 election.

15 As Allardt and Pesonen (1967: 343) and Alapuro (1982: 150–53) state, Finland acquired its independence in 1917 when the Russian Empire collapsed under the Communist Revolution. The following year, a short but bitter civil war overwhelmed the country, opposing the Social Democrats (forming the Red Army) and the bourgeois parties (joined to form the White Army). The Whites prevailed, but the Civil War had a profound effect on Finnish society: having embraced the revolutionary movement led by the Social Democrats, the working class became almost entirely excluded from the national culture, defined in bourgeois terms.

16 Since 1946, the Swedish People's Party has always been included within the parliamentary majorities. As referred by Tronconi (2009: 54), this is a very anomalous case, since no other ethnoregionalist party in Europe has similar steady attendance in government. The integration of this party into the national political system is a further evidence of the politics of accommodation carried out by the ruling elites.

17 This geographical distribution of the Catholic population is still valid today: for further details, see the map by Guillorel (1981: 411) on the level of church attendance in 1979 at the level of the department.

18 Even the urban-rural cleavage did not lead to the emergence of a rural party. On the reasons for this phenomenon, see Tarrow (1971).

19 Dogan (1967: 134–35) underlines the presence of two types of communist vote, one industrial and the other agrarian. The latter one is predominant in some rural areas, such as that of the Massif Central and in particular some departments of Limousin (Corrèze, Creuse) that are heavily agricultural and where the majority of communist voters are small farmers.

20 As reported by Hanley (1999: 61), the PCF represents today only inner-city ghettos and some old mining seats.

21 Russo, Laurent and Dolez (2013) confirm this finding of increasing nationalisation over time. They postulate that this increase is partly due to a shaping effect that the presidential elections have on the legislative ones. Basically, the dynamic of the shaping effect consists of using the legislative elections in order to give the parliamentary majority to the president, and this apparently reduces the local dimension of the legislative elections.

22 Unlike the other Protestant countries, the Reformation did not foster the process of nation-building. On the contrary, religious divisions served to consolidate the barriers against territorial unification. According to Hurstfield (1968: 130), 'the Protestant Reformation which might have unified Germany against the Pope divided Germany against the Emperor'.

23 With the creation of the Federal Republic of Germany in 1949 and the exclusion of the eastern *Landër* (mainly Protestant and highly secularised), the two religious denominations became more evenly balanced, with the Catholics that constituted almost 46 per cent of the population (Urwin 1982b: 210). In the following decades, the proportion of Catholics continued to increase so that in 1985 there were more Catholics than Protestants (Pappi and Mnich 1992: 184).

24 Respectively, Socialist and Catholic-Conservative areas of predominance.

25 Another new party emerged after the reunification deserves to be mentioned: Alliance 90. It was the expression of the civil right movements and contested the 1990 election only in the eastern *Landër*, before merging with the Greens in the 1994 election.

26 The current study follows the choice of Caramani (2004) and treats the CSU as an independent party since it is an independent party list that contests seats and fulfils both the two criteria to be included in the data set (3 per cent of the votes nationwide or 4 per cent in a constituency). Other scholars consider the CDU-CSU electoral alliance as one only party (Rose and Urwin 1975) or treat the CSU as a 'related party', thus counting the CDU-CSU alliance as one party and a half (Lijphart 1999).

27 Seferiades (1986: 80) argues that Greece had a format of limited pluralism (three to four relevant parties) but displaying a high ideological polarisation and a centrifugal competition: it indeed represented a paradox that defied the 'normal' features of such type of system, as defined by Sartori (1976).

28 The 1981 election can be placed in the category of typically 'critical' in Key's (1955) sense: it represented a real electoral earthquake, and it signified the passage from party fragmentation to the high concentration of political forces (Pappas 2003).

29 The quasi-two-party outcome of the Greek elections is also strengthened by the highly disproportional electoral system (Seferiades 1986; Bolgherini 2002: 49–50). Even if it is reshaped in almost every election, its general structure consists of a proportional system with different national thresholds for party lists and with some seats allocated in upper tiers. In 2007, a majority bonus of 40 seats for the party winning the relative majority of votes was introduced. In 2012, this bonus increased to 50 seats, leaving 250 seats to be allocated by PR. In essence, this system has almost always

guaranteed the winning party to achieve the absolute majority of seats with a relative majority of votes.

30 As reported by Pierides (2009: 6), '98 per cent of Greece's population declare themselves as Christian Orthodox believers'.

31 Even though a specific religious party has never existed, since the 1990s the left-right axis and the religious dimension have taken an outright parallelism, with the strong believers that seem more likely to vote for New Democracy, while the occasional believers and the lay people tending to prefer the PASOK and the KKE (Bolgherini 2002: 81–82).

32 As stated by Pierides (2009: 9), besides the left-right axis, there is another newly emerged line of opposition, the ethical division between 'Catharsis and Corruption'. Recently, in the wake of corruption scandals that have involved Greek politics, this dimension has acquired great importance.

33 In 1921, the Irish Free State had only a limited independence from Britain, but the remaining limitations 'were gradually eroded during the course of the 1930s, the changes being formalised in the new Constitution of 1937. Ultimately, in 1948, Ireland left the Commonwealth and the Republic was declared' (Farrell 1999: 30).

34 For an excellent account of why the Irish left is traditionally so weak, see Mair (1992).

35 After a cross-national analysis, looking for possible constellations of party systems in Europe, Laver (1992: 373–74) finds that the Irish case best fits the Mediterranean constellation and illustrates this by superimposing the Irish system over that of France: in particular, *Fianna Fáil* fulfils the same role as the Gaullists (RPR), *Fine Gael* the same as the UDF and the socialists are similar in both systems.

36 For different viewpoints, see Garvin (1974) and Sinnott (1995).

37 As noted by Carey (1980: 272), '*Fianna Fáil* is notably the party of Irish language restoration'.

38 According to Farrell (1992: 389), the Irish party system has oscillated between a multiparty tendency and a two-and-a-half party one.

39 Note that for the election of 2011, Lago and Lago (2016) report a weird result of the Bochsler's index (0.390), which is radically inconsistent with our calculations and also completely deviating from the rest of Irish elections. A quick look to the territorial distribution of votes for the main Irish parties in 2011 is sufficient to exclude that such score is reliable.

40 Although not reported in the table, independent candidates have been aggregated in a separate category to calculate the systemic measure of vote nationalisation. At any rate, the scores are very similar if they are instead included in the residual 'other' category.

41 Part of this section is an excerpt from Emanuele (2015a).

42 The PCI exceeded the sensational quota of two million of direct members in the early 1950s (Bardi and Morlino 1992).

43 On the relation between Christian Democracy and clientelism, see Caciagli (1977).

44 Alternative explanations are offered by Galli's (1966) model of 'imperfect two-party system' and Farneti's (1983) 'centripetal pluralism'.

45 On the Italian electoral geography during the First Republic, see Dogan (1967), Galli et al. (1968), Pavsic (1985), Corbetta, Parisi and Schadee (1988) and Agnew (1988).

46 In 1991, the PCI became the Democratic Party of the Left (PDS), replacing the former communist ideology with a more pragmatic Social Democratic platform. The left wing of the party opposed this change and split away to form the Communist Refoundation (PRC). Similarly, in 1995 the MSI became National Alliance (AN) moving away from fascist inheritance towards a mainstream conservative appeal.

47 The DC changed its name to Italian People's Party (PPI) in 1993 and progressively entered into the centre-left camp. The right-wing factions abandoned the party and formed the Christian Democratic Centre (CCD) and the United Christian Democrats (CDU), which allied with the conservative bloc.

48 For this reason, Chiaramonte (2007) has defined the new party system in the Second Republic as a case of 'fragmented bipolarism'.

49 The electoral system changed again in 2005, with the introduction of a PR system with a majority bonus for the winning coalition. This change did not alter the bipolar structure of the competition (see D'Alimonte 2007).

50 This change occurred after the creation of two new large parties: the centre-left Democratic Party (PD), by the merger of the two main centre-left parties, the post-communist Left Democrats (DS, successor of the PDS) and the Christian Democratic *La Margherita*; the conservative People of Freedom (PDL), by the merger of *Forza Italia* and National Alliance.

51 The reference is Diamanti (2009), the first to define as 'green zone' (from the colour of the Northern League) the northeastern regions of the country, formerly characterised by a deeply rooted Catholic subculture.

52 Empirical analyses brought by Bartolini (1976), Pavsic (1985) and Agnew (1988) support this interpretation.

53 Like all the other parties fitting the criteria only in one election, the score of the M5S is not reported in table A.9.

54 The segmentation of Dutch society into these different subcultures is called *verzuiling* or pillarisation. Quoting Rokkan (1990: 142), *verzuiling* refers to the 'interlocking between cleavage-specific organisations active in the corporate channel and party organisations mobilising for electoral action'.

55 As reported by Flora (1983: 61), the Catholics were settled in the southern, bordering Belgium, provinces of Limburg and North Brabant, while the Protestants were rooted in the three northern provinces of Drenthe, Friesland and Groningen, but they suffered for an increasing secularisation after World War II (in 1971 the Protestant population in these provinces was strongly reduced). For a more detailed analysis, see Daalder (1981: 228–29).

56 This was particularly true for the Catholic segment of the population: according to Irwin (1980: 167), between 1917 and 1967, some 80–90 per cent of all Catholics supported the Catholic People's Party (KVP).

57 This name derives from the opposition of the party to the ideals of the French Revolution advocated by the Liberals (Caramani 2004: 142).

58 However, the consensual attitude of Dutch politics (see Lijphart 1968) has never disappeared, as the two parties have governed together until 2017 in a so-called purple cabinet (named after the merger of the colours representative of the two parties, red for the PvdA and blue for the VVD).

59 Nevertheless, some authors argue that from 1970s there has been a 'swing to the right' (*hoyrebolgen*) in the Norwegian electoral results. Another interesting trend has been the polarisation between the two largest parties, Labour and Conservatives: until the end of the 1960s, the system had one large and four middle-sized parties; in the 1980s, there were two large parties and a number of small parties (Valen 1992: 308).

60 'The *cacique* was the local boss, usually a landowner, a local priest or some other influential figure able, through his influence in the village, to offer a supply of votes to the government and to gain favours in return' (Magone 1999: 233).

61 On this point, see Mair and Van Biezen (2001), Lisi (2007: 203–4) and Espírito Santo (2014).

62 However, in the urban western district of Lisbon, Almada and above all of Setubal, the Communists hold a strong and sometimes majoritarian support.

63 From 1980 to 1983, also the CDS entered the government after winning the 1979 and later the 1980 elections as an ally of the PSD in the joint list called *Alianca democrática*.

64 For a detailed overview of the origins of the Spanish party system from the nineteenth century up to the civil war of 1936–1939, see Linz (1967a).

65 On Basque nationalism, see Linz (1981), Heiberg (1982) and Díez Medrano (1995).

66 Spain is a semi-federal system (Lijphart 1999) where each of the nineteen regions (*Comunidades autónomas*) has large powers and could claim for further competencies, as established by the Constitution of 1978.

67 On the Galician distinctiveness and its party system, see Díaz López (1982).

68 The importance of the regionalist parties is reinforced by the electoral law, a proportional system with small districts that tend to favour large national parties as well as parties with geographically concentrated support, while it underrepresents smaller national parties. This institutional incentive encourages the further territorial fragmentation of the party system.

69 On this point, see Rokkan's (1970: 115) eightfold typology of basic political opposition in Europe.

70 On this point, see Caciagli (1986: 20).

71 In the computation of territorial coverage, instead, bigger and smaller parties are weighted one to one. On this point, see Caramani (2004: 113).

72 The electoral strength and the monopoly of governmental power of the SAP led Sartori (1976: 198) to classify the Swedish case as a predominant party system.

73 The erosion of the class-cleavage voting has been reflected in the progressive drop in the Social Democratic share of votes: after 1994 the SAP has never reached 40 per cent, and in the 2010 election, it has fallen to its lowest result since 1920 (30.7 per cent).

74 Romandie includes Geneva, Jura, Neuchatel, Vaud, Valais, Fribourg and the northern part of Bern.

75 The cantons of Basel (*Land and Stadt*), Thurgau, Glarus, Bern, Neuchatel, Schaffhausen, Vaud, Zurich and *Appenzell Ausserrhoden* consist of a majority of Protestant population. The cantons of Ticino, Uri, Valais, Schwyz, *Appenzell Innerrhoden*, Luzern, Zug, Solothurn, Fribourg, Obwalden, Nidwalden, St. Gallen and Geneva are composed of a majority of Catholic population. Aargau and Grisons are religiously balanced. See Caramani (2004: 280).

76 As accurately defined by Daalder (1971: 355), '"Consociational" has been increasingly used to characterise a certain pattern of political life in which the political elites of distinct social groups succeed in establishing a viable, pluralistic State by a process of mutual forbearance and accommodation'. As underlined by Kerr (1987: 107), 'Swiss political practice transforms opposition into coalition, conflict into consensus and diversity into unity'.

77 On the Swiss referendum experience, see Uleri (2003).

78 For a fascinating analysis of the policy change occurred in Britain during the 1970s, see Hall (1993).

79 According to Franklin (1992: 102), 'The class cleavage had already lost much of its ability to structure voting choice by 1970'.

80 The decline of the Conservative Party in Scotland and Wales is explained by the antidevolution positions assumed by the party.

81 According to Emanuele's (2015b) database, the 2015 election recorded the highest level of electoral volatility in the United Kingdom's post–World War II history (18.2). Moreover, note that the rise of the UKIP has been remarkable in the electoral arena (it became the third-largest party with 12.6 per cent of the national share), but negligible in the parliamentary arena (one seat); conversely, the SNP, thanks to its regional concentration, secured fifty-six seats with only 4.7 per cent of the votes. This evidence suggests a relation between the features of the electoral system and vote nationalisation, which is investigated in chapter 5.

References

Aarebrot, F. H. (1982) 'Norway: Centre and periphery in a peripheral state' in S. Rokkan and D.W. Urwin (eds.) *The Politics of Territorial Identity: Studies in European Regionalism*, London: Sage, pp. 75–111.

Agnew, J. (1987) *Place and Politics. The Geographical Mediations of State and Society*, London: Allen and Unwin.

——— (1988) '"Better thieves than Reds"? The nationalization thesis and the possibility of a geography of Italian politics', *Political Geography Quarterly*, 7(4): 307–21.

Aguiar, J. (1985) 'The hidden fluidity in a ultra-stable system' in E. Sousa Ferreira and W.C. Opello Jr. (eds.) *Conflict and Change in Portugal 1974–1984*, Lisbon: Editorial Teorema, pp.101–27.

Alapuro, R. (1982) 'Finland: An interface periphery' in S. Rokkan and D.W. Urwin (eds.) *The Politics of Territorial Identity: Studies in European regionalism*, London: Sage, pp. 113–64.

Aldrich, J. (1995) *Why New Parties? The Origins and Transformations of Political Parties in America*, Chicago: University of Chicago Press.

Alemán, E. and Kellam, M. (2016) 'The nationalization of presidential elections in the Americas', *Electoral Studies*, doi:10.1016/j.electstud.2016.11.015.

Alesina, A., Devleeschauwer, A., Easterly, W., Kurlat, S. and Wacziarg, R. (2003) 'Fractionalization', *Journal of Economic Growth*, 8(2): 155–94.

Alesina, A. and Zhuravskaya, E. (2011) 'Segregation and the quality of government in a cross section of countries', *The American Economic Review*, 101(5): 1872–911.

Allardt, E. and Pesonen, P. (1967) 'Cleavages in Finnish politics' in S. M. Lipset and S. Rokkan (eds.) *Party Systems and Voter Alignments: Cross-national Perspectives*, New York: The Free Press, pp. 325–66.

Allik, M. (2006) *Parteisu¨ steemid Fö deraalriikides*, unpublished thesis, University of Tartu.

Andreadis, I. (2011) 'Indexes of party nationalization', paper presented at the True European Voter Conference, Vienna, September.

Bagehot, W. (1963) *The English Constitution*, London: Ed. RHS Crossman.

Balassa, B. (1961) *The Theory of Economic Integration*, Homewood, Illinois: Irwin.

Bardi, L. and Morlino, L. (1992) 'Italy' in R. S. Katz and P. Mair (eds.) *Party Organizations in Western Democracies: A Data Handbook*, London: Sage, pp. 458–618.

Bartolini, B. (1976) 'Insediamento subculturale e distribuzione dei suffragi in Italia', *Rivista Italiana di Scienza Politica*, 6: 481–514.

Bartolini, S. (1993) 'On time and comparative research', *Journal of Theoretical Politics*, 5: 131–67.

——— (1999) 'Collusion, competition and democracy Part I', *Journal of Theoretical Politics*, 11(4): 435–70.

——— (2000) *The Political Mobilization of the European Left, 1860–1980. The Class Cleavage*, Cambridge: Cambridge University Press.

——— (2005) *Restructuring Europe: Centre Formation, System Building, and Political Structuring between the Nation State and the European Union*, Oxford: Oxford University Press.

Bartolini, S. and Mair, P. (1990) *Identity, Competition, and Electoral Availability: The Stabilisation of European Electorates, 1885–1985*, Cambridge: Cambridge University Press.

Beck, N. (2001) 'Time-series-cross-section data: What have we learned in the past few years?', *Annual Review of Political Science*, 4: 271–93.

——— (2008) 'Time-series-cross-section methods' in J. M. Box-Steffensmeier, H. E. Brady and D. Collier (eds.) *The Oxford Handbook of Political Methodology*, Oxford: Oxford University Press, pp. 475–93.

Beck, N. and Katz, J. (1995) 'What to do (and not to do) with time-series-cross-section data', *American Political Science Review*, 89: 634–47.

——— (2004) 'Time-series-cross-section issues: Dynamics', draft paper, July.

——— (2007) 'Random coefficient models for time-series—cross-section data: Monte Carlo experiments', *Political Analysis*, 15: 182–95.

Berglund, S. and Lindström, U. (1978) *The Scandinavian Party System(s): A Comparative Study*, Lund: Studentlitteratur.

Bergström, H. (1991) 'Sweden's politics and party system at the crossroads', *West European Politics*, 14(3): 8–30.

Beyme, K. von (1985) *Political Parties in Western Democracies*, Aldershot: Gower.

Bille, L. (1992) 'Denmark' in R. S. Katz and P. Mair (eds.) *Party Organizations in Western Democracies: A Data Handbook*, London: Sage, pp. 199–272.

Blondel, J. (1968) 'Party systems and patterns of government in Western democracies', *Canadian Journal of Political Science*, 1: 180–203.

——— (1981) 'Political integration and the role of political parties: The case of Spain' in P. Torvsik (ed.) *Mobilization, Center-Periphery Structures and Nation Building: A Volume in Commemoration of Stein Rokkan*, Oslo: Universitetsforlaget, pp. 319–34.

Bochsler, D. (2010) 'Measuring party nationalisation: A new Gini-based indicator that corrects for the number of units', *Electoral Studies*, 29: 155–68.

Bochsler, D., Mueller, S. and Bernauer, J. (2016) 'An ever closer union? The nationalisation of political parties in Switzerland, 1991–2015', *Swiss Political Science Review*, 22(1): 29–40.

Bolgherini, S. (2002) 'Elezioni, famiglie politiche e sistema partitico nella Grecia democratica (1974–2000)', *Quaderni dell'Osservatorio Elettorale*, 47: 33–86.

Borioni, P. (2005) *Svezia*, Milano: Unicopli.

Bormann, N-C. and Golder, M. (2013) 'Democratic electoral systems around the world 1946–2013', *Electors Studies*, 32: 360–69.

Borre, O. (1992) 'Denmark' in M. Franklin, T. Mackie and H. Valen (eds.) *Electoral Change: Responses to Evolving Social and Attitudinal Structures in Western Countries*, Cambridge: Cambridge University Press, pp. 153–72.

Brambor, T., Clark, W. R. and Golder, M. (2006) 'Understanding interaction models: Improving empirical analyses', *Political Analysis*, 14: 63–82.

Brancati, D. (2006) 'Decentralization: Fueling or dampening the flames of ethnic conflict and secessionism', *International Organization*, 60: 651–85.

——— (2007) 'The origins and strengths of regional parties', *British Journal of Political Sciences*, 38(1):135–59.

Broughton, D. and Donovan, M. (eds.) (1999) *Changing Party Systems in Western Europe*, London and New York: Pinter.

Caciagli, M. (1977) *Democrazia Cristiana e Potere nel Mezzogiorno: Il sistema democristiano a Catania*, Firenze: Guaraldi.

——— (1986) *Elezioni e Partiti Politici nella Spagna Postfranchista*, Padova: Liviana.

——— (2006) *Regioni d'Europa: Devoluzioni, regionalismi, integrazione europea*, Bologna: Il Mulino.

Cameron, A. C. and Trivedi, P. K. (2009) *Microeconometrics Using Stata*, 5, College Station, TX: Stata press.

Caramani, D. (1994) 'La nazionalizzazione del voto', *Rivista Italiana di Scienza Politica*, 24: 237–86.

——— (1996) 'The nationalization of electoral politics: A conceptual reconstruction and review of the literature', *West European Politics*, 19(2): 205–24.

——— (2004) *The Nationalization of Politics: The Formation of National Electorates and Party Systems in Western Europe*, Cambridge: Cambridge University press.

——— (2005) 'The formation of national party systems in Europe: A comparative-historical analysis', *Scandinavian Political Studies*, 28(4): 295–322.

——— (2015) *The Europeanization of Politics: The Formation of a European Electorate and Party System in Historical Perspective*, Cambridge: Cambridge University Press.

Carey, J. M. (1980) 'Ireland' in P. H. Merkl (ed.) *Western European Party Systems*, New York: Free Press, pp. 257–77.

Carey, J. M. and Shugart, M. S. (1992) *Presidents and Assemblies. Constitutional Design and Electoral Dynamics*, Cambridge, Cambridge University Press.

——— (1995) 'Incentives to cultivate a personal vote: A rank ordering of electoral formulas' *Electoral Studies*, 14(4): 417–39.

Casal Bértoa, F. (2014a) 'Party systems and cleavage structures revisited: A sociological explanation of party system institutionalization in East Central Europe', *Party Politics*, 20(1): 16–36.

——— (2014b) ‘Seismic wave or tsunami? Assessing party system change in times of crisis’, paper presented at the ECPR General Conference, Glasgow, September.

Castañeda-Angarita, N. (2013) ‘Party system nationalization, presidential coalitions, and government spending’, *Electoral Studies*, 30(1): 1–12.

Chiaramonte, A. (2007) ‘Il nuovo sistema partitico italiano tra bipolarismo e frammentazione’ in R. D’Alimonte and A. Chiaramonte (eds.) *Proporzionale ma non solo. Le elezioni politiche del 2006*, Bologna: Il Mulino, pp. 369–406.

——— (2010) ‘Dal bipolarismo frammentato al bipolarismo limitato? Evoluzione del sistema partitico italiano’ in R. D’Alimonte and A. Chiaramonte (eds.) *Proporzionale se vi pare. Le elezioni politiche del 2008*, Bologna: Il Mulino, pp. 203–28.

Chhibber, P. and Kollman, K. (1998) ‘Party aggregation and the number of parties in India and the United States’, *American Political Science Review*, 92: 329–42.

——— (2004) *The Formation of National Party Systems: Federalism and Party Competition in Canada, Great Britain, India, and the United States*, Princeton: Princeton University Press.

Chiaramonte, A. and De Sio, L. (eds.) (2014) *Terremoto elettorale: le elezioni politiche del 2013*, Bologna: Il Mulino.

Chiaramonte, A. and Emanuele, V. (2013) ‘Volatile and tripolar: the new Italian party system’ in L. De Sio, V. Emanuele, N. Maggini and A. Paparo (eds.) *The General Election of 2013. A Dangerous Stalemate*, Rome: CISE, pp. 63–68.

——— (2014) ‘Bipolarismo addio? Il sistema partitico tra cambiamento e de-istituzionalizzazione’ in A. Chiaramonte e L. De Sio (eds.), *Terremoto elettorale. Le elezioni politichedel 2013*, pp. 233–62.

——— (2015) ‘Party system volatility, regeneration and de-institutionalization in Western Europe (1945–2015)’, *Party Politics*, doi:1354068815601330.

——— (2017) ‘Towards turbulent times: measuring and explaining party system (de-)institutionalization in Western Europe (1945–2015)’, *Italian Political Science Review*, forthcoming.

Christensen, D. A. (1997) ‘Adaptation of agrarian parties in Norway and Sweden’, *Party Politics*, 3(3): 391–406.

Claggett, W., Flanigan, W. and Zingale, N. (1984) ‘Nationalization of the American electorate’, *American Political Science Review*, 78: 77–91.

The Conference Board (2015) *Total economy database*. http://www.conference-board.org/data/economydatabase (accessed 30 August 2016).

Cook, C. (1989) *A Short History of the Liberal Party 1900–88*, Basingstoke: Palgrave Macmillan.

Corbetta, P., Parisi, A. and Schadee, H. (1988) *Elezioni in Italia: Struttura e tipologia delle consultazioni politiche*, Bologna: Il Mulino.

Cornford, J. (1970) ‘Aggregate Election Data and British Party Alignments, 1885–1910’ in E. Allardt and S. Rokkan (eds.) *Mass Politics*, New York: Free Press, pp. 107–16.

Cox, G. W. (1997) *Making Votes Count: Strategic Coordination in the World’s Electoral Systems*, Cambridge: Cambridge University Press.

——— (1999) ‘Electoral rules and electoral coordination’, *Annual Review of Political Science*, 2: 145–61.

Cox, G. W. and Knoll, J. S. (2003) 'Ethnes, fiscs and electoral rules: The determinants of party-system inflation', paper presented at the Annual Meeting of the APSA, Chicago, September.

Cox, K. R. (1969) *The Spatial Evolution of National Voting Response Surfaces: Theory and Measurement*, Columbus: Ohio State University.

Crisp, B. F., Olivella, S. and Potter, J. D. (2013) 'Party-system nationalization and the scope of public policy: The importance of cross-district constituency similarity', *Comparative Political Studies*, 46(4): 431–56.

Daalder, H. (1966a) 'Parties, elites, and political development in Western Europe' in J. La Palombara and M. Weiner (eds.) *Political Parties and Political Development*, Princeton: Princeton University Press, pp. 43–77.

——— (1966b) 'The Netherlands: Opposition in a segmented society' in R. Dahl (ed.) *Political Oppositions in Western Democracies*, New Haven: Yale University Press, pp. 188–236.

——— (1971) 'On building consociational nations: The cases of the Netherland and Switzerland', *International Social Science Journal*, 23(3): 355–70.

——— (1981) 'Consociationalism, center and periphery in the Netherlands' in P. Torvsik (ed.) *Mobilization, Center-Periphery Structures and Nation Building. A Volume in Commemoration of Stein Rokkan*, Oslo: Universitetsforlaget, pp. 181–240.

——— (1990) 'The "reach" of the party system' in P. Mair (ed.) *The West European Party System*, Oxford: Oxford University Press.

Daalder, H. and Koole, R. (1988) 'Liberal parties in the Netherlands' in E. J. Kirchner (ed.) *Liberal Parties in Western Europe*, Cambridge: Cambridge University Press, pp. 151–77.

Dahl, R. A. (1971) *Poliarchy: Participation and Opposition*, New Haven: Yale University Press.

D'Alimonte, R. (2007) 'Il nuovo sistema elettorale. Dal collegio uninominale al premio di maggioranza' in R. D'Alimonte and A. Chiaramonte (eds.) *Proporzionale ma non solo. Le elezioni politiche del 2006*, Bologna: Il Mulino, pp. 51–88.

Dalton, R. J. (2002) 'Political cleavage, issues, and electoral change' in L. Le Duc, N. G. Niemi and Norris, P. (eds.) *Comparing Democracy 2: New Challenges in the Study of Elections and Voting*, London: Sage, pp. 319–42.

Dalton, R. J., Flanagan, S. C. and Beck, P. A. (1984) *Electoral Change in Advanced Industrial Democracies*, Princeton: Princeton University Press.

Daniels, P. (1999) 'Italy: rupture and regeneration?' in D. Broughton and M. Donovan (eds.) *Changing Party Systems in Western Europe*, London and New York: Pinter, pp. 71–95.

Dargent, C. (2005) *Les Protestants en France Aujourd'hui*, Paris: A. Colin.

Dassonneville, R. and Hooghe, M. (2015) 'Economic indicators and electoral volatility: Economic effects on electoral volatility in Western Europe, 1950–2013', *Comparative European Politics*, doi:10.1057/cep.2015.3.

Delwit, P. (2013) 'The end of voters in Europe? Electoral Turnout in Europe since WWII', *Open Journal of Political Science*, 3: 44–52. doi:10.4236/ojps.2013.31007.

De Miguel, C. (2016) 'The role of electoral geography in the territorialization of party systems', *Electoral Studies*, doi:10.1016/j.electstud.2016.11.013.

Deschouwer, R. (1989) 'Patterns of participation and competition in Belgium', *West European Politics*, 12(4): 28–41.

——— (1992) 'Belgium' in R. S. Katz and P. Mair (eds.) *Party Organizations in Western Democracies: A Data Handbook*, London: Sage, pp. 121–98.

——— (2009) 'Towards a regionalization of statewide electoral trends in decentralized states? The cases of Belgium and Spain' in W. Swenden and B. Maddens (eds.) *Territorial Party Politics in Western Europe*, Houndmills: Palgrave Macmillan, pp. 31–46.

Dewachter, W. (1987) 'Changes in a particratie: The Belgian party system from 1944–1986' in H. Daalder (ed.) *Party Systems in Denmark, Austria, Switzerland, the Netherlands and Belgium*, London: Frances Pinter, pp. 285–363.

De Winter, L. and Dumont, P. (1999) 'Belgium: Party system(s) on the eve of disintegration?' in D. Broughton and M. Donovan (eds.) *Changing Party Systems in Western Europe*, London and New York: Pinter, pp. 183–206.

De Winter, L. and Türsan, H. (eds.) (1998) *Regionalist Parties in Western Europe*, London: Routledge.

Diamanti, I. (2009) *Mappe dell'Italia Politica: Bianco, rosso, verde, azzurro e . . . tricolore*, Bologna: Il Mulino.

Diamond, L. (1988) *Class, Ethnicity, and Democracy in Nigeria: The Failure of the First Republic*, Syracuse: Syracuse University Press.

Díaz López, C. (1982) 'The politicization of Galician cleavages' in S. Rokkan and D. W. Urwin (eds.) *The Politics of Territorial Identity: Studies in European Regionalism*, London: Sage, pp. 389–424.

Díez Medrano, J. (1995) *Divided Nations: Class, Politics and Nationalism in the Basque Country and Catalonia*, Ithaca: Cornell University Press.

Dimitras, P. (1992) 'Greece' in M. Franklin, T. Mackie and H. Valen (eds.) *Electoral Change: Responses to Evolving Social and Attitudinal Structures in Western Countries*, Cambridge: Cambridge University Press, pp. 205–18.

Dogan, M. (1967) 'Political cleavage and social stratification in France and Italy' in S. M. Lipset and S. Rokkan (eds.) *Party Systems and Voter Alignments: Cross-national Perspectives*, New York: The Free Press, pp. 129–95.

Dorrucci, E., Firpo, S., Fratzscher, M. and Mongelli, F. P. (2002) 'European Integration: What Lessons for Other Regions? The Case of Latin America', ECB Working Paper 185, Frankfurt: European Central Bank.

Downs, A. (1957) *An Economic Theory of Democracy*, New York: Harper.

Drukker, D. M. (2003) 'Testing for serial correlation in linear panel-data models', *The Stata Journal*, 3(2): 168–77.

Drummond, A. J. (2006) 'Electoral volatility and party decline in western democracies: 1970–1995', *Political Studies*, 54: 628–47.

Emanuele, V. (2011) 'Riscoprire il territorio: dimensione demografica dei comuni e comportamento elettorale in Italia', *Meridiana—Rivista di Storia e Scienze Sociali*, 70: 115–48.

——— (2015a) 'Vote (de)-nationalisation and party system change in Italy (1948–2013)', *Contemporary Italian Politics*, doi:23248823.2015.1076617.

——— (2015b) *Dataset of electoral volatility and its internal components in Western Europe (1945–2015)*, Rome: Italian Centre for Electoral Studies. http://cise.luiss.it/cise/dataset-of-electoral-volatility-and-its-internal-components-in-western-europe-1945-2015/ (accessed 30 August 2016).

Emanuele, V. and Chiaramonte, A. (2016) 'A growing impact of new parties: Myth or reality? Party system innovation in Western Europe after 1945', *Party Politics* Online First, doi:10.1177/1354068816678887.

Ersson, S., Janda, K. and Lane, J. E. (1985) 'Ecology of party strength in Western Europe: A regional analysis, *Comparative Political Studies*, 18: 170–205.

Espírito Santo, P. (2014), 'Party membership figures. Portugal 1921–2014', *MAPP dataset*. www.projectmapp.eu (accessed 30 August 2016).

Evans, G. (2000) 'The continued significance of class voting', *Annual Review of Political Science*, 3(1): 401–17.

Fabbrini, S. (2008) *Politica Comparata*, Roma-Bari: Laterza.

Farneti, P. (1983) *The Italian Party System*, London: Pinter.

Farrell, B. (1970) 'Labour and the Irish political party system: A suggested approach to analysis', *Economic and Social Review*, 1: 477–502.

Farrell, D. M. (1992) 'Ireland' in R. S. Katz and P. Mair (eds.) *Party Organizations in Western Democracies: A Data Handbook*, London: Sage, pp. 389–457.

——— (1999) 'Ireland: A party system transformed?' in D. Broughton and M. Donovan (eds.) *Changing Party Systems in Western Europe*, London and New York: Pinter, pp. 30–47.

Finer, S. (1974) 'State-building, state boundaries, and border control: An essay on certain aspects of the first phase of state-building in Western Europe considered in the light of the Rokkan-Hirschman model', *Social Science Information*, 10: 151–65.

Flora, P. (1999) *State Formation, Nation-Building, and Mass Politics in Europe: The Theory of Stein Rokkan*, Oxford: Oxford University Press.

Flora, P., Alber, P. J. and Kraus, F. (1983) 'The Growth of Mass Democracies and Welfare States' in P. Flora (ed.), *State, Economy, and Society in Western Europe 1815–1975: A Data Handbook in Two Volumes*, Frankfurt-am-Main: Campus.

Floridia, A. (2008) '"Scendere in campo": l'accesso alla competizione elettorale tra barriere formali e incentivi politici' in R. D'Alimonte and C. Fusaro (eds.) *La Legislazione Elettorale Italiana*, Bologna: Il Mulino, pp. 69–109.

Franklin, M. (1992) 'Britain' in M. Franklin, T. Mackie and H. Valen (eds.) *Electoral Change: Responses to Evolving Social and Attitudinal Structures in Western Countries*, Cambridge: Cambridge University Press, pp. 101–22.

——— (2004) *Voter Turnout and the Dynamics of Electoral Competition in Established Democracies since 1945*, New York: Cambridge University Press.

Franklin, M., Mackie, T. and Valen, H. (eds.) (1992) *Electoral Change: Responses to Evolving Social and Attitudinal Structures in Western Countries*, Cambridge: Cambridge University Press.

Frognier, A. P., Quevit, M. and Stenbock, M. (1982) 'Regional imbalances and centre-periphery relationships in Belgium' in S. Rokkan and D. W. Urwin (eds.)

The Politics of Territorial Identity: Studies in European Regionalism, London: Sage, pp. 251–78.

Gallagher, M. (1998) 'Il comportamento elettorale in Irlanda dal 1969 al 1997', *Quaderni dell'Osservatorio Elettorale*, 40: 71–98.

——— (2016) *Election indices dataset*. http://www.tcd.ie/Political_Science/staff/michael_gallagher/ElSystems/index.php (accessed 30 August 2016).

Galli, G. (1966) *Il Bipartitismo Imperfetto*, Bologna: Il Mulino.

Galli, G., Capecchi, V., Cioni Polacchini, V. and Sivini, G. (1968) *Il Comportamento Elettorale in Italia*, Bologna: Il Mulino.

Garrett, G. (1998) *Partisan Politics in the Global Economy*, New York: Cambridge University Press.

Garvin, T. (1974) 'Political cleavages, party politics and urbanisation in Ireland: The case of the periphery-dominated centre', *European Journal of Political Research*, 2: 307–27.

Garzia, D. (2014) *Personalization of Politics and Electoral Change*, Basingstoke: Palgrave Macmillan.

Gerlich, P. (1987) 'Consociationalism to competition: The Austrian party system since 1945' in H. Daalder (ed.) *Party Systems in Denmark, Austria, Switzerland, the Netherlands and Belgium*, New York: St. Martin's Press, pp. 61–106.

Golosov, G. V. (2010) 'The effective number of parties: A new approach', *Party Politics*, 16(2): 171–92.

——— (2014) 'Party system nationalization: The problems of measurement with an application to federal states', *Party Politics*, doi:1354068814549342.

——— (2016a) 'Party system nationalisation in Sub-Saharan Africa: Empirical evidence and an explanatory model', *International Area Studies Review*, doi:2233865916629383.

——— (2016b) 'Factors of party system nationalization', *International Political Science Review*, 37(2): 246–60.

——— (2016c) 'Party nationalization and the translation of votes into seats under single-member plurality electoral rules', *Party Politics*, doi:1354068816642808.

Guillorel, H. (1981) 'France: Religion, periphery, state and nation-building' in P. Torvsik (ed.), *Mobilization, Center-Periphery Structures and Nation Building. A Volume in Commemoration of Stein Rokkan*, Oslo: Universitetsforlaget, pp. 390–428.

Hall, P. A. (1993) 'Policy paradigms, social learning and the state: The case of economic policymaking in Britain', *Comparative Politics*, 25(3): 275–96.

Hancock, M. D. (1980) 'Sweden' in P.H. Merkl (ed.) *Western European Party Systems*, New York: Free Press, pp. 185–204.

Hanley, D. (1999) 'France: Leaving with instability' in D. Broughton and M. Donovan (eds.) *Changing Party Systems in Western Europe*, London and New York: Pinter, pp. 48–70.

——— (2002) *Christian Democracy and the Paradoxes of Europeanization*, London: Sage.

Harbers, I. (2010) 'Decentralization and the development of nationalized party systems in new democracies', *Comparative Political Studies*, 43: 606–27.

Heiberg, M. (1982) 'Urban politics and rural culture: Basque nationalism' in S. Rokkan and D. W. Urwin (eds.) *The Politics of Territorial Identity: Studies in European Regionalism*, London: Sage, pp. 355–88.

Hernández, E. and Kriesi, H. (2016) 'The electoral consequences of the financial and economic crisis in Europe', *European Journal of Political Research*, 55(2): 203–24.

Hicken, A., Kollman, K. and Simmons, J. (2016) 'Party system nationalization and the provision of public health services', *Political Science Research and Methods*, 4(3): 573–94.

Hirschman, A. (1970) *Exit, Voice and Loyalty: Responses to Decline in Firms, Organizations and States*, Cambridge, MA: Harvard University Press.

Hooghe, L. and Marks, G. (2001) *Multi-Level Governance and European Integration*, Oxford: Rowman & Littlefield.

Hooghe, L., Marks, G. and Schakel, A. H. (2010) *The Rise of Regional Authority: A Comparative Study of 42 Democracies*, London: Routledge.

Hooghe, L., Marks, G., Schakel, H., Chapman Osterkatz, S., Niedzwiecki, S. and Shair-Rosenfield, S. (2016) *Measuring Regional Authority: A Postfunctionalist Theory of Governance*, I, Oxford: Oxford University Press.

Hopkin, J. (1999) 'Spain: Political parties in a young democracy' in D. Broughton and M. Donovan (eds.) *Changing Party Systems in Western Europe*, London and New York: Pinter, pp. 207–31.

——— (2003) 'Political decentralisation, electoral change and party organisational adaptation: A framework for analysis', *European Urban and Regional Studies*, 10(3), 227–37.

——— (2009) 'Party matters: Devolution and party politics in Britain and Spain', *Party Politics*, 15(2): 179–98.

Huntington, S. (1991) *The Third Wave: Democratization in the Late Twentieth Century*, Norman: University of Oklahoma Press.

Hurstfield, J. (1968) 'Social structure, office-holding and politics, chiefly in Western Europe' in R. B. Wernham (ed.) *The Counter-Reformation and the Price Revolution, 1559–1610*, London: Cambridge University Press, pp. 126–48.

Inglehart, R. (1977) *The Silent Revolution: Changing Values and Political Styles among Western Publics*, Princeton: Princeton University Press.

Irwin, G. A. (1980) 'The Netherlands' in P. H. Merkl (ed.) *Western European Party Systems*, New York: Free Press, pp. 161–84.

Johnson, J. W. and Wallack, J. S. (2012) *Electoral systems and the personal vote*. https://dataverse.harvard.edu/dataset.xhtml?persistentId=hdl:1902.1/17901 (accessed 30 August 2016).

Jones, M. P. and Mainwaring, S. (2003) 'The nationalization of parties and party systems: An empirical measure and an application to the Americas', *Party Politics*, 9: 139–66.

Jurado, I. and Leon, S. (2017) 'Economic crisis and the nationalisation of politics', *European Journal of Political Research*, doi:10.1111/1475-6765.12198.

Karvonen, L. (1993) 'In from the cold: Christian parties in Scandinavia', *Scandinavian Political Studies*, 16: 25–48.

——— (2010) *The personalisation of politics: a study of parliamentary democracies*, Colchester: ECPR Press.

Kasuya, Y. and Moenius, J. (2008) 'The nationalization of party systems: Conceptual issues and alternative district-focused measures', *Electoral Studies*, 27: 126–35.

Katz, R. (1973) 'The attribution of variance in electoral returns: An alternative measurement technique', *American Political Science Review*, 67: 817–28.

Kawato, S. (1987) 'Nationalization and partisan realignment in congressional elections', *American Political Science Review*, 81: 1235–50.

Keating, M. (1998) *The New Regionalism in Western Europe: Territorial Restructuring and Political Change*, Cheltenham: Edward Elgar.

Kerr, H. H. (1987) 'The Swiss party system: Steadfast and changing' in H. Daalder (ed.) *Party Systems in Denmark, Austria, Switzerland, the Netherlands and Belgium*, London: Frances Pinter, 107–92.

Key, V. O. (1955) 'A theory of critical elections', *Journal of Politics*, 17(1): 3–18.

Kirchheimer, O. (1966) 'The transformation of the Western European party system' in J. La Palombara and M. Weiner (eds.) *Political Parties and Political Development*, Princeton: Princeton University Press, pp. 177–200.

Knutsen, O. (2004) *Social Structure and Party Choice in Western Europe. A Comparative Longitudinal Study*, Basingstoke: Palgrave Macmillan.

——— (2010) 'The regional cleavage in Western Europe: Can social composition, value orientation and territorial identities explain the impact of region on party choice?', *West European* Politics, 33(3): 553–85.

Krieger-Boden, C. and Soltwedel, R. (2013) 'Identifying European economic integration and globalization: A review of concepts and measures', *Regional Studies* 47(9): 1425–42.

Kriesi, H. (1998) 'Il Cambiamento dei Cleavages Politici in Europa', *Rivista Italiana di Scienza Politica*, 28(1): 55–80.

——— (2015) 'Conclusion: The political consequences of the polarization of Swiss politics', *Swiss Political Science Review*, 21(4): 724–39.

Kriesi, H., Grande, E., Dolezal, M., Helbling, M., Höglinger, D., Hutter, S. and Wüest, B. (2012) *Political Conflict in Western Europe*, Cambridge: Cambridge University Press.

Kübler, D., Scheuss, U. and Rochat, P. (2013) 'The metropolitan bases of political cleavage in Switzerland' in J. M. Sellers, D. Kübler, M. Walter-Rogg, and R. A. Walks, (eds.) *The Political Ecology of the Metropolis: Metropolitan Sources of Electoral Behaviour in Eleven Countries*, Colchester: ECPR Press, pp. 199–226.

Laakso, M. and Taagepera, R. (1979) '"Effective" number of parties: A measure with application to West Europe', *Comparative Political Studies*, 12: 3–27.

Ladner, A. (2001) 'Swiss political parties: Between persistence and change', *West European Politics*, 24(2): 123–44.

Lago, I. (2011) 'Why (not) National Party Systems?' Estudio/Working Paper 2011/259, Instituto Juan March de Estudios e Investigaciones.

Lago, I. and Lago, S. (2010) 'Decentralization and Nationalization of Party Systems', International Studies Program Working Paper 10–06, Atlanta: Andrew Young School of Policy Studies.

——— (2016) 'An economic explanation of the nationalization of electoral politics', *Electoral Studies*, 44: 409–18.

Lago, I. and Montero, J. R. (2014) 'Defining and measuring party system nationalization', *European Political Science Review*, 6(2): 191–211.

Lancaster, T. (1992) 'Spain' in M. Franklin, T. Mackie and H. Valen (eds.) *Electoral Change: Responses to Evolving Social and Attitudinal Structures in Western Countries*, Cambridge: Cambridge University Press, pp. 327–38.

Lanza, O. (2007) 'Spagna: Sistema partitico o sistemi partitici?' in P. Grilli di Cortona and G. Pasquino (eds.) *Partiti e Sistemi di Partito nelle Democrazie Contemporanee*, Bologna: Il Mulino, pp. 117–49.

Laver, M. (1992) 'Are Irish parties peculiar?' in J. H. Goldthorpe and C. T. Whelan (eds.) *The Development of Industrial Society in Ireland*, Oxford: Oxford University Press, pp. 359–81.

Lee, A. (1988) 'The persistence of difference: Electoral change in Cornwall', paper presented at the Political Studies Association Conference, Plymouth.

Lewis-Beck, M. and Skalaban, A. (1992) 'France' in M. Franklin, T. Mackie and H. Valen (eds.) *Electoral Change: Responses to Evolving Social and Attitudinal Structures in Western Countries*, Cambridge: Cambridge University Press, pp. 167–78.

Liang, K-Y. and Zeger, S. L. (1986) 'Longitudinal data analysis using generalized linear models', *Biometrika*, 73(1), 13–22.

Lijphart, A. (1968) *The Politics of Accommodation: Pluralism and Democracy in the Netherlands*, Berkeley: University of California Press.

——— (1999) *Patterns of Democracy: Goverment Forms and Performance in Thirty-six Countries*, New Haven and London: Yale University Press.

Linz, J. J. (1967a) 'The party system of Spain: Past and future' in S. M. Lipset and S. Rokkan (eds.) *Party Systems and Voter Alignments: Cross-national Perspectives*, New York: The Free Press, pp. 197–282.

——— (1967b) 'Cleavage and consensus in West German politics: The early fifties' in S. M. Lipset and S. Rokkan (eds.) *Party Systems and Voter Alignments: Cross-national Perspectives*, New York: The Free Press, pp. 283–321.

——— (1976) 'Pattern of land tenure, division of labor and voting behavior in Europe', *Comparative Politics*, 8: 365–430.

——— (1980) 'The new Spanish party system' in R. Rose (ed.) *Electoral Participation: A Comparative Analysis*, London: Sage, pp. 101–90.

——— (1981) 'Peripheries within the periphery' in P. Torvsik (ed.) *Mobilization, Center-Periphery Structures and Nation Building. A Volume in Commemoration of Stein Rokkan*, Oslo: Universitetsforlaget, pp. 335–89.

Linz, J. J. and Montero, J. R. (1999) 'The Party System of Spain: Old Cleavages and New Challenges', Estudio/Working Paper 138, Madrid: Juan March Institute.

Lipset, S. M. and Rokkan, S. (1967) 'Cleavage structures, party systems and voter alignments: An introduction' in S. M. Lipset and S. Rokkan (eds.) *Party Systems and Voter Alignments: Cross-national Perspectives*, New York: The Free Press, pp. 1–64.

Lisi, M. (2007) 'Portogallo: Un sistema di partito ultrastabile?' in P. Grilli di Cortona and G. Pasquino (eds.) *Partiti e Sistemi di Partito nelle Democrazie Contemporanee*, Bologna: Il Mulino, pp. 183–212.

Lupu, N. (2015) 'Nacionalizacion e institucionalizacion de partidos en la Argentina del siglo XX' in M. Torcal (ed.) *Institucionalizacion de los Sistemas de Partidos en America Latina: Causas y Consecuencias*, Buenos Aires: Anthropos/Siglo XXI.

Luther, K. R. (1999) 'Austria: From moderate to polarized pluralism' in D. Broughton and M. Donovan (eds.) *Changing Party Systems in Western Europe*, London and New York: Pinter, pp. 118–42.

Maggini, N. and Emanuele, V. (2015) 'Contextual effects on individual voting behaviour: The impact of party system nationalization in Europe', *Italian Political Science Review/Rivista Italiana di Scienza Politica*, 45(2): 105–30.

Magone, J. M. (1999) 'Portugal: Party system installation and consolidation' in D. Broughton and M. Donovan (eds.) *Changing Party Systems in Western Europe*, London and New York: Pinter, pp. 232–54.

Mainwaring, S. and Scully, T. R. (1995) *Building Democratic Institutions: Party systems in Latin America*, Stanford: Stanford University Press.

Mainwaring, S. and Zoco, E. (2007) 'Historical sequences and the stabilization of interparty competition: Electoral volatility in old and new democracies', *Party Politics*, 13: 155–78.

Mainwaring, S., Gervasoni, C. and España-Najera, A. (2016) 'Extra- and within-system electoral volatility', *Party Politics*, doi:10.1177/1354068815625229.

Mair, P. (1992) 'Explaining the absence of class politics in Ireland' in J. H Goldthorpe and C. T. Whelan (eds.) *The Development of Industrial Society in Ireland*, Oxford: Oxford University Press, pp. 383–410.

——— (2011) 'The election in context' in M. Gallagher and M. Marsh (eds.) *How Ireland Voted 2011: The Full Story of Ireland's Earthquake Election*, Basingstoke: Palgrave, pp. 283–97.

Mair, P. and Van Biezen, I. (2001) 'Party membership in twenty European democracies, 1980–2000', *Party Politics*, 7(1): 7–21.

Marini, L. (2011) 'I ghiacci si sciolgono. Lo scongelamento del comportamento di voto nei tre sistemi scandinavi', *Quaderni dell'Osservatorio Elettorale*, 65: 65–119.

Marsh, M. (1992) 'Ireland' in M. Franklin, T. Mackie and H. Valen (eds.) *Electoral Change: Responses to Evolving Social and Attitudinal Structures in Western Countries*, Cambridge: Cambridge University Press, pp. 219–37.

——— (2002) 'Electoral context', *Electoral Studies*, 21: 207–17.

Mendes, S. M., Camões, P. J. and McDonald, M. D. (2001) 'The changing face of the Portuguese parties: Strategic innovation and the dimensionality of the party policy space', paper presented at the ECPR Joint Session Conference, Grenoble.

Miller, W. (1983) 'The denationalization of British politics: The reemergence of the periphery', *West European Politics*, 6: 103–29.

Moenius, J. and Kasuya, Y. (2004) 'Measuring party linkage across districts: Some party system inflation indices and their properties', *Party Politics*, 10: 543–64.

Mommen-Reindl, M. (1980) 'Austria' in P. H. Merkl (ed.) *Western European Party Systems*, New York: Free Press, pp. 279–97.

Mongelli, F. P., Dorrucci, E. and Agur, I. (2005) 'What Does European Institutional Integration Tell Us About Trade Integration?' ECB Occasional Paper No. 40, Frankfurt: European Central Bank.

Morgenstern, S., Polga-Hecimovich, J. and Siavelis, P. M. (2014) 'Seven imperatives for improving the measurement of party nationalization with evidence from Chile', *Electoral Studies*, 33: 186–99.

Morgenstern, S. and Pothoff, R. (2005) 'The components of elections: District heterogeneity, district-time effects, and volatility', *Electoral Studies*, 24(1): 17–40.

Morgenstern, S., Smith, N. and Trelles, A. (2017) 'How party nationalization conditions economic voting', *Electoral studies*, doi:10.1016/j.electstud.2016.11.014.

Morgenstern, S., Swindle, S. M. and Castagnola, A. (2009) 'Party nationalization and institutions', *Journal of Politics*, 71: 1322–341.

Mouzelis, N. (1986) *Politics in the Semi-periphery: Early Parliamentarianism and Late Industrialization in the Balkans and Latin America*, Basingstoke: Palgrave Macmillan.

Müller, W. C. (1992) 'Austria' in R. S. Katz and P. Mair (eds.) *Party Organizations in Western Democracies: A Data Handbook*, London: Sage, pp. 21–120.

Müller, W. C. and Fallend, F. (2006) 'Dal multipolarismo al bipolarismo: Il cambiamento del sistema partitico in Austria' in L. Bardi (ed.) *Partiti e Sistemi Di Partito*, Bologna: Il Mulino, pp. 287–311.

Nikoleny, C. (2008) 'The impact of institutional design on the nationalization of post-communist party systems: party inflation in the Czech Republic, Hungary, Poland and Slovakia', paper presented at the EJPR Joint Sessions of Workshops, Rennes.

Nilson, S. S. (1980) 'Norway and Denmark' in P. H. Merkl (ed.) *Western European Party Systems*, New York: Free Press, pp. 205–34.

Orriols, L. and Cordero, G. (2016) 'The breakdown of the Spanish two-party system: The upsurge of Podemos and Ciudadanos in the 2015 general election', *South European Society and Politics*, doi:13608746.2016.1198454.

Oskarson, M. (1992) 'Sweden' in M. Franklin, T. Mackie and H. Valen (eds.) *Electoral Change: Responses to Evolving Social and Attitudinal Structures in Western Countries*, Cambridge: Cambridge University Press, pp. 339–59.

Pappas, T. S. (2003) 'The transformation of the Greek party system since 1951', *West European Politics*, 26(2): 90–114.

Pappi, F. U. and Mnich, P. (1992) 'Germany' in M. Franklin, T. Mackie and H. Valen (eds.) *Electoral Change: Responses to Evolving Social and Attitudinal Structures in Western Countries*, Cambridge: Cambridge University Press, pp. 179–204.

Parks, R. W. (1967) 'Efficient estimation of a system of regression equations when disturbances are both serially and contemporaneously correlated', *Journal of American Statistical Association*, 62: 500–509.

Paulis, E., Sierens, V. and Van Haute, E. (2015) 'Explaining variations in party membership levels', paper presented at the ECPR General Conference, Montreal, August.

Pavsic, R. (1985) 'Esiste una tendenza all'omogeneizzazione territoriale dei partiti italiani?', *Rivista Italiana di Scienza Politica*, 15: 69–97.

Pedersen, M. (1979) 'The dynamics of European party systems: Changing patterns of electoral volatility', *European Journal of Political Research*, 7: 1–26.

——— (1983) 'Changing patterns of electoral volatility in European party systems, 1948–1977: Explorations in explanations' in H. Daalder and P. Mair (eds.) *Western European Party Systems: Continuity and Change*, London: Sage, pp. 29–66.

Pierides, C. (2009) 'Changing social cleavages and the formation of electoral behaviour in Greece of the late "Metapolitefsis" (1996–2007)', paper presented at the fourth Hellenic Observatory PhD Symposium, Athens.

Plasser, F., Ulram, P. and Grausgruber, A. (1992) 'The decline of "Lager Mentality" and the new model of electoral competition in Austria' in K. R. Luther and W. C. Müller (eds.) *Politics in Austria: Still a Case of Consociationalism?* London: Frank Cass, pp. 16–44.

Poli, A. (2007) 'Svezia: Da modello a eccezione?' in P. Grilli di Cortona and G. Pasquino (eds.) *Partiti e Sistemi di Partito nelle Democrazie Contemporanee*, Bologna: Il Mulino, pp. 151–82.

Powell, J. B., Jr. (2000) *Elections as Instruments of Democracy: Majoritarian and Proportional Visions*, New Haven and London: Yale University Press.

Pridham, G. (1984) *The New Mediterranean Democracies*, London: Frank Cass.

Pugh, M. (1992) *The Making of Modern British Politics*, Oxford: Basil Blackwell.

Pulzer, P. (1967) *Political Representation and Elections in Britain*, London: Allen and Unwin.

Renwick, A. and Pilet, J. B. (2016) *Faces on the Ballot: The Personalization of Electoral Systems in Europe*, Oxford: Oxford University Press.

Roberts, K. M. and Wibbels, E. (1999) 'Party systems and electoral volatility in Latin America: A test of economic, institutional, and structural explanations', *American Political Science Review*, 93: 575–90.

Rokkan, S. (1967) 'Geography, religion and social class: Crosscutting cleavages in Norwegian politics' in S. M. Lipset and S. Rokkan (eds.) *Party Systems and Voter Alignments: Cross-national Perspectives*, New York: The Free Press, pp. 367–444.

——— (1970) *Citizens, Elections, Parties*, Oslo: Universitetsforlaget.

——— (1990) 'Towards a generalised concept of verzuiling' in P. Mair (ed.) *The West European Party System*, Oxford: Oxford University Press, pp. 139–49.

Rokkan, S. and Urwin, D. W. (eds.) (1982) *The Politics of Territorial Identity: Studies in European Regionalism*, London: Sage.

Rokkan, S. and Urwin, D. W. (1983) *Economy, Territory, Identity: Politics of West European Peripheries*, London: Sage.

Rokkan, S. and Valen, H. (1970) 'Regional contrast in Norwegian politics: A review of data from official statistics and from sample surveys' in E. Allardt and S. Rokkan (eds.) *Mass Politics*, New York: Free Press, pp. 190–247.

Rose, R. and Urwin, D. W. (1970) 'Persistence and Change in Western Party Systems since 1945', *Political Studies*, 18(3): 287–319.

——— (1975) *Regional Differentiation and Political Unity in Western Nations*, London and Beverly Hills, Sage Professional Papers in Contemporary Political Sociology (no. 06–007).

Russo, L., Dolez, A. and Laurent, B. (2013) 'Presidential and legislative elections: How the type of election impacts the degree of nationalization: The case of France (1965–2012)', *French Politics*, 11(4): 356–72.

Sartori, G. (1976) *Parties and Party Systems: A Framework for Analysis*, New York: Cambridge University Press.

——— (1984) 'The influence of electoral systems: faulty laws or faulty method?' in B. Grofman and A. Lijphart (eds.) *Electoral Laws and Their Political Consequences*, New York: Agathon Press.

——— (1994) *Comparative Constitutional Engineering: An Inquiry into Structures, Incentives and Outcomes*, New York: New York University Press.

Schakel, A. J. (2012) 'Nationalization of multilevel party systems: A conceptual and empirical analysis', *European Journal of Political Research*, 52: 212–36.

Schattschneider, E. E. (1960) *The Semi-Sovereign People: A Realist's View of Democracy in America*, New York: Holt, Rinehart, and Winston.

Seferiades, S. (1986) 'Polarization and nonproportionality: The Greek party system in the postwar era', *Comparative Politics*, 19(1): 69–93.

Sellers, J. M., Kübler, D., Walter-Rogg, M. and Walks, R. A. (eds.) (2013) *The Political Ecology of the Metropolis: Metropolitan Sources of Electoral Behaviour in Eleven Countries*, Colchester: ECPR Press.

Selway, J. S. (2011) *Cross-national Indices of Multidimensional Measures of Social Structure*. https://sites.google.com/site/joelsawatselway/CROSS-CUTTING-CLEAVAGES-DATA (accessed 30 November 2016).

Sikk, A. (2005) 'How unstable? Volatility and the genuinely new parties in Eastern Europe', *European Journal of Political Research*, 44(3): 391–412.

Sikk, A. and Bochsler, D. (2008) 'Impact of ethnic heterogeneity on party nationalization in the Baltic States: The nationalisation of party systems in Central and Eastern Europe', paper presented at the ECPR Joint Sessions of Workshop, Rennes.

Simmons, J., Hicken, A., Kollman, K. and Nooruddin, I. (2016) 'Party system structure and its consequences for foreign direct investment', *Party Politics*, doi:1354068816644762.

Simón, P. (2013) 'The combined impact of decentralization and personalism on the nationalisation of party systems', *Political Studies*, 61: 24–44.

Simón, P. and Gunjoan, M. (2017) 'The short-term and long-term effects of institutional reforms on party system nationalization', *Comparative European Politics*, doi:10.1057/s41295-017-0100-3.

Sinnott, R. (1995) *Irish Voters Decide: Voting Behaviour in Elections and Referendums since 1918*, Manchester: Manchester University Press.

Smith, G. (1976) 'West Germany and the Politics of Centrality', *Government and Opposition*, 11: 387–407.

Stepan, A. C. (2001) *Arguing Comparative Politics*, Oxford: Oxford University Press.

Stimson, J. (1985) 'Regression in time and space: A statistical essay', *American Journal of Political Science*, 29(4), 914–47.

Stokes, D. E. (1965) 'A variance components model of political effects' in J. M. Claunch (ed.) *Mathematical Applications in Political Science*, Dallas: Arnold Foundation.

——— (1967) 'Parties and the nationalization of electoral forces' in W.Chambers and W. D. Burnham (eds.) *The American Party Systems: Stages of Political Development*, New York: Oxford University Press.

Su, Y-P. (2017) 'Personal vote, spatial registration rules, and party system nationalization in Latin America', *International Political Science Review*, doi:10.1177/0192512116676354.

Suhonen, P. (1980) 'Finland' in P. H. Merkl (ed.) *Western European Party Systems*, New York: Free Press, pp. 235–56.

Sundquist, J. (1973) *Dynamics of the Party System: Alignment and Realignment of Political Parties in the United States*, Washington, DC: The Brooking Institution.

Szöcsik, E. and Zuber, C. I. (2012) 'Ethnicity, territory and party competition: Toward a unified approach', outline of the workshop held at the ECPR Joint Sessions, Antwerp.

Taagepera, R. and Shugart, M. (1989) *Seats and Votes: The Effects and Determinants of Electoral Systems*, New Haven: Yale University Press.

Tarrow, S. (1971) 'The urban-rural cleavage in political involvement: The case of France', *American Political Science Review*, 65(2): 341–57.

Tavits, M. (2005) 'The development of stable party support: Electoral dynamics in post-communist Europe', *American Journal of Political Science*, 49(2): 113–34.

——— (2008) 'On the linkage between electoral volatility and party system instability in Central and Eastern Europe', *European Journal of Political Research*, 47(5): 537–55.

Taylor, P. and Johnston, R. (1979) *Geography of Elections*, New York: Holmes and Meier.

Ten Napel, H.-M. (1999) 'The Netherlands: Resilience amidst change' in D. Broughton and M. Donovan (eds.) *Changing Party Systems in Western Europe*, London and New York: Pinter, pp. 163–82.

Thomas, D. R. and Rao, J. N. K. (1985) 'On the Power of Some Goodness-of-Fit Tests under Cluster Sampling', *Proceedings of the Survey Research Methods Section*, Alexandria, VA: American Statistical Association, pp. 291–96.

Thorlakson, L. (2007) 'An institutional explanation of party system congruence: Evidence from six federations', *European Journal of Political Research*, 46(1): 69–95.

Tilly, C. (ed.) (1975) *The Formation of National States in Western Europe*, Princeton: Princeton University Press.

Torvsik, P. (ed.) (1981) *Mobilization, Center-Periphery Structures and Nation Building. A Volume in Commemoration of Stein Rokkan*, Oslo: Universitetsforlaget.

Treiman, D. J. (2009) *Quantitative Data Analysis: Doing Social Research to Test Ideas*, San Francisco: Jossey-Bass.

Tronconi, F. (2009) *I Partiti Etnoregionalisti: La politica dell'identità territoriale In Europa Occidentale*, Bologna: Il Mulino.

Tukey, J. W. (1949) 'Comparing individual means in the analysis of variance', *Biometrics*, 5(2): 99–114.

Uleri, P. V. (2003) *Referendum e Democrazia. Una prospettiva comparata*, Bologna: Il Mulino.

Urwin, D. (1980) *From Ploughshare to Ballotbox: The Politics of Agrarian Defence in Europe*, Oslo: Universitetsforlaget.

——— (1982a) 'Territorial structures and political development in the United Kingdom' in S. Rokkan and D. W. Urwin (eds.) *The Politics of Territorial Identity: Studies in European Regionalism*, London: Sage, pp. 19–74.

——— (1982b) 'Germany: From geographical expression to regional accomodation' in S. Rokkan and D. W. Urwin (eds.) *The Politics of Territorial Identity: Studies in European Regionalism*, London: Sage, pp. 165–249.

Valen, H. (1992) 'Norway' in M. Franklin, T. Mackie and H. Valen (eds.) *Electoral Change: Responses to Evolving Social and Attitudinal Structures in Western Countries*, Cambridge: Cambridge University Press, pp. 307–26.

Van Biezen, I., Mair, P. and Poguntke, T. (2012) 'Going, going, . . . gone? The decline in party membership in contemporary Europe', *European Journal of Political Research*, 51: 24–56.

van der Eijk, C. and Niemöller, K. (1992) 'The Netherlands' in M. Franklin, T. Mackie and H. Valen (eds.) *Electoral Change: Responses to Evolving Social and Attitudinal Structures in Western Countries*, Cambridge: Cambridge University Press, pp. 255–83.

Van Haute, E., et al. (2016) *MAPP dataset.* www.projectmapp.eu (accessed 30 August 2016).

Ventura, S. (2007) 'Francia: Bipolarismo a formato variabile' in P. Grilli di Cortona and G. Pasquino (eds.) *Partiti e Sistemi di Partito nelle Democrazie Contemporanee*, Bologna: Il Mulino, pp. 83–116.

Visser, J. (2015) *ICTWSS Data base. Version 5.0. Amsterdam: Amsterdam Institute for Advanced Labour Studies AIAS.* http://www.uva-aias.net/en/ictwss (accessed 30 June 2016).

Voulgaris, I. (2007) *Greece of the Metapolitefsis Era, 1974–1990*, Athens: Themelio.

Webb, P. and Fisher, J. (1999) 'The changing British party system: Two-party equilibrium or the emergence of moderate pluralism?' in D. Broughton and M. Donovan (eds.) *Changing Party Systems in Western Europe*, London and New York: Pinter, pp. 8–29.

West, D. M. (2013) *Air Wars: Television Advertising and Social Media in Election Campaigns, 1952–2012*, London: Sage.

Whyte, J. (1974) *Church and State in Modern Ireland, 1923–1979*, Dublin: Gill and Macmillan.

Wiarda, H. J. (1980) 'Spain and Portugal' in P. H. Merkl (ed.) *Western European Party Systems*, New York: Free Press, pp. 298–328.

Zuffo, E. (2001) 'L'introduzione del sistema proporzionale nelle elezioni italiane del 1919: Il contenuto della nuova legge ed i risultati della consultazione', *Quaderni dell'Osservatorio Elettorale*, 44: 57–98.

Index

About the Author

Vincenzo Emanuele is Post-doctoral Fellow in Political Science at LUISS Guido Carli in Rome. He is a member of CISE (Italian Centre for Electoral Studies) and ITANES (Italian National Election Studies). His research has appeared in *Comparative Political Studies*, *Party Politics*, *Regional and Federal Studies*, *Journal of Contemporary European Research*, *Italian Political Science Review*, *Contemporary Italian Politics*.

Printed in Great Britain
by Amazon

11882872R00174